The Age
of
Transformation
1789 – 1871

BLANDFORD HISTORY SERIES

(General Editor R. W. Harris)

THE HISTORY OF ENGLAND

HISTORY OF EUROPE

PROBLEMS OF HISTORY

HISTORY AND LITERATURE

1789–1871

The Age
of
Transformation

R. F. LESLIE

*Professor of Modern History
and Head of the Department of History
in the University of London
at Queen Mary College*

Blandford Press London

First published 1964
Revised edition 1969
Reprinted 1975

© Copyright by Blandford Press Ltd
167 High Holborn London WC1V 6PH

ISBN 0 7137 0355 5 (Trade edition)
ISBN 0 7137 0359 8 (School edition)

*Printed in Great Britain by
Fletcher & Son Ltd, Norwich*

Contents

List of Illustrations

(between pages 248 and 249)

ACKNOWLEDGMENTS

The illustrations have been reproduced by permission of the following:

1-9, 11, 14-21, 23-25   Radio Times Hulton Picture Library
10, 12   Science Museum, London, S.W.7
13   Imperial War Museum, London
22   United States Information Service, London
26   Ministry of Works: Crown Copyright

LIST OF MAPS
Drawn by A Spark

Introduction:
The Transformation of Europe

Between the end of the eighteenth century and the events of 1870–1 European society was transformed. All ages are periods of transition, but between the French revolution of 1789 and the Franco-German War of 1870–1 change occurred with a rapidity which made all previous ages seem relatively static. Already by the sixteenth century the peoples of Europe had begun to differ sharply from the nations of the rest of the world who often enjoyed more stable conditions. European society then achieved a dynamism which accelerated its progress. Already this energy had become so restless that it could not be confined within the limits of a single continent. The creative and at the same time destructive force of Europe by the end of the eighteenth century had produced the conditions of a social explosion. The twentieth century is accustomed to the phenomenon of rapid change, but the speed of development may easily give rise to an historical illusion. It may be a matter of wonder that a man may travel by air from London to New York, leaving at breakfast time and arriving in time to enjoy another breakfast, but it was of incomparably greater significance that in the first three-quarters of the nineteenth century the peoples of Europe were freed from the speed of the ox-cart by the railways and from the speed of the sailing ship, dependent upon the force of the winds, by the invention of the steamship. The localism of Europe was destroyed and Europe in its turn began to penetrate the entire world, setting in motion outside the European continent developments similar to and often more rapid than its own.

The explosion of Europe has many origins, and it would be easy to confuse symptoms and causes. The most impressive of European achievements was engineering technology. The most famous of all

inventions was James Watt's steam engine, which freed men from
their dependence upon wind and water and permitted them to concentrate industry where they wished, but the very fact that it was
invented reveals that a need for it was already felt. In short, the
invention of the steam engine was the response to an urgent need for a
technology to match the opportunities which had been opened to
Europe and more especially to Great Britain. Already by the middle
years of the eighteenth century powerful sections of opinion in
Britain were demanding that the government should turn its back
upon Europe and the traditional struggle to maintain the balance
of power on the continent. Beyond Europe, they argued, was the
wider world of America and the East. They demanded that Britain
should seek to defeat France overseas. The object was not to win
territory, but rather to capture sources of raw materials and markets
of unimaginable proportions. The Seven Years War gave Britain a
short-lived political domination in North America, which came to
an end with the grant of independence to the thirteen mainland
colonies which were to form the United States, but Britain nevertheless remained the dominant commercial power in North America.
In India a commercial hegemony was established and linked with the
profitable Chinese market through the port of Canton. The other
great colonial powers, Spain and the United Provinces, did not reap
the rewards of their efforts to the same extent. Central and Southern
America were controlled by Spain, but they were poor and intractable
territories. The Dutch East India Company in the eighteenth century
was meeting with grave difficulties in its attempts to exploit the
islands of south-east Asia and was never far from bankruptcy.
Portugal had long passed the zenith of her influence as a commercial
and maritime power. It was upon Britain that the pressure of demand
fell, compelling her to supplement her relatively meagre sources of
manpower with the power of steam.

The central factor in the British industrial expansion was the
manufacture of cotton fabrics. Raw cotton from traditional sources
soon could not meet the demands of the great British mills, and the
southern planters of the United States began to extend their cultivation, largely with the use of African slave labour. The steam engines
which drove the mills of Britain could be turned to other purposes.
Lathes could be constructed to achieve a precision beyond the skills

of even the most competent ironmasters of previous centuries. Thus the cotton revolution was succeeded by a metallurgical revolution, in which the world began to demand ever greater quantities of iron and steel. The steam engine could be made to turn wheels on rails and thus the locomotive was constructed. In 1825 Stockton and Darlington were connected by rail and Liverpool and Manchester by 1830. It was not long before the continental states themselves began to construct railways. Even more startling was the development of railways in the United States, which began to open up before men's eyes the possibility of developing an almost virgin continent. Thus the steam engine, created to supply power for a growing industry, itself extended the market by reaching out to areas which the waterways, canals and rivers had in the past been unable to open to European commerce. Water, nevertheless, to this day provides the cheapest and quickest method of carrying goods in bulk. At the end of the Napoleonic Wars in 1815 the largest vessels employed by the East India Company were about 1300 tons. Shipbuilders soon began to experiment with metal hulls. In 1829 John Laird of Birkenhead launched the first iron ship, and in 1837 the first iron ocean-going ship, powered with a steam engine, the *Rainbow*, was constructed. The size of the ocean-going steamer was gradually increased. Improved boilers and the screw propeller, which replaced the paddle, permitted ships of 3,500 tons to be built. In 1858 *The Great Eastern* was launched, a vessel of 22,500 tons. Freed from their dependence upon wood, the shipbuilders could provide for the transportation of goods in quantities far in excess of those conceived in the eighteenth century. Goods could, moreover, be conveyed to their destination more quickly. With the opening of the Suez canal on 17 November 1869 the hazards of trade with the Orient were greatly reduced. With the increase in the speed of transport went a desire for an increase in the speed of communication. By the 1830s the telegraph was operating on the British railways to assist signalling, but it was obvious that this means of communication could be used for other purposes. In November 1851 London and Paris were linked by a telegraphic cable. By 1866 a cable had been laid across the Atlantic to join Europe and North America. This was not yet the age of the telephone and the wireless, but the basic problem of obtaining information had been solved. What was being constructed was a system of multinational trade with a complexity which often defeated the ingenuity of its creators to control it.

There was never such an age, and the men who made the new civilization tended to be self-congratulatory for all their persistent inquiry into the methods of improving their achievements. The industrial development of Europe was not an unmixed blessing. The political imperfections of the eighteenth century were indeed enlarged. The armies of the French Revolutionary and Napoleonic Wars were usually about 100,000 men strong. In 1870 the North German Confederation and its allies put over 1,000,000 men into the field for the war against France. The increase in the total productivity of Europe, making possible an increase in the well-being of mankind, went hand in hand with the possibility of mass-destruction. All Europe was thrown into confusion. This confusion extended itself beyond Europe to the two Americas, India, China and Japan. The validity of ancient ways of life was called into question.

The social and economic transformation of Europe was in fact uneven. The fundamental factor in industrialization based upon the steam engine was the supply of coal. At first the tempo of development was most intense in the coal belts of Europe. The density of the European population to this day reveals how industry began to grow along the great coal belt which stretches through Britain, Northern France, along the Meuse through the province of Liège and thence into Germany, where the Ruhr became a great industrial basin. A subsidiary area of development was to appear in the coal belts of Upper Silesia. The development of industry in the Russian coal belts was retarded by the perennial difficulty of Tsardom, the shortage of capital for investment. To these new industrial areas were attracted labourers. The populations of the cities began to grow. It was an age of the masses. The industrial workers, herded into bleak cities and at the mercy of the uncertainties attendant upon the brilliant but haphazard expansion of production, began to entertain political aspirations of their own. The eighteenth century was an aristocratic age, in which the possession of political power and social pre-eminence by the upper classes was not seriously challenged anywhere except in France in 1789. Europe was still essentially rural, and the principal occupation of all countries was agriculture. The landed proprietors, farmers and peasants had their

differences which frequently rose to the surface. The power of the
civic authorities might from time to time be challenged by the
journeymen of the handicraft industries. It is nevertheless broadly
true to say that rarely did a disturbance, which contained the elements
of a social revolution, prove difficult for the state to suppress. By
the middle of the nineteenth century, however, the power of the
state to control the inflated populations of the cities was much
reduced. A challenge was issued by the industrial workers to what
had seemed a natural principle that nobility of birth and inherited
wealth should carry with them a prescriptive right to a monopoly of
political power.

The change in the climate of progressive opinion may be measured
by a comparison of two famous political thinkers, Rousseau and
Marx. Rousseau published his *Social Contract* in 1762, a work which
probably had little influence upon the events in France in 1789,
but which represents the high point in the thinking of the Contractual
School of political thought. At the beginning of the *Social Contract*
Rousseau wrote:

> Man is born Free; and everywhere he is in chains. One thinks himself
> the master of others and still remains a greater slave than they. What
> can make it legitimate? That question I think I can answer.

In spite of his own personal timidity, Rousseau was a thinker of
revolutionary importance. The Contractual School of thought, which
deduced its system from the idea that government was based upon a
fundamental agreement between the ruler and the ruled, was obsessed
with the problem of sovereignty. Thus Thomas Hobbes, in his
Leviathan (1651), had argued that men in order to avoid the brutalities
of life in the natural order accepted civil society; their solution was
'to confer all their power and strength upon one man, or upon one
assembly of men, that may reduce all their wills, by plurality of
voices, unto one will'. This surrender of men's individual rights was
in Hobbes' view irrevocable. Such an intellectual solution raised
many difficulties. By the eighteenth century thinkers had grown
discontented with a concept which seemed to deprive the individual
of all his rights. Many European monarchs had in fact begun the
work of legal codification, which they considered would establish
the rule of law and thus to some extent put men in possession of

their natural rights and free them from arbitrary judicial decisions. Rousseau went a stage further. Instead of conferring sovereignty upon one man, or upon an assembly, he conferred it upon the people as a whole, who as the sovereign might decide for themselves what conditions they should impose upon themselves; for Rousseau the ruler was merely a magistrate responsible to the sovereign people and removable by it.

By 1848 a new aspiration had appeared in the thinking of the European Left. In the *Manifesto of the Communist Party* Karl Marx urged the working classes of the towns to seize power and exercise it in the interests of humanity at large:

> The Proletarians have nothing to lose but their chains. They have a world to win. Working men of all countries, unite!

Both Rousseau and Marx used the word *chains*. For Rousseau these were the chains of an unjust political system. For Marx they were the chains of an unjust social and economic order. In his *Theses on Feuerbach*, which he jotted down in 1845, among the points he made were two which illustrate his point of view:

> X. The standpoint of the old materialism is 'civil society'; the standpoint of the new is *human* society or socialized humanity.
> XI. The philosophers have *interpreted* the world in various ways; the point however is to *change* it.

When the people of Paris for a few months in 1870–1 took power into their own hands upon the collapse of the French Second Empire, Marx believed that he saw for the first time a practical expression of his ideas.

Marx was the most advanced left-wing thinker of the nineteenth century. It was he who presented the most radical solution of the great industrial crisis. Most thinkers did not envisage a system in which the people themselves actually exercised political power, but there were many who were prepared to take power out of the hands of the kings and princes and transfer it to the representatives of the people. This in part is the theme with which this book will occupy itself, the great struggle for power within the European states. A subsidiary, but no less important, theme is the impact of Europe upon the peoples of the world, who were external to the details of European politics, but to whom the material progress of Europe administered a shock from which only in our own age are they recovering.

1: Europe in Turmoil

The Crisis of the Old Régime

In the 1780s the Old Régime in Europe everywhere was faced with a crisis. The revolution which was to break out in France in 1789 was only the most dramatic of a series of disturbances which suggest that the political malaise was a phenomenon of European dimensions. In Spain, Hungary, the United Provinces, the Austrian Netherlands and Poland discontent boiled over. Everywhere the old régime was compelled to meet a challenge of one form or another. The term *old régime* is in fact a bad one. The very word *old* carries with it an implication of decay and suggests that the régimes of the epoch which preceded the crisis were moribund and deserved to be destroyed. In Joseph II the Habsburg dominions had found a monarch whose enthusiasm for reform exceeded that of his subjects. Leopold, the Grand Duke of Tuscany, who succeeded him, could write in 1790:

> I think the Sovereign, though hereditary, is only the delegate and servant of the people . . . For every country there ought to be a fundamental law between the people and the Sovereign, which defines the authority and power of the latter . . . Executive power lies with the Sovereign, but the legislative power lies with the people and its representatives . . . The Sovereign must give an exact and annual account to the people of the application of the public revenue. He has no right at all to impose arbitrary taxes. He should render an account and obtain approval for all the changes in the structure of the state, new laws etc. Finally, I think that the Sovereign ought to reign only in accordance with the laws . . .

This theory of government perhaps represents the culmination of a theory, but there were other monarchs who were not far behind him. Certainly the famous Don Carlos, who between 1735 and 1759 was king of Sicily, as king of Spain from 1759 to 1788 was a better monarch than his surly subjects deserved to obtain, attempting in spite of them to induce reasonableness in a clergy unrivalled in Europe for its ignorance and bigotry.

The prestige of the monarchs was high in Europe. Everywhere, with the exception of Poland, the monarchies had brought the turbulent feudal nobility under control. The role of the absolute monarch had been to destroy particularist opposition and reduce all his subjects, whether great or small, to obedience to the state. This had in essence been a struggle for political power. In the eighteenth century there had appeared a new type of monarchy to which the inadequate term 'Enlightened Despotism' has been applied. Frederick II of Prussia had declared: 'I am the first servant of the state.' Here was a conception of service to the community. The progressive monarchs of Europe were attempting with varying degrees of success to use the political victory which their predecessors had won in order to mitigate the severity of absolutism, to systematize, to reform, to eradicate the barbarisms of the past. In the Roman Catholic countries the monarchies had adopted the logical attitude that, if the nobility had been reduced to order, then the other element in the state which had challenged the civil authority, the Church, might be reduced to subjection. In Portugal, Spain, Naples, Austria, Parma and Tuscany the extra-territorial rights of the Church had been circumscribed. Even in the ecclesiastical states of Germany the authority of the Pope was severely limited. In 1773 the Jesuit Order had been suppressed, to survive only in the great centre at Polotsk, where the Order, having come within the jurisdiction of Russia as a result of the first partition of Poland in 1772, was permitted to remain on condition of its giving full support to the political authority of Orthodox Russia. Everywhere efforts were made to reform the penal codes. Reform of the civil law was proceeding apace. In Austria Joseph II lightened serfdom, while in Prussia the extreme form of serfdom, *Leibeigenschaft*, was replaced by the modified condition of subjection, *Unterthänigkeit*. Where economic serfdom survived in the performance of labour services, some progress was being made. Under the system of the Prussian *Allgemeine Landrecht* security of tenure was secured, while in Austria there was some reduction of labour services. It is broadly true to say that the monarchies of the Old Régime were attempting to march in step with progressive opinion and certainly exceeded the wishes of the conservative sections of the upper classes.

There was, however, an inherent weakness in monarchical

government in continental Europe. Reform proceeded slowly only after painstaking discussions among officials. It has been said that the monarchs in fact adopted the principle of 'Everything for the people and nothing by the people'. Much might depend upon the personality of the monarch. A vigorous monarch could hasten the movement towards reform, but not all monarchs were themselves moved by the zeal which was apparent in Joseph II of Austria. Frederick II, for all the prestige of his military successes, exhibited a tendency towards conservatism, for which Prussia was to pay dearly in the great crisis. The monarchs of the eighteenth century gave an impetus to change from the top, and in spite of themselves encouraged a desire for change from the bottom. It was in the midst of this movement for reform, tentative though it was, that the French Revolution of 1789 broke upon Europe and transmitted to Europe a political revolution, which in any case the technological revolution appearing in Britain would have compelled.

The French Revolution of 1789

France was the richest country in Europe. Her human resources and civilization by far outstripped those of any other European country. Her political organization, however, had not matched her material and cultural achievements. France was a victim of the success of the Bourbon dynasty. Louis XIV had followed the policy of the great ministers, Richelieu and Mazarin, and reduced the great feudal lords to a position of political impotence. His success was so complete that the urge to reform, which was to be seen in less powerful monarchies, was less apparent under Louis XV and Louis XVI. The United Provinces had survived in the seventeenth century by their acceptance of modern capitalism. England and her dependencies, Ireland and Scotland, had won their place in the world by achieving a degree of centralization which was unknown elsewhere in Europe. For all the power of France there was in her social system much to be desired. The paradox of the late eighteenth century was that France, rich and powerful, had fallen behind her poorer and weaker neighbours in her social and political organization. If France had experienced some form of Enlightened Despotism the revolution of 1789 might never have broken out. The fault lay not with the French bureaucracy, which desired reform and which transmitted to the Revolution and the Empire its reforming zeal. The political malaise in France may be ascribed to a monarchy which lacked the energy and will to transform itself. The French monarchy fell, but the vigour inherent in French society re-emerged from the confusion of 1789 to prove that France, no less than the France of the seventeenth century, had the dominion of Europe almost within her grasp.

In 1789 French society burst the bonds of restraint placed upon it by the monarchy of Louis XIV. The origins of the revolution of 1789 have frequently been seen in the intellectual movements of the eighteenth century which implanted in men's minds the desire for freedom, but the truth is more mundane. The French bourgeoisie may have benefited from and may in varying degrees have been under the influence of the new learning, but it was not they who set in motion the struggle which culminated in the assembly of the States General in May 1789. The origin of the civil conflict lay much deeper in the very structure of the political and social system. France was a top-heavy society which in law consisted of three estates: the clergy, numbering about 135,000, and the nobles, of whom there were 400,000, these two elements constituting the first and second estates and enjoying exemption from taxation, who confronted the Third Estate, which embraced everyone else in the realm, about 1,000,000 bourgeoisie, 2,000,000 working men and 23,000,000 peasants, upon whom the burden of taxation fell without at the same time affording them the traditional redress of grievance associated with it. In the face of this fact it might at first sight appear obvious that revolution should spring from the Third Estate, but it was in fact the privileged orders which first offered the challenge to the French crown and unwittingly destroyed the system from which they themselves drew so much profit.

The Noble Opposition

France was a country in which old scores were not easily forgotten. The privileged elements in French society had never forgiven Louis XIV for curtailing their privileges. In the growing weakness of French absolutism in the eighteenth century the descendants of the men who fought against the Valois in the second half of the sixteenth century and the men who had been the authors of the Frondes in the seventeenth sensed an opportunity to reassert their claims against the crown.

The only vocal expression at first came from the law courts, or *parlements*, relics of the medieval constitution which had orginally been a means of ensuring unity in France in contrast with Germany, which had fallen into pieces in the absence of a strong monarchy. The most important of these was the *Parlement de Paris* with a membership of about 1,100 and a jurisdiction embracing about one-third of France. In fact, the *parlements* were institutions controlled by powerful families. Originally bourgeois in origin the lawyer class constituted itself the *noblesse de la robe*. A degree of Law could be bought and the office of the *parlementaire* became a piece of property in virtue of the *paulette*, a tax amounting to one-sixtieth of its value, in return for which it was made hereditary. By the eighteenth century the crown had lost control over the personnel of the *parlements*, which still continued to exercise important functions. Apart from judicial duties the *parlements* still had some control over the police. Prices, morals and censorship fell within their competence. Their most important function, however, was the registration of royal edicts, which, if they considered them inconsistent with the laws of France, they could refuse registration. In the event of a remonstrance by the *parlements* a number of courses were open to the King. He could either order the registration of an edict by a *lettre de jussion*, or as the fountainhead of justice make a personal appearance to register the edict himself by the procedure known as a *lit de justice*. If all efforts failed to obtain satisfaction the final course was the exile of the *parlementaires*. Louis XIV never forgave the *parlementaires* for their part in the Frondes and tolerated no nonsense from them, but his successors, Louis XV and Louis XVI, were not men of the same energy. In their reigns the *parlements* were able to recover some of their old confidence and once more offer a challenge to the crown.

The initial cause of their resistance arose from an obscure doctrinal issue connected with Jansenism. Jansenism was no longer the old style dissent which had led Louis XIV to enforce the Bull *Unigenitus*. Under Louis XV it exhibited a certain Gallicanism. In this sense the Jansenists saw eye to eye with the chief opponents of papal influence in France, the lawyer class. In such a matter the monarchy was neutral. The crisis came when the Archbishop of Paris ordered that no Jansenist should receive the last sacrament, a serious act in a Roman Catholic country. This was the signal for a protracted guerrilla warfare between the lawyers and the clergy. In the absence of intervention by the crown and indeed with some support from the King's mistress, Madame de Pompadour, and the chief minister, Choiseul, the confidence of the *parlements* in their own powers grew. In 1764 the *parlements* achieved a great success in forcing the expulsion of the Jesuits from France.

With equal enthusiasm, however, the *parlements* approached the question of finance. In this respect they were the spokesmen of the privileged classes, refusing to register new financial edicts and thus blocking the way to reform, which the French bureaucracy in the eighteenth century would gladly have undertaken. The crown feared to exile the *parlementaires*, because there were many vested interests which would be disrupted if the work of the *parlements* ceased, while the actual dislocation of justice could not readily be faced by the monarchy. Confident in their strength, the *parlementaires* began to develop a political theory of their own, taking as their point of departure the historic rights of the French nation. In 1753 was produced by the *Parlement de Paris* a Grand Remonstrance, which contained the idea that people owed obedience to the king, but the king himself was subject to the laws. Essential to the Remonstrance was the concept of contract between the sovereign and the governed and therefore of the limitation of monarchical powers. The same argument was developed in the local *parlements* in the struggle against the royal intendants. In fact, the *parlementaires* acted in opposition to the ideas of most *philosophes* who wished to strengthen the monarchy in order to make drastic reform possible. On the other hand, they gave wide publicity to the concepts of the contractual theorists, the enemies of unlimited monarchy.

The turning point came in 1770 when Louis XV for once roused himself to a policy of reform. The *parlements* were dissolved and six new courts were established. The Chancellor, Maupeou, and the Controller-general, the Abbé Terray, were empowered to reorganize the structure of the French state. Louis XV was guilty of many disservices to France, of which the worst perhaps was dying when he did. His successor, Louis XVI, believed that the old king had been disreputable, an opinion well grounded in fact. In consequence, he attempted a policy of conciliation and in doing so threw away all the advantages which Maupeou and Terray had won for the Crown. Chancellor and Controller-general were alike dismissed, the *parlements* restored and the Old Régime brought back into force again. Unfortunately for Louis XVI his well-intentioned moves coincided with a major effort in the field of foreign affairs. In 1778 France entered into the war against Great Britain on the side of the American settlers in an effort to reverse the defeats which she had suffered during the Seven Years' War. The ordinary income of the Crown was not enough and recourse was had to borrowing. The debt service became so heavy that after the restoration of peace borrowing was continued in order to finance the royal administration. This policy is associated with the Director-general, the protestant Swiss banker, Necker, who enjoyed a considerable reputation with the financial classes. It was Necker who in 1781 painted a false picture of the state of royal finances in his celebrated *Compte-rendu au Roi*, which declared that revenue was buoyant. Having been guilty of this deception and placed himself in a very difficult position, he contrived his own dismissal by claiming a place in the *Conseil-d'en haut*, which could not be granted because the other ministers refused to accept such an unjustified elevation. Necker saddled his successors with the policy of borrowing, for confession of near bankruptcy would cause all loans to dry up. Calonne continued the policy of borrowing until August 1786, when loans at length could no longer be negotiated. The position of French finances in March 1788 reveals that the expenditure of the Crown was 629,000,000 livres, but its income was only 503,000,000, thus leaving a deficit of 126,000,000. Much has been said of the extravagance of the court at Versailles, but its expenditure was a mere drop in the ocean by comparison with the debt service, which amounted annually to 318,000,000 livres. One course open to the Crown was the repudiation of the debt, but this would have led to the alienation of the bourgeoisie. The only feasible course of action was to increase taxation, but this raised a delicate question—who should be required to pay it?

The contemporary impression was that existing sources could be made to yield no more. Modern research shows that between the two periods 1726–41 and 1785–9 prices had risen 65 per cent, but wages only 22 per cent. The only solution, it appeared, was to revise the taxation system, which in effect meant the abolition of exemptions and compelling the clergy and nobles to pay. On 20 August 1786 Calonne in a memorandum proposed measures should be taken to improve the income of the Crown. The *vingtième*, a tax of one-twentieth on incomes, should be made to apply to all classes, while some relief should be given to the poorer classes. It was suggested, moreover, that all internal tariffs should be abolished and restrictions upon the grain trade removed in the interest of encouraging agriculture, while the sale of church properties could help to clear the debts of the Crown. The only difficulty was that the *parlements* could not be made to register edicts sanctioning such radical measures. Instead Calonne attempted an indirect method by summoning an Assembly of Notables for February 1787, whom he hoped to persuade to concede the abolition of the tax exemptions. Thus the traditional enemy of the Crown, the French nobility, was invited to save it from its embarrassments by foregoing the most cherished of its privileges. The Assembly refused all co-operation and Calonne was compelled to resign.

His place was taken by the Archbishop of Toulouse, Loménie de Brienne, ready to carry out a policy of drastic reform. When the *parlement* of Paris rejected his proposals for fiscal reform he exiled the *parlementaires* to Troyes in August 1787, but the protests were too great and the *parlement* was recalled to Paris. For a few months a desultory struggle took place between the Crown and the *parlements*, until at length even the mild Louis XVI perceived that the only course was to adopt the advice of Lamoignon and revert to the scheme of Maupeou and the Abbé Terray. On 8 May 1788 the *parlements* were suspended and in their place set up seven new courts, with a plenary court to register royal edicts. From this moment dates the reactionary revolution. The Church and the nobility combined to offer resistance to the monarchy. There were widespread disorders throughout provincial France. In the Dauphiné the nobles were completely out of control, while in Brittany there was a state almost of open insurrection.

The Calling of the French States General

The French monarchy was obliged to go back on the scheme of Lamoignon. The treasury was empty and the government utterly dependent upon the *parlements*. There was no alternative but to reinstate Necker, restore the *parlements* and call the States General for 1 May 1789. This was a crisis which in every way had been produced by the representatives of the old order of society, the elements which Louis XIV had reduced to subservience. The privileged orders during the eighteenth century had found their way back into the royal administration. Such was their power that the royal intendants could not enforce their authority. The situation was not, however, hopeless for the King. The nobles were intent upon obtaining more power for themselves by means of their control of the provincial estates and the States General, but they were to be in a poor tactical position if they insisted upon the preservation of their tax immunities. The calling of the States General, moreover, admitted the Third Estate to a voice in the affairs of the kingdom. In short, the French Crown had the opportunity of appealing from its historic enemy, the nobility, to its historic ally, the bourgeoisie.

It should not be imagined that the French bourgeoisie were a homogeneous class. There were among them financiers and merchants trading overseas whose political attitudes were often equivocal. The largest part of the bourgeoisie, however, consisted of men from the liberal professions, especially lawyers. The majority were men of modest means, in close contact with the common people and appreciating their aspirations. For themselves they hoped that they might achieve equality with the nobility, which had insisted upon its own class exclusiveness, but they nevertheless felt a sense of mission. In common with most liberally minded persons in the eighteenth century they thought that they ought to work for the good of humanity. At first they had shown some sympathy for the *parlements*, especially when it was suggested that the States General should be called. The bourgeoisie would thus be able to air their grievances for the first time since 1614, the last occasion on which the States General had met. The cardinal error of the *parlements* was their insistence upon the medieval procedure of the States General. In a declaration of 23 September 1788 it was proposed that the rules of 1614 should apply, by

which the States should vote by order. In other words, the two
privileged orders, the clergy and the nobility, would be able to out-
vote the Third Estate. The popularity of the *parlements* collapsed
overnight. The bourgeoisie ceased to be anti-monarchical. It was now
to be a struggle between the bourgeoisie and the privileged orders for
reform. In this situation the Crown might have given some leadership,
but no steps were taken to resolve the important question of whether
the States General should vote by order or vote as individuals. Upon
this question of procedure hung the vital political and social questions
which vexed France under the old régime. The indecision of the
monarchy led to a growth of radicalism among the bourgeoisie.
Everywhere in France clubs were established to organize resistance
to the privileged classes.

In one sense the antique institutions and social philosophies of
France assisted the bourgeoisie. Under the terms of the electoral
ordinance of 29 January 1789 the territorial divisions upon which
elections to the States General were to be based were the secondary
and principal bailiwicks. For the Third Estate there was to be a
system of indirect election. Deputies, moreover, were required to
possess certain property qualifications. The peasants themselves
could not provide leadership, and therefore tended to insist upon
men whom they knew, in general, men who were respected for their
grasp of affairs. This meant that they selected men who had taken
part in the defence of the peasants' interests in the innumerable
disputes which had arisen in connection with exploitation of feudal
dues by the seigneurial agents during the eighteenth century. Such
men were known not to be subject to seigneurial pressure and could
be relied upon to speak freely. The Third Estate was thus likely to be
composed of men who would adopt vigorous attitudes. To some
extent the method of selecting representatives from the clergy
favoured the bourgeoisie. All bishops and clergy could take part in
the elections, but for the religious orders only one vote was permitted
for each house. In consequence, the highly privileged element among
the clergy was under-represented, but the system of voting by head
favoured the anti-episcopal element, namely the parish priests, who
just as the peasants suffered under pressure from their superiors.
Among the nobles the caste feeling, which had in some measure been
responsible for the initial crisis, caused the election of men whose

merits were measured by the length of their family trees. There was a dislike of men of recent origin, who were considered unfit to represent the true interests of the nobility. For this reason men were elected to represent the nobility who had little talent and small capacity for public speaking. A disproportionate influence was exercised by nobles like La Fayette, who were in favour of reform and prepared to join hands with the bourgeoisie to obtain it. In such a situation it is difficult to argue that the Crown was powerless. The *cahiers de doléances*, or petitions, gave a clear indication of what the mass of the Third Estate wanted from it. The way was open for a modicum of reform, coupled with a minimum of representation. In practice, the Crown was to make the wrong choice. It would not break with the nobility and therefore missed an opportunity of surmounting the crisis, even perhaps with its real power enhanced.

The States General met in the magnificent palace at Versailles. This atmosphere intensified the dislike of the Third Estate for the apparently parasitic life of the courtier. There was enough encouragement from the city of Paris to bolster their morale and sustain them in a strong course of action. The tactics of the bourgeoisie were those of obstruction. They refused to declare themselves in session until it had been granted that the States General should vote by head. As long as the States General were not in session, no taxes could be voted, the prime purpose of their being summoned. On 11 May 1789 the nobles voted against any form of conciliation and announced their determination to sit as a separate house. The clergy, however, wavered and at length, having failed to win over the nobles, some of them decided to join the Third Estate. The nobles still refused to modify their attitude. On 10 June the Abbé Siéyès proposed that a summons should be issued to the privileged orders to come to a joint session with the Third Estate and that, if they refused, they should be considered to have defaulted. This was nothing less than a proposal to set up a national representative body with or without the consent of the King; in the meantime the collection of existing taxes was to be granted, the assumption being that the States General could withdraw this grant if they so desired. On 17 June the Third Estate declared that it was 'The National Assembly', which was a virtual claim that it alone spoke for France, whereas the nobles and the clergy spoke only for particular interests. This was a radical move to make, but all was not lost for the King. Necker was willing to submit, but the minister of war was opposed, lest control over appointments in the army should pass out of the King's hands. The King's brothers, too, offered their resistance. The Third Estate felt itself in danger. On 20 June 1789 the Third Estate met in the tennis court at Versailles and took a solemn oath that they would not disperse until the future constitution of France was laid upon a firm foundation. Royal vacillation had compelled the bourgeoisie to throw down a direct challenge to the King.

The Bourgeois Revolution

The challenge to the King was also an opportunity for him to re-assert the royal initiative. Under pressure of Necker it was agreed to summon a royal session of the States General on 23 June at which a royal plan of reform should be presented, but the plan which the King offered was one which revealed the influence which the privileged orders had upon his mind. The King was prepared to permit the States General to vote taxes and, in cancelling the mandates of the representatives, he removed obstacles to voting by head in joint deliberations of matters of common interest, but he declared that he excluded from discussion the rights of the three orders; the three orders were to retain their separate identity, which meant only one thing, that any modification of fiscal immunities would be determined by the minimum which the nobles were willing to concede. The King declared, moreover, that the decisions of the Third Estate on 17 June were without validity.

If the King had met the States General with such proposals when it first assembled he might have obtained support, but procrastination and delay gave rise to suspicion that in fact no reform was intended. Yet the King refused to coerce the bourgeoisie. Already part of the clergy had joined the Third Estate and on 25 June they were joined by a group of liberal nobles. The recalcitrant privileged orders were becoming increasingly isolated. Suddenly on 27 June the King, perhaps fearing that he would provoke a crisis, bowed before the storm and ordered the privileged orders to seat themselves with the Third Estate. The bourgeoisie by its own recalcitrance and stubbornness had won a bloodless victory. Without the use of force they had achieved legislative supremacy in France. The way was opened once more for an alliance between the King and the Third Estate.

The momentary popularity of Louis XVI soon gave way to distrust. The bourgeoisie merely proposed the indivisibility of sovereignty between the Monarch and the Nation, a partnership in which the King might retain the right of veto and control of the executive. In short, the King might easily have saved the substance of his power and led France forward from Absolutism to an Enlightened Despotism which accepted some representation of the people. The King, however, listened to other counsels current in the Court Party. There was every appearance that the Court intended to carry out a coup d'état. On the pretext that food shortages were likely to lead to disturbances some 18,000 troops were brought up to the region of Paris. The plan of the Court Party was to dissolve the States General and to rely upon the *parlements* to declare a bankruptcy. On 11 July Necker, the symbol of bourgeois respectability, was dismissed and a ministry established under Breteuil, a courtier. It was thus the aristocratic party which appealed to force to combat the bloodless revolution achieved by the Third Estate.

The Urban Revolution

The bourgeoisie were a less united class than might be supposed, but the danger of a coup d'état gave them a solidarity which they might not otherwise have possessed. The holders of government stock were frightened lest they be ruined by a bankruptcy. They were therefore willing to call upon the people to protect them. The lesser bourgeoisie were not influenced to any great extent by the class conflicts which bedevilled French society in the nineteenth century. They were still under the influence of the highly ethical theories of eighteenth-century philosophy, that it was the duty of enlightened men to promote the interests of humanity. From their point of view the proletarians of the cities ought to obtain the opportunity of acquiring property. There was in fact no word in French for *proletariat*.

This does not mean an absence of economic strains and stresses. The general tendency in eighteenth-century France was for wages to have risen less quickly than prices. Probably rising prices hit the countryside more severely than the towns. Rents had risen by 90 per cent, while prices had risen by 65 per cent, the index of the so-called 'feudal reaction' which was taking place. Large numbers of peasants supplemented their incomes by wage-labour, but wages had risen only by 22 per cent. There was therefore a declining purchasing power in the countryside. This inevitably had its repercussions upon the towns. The grain system of the Old Régime in France was governed by the ideal of local self-sufficiency. People disliked grain moving out of the local area and there were internal customs barriers to ensure that each region was kept well supplied. Within the local market there was a compulsory place of sale and a recognized order of sale; the local inhabitants might buy grain first, followed in turn by the bakers and the merchants. The local authorities intervened to fix prices. This was essentially a town policy, with a history stretching back into the Middle Ages. The Physiocratic economists of eighteenth-century France, however, wanted to free the grain trade, because the removal of controls would send up prices and encourage investment in agriculture. Experiments in the abandonment of controls were made in 1763 and 1774, but on each occasion they were abandoned. In 1787, however, Brienne repeated this experiment. There was therefore a boom in the grain trade in a year of poor harvest. The poor yields of 1788 caused prices again to rise. A complicating fact, however, was the good grape harvest in the wine districts of Southern France. As a result the price of wine fell at a moment when the price of bread was rising. In such a situation all the advantages were with the large landed proprietors who had a surplus of grain and the right to move it wherever they might find attractive prices. More grain than ever was visible on the roads and on the rivers. In the universal crisis which afflicted France it was supposed that the landed proprietors, in other words, the nobles, were responsible for the miseries of the people. In the countryside the peasants frequently had to buy back corn which they had paid in rents to the proprietor. In the towns unemployment increased because the peasants lacked the money to make purchases of manufactured goods.

The traditional policy of the government was to control prices in times of scarcity. Therefore in all the towns of France there were demands for the regulation of prices. These demands were presented to the town halls, and discontents soon transformed themselves into attacks upon the municipal authorities. There was thus a breakdown of order. At the centre the monarchy was paralysed by the political crisis at Versailles. The disorders were in fact too widespread for the army to control them. Indeed, the army itself was unreliable. Many of the junior officers were denied promotion in a system under which preference was given according to the length of the officers' family trees. The men, moreover, were not in barracks, but billeted upon the population and given a subsistence allowance. They were exposed to exactly the same economic pressures as the people, whose aspirations they shared. The only units absolutely loyal to the Crown were the foreign troops, a dubious advantage in a dangerous situation.

All over France an urban revolution took place. Municipalities were either taken over by new rulers, or the old oligarchical town governments wisely admitted new members. In Paris the 407 electors to the States General decided to remain in close contact after they had appointed their representatives and on 25 June established themselves in the Hôtel de Ville as an unofficial government of Paris. Distrustful of the security forces, the Watch and the Gardes Françaises, the bourgeoisie began to agitate for a National Guard controlled by officers of its own. It was in this explosive situation that on 12 July the news reached Paris that Necker had been dismissed. There were spontaneous gatherings at which speakers demanded arms for the people, but there were no arms to be had. On 14 July a search was made for arms in the public buildings and above all at the fortress of the Bastille. Here the royal troops lost their nerve and fired into the crowd and an assault was threatened, whereupon the governor surrendered the fortress to the mob. The so-called Storming of the Bastille was subsequently considered symbolic of freeing France from tyranny and 14 July has become the National Day of France, but for the King in 1789 the events of that day had an immediate practical importance. He had lost control of the greatest city in France which it would take a full-scale siege to regain. The aristocratic factions at court advised the use of the army, but Louis XVI decided that he must submit. Breteuil was dismissed and Necker recalled. On 17 July as a gesture of conciliation Louis XVI visited Paris, where he received from Bailly, the president of the Third Estate, the national red, white and blue cockade, the red and the blue representing Paris, and the white the House of Bourbon, symbolic of a renewed alliance of the people and the King. The commune of Paris was in fact the master of the King. It was more than a town government. Under its mayor, Bailly, it was pre-eminent among the new town governments of France and with its National Guard under La Fayette it had the means to impose its will.

The Rural Revolution

For the moment there was an illusion of law and order, but it was apparent only in the towns. As yet the peasants of the countryside had not made their voices heard. Serfdom was not the problem of rural France. There were for practical purposes no serfs in France. The fundamental social problem was land hunger resulting from the division of holdings. There were some peasants, possibly a third of the total, who owned their own land, living mainly in the north of France, but representing a substantial element everywhere in the country. The majority of the peasants, however, owned no land, but rented holdings. A common system was *métayage* or share-cropping, by which the peasant paid a portion of the yield to the proprietor. Holdings were small, methods backward and subdivision under the pressure of a growing rural population proceeding apace. There was little idea among the peasants of attacking property. Their real grievances were the rural obligations. Under the 'feudal reaction' proprietors attempted to extract the last possible profit from their seigneurial rights. Manorial courts invariably found in favour of the seigneur in disputes, while appeal to the *parlements* was merely reference to judges who themselves were often seigneurs. Some of the seigneurial rights were in fact absurd and long out of date, but by the eighteenth century they had become a powerful weapon for the extortion of money from the peasants. Objection was made also to the tithes, which did not benefit the parish priests, but went to the bishops and the orders and, being collected in kind, gave the recipient the opportunity of making considerable gains in times of crisis. The landlords, moreover, were encroaching everywhere upon the collective rights of the villagers, which gave offence to the propertied peasants. On top of all these obligations were the taxes due to the state, the *taille, capitation, vingtième* and the *corvée des routes*. The grievances of the peasants were not those of the towns, for whom the urban revolution promised justice. The peasants none the less were interested in the outcome of the States General. It was believed that at last the King, by calling the States General, had recognized the wrongs done to the peasants and would give them redress against the landlords. The absence of any mention of the peasants in the States General was considered evidence of aristocratic intrigue, but the King had visited Paris on 17 July and received the red-white-and-blue cockade, which was considered proof that he at least did not side with the nobles. Towards the end of July 1789 the countryside began to seethe with discontent and local riots began to merge into a vast peasant uprising, the *Grande Peur*.

What the peasants were alleged to fear was an aristocratic plot in which brigands would lay waste the villages of France. A *jacquerie* spread through France from several different centres. There was nothing fanciful in the action which the peasants took. They attacked castles and destroyed the manorial rolls, which had been the instruments of their misery. They overthrew the enclosures which barred them from the common pastures and took timber from the seigneurial woods. The disturbances which took place were on far too wide a scale for the leaders of the Third Estate to suppress. Indeed, suppression would have given the King forces with which to overthrow the gains which the bourgeoisie had extracted from him. For this reason it was decided that concessions must be made to the peasants in order to restore tranquillity. On 4 August a group of liberal nobles in alliance with the Third Estate rose to make a voluntary resignation of their privileges. It has been said that 'a contagion of sentimental feeling carried them away'. Noble vied with noble to renounce manorial rights before the National Assembly. In the days after this historic session there was a diminution of enthusiasm and an attempt was made to draw a distinction between *feudal* rights and dues which owed their origin to a freely negotiated contract, the former to be abolished outright and the latter to be subject to compensation for the landlords, but in practice the peasants achieved their emancipation without onerous burdens being placed upon them. Everywhere their immediate economic demands were satisfied and the agrarian question receded into the background.

The King and the Revolution

For all the changes which were brought about by the National Assembly there remained the problem of obtaining the King's sanction. In spite of the crisis the King still clung to the conception that his allies were the nobles and the people his enemy. The King delayed and refused his assent to constitutional changes. The arrival of the Flanders Regiment at Versailles on 1 October did nothing to allay the suspicion that the King was waiting merely for an opportunity to restore the Old Régime. The dilemma of the bourgeoisie was solved in a manner which was almost absurd. On 5 October a gathering of women before the Hôtel de Ville in Paris clamoured for bread, and the idea arose that they should march to Versailles to petition the King, The National Guard under La Fayette was completely nonplussed by this turn in events. The Municipal Council decided in the afternoon that the National Guard must itself march to Versailles and bring the King to Paris. In the early hours of 6 October the motley gathering from Paris invaded the quarters of the King. In the face of this spontaneous demonstration the King decided that he must return with his family to Paris. Louis XVI on 6 October was carried back by his people to Paris, to escape from which after the experience of the Frondes Louis XIV had ordered the construction of Versailles. Paris had exerted its supremacy and the King was henceforth to be the prisoner of the Revolution, lodged in the old palace of the Tuileries. Laid bare for all to see was the power of the mob in a capital city, which could at will make and unmake governments.

The French Revolution and Reform

In a France in the mood of 1789 there was no place for the leaders of the Old Régime. The Comte d'Artois, the King's brother, and his followers, who had planned for a military suppression of the revolution, chose to leave the country in order to do it as much harm as they could from abroad. Having done so much to prevent the victory of the Third Estate, they now left it to give form and shape to its principles. These principles were first formulated in the Declaration of the Rights of 27 August 1789, which listed the attributes of men in society. Men, it announced, were free and equal in their rights, enjoying freedom of opportunity and opinion, freedom from arbitrary arrest and liberty of opinion; law was to be the expression of the general will, by which it was understood that a representative assembly was to give expression to the aspirations of the people.

When the King was brought back to Paris a supplementary decree declared him to be 'Louis, by the grace of God and the constitutional law of the state, King of the French'; no longer could he claim to rule in virtue of his hereditary titles, for the Declaration of Rights affirmed that the source of sovereignty lay with the French nation. There was little that was original in the Declaration of Rights. It represented no more than the lowest common denominator of opinion common to the school of thought which began its thinking from the concept of Natural Law. It was nevertheless influential, for it was not only a manifesto, but one which could be tested by the practical reforms which the Revolution of 1789 undertook.

The National Assembly of 1789 transformed itself into a Constituent Assembly to draw up a constitution for the new France. There was much talk of the rights of the people, but, though all adult males were citizens, not all were to come within the pale of the constitution. Only men who paid direct taxes to the value of three days' labour in the year were to be given the right to vote, while membership of the electoral assemblies and the future Legislative Assembly were to be subject to severe property qualifications. Behind all the enthusiasm engendered by the Revolution lay a narrow design among the majority of the bourgeoisie to keep effective political power in the hands of the propertied classes. This did not mean that the aristocratic privileges of the Old Régime were to remain. A clean sweep was made of the historic provinces. The besetting evil of France under the Bourbons had been its provincialism. The events of 1789 had brought into existence all over France a system of communes, which were now retained, and in place of the historic divisions of France were established eighty-three departments, more or less equal in their populations. Local officials were henceforth to be elected, subject to their possessing the requisite property qualifications. The reform of local government was permanent and constitutes the system in force in France to this day, but the new local authorities lacked financial powers when they were first established, and therefore for a short period there was some confusion.

Indeed, the question of finance lay at the root of France's troubles in 1789. The Constituent Assembly assumed responsibility for the royal debt and even increased it by abolishing the system of the sale of offices by the Controller-General, with compensation for their holders, who were of course members of the bourgeois class. Obviously the members of the Constituent Assembly had no intention of imposing fresh burdens upon the Third Estate. In common with the Enlightened Despots of the eighteenth century they turned their attention to the estates of the Church. On 2 November 1789 the lands of the clergy were placed at the disposal of the nation, and on 14 December 1789 the decision was taken to issue *assignats*, or bonds, to the value of 400,000,000 livres carrying an interest of 5 per cent and secured upon the property of the clergy. In the first half of 1790 the monasteries were suppressed and the clergy deprived of the administration of their property; the clergy were to be paid by the state and ecclesiastical property to be placed upon the market for sale. To meet the current needs of the treasury the *assignat* became a bank note, of which an issue of up to 1,200,000,000 livres was authorized in August 1790. In theory the lesser clergy stood to gain by the receipt of a regular salary, but the state ran the risk of future financial troubles. The issue of what was in effect a paper currency inevitably led to inflation and a fall in the face value of the *assignat*, which in its turn caused the hard currency of France to disappear. By the summer of 1791 the *assignat* had fallen to about 75 per cent of its nominal value.

Hand in hand with the confiscation of ecclesiastical property went the reorganization of the Church itself. Little opposition was to be expected of a Pope as weak as Pius VI, whom the monarchs of Europe treated as a nonentity. Indeed, the clergy of France had no basic objection to loosening the ties with Rome. On 12 July 1790 was voted the Civil Constitution of the Clergy. Bishops and priests were, like other officials of the state, to be elected. Provincial synods were to be held and the bishop was to be assisted by a council with whose decisions he must accord. The Pope was forbidden to receive money from France and, though his primacy was recognized, he was deprived of all jurisdiction within France. The Civil Constitution of the Clergy was not to the liking of the King, who hesitated to ratify it. The bishops wished to know where authority lay within the French Church, whether with the Pope or with a council. The Constituent Assembly feared to create a council of bishops, because that would erect a centre of opposition to itself. On 27 November 1790 the Constituent Assembly demanded from the clergy an oath of allegiance to the Constitution of France, of which the Civil Constitution of the Clergy was an integral part. Only seven out of 160 bishops took the oath, and less than half the clergy followed their example. The Assembly had made the same mistake as many European monarchs in underestimating the strength of attachment to the traditional organization of the Church. In the spring of 1791 Pope Pius VI proclaimed his opposition to the principles of the Revolution and the Civil Constitution of the Clergy. Open defiance of the Civil Constitution appeared in northern France, Brittany, the Loire Valley and in Alsace. The pliant bishop of Autun, Talleyrand, and Gobel, the bishop of Lydda, agreed to consecrate elected bishops for the Constitutional Church, but for fear of destroying the fabric of the Church altogether the recalcitrant clergy was left in possession of their benefices. By the zeal of its anti-clericalism the Constituent Assembly caused a cleavage in French society which has never entirely been healed.

Less controversial were the attempts of the Constituent Assembly to reform the civil and criminal laws. The *parlements* were abolished and replaced with new courts. With the *parlements* went all the barbarous punishments which they had inflicted upon criminals and prosecutions for heresy and witchcraft. Jews were given full rights of citizenship, in spite of opposition from the Germans of Alsace-Lorraine, but paradoxically slavery was maintained in the West Indies for fear of antagonizing the sugar planters and merchants engaged in the colonial trade. The commercial and industrial corporations were abolished with the aim of removing the shackles from economic development, but no freedom of association was granted to the workers to strike. Similarly, while all the internal customs barriers were removed and a single tariff applied to all France, the Constituent Assembly remained strongly protectionist in its attitude towards the importation of foreign goods, especially English manufactures, and stoutly upheld the monopoly system of the French colonial trade. Only in its anti-clericalism can the Constituent Assembly be said to have overstepped the limits of French tolerance.

France in October 1791

On 1 October the new constitution came into force and the Legislative Assembly met. Under this system the King controlled foreign policy and had the power to appoint the six principal ministers, army commanders and ambassadors. In addition, he might exercise a suspensive veto over the decisions of the Legislative Assembly. There were, however, limitations upon the King's power. He could not issue an order without the countersignature of the minister responsible to the Assembly, nor could he leave Paris without permission. The King had no power to dissolve the Assembly. The system of indirect election ensured that it would consist of well-to-do bourgeoisie. Thus inherent in the constitution was a potential clash between the King and his ministers, on the one hand, and the bourgeoisie of the Assembly, on the other. The Constituent Assembly, moreover, had taken a fatal step before its dissolution. Upon the proposal of Robespierre, a radical lawyer from Arras, the members of the Constituent Assembly in a self-denying ordinance voted that they should not be eligible for election to the Legislative Assembly. In this way those members of the Constituent Assembly who had accumulated some experience of parliamentary government were unable to transmit it to the Legislative Assembly, which was composed entirely of new men, who were required to learn from the beginning the techniques of management and statesmanship.

Already therefore there were signs of fragmentation in the edifice constructed by the Revolution. The Church was disaffected by the Civil Constitution. There was, moreover, a growing left-wing which disliked a constitution which in effect created a bourgeois republic. There was the Cordeliers Club, of which Danton was the most prominent member, but more important was the Jacobin Club. The Jacobins had a large influence not only in Paris but also in the provinces. By corresponding with the provincial clubs, which often took its name, it gradually won an authority which enabled it to rival the state itself. The Jacobin Club became an alternative government. It saw its task as the representation of popular wishes, protecting the poor against the rich, though the membership of the Jacobin Club was itself decidedly middle-class. It is perhaps too much to claim complete political coherence for the Jacobins, but they foreshadowed a new form of political organization in which the state and the party were to be so closely identified that they might scarcely be distinguished.

The greatest enemy of the Revolution, however, was the King

himself. One aristocrat at least, Mirabeau, had seen that the monarchy must take the initiative and steer a course between the Scylla of aristocratic intrigue and the Charybdis of left-wing extremism. Mirabeau knew that the majority of the representatives in the Constituent Assembly would have accepted a working partnership with the Crown, but Louis XVI and his queen, Marie Antoinette, were not persons with a great political insight and would not accept his advice. Mirabeau, moreover, advised the King to leave Paris and establish himself in a loyal province from which he could speak with greater freedom. Mirabeau was unfortunately a man with a notorious past which detracted from his authority. Exhausted by his efforts to defend the monarchy in the Assembly, he died on 2 April 1791. On 20 June 1791 the King and the royal family did attempt to seek refuge in the provinces, but they drove out eastwards in the direction of Metz, where they believed they could rely upon the loyalty of its garrison and, if they were compelled to flee, could reach with ease the eastern frontier of France. On the following day they were detected at Varennes and brought back to Paris under an escort of the National Guard. The immediate effect of the flight to Varennes was to give an impulse to the growth of republican feeling. The event occurred at an unfortunate juncture in the external affairs of France and the foreign relations of Europe. Louis XVI gave the impression that he was deserting his subjects to seek the aid of the foreigner. On 17 July 1791 a great demonstration was held on the Champ de Mars to demand the abdication of the King. Martial law was proclaimed and a detachment of the National Guard dispersed the mob with considerable bloodshed. The King was, however, not long to survive his final act of folly.

The International Crisis

The flight of Louis XVI to Varennes had a significance for France which owed much to factors which had little to do with French internal conditions. With the consummation of the Revolution in France emergent French aspirations blended with the conflicts of Europe as a whole. The political class in France had not forgotten that Louis XIV had brought his power to the point where the domination of all Europe had lain within his grasp, but his successors had manifestly failed to fulfil the promise which French prowess in arms seemed to foreshadow. French historians, proud of the dynamic role which France has played in Europe, are inclined to give their country pride of place in the events of the late eighteenth century, but the fact remains that in the early stages of the Revolution France was a cypher in international relations. France was a military monarchy which was temporarily at the nadir of her fortunes. In Russia the military monarchy of Peter the Great was still groping for a solution of problems which belonged to another age.

Russia at the Outbreak of the French Revolution

Russia in the 1780s had an influence which stretched far beyond her frontiers, but her social and political organization had only recently become effective beyond the frontiers of the Muscovy of Peter the Great. When Catherine II assumed supreme power in 1762 there was much to be done. The so-called 'Northern System' of Panin proved a failure, but Catherine II had emerged triumphant from her troubles. Austria and Prussia had nibbled at Russia's sphere of influence under the terms of the First Partition of Poland of 1772, but Russia had restored her position. The cession of parts of Western Poland to Prussia and southern Poland to Austria had enabled Russia to bring the war against Turkey to a successful conclusion by the treaty of Kutchuk Kajnardji in 1774. The Russian frontier was advanced to the river line of the southern Bug and the possession of the fortress of Kinburn, ensuring the security of the estuary of Dniepr, and the acquisition of Kerch and Yenikale at the eastern end of the Crimean Peninsula gave Russia effective control over the Crimean Khanate; in 1783 the Khanate, already technically independent of Turkey, was occupied by Russia as a result of a dispute within the ruling Girej family. For the first time Russia appeared on the Black Sea in strength. Behind the line of advance of Russian sovereignty the authority of the state was widening and expanding.

It is customary to point to the limitations upon the enlightenment of Catherine II, but in spite of all her deficiencies, imposed upon her as much by her own caution as by the backward condition of Russia's social development, there were many solid achievements, for which less than due credit has been given. Catherine II was a usurper when she came to the throne in 1762, and there had been no guarantee that her reign would last long. The whole structure of

THE ADVANCE OF RUSSIA
TO THE WEST (to 1795)

GAINS FROM POLAND 1772
" " 1793
" " 1795

VIBORG

REVEL

ESTONIA

ST. PETERSBURG

NOVGOROD

VOLOGDA

LIVONIA

PSKOV

KOSTROMA

KURLAND
1795

RIGA

DUNABURG

1772

POLOTSK

MOSCOW

KÖNIGSBERG

1795

KOVNO

VILNA

VYAZMA

SMOLENSK

KALUGA

1772

To PRUSSIA

GRODNO

MINSK

1793

MOGILEV

WARSAW

GAINS FROM POLAND

GOMEL

OREL

TAMBOV

RADOM
1795

LUBLIN

BREST-LITOVSK

1793

1795

CHERNIGOV

KURSK

VORONEZH

To AUSTRIA

1772

GALICIA

LVOV

ZHITOMIR

KIEV

BELGOROD

SLOBODSKAYA

AUSTRIA

R. Dniestr

BAR
KAMENETS
PODOLSK

1793

R. Dniepr

UKRAINA

R. Donets

BUKOVINA

1775

MOLDAVIA

JASSY

1792

R. Bug

OCHAKOV

NEW RUSSIA

ZAPOROZHE
1775 COSSACKS

TERRITORIES
OF THE
DON
ARMY

WALLACHIA

FOCSANI

ISMAIL

Dniestr

AKKERMAN

1783

SEA OF
AZOV

KERCH

1774

1783

BUCHAREST

R. Danube

KUTCHUK-KAJNARDJI

CRIMEAN
KHANATE

BAKHISERAI

KUBAN HORDE

CIRCASSIANS

OTTOMAN
EMPIRE

BLACK SEA

0   50   100   200
Miles

Tsarist Russia was threatened with destruction by the Pugachev rebellion of 1773–5, which had coincided with a crisis in the conduct of Russia's foreign policy. The lesson which Catherine II learned from the Pugachev rebellion was that Russia was in need of closer supervision from the centre. This was the reason for the reform of the internal administration of Russia in 1775, by which Russia was divided into fifty governments, or *gubernii*; each *gubernia* contained 300,000 to 400,000 inhabitants and was subdivided into districts (*uyezdy*), each of which contained 20,000 to 30,000 inhabitants. The basis of the administrative division of Russia was therefore numerical, often defying historical and geographical considerations. The *gubernii* were usually linked in pairs or threes under a general-governor, but within each *gubernia* was a *gubernator* responsible for the civil administration. The financial and judicial organs of the local administration were uniform throughout the *gubernii* and districts of Russia. The provinces of the Ukraine were gradually absorbed into the Russian system. The *hetmanshchina* had long been subject to close supervision, and in 1764 the office of hetman was abolished. In 1765 the regimental organization (*polkovoye upravleniye*) was abolished in the Slobodskaya Ukraina, which lost its Cossack privileges. In 1775 the Sech at Zaporozhe was occupied and the Zaporozhe army was disbanded. Only the Don Cossacks were to retain their peculiar organization.

Hand in hand with this eradication of regional peculiarities and the strengthening of the central government's power had gone a policy of conciliating the gentry. In 1785 a charter of privileges was granted to the nobility. The charter contained nothing new in principle, but it confirmed a series of individual measures which had already been taken. The nobility were freed from compulsory service, the payment of taxes, corporal punishment and the obligation of billeting troops. They were granted complete economic freedom, with a monopoly of holding land and owning serfs. At the same time a charter of liberties was granted to the oligarchies of the towns. There was no alleviation of serfdom. In fact, it was extended with the advancement of the government's authority in the Ukraine. With the suppression of the Cossack privileges and the conversion of the Cossack forces into units of the regular army it was necessary to conciliate the Cossack senior officers. Thus in May 1783 in the left-bank Ukraine serfdom was imposed upon the common people. In contrast with the French Revolution, which destroyed noble privileges, the Russia of Catherine II extended them, but at the same time even before the French Revolution adopted a system of local government which gave the Empire a unity unknown in the France of the Old Régime. In the 1770s and 1780s organized life was to extend into the more than half-empty lands of the south. In 1778 was founded Kherson, Maryupol in 1784, Yekaterinoslav (Dnepropetrovsk) in 1787, Nikolayev in 1789 and Odessa in 1794. At last the effective authority of the Russian state was reaching out beyond the confines of medieval Muscovy. Russia, moreover, had an army, national in its composition and larger than any other in Europe.

It had long been a rule of Russian foreign policy that a war on two fronts should be avoided. After the conclusion of the treaty of Kutchuk Kainardji Russia began to strengthen her position in the west. Her domination over Poland was quickly re-established in 1775 when Poland was given a modern government for the first time in the form of the 'Permanent Council', which was to be the instrument of maintaining order in the Polish Commonwealth and preventing disturbances upon the scale of the Confederation of Bar in 1768. The pretensions of Frederick II were likewise given a severe check. In July 1778 he had invaded Bohemia in order to prevent the exchange of the Austrian Netherlands for Bavaria, to which Charles Theodore of Bavaria had agreed with Joseph II, on the grounds that this transfer would upset the balance of power in Germany. France and Russia combined to restore the *status quo* in the Empire and offered their mediation, which resulted in the peace of Teschen of 1779, under the terms of which both France and Russia became guarantors of the Imperial German constitution. In this way Russia obtained a treaty right to maintain the system of parcelization in Germany and restrain Prussian expansionism. In 1780 Catherine II stood at the head of the first Armed Neutrality of the North in defiance of Great Britain's claim to the Right of Search upon the seas. Thus Catherine II reached the zenith of her power. It was not until the death of Frederick II in August 1786, however, that serious consideration could again be given to plans of settling accounts with the Turks. In the May of 1787 Catherine II met Joseph II in the Crimea, where the Balkan Question was discussed.

The Ottoman Empire had long experience of the laborious preparations of Russian diplomacy. On 26 July 1787 an ultimatum was
delivered to Russia demanding the recognition of Turkish sovereignty
in Georgia, where Russia was extending her influence, and the
admission of Turkish consuls to the Crimea. Catherine II would have
been glad to postpone a conflict with Turkey, but the Turks declared
war on 15 August 1787 in order to obtain the advantage of surprise.
It was not until February 1788 that Austria declared war upon
Turkey in support of Russia, but the aid which Austria brought to
Russia was offset by the Swedish declaration of war upon Russia in
July 1788. At the same time as the crisis was growing in France the
whole of eastern Europe was involved in a great war.

The Polish Revolt of 1788

Poland had been a power vacuum controlled by Russia since 1717 and
had only on occasions slipped from her grasp. The re-assertion of
Russian authority in Poland in 1775 had not been any the more
acceptable to the Poles for the good government and tranquillity
it brought with it. The King, Stanisław August Poniatowski, had
sought to associate Poland with the great war against the Turks,
but Catherine II was not willing to pay the price even of minor
modifications in the system of Russian domination. It was a tradition
of Polish politics that each party would seek the aid of neighbouring
powers to supplement its strength. The power to which the Polish
opposition now looked was Prussia. When the Polish Diet assembled
in 1788 the Prussian ambassador offered the Polish Republic an
alliance. This step was sufficient for all the groups opposed to
Russia, whether reactionary or progressive, to combine to overthrow
the system imposed upon Poland in 1775. An army of 100,000 men
was voted in order that Poland might once more enjoy a separate
and independent foreign policy. The War Department of the Permanent Council was overthrown and military affairs placed in the
hands of the Diet. In January 1790 the Permanent Council itself was
abolished and the last vestige of Russian influence removed.

Behind the Prussian offer of an alliance lay diplomatic complications which involved the whole of Europe. Prussia was scarcely
content with the restoration of the *status quo* in Germany by the
peace of Teschen of 1779, which, though it prevented the exchange

of Bavaria for the Austrian Netherlands, was none the less a hindrance to Prussian expansionism. Great Britain, moreover, was deeply conscious of her own isolation in the years during the War of American Independence and the fact that her weakness in Europe had compelled her to sue for peace. The Younger Pitt was from the outset seeking for allies in Europe. In the summer of 1787 the unresolved conflict between the Stadholder and the merchant classes in the United Provinces once more reached a point of crisis. In September 1787 Frederick William II intervened in the dispute by sending 24,000 troops into the United Provinces in support of his brother-in-law, William V of Orange. This action was accompanied by a British naval demonstration, because the opponents of William V had looked towards France in conducting their foreign policy since the alliance of the Dutch States General of November 1785 by the treaty of Versailles. A virtual dictatorship of the Stadholder was established when his office was made hereditary and the United Provinces removed from the French field of influence. Though the Dutch opposition continued to look towards France, the first fruit of this action was an alliance between Britain and the United Provinces in April 1788 and Britain and Prussia in August 1788. In this manner a new alliance system was born, to which the Prussian government hoped to add Poland. There was no altruism in the policy of Prussia. Her plan was to obtain from Poland the towns of Danzig and Toruń, in return for which she would wrest from Austria her gains under the First Partition of 1772, the province of Galicia, and restore it to Poland. In January 1790 Prussia concluded an alliance with Turkey and with Poland in March 1790.

The Crisis in the Habsburg Dominions

The war in the east and the internal policies of Joseph II threw the whole of the Habsburg dominions into confusion. In 1789 the conservatives in the Austrian Netherlands under van der Noot and van Eupen, defending the vested interests of the guilds and the Church, joined hands with the constitutional democratic party of de Vonck to throw off the Habsburg suzerainty. On 7 January 1790 the States General in Brussels proclaimed the independence of Belgium, or rather the United States of Belgium. This new state looked to the support of Britain, Prussia and the United Provinces.

At the same time in Hungary the centralizing measures of Joseph II had lost for the dynasty the support which the cautious policy of Maria Theresa had won. When Joseph II attempted in addition to abolish the fiscal immunities of the gentry and with them the whole system of serfdom, Hungary was plunged into a state of disorder and like Belgium brought to the point of revolt. In the midst of this crisis Joseph II died on 20 January 1790. Faced with internal problems and the threat of a Prussian attack in the rear, his successor, Leopold II, decided to yield in everything. Joseph II himself had before his death conceded that his policy in Hungary could no longer be upheld and had decided to revert to the policy of conciliation. By the end of 1790 Leopold II was able to resume control in the Austrian Netherlands, though at the price of conciliation by granting a restoration of the system of government in the country as it had existed under Maria Theresa. The external crisis was solved by a direct approach to Prussia. At the vital moment the nerve of Frederick William II failed. There was no indication that Polish opinion would permit the exchange of Toruń and Danzig for Galicia, nor was there much to be gained in reviving an Austro-Prussian hostility which had cost Prussia dear in the past. For these reasons Austria and Prussia ostensibly composed their differences by the convention of Reichenbach of 27 July 1790, by which Prussia undertook to support the restoration of Austrian authority in the Low Countries and the election of Leopold II as Emperor in return for Austria's withdrawal from the war against Turkey on the basis of maintaining the existing frontiers. Not for the first time did Austria abandon Russia to a solitary struggle with the Ottoman Empire. On 4 August 1791 Austria concluded with Turkey the Peace of Sistova.

Britain did not long enjoy the freedom of manoeuvre which her association with Prussia gave her. In 1790 British fishing vessels were seized by Spain in Nootka Sound, off Vancouver Island, and the British government was able to adopt a belligerent attitude. Spain appealed to France for aid, but France could not lend her diplomatic support on account of the Constituent Assembly's hostility to an adventure in foreign policy. Spain was obliged to yield and submit to the British demands by the convention of 24 July 1790. When, however, the Younger Pitt attempted to adopt a forward policy in

March 1791 in response to the appeal of Prussia for assistance against Russia and a demand was to be made that Russia should restore to Turkey the fortress of Ochakov on the north-western shore of the Black Sea, there was an outcry among the British opposition and merchant classes against an aggressive policy in an area where Britain had no obvious interests, and the stability of the British administration itself was severely shaken. Accordingly, a messenger was hastily sent to St Petersburg with the order that the ultimatum to surrender Ochakov should not be presented to the Russian government. The Anglo-Prussian alliance was revealed to have no force behind it.

Though Austria concluded the peace of Sistova with the Porte, Russia was not under the same pressure to accept the formula of the *status quo ante bellum*. She had been too heavily involved in the south to make much progress against the Swedes, but the peace of Varëla was concluded in August 1790 and Russia was freed from fear of attack in the rear. The Russian army had in fact once more shown its skill in the war against the Turk. In July 1789 the great Russian soldier, Suvorov, defeated the Turks at Focsany and in September at Rymnik. In December 1790 Suvorov took the fortress of Ismail by storm. The prospect of aid from Britain encouraged the Turks to hold out, but the failure of Pitt to carry out his policy permitted the Russian army to take the field against the Turks in the summer of 1791. Fresh defeats compelled the Turks to sign the Preliminaries of Galatz in August 1791. On 9 January 1792 after much hard bargaining the treaty of Jassy was signed, which renewed all the provisions of the treaty of Kutchuk-Kajnardji and subsequent agreements and made the river Dniestr the frontier between Turkey and Russia. Russia might have made more of her successes to secure territory beyond the Dniestr, but her attention was directed to the Polish Republic and the West.

In the midst of Russia's preoccupations the Poles had slipped from her control. A policy opposed to Russia united all Polish parties, but the question of reform soon divided them. There were the oligarchical factions which supposed freedom to mean a return to the anarchy of the past, in which the great aristocratic families divided the spoils of office between them. There were, on the other hand, patriots who knew that Poland could not survive unless she put her house in order. The 'Patriotic Party' under Ignacy Potocki came to terms with the King in the winter of 1790–1 and a new constitution was drawn up, which was to establish a hereditary constitutional monarchy, the future king to be the elector of Saxony and his successors. The reformers were, however, uncertain of their plan's reception, and they therefore waited until the Easter of 1791, when a large number of senators and deputies would return to their homes for the festival. Out of 500 senators and deputies only 182 remained in the city during Easter, but of these 110 were in favour of reform. The new constitution was brought before the Diet (*Sejm*) on 3 May 1791. Legalized rebellion, the *liberum veto* and all the paraphernalia of the Polish constitution were swept aside and the elective kingship abandoned by a trick which offended the great territorial magnates of Poland. Far from solving Poland's troubles, it introduced elements of civil war into Polish society. Already the Polish opposition under Rzewuski, Branicki and Szczęsny Potocki were appealing to Catherine II for aid, but it was only on 28 March 1792 after the treaty of Jassy that Catherine II made known her refusal to recognize the Constitution of 3 May 1791. From that moment intervention by Russia in Poland became certain. Catherine II could now use the troubles in western Europe to secure a settlement designed by herself.

The Powers and the French Revolution

It would give a false picture of the policies adopted by the states of Europe under the Old Régime if it were stated that they exhibited irreconcilable hostility towards the events which took place in France in the years between 1788 and 1791. The Younger Pitt and his followers in Britain welcomed the French Revolution for the freedom of manoeuvre it gave British policy. Russia and Austria were absorbed by the war against Turkey and the possibilities which it seemed to offer. Prussia looked with greedy eyes upon Poland and was for that reason suspected by Austria who had troubles enough of her own in Hungary and the Netherlands. Russia was compelled as a result of Prussian intrigue once more to look to the security of her western frontier. The powers were too divided to present any common front to France and too anxious to look to their own immediate advantages to express more than a mild distaste for the actions of the Revolution.

The sources of conflict between France and the rest of Europe must be sought within France herself.

The Outbreak of War

Leopold II of Austria was anxious to minimize his dangers and decided upon conciliation with Prussia. The flight of Louis XVI and his Queen, Marie Antoinette, to Varennes on 20 June 1791 not unnaturally troubled Leopold II, for Marie Antoinette was his sister, but he knew that he could undertake no measures on behalf of the French royal family, except at the price of permitting Prussia and Russia to settle the Polish Question at their will. The best which Leopold could do was to pursue a policy of intimidation. Thus by the Circular of Padua of 6 July 1791 Leopold II invited the powers to adopt a common policy towards the French Revolution. On 25 July a preliminary agreement was reached between Austria and Prussia for a defensive alliance and a guarantee of one another's territories; to this was added support for the Polish constitution of 1791 and a common policy towards France. As a result of a conference at Pilnitz between Leopold II and Frederick William II a declaration was made on 27 August 1791 that war should be made upon France if Louis XVI were not restored to his full powers, but this was recommended only if the other sovereigns were willing to collaborate. This policy of intimidation contained no substantial threat, but it was sufficient to arouse in French minds fears of an attack. Nevertheless, all cause for intervention was removed when on 14 September 1791 Louis XVI himself accepted the new French constitution. If the King were content with the new system, then the powers could hardly intervene to cause him to change his mind.

The French Legislative Assembly, October 1791

The French Legislative Assembly met in Paris on 1 October 1791. The majority of the deputies were royalist in their outlook in spite of the King's flight to Varennes. Politically its composition was different from that of the Constituent Assembly because the old right wing of nobles and conservatives had disappeared. The new right wing were the supporters of constitutional monarchy. About 260 deputies of this persuasion were enrolled in the club of the Feuillants, whereas the extreme left was represented by about 150

members of the Jacobins or Cordeliers. There was a loose un-
committed centre which consisted of about 350 members, looking
both to right and to left in matters of legislation and policy. In such a
situation an individual could easily exercise leadership. An undue
initiative was enjoyed by Brissot, a man of dubious antecedents,
who allied himself with a group of deputies from the constituencies
in the valley of the Gironde, the so-called Girondins.

Brissot's aim was to exploit the dissatisfaction of the Assembly
with the conduct of French foreign policy in the years before the
revolution. It rankled that the British and Prussians had been able to
detach the United Provinces from their alliance with France by the
intervention of 1787. The arbitrary manner in which Britain had
dealt with Spain in the Nootka Sound dispute seemed to point to the
powerlessness of France in the field of foreign affairs. Brissot wanted
personal power and war seemed the means to that end. In this policy
the Brissotins, as they came to be called, were supported by the
Comte de Narbonne, the minister of war, reputed to be a bastard
of Louis XV and at this time definitely the lover of Necker's daughter,
Madame de Staël. Narbonne believed that if France were to go to
war power would be placed in the hands of the Crown and it would
therefore be able to restore its authority. This was clearly appreciated
by the left-wing Robespierre, who after some flirtation with the idea
of war perceived that it might lead to the destruction of the Revolution's work. In the first instance, however, the Jacobin Club gave its
ear to Brissot rather than to Robespierre.

Under the pressure of the Brissotins a new ministry was brought
into power in the March of 1792. Narbonne himself had already lost
office. The most important figure in the new government was
Dumouriez, the minister of foreign affairs, a man who was not only a
professional officer, but who had also served in the secret missions of
Louis XV. Dumouriez was both an advocate of war and a born
intriguer who suited the purposes of the Brissotins and Girondins,
though their support did not prevent him from clandestine relations
with the Court. A pretext for declaring war was easy to find. Groups
of *émigrés* were assembling their forces beyond the eastern frontier
of France. The French Revolution, moreover, treated France as an
integral whole and wished to set aside the rights which the German
princes still exercised in the enclaves in Alsace and Lorraine. Quickly

the idea gained currency that the French Revolution could appeal to the peoples beyond the frontiers of France. There was obviously discontent to be exploited in the Austrian Netherlands, while beyond them in the United Provinces the opposition chafed under the régime of the prince of Orange. There were, moreover, Catalans, Basques and Savoyards to be freed from tyranny. Imagination might stretch as far as the Bohemians, not distinguished in the eighteenth century for their loyalty to the Habsburgs. It was to be a war of the peoples against the kings, which lent a certain idealistic respectability to the traditional policy of the Bourbon kings. On 25 January 1792 a demand was made to the Emperor Leopold II that he should declare that he had no hostile intent against France by 1 March and that the forces assembling in the Rhineland should be dispersed, but Leopold II protested his pacific intentions. Leopold, however, died on 1 March 1792 and was succeeded by his son, Francis II, who adopted a less pliant policy. On 20 April 1792 the Legislative Assembly voted a declaration of war against the Emperor. The army commanders, however, were by no means in favour of this venture. The condition of the army was deplorable; out of 9,000 officers 6,000 had deserted from their posts. There was a complete lack of discipline and supplies had not been accumulated. The appreciation of the army commanders proved correct when a small force of French troops of 3,000 men crossed into the Austrian Netherlands with the object of taking Tournai. On meeting the enemy they panicked and withdrew ignominiously, adding scandal to defeat by murdering their commander and the prisoners they had taken from the Austrians. The Brissotins, therefore, were hoist with their own petard. France was beset with economic difficulties in which the *assignat* had fallen to below 50 per cent of its face value in the spring of 1792. Everywhere there was a shortage of food, because the peasants in a period of rapid inflation would not market their produce. Throughout the country there were disturbances. The utter failure of the Brissotins enabled the King on 12 June 1792 to dismiss the Minister of the Interior, Roland, and two of his colleagues, who were replaced by men of more malleable disposition from the Feuillants. In spite of the fact that the mob invaded the Tuilleries, the King stuck to his decision and refused to restore the Brissotin and Girondin ministers. The Brissotins therefore began to launch attacks upon the King in the hope that by intimidation of him they would regain their positions. One of their measures was to demand that the provincial National Guard should be called to Paris to strengthen their position, and at the beginning of July the *fédérés* began to arrive, but they brought no accretion of strength to the Brissotins. Rather they were quickly indoctrinated by the Parisian left wing. Thus tension began to mount in Paris at the very moment when the sovereigns of Europe were deciding upon what course of action they must take.

Poland and the Events in France

Catherine II had by now made her pact with the leaders of the Polish reactionary opposition, Szczęsny Potocki, Rzewuski and Branicki, who had agreed to raise the standard of rebellion in Poland against the lawful government. On 14 May 1792 the Confederation of Targowica, a small town in the eastern regions of the Polish Republic, was assembled. In support of this rebellion the Russians invaded Poland. Poland's ally, Prussia, now refused to honour the treaty of alliance. Both Austria and Prussia looked to Russia for enlargement of their own territories at the expense of Poland. Both agreed to restore the old régime in Poland. At the very moment when Austria and Prussia were considering intervention in France they had their eyes turned towards the east. It was clearly the intention of Frederick William II that he should obtain compensation for his support of Austria in the west by the annexation of Danzig (Gdańsk), Toruń and parts of Poznania. Russia encouraged this idea in order to draw off the hostility of Prussia, but it yet remained to find some means of satisfying the territorial aspirations of Austria. The Russian ambassador in Vienna, Razumovsky, was instructed to propose to Austria that she should revive the project of Joseph II for exchanging the Austrian Netherlands for Bavaria, a solution which was not to the taste of Britain, who did not believe that an independent Southern Netherlands could constitute an adequate barrier to French expansionism. Essential to the diplomacy of intervention in France was the fact that Poland was about to be partitioned.

The Austro-Prussian Intervention, 1792

The plan of Austria and Prussia was the raising of 150,000 troops for the invasion of France under the aged Duke of Brunswick, a hero of the Seven Years' War, who was by no means enamoured of his task. The line of advance was to be in the direction of Verdun. On 25 July the Duke of Brunswick against his better judgment was compelled by Francis II to set his signature to the so-called 'Brunswick Manifesto'. The army was declared to be entering France to protect the rights of the German princes in Alsace and to restore the power of the King of France which had been overthrown by the French factions. Punishments were threatened against any persons not of the French armed forces who resisted the invaders. It declared that the members of the Assembly and the municipality of Paris would be held responsible for any disorders and that they would answer with their lives. If, moreover, any violence were shown to the King and the royal family, the allies would make an example of the malefactors.

All those who had been prominent in French politics now began to fear for their safety. Demands for the deposition of the King were current. On 29 July 1792 Robespierre demanded at the Jacobin Club a National Convention elected by universal manhood suffrage. The Brunswick Manifesto thus provoked the French Left. The mayor of Paris, Pétion, had distributed 50,000 arms to the people of the city, so that the French Left now had in its hands the weapons with which to execute a coup d'état. On the night of 9 August there occurred a fresh revolution. The mob penetrated into the Tuileries, and in the confusion there was an outbreak of firing, which developed into a general battle. In the fighting 373 of the mob were killed, but the casualties among the nobles of the Court and the Swiss guards amounted to no less than 800. On 10 August the Legislative Assembly admitted that it no longer controlled the situation. The King was suspended in his functions and orders were given for the calling of a National Convention to be elected by universal suffrage. In theory the Brissotins and the Girondins returned to power, but the insurgents insisted that the radical lawyer, Danton, be appointed to the Ministry of Justice. The victory in fact lay with the Parisian left wing.

The invasion of France by the Duke of Brunswick with a small corps of Prussian troops began in its own leisurely fashion on 19 July. Brunswick crossed the frontier and marched between the two French armies of Sedan and Metz and arrived at the fortress of

Longwy. Longwy in fact offered no resistance, and on 20 August its garrison marched out on condition that it took no further part in the war. Brunswick then moved on to Verdun, which fell with even less ado on 31 August. The ease of the advance began to alarm Paris. Such was the confusion of France that La Fayette in command of the army conceived the plan of taking back his troops to restore order, but no one would follow him and he increased the suspicions of the people by himself fleeing to the Austrians. Everywhere it was supposed that there was a noble plot. The climax was reached on 2 September when Paris discovered that Verdun had fallen. Once more the people of Paris rose and there followed the so-called 'September Massacres', which continued until 6 September. The victims were priests, Swiss guards, political prisoners and ordinary criminals. A maximum estimate of the number of persons killed is 1,400. The episode was an example of the abnormal psychology of Paris in the face of invasion. The influence of the Brissotins was now at an end in Paris, and leadership passed into the hands of that leader who could control the excited people of the capital.

It should not be imagined that the National Convention, which assembled on 20 September 1792 and which continued to rule France until it was replaced by the Constitution of 1795, in any way represented the will of the masses. There were in fact very few voters, in spite of the application of universal suffrage. Possibly only 10 per cent of the primary voters went to the polls at all, while in the secondary elections the electors often absented themselves. What the elections to the Convention did give birth to was a revolutionary élite. Brissotins and non-party deputies were returned in the provinces, but they were out of tune with the Parisian mob, which gave its allegiance to the Left. France had no tradition of parliamentary government. The Convention bequeathed to France and subsequently to the world a concept of a system in which a dedicated minority, divorced from the people, nevertheless devoted its energy to the government of the people and, according to its own interpretation of events, served their interests.

The Duke of Brunswick continued his march through the forest of Argonne and outflanked Dumouriez, who had now joined the army as its commander-in-chief. Brunswick expected the French to make an orderly withdrawal, but Dumouriez took his stand against the invaders by interposing his forces between Brunswick's army and his base at Verdun. From the outset Brunswick had approached the intervention with some nervousness. On the morning of 20 September the two armies met at Valmy in Champagne and the Prussians came under the bombardment of General Kellerman's artillery. In the exchanges only some 500 casualties were sustained in the total forces involved. What was significant was that the French had not melted away, but had stood their ground. They were in fact troops of the old army, many of whom had seen service in America; Brunswick's Prussian troops for the most part had no battle experience and panicked. The weather was bad and Brunswick was cut off from his supplies. In accordance with the best rules of contemporary German generalship he began to withdraw. Dumouriez, however, did not attack him. War and diplomacy were inextricably interwoven. Dumouriez moved parallel to Brunswick, but with the intention of attacking the Austrian Netherlands, in conformity with the policy which he had promoted while he was minister of foreign affairs and indeed which he sought now to promote by discussions with the Prussian officers. The military leaders were looking for some understanding with Prussia which would permit them to concentrate all their forces upon the Austrians. By 23 October 1792 the Prussians had crossed back into Germany and the political situation of France transformed.

The Convention and the French Republic

On the day that the battle of Valmy was fought, 20 September 1792, the Convention met and the following day proclaimed the abolition of the Monarchy. The Gregorian calendar was abolished subsequently in 1793 and a revolutionary calendar introduced with effect from 22 September 1792. France was fired with a revolutionary fervour. It was believed that the dawn of a new epoch had been witnessed. It seemed even more certain when Dumouriez opened his offensive against the Austrians and French forces entered Savoy and Nice. In October French troops under General Custine entered Germany and took the towns of Speyer, Worms, Mainz and Frankfort. On 6 November 1792 Dumouriez achieved his greatest triumph when he defeated the Austrians at Jemappes and marched into Brussels to the acclamation of the population.

Victory is a heady wine for revolutionaries to drink. The correspondence of Louis XVI with the enemies of France had been discovered in the Tuileries, and he was condemned to death by the Convention. On 21 January 1793 Louis XVI was led to his execution by the guillotine. The regicides who had voted for his death had committed themselves with their own lives to the success of the Republic. Failure would mean that they, too, would pay with their lives for their audacity. On 27 November 1792 Savoy was incorporated in France. On 19 November a decree of the Convention offered French aid to all peoples struggling for freedom. Danton, the principal figure in the Convention, pronounced in January 1793 the doctrine that France should seek her natural frontiers, by which it was understood that the Republic would fight for the left bank of the Rhine. Caution was now being thrown to the winds. Efforts had hitherto been made to secure the neutrality of Great Britain. On 16 November, however, the Scheldt was, in defiance of the treaty of Münster of 1648, opened to the shipping of all countries. The flames of Anglo-French hostility were fanned when upon the execution of Louis XVI the French envoy was requested by the British government to leave London. On 1 February 1793 the Convention voted that a declaration of war upon Britain and Holland should be made. For good measure war was declared upon Spain on 7 March 1793. The French Republic in its supreme self-confidence was prepared to lay down a challenge to all Europe.

2: The Great War of the Revolution with Europe

The French Convention in 1793, for all its idealistic enthusiasm reverted to the policy of Louis XIV. Aggrandizement was no longer that of a monarch, but rather associated with an ill-defined creed. The French revolutionaries were calling into existence the people, but no exact definition could be given to the peoples to whom the appeal was made. It was certainly not the common people of Europe, whose aid France wished to enlist. The problem may perhaps be more easily formulated by pointing to the enemies of France, the traditional possessors of power, whom the educated classes without mass support aspired to challenge. France was to appear as the liberator to give the European bourgeoisie a glimpse of power, but there was small thought even among the most advanced revolutionaries that power should descend to the actual toiling masses, who were everywhere in Europe inarticulate. Europe remained at the bottom local and isolated. Events might take a radical course in the cities, but from one year's end to another the peasants continued to till their fields and resented the intrusion of war upon their life. Political Europe was still very much the Europe of courts and cabinets. The war begun by the Revolution was to continue until 1814, but the actual physical condition of Europe was to remain largely unchanged. The great conflicts of 1793–1814 were to be fought at an early stage in the era of technological advancement and before the complete breakdown of rural isolation. No country in Europe enjoyed greater freedom from war than France itself. Great though the influence upon France of the Revolution was, it was the states beyond France which received the greater impulse. France was for all its troubles basically a rich country, but the poorer countries of Europe were levered out of their sloth and as a result forced into a new social organization in which they equalled France and in the end were to overtake her.

The Coalition Against France 1793

The formidable coalition which was assembled against France in 1793 was largely the work of the Younger Pitt, who brought together Russia, Sardinia, Spain, Naples and Sicily, Prussia, Austria, Portugal, the Empire, Baden and the two Hesses in a league against France. Britain was already in alliance with the United Provinces, and George III automatically brought his Electorate of Hanover into the war. The solidarity of the allies was more apparent than real. The sole unifying factor was Great Britain. Some countries entered the coalition merely as mercenaries. The Dutch gave some financial support, but did not contribute large numbers of troops. Russia and Spain merely adhered to the blockade of France. Austria and Prussia were willing to accept British money, but they were not inclined to take orders from their paymaster. What was lacking was a common plan for the defeat of France. There was, moreover, no concept of the principles upon which the war was to be fought. France was declaring war upon Europe in the name of Liberty. A few thinkers in Europe, like Burke in England, saw the struggle as one against precipitous innovation and the destruction of the aristocratic political predominance. The official British attitude was the traditional one, that Britain was fighting for the maintenance of the balance of power in Europe, though Pitt would not have looked askance in addition at some form of limited monarchy in France. The majority of the states of Europe were concerned neither with ideologies nor principles of action. They were looking simply for opportunities of enlarging their territories. Already even before the formation of the coalition the principle of territorial compensation was under consideration by the continental states, and the chief victim of this policy was to be Poland.

The war opened in the usual leisurely fashion of the eighteenth-century generals. At once France found herself in a crisis. On 18 March 1793 Dumouriez was defeated at the battle of Neerwinden, between Louvain and Liège. All the gains of the previous year were now lost and Dumouriez reverted to the policy of combining war with diplomacy. In order to save France from invasion he concluded an armistice with the allied commander, Coburg, which would permit him to lead his troops back into France and overthrow the

Convention, but Dumouriez's troops refused to follow him, and on 5 April 1793 he and his staff defected to the Austrians. The allies now had the opportunity to overrun France, but Coburg did not press his advantage. He had an army of 110,000 men between the North Sea and the Meuse. The King of Prussia was attacking Mainz with 42,000 men with Austrian support. In the south 20,000 Sardinians supported by 6,000 Neapolitans entered France. An army of 50,000 Spaniards supported by a Portuguese division had taken the field. Revolt, moreover, had broken out in the Vendée. On 27 August 1793 the port of Toulon was surrendered to the British fleet by the royalists. Lyons rose in revolt against the French government. These events should have been enough to have overthrown the Convention and restored the Old Régime in France.

The allies, however, did not pursue the war with vigour. Coburg settled down to a war of sieges in the Low Countries. The Prussians encircled Mainz and the Austrians under Wurmser crossed the Rhine south of Mannheim, but small progress was made. The British contribution to the war was pitiful. In February 1793 the Duke of York had only four battalions under his command and by April still only 6,500 men, who were assigned to the siege of Dunkirk. No real effort was made by the British to exploit the capture of Toulon. The eyes of Britain were not upon Europe, but upon the colonial possessions of France. The French were thus able to re-group their forces. The Duke of York was driven back from Dunkirk and Coburg defeated at Hondschoote on 6–8 September and Wattignies on 16 October. The allies made no progress in the south. Lyons fell and the Sardinians were driven back into Savoy. Toulon was besieged and fell to French attack. All that the allies could claim for their efforts in 1793 was that they had recovered the left bank of the Rhine and the Austrian Netherlands and held three French fortresses on the northern frontier of France. They had, however, set in motion within France events which were in startling contrast to the passive generalship of the allies.

The Crisis in France and the Rule of the Left

The desertion of Dumouriez and the royalist rising in the Vendée re-created in the minds of the citizens of Paris the uncertainties and fears of August–September 1792. Inflation and the food crisis, coupled with the conviction that France was being betrayed from within, once more produced a revolutionary situation. On 6 April 1793 was created the Committee of Public Safety with the task of supervising the Executive Council. This body was to be elected for one month at a time, and at first the moderate elements predominated. The leading figure in it, Danton, was in effective control of French foreign policy and sought to save France from invasion by conciliation of the opposing powers. On 13 April 1793 by a decree of the Convention it was proclaimed that France would not interfere in the government of other nations. Within France the Committee decided upon a system of price and wage control, to implement which the Decree of the Maximum was issued on 3 May. This was not enough to satisfy the extreme left wing, the so-called Mountain, the deputies who sat upon the upper seats of the Convention. Behind them were the Paris Commune and its sections, demanding a purge of political opponents. On 2 June 1793 the mob and part of the National Guard had appeared before the Tuileries and demanded the arrest of the factious members of the Convention, by whom they meant the Girondins and the Brissotins. The Convention could do no other than submit. The less resolute members departed from Paris and the Jacobins left in control.

From July 1793 the composition of the Committee of Public Safety changed. New and ruthless men of great ability now entered it, to form the effective government of France until July 1794. This was not a dictatorship of any one particular member, but the committee certainly exercised the powers of a dictatorial régime. Robespierre, the lawyer from Arras, was perhaps the most prominent member of the Committee and the one whose reputation suffered most at the hands of posterity. He was in fact a man of great personal integrity and like many puritans pushed his purity to extremes, which revolted men with more accommodating moral standards, but he was not alone in the vigour which was now displayed. In effect, the resistance of France depended upon Paris. In the provinces disintegration was everywhere apparent. The revolt in the Vendée had made progress and Nantes was actually besieged by the rebels, while disturbances were evident in Brittany and Normandy. Bordeaux, Marseilles, Lyons and Toulon had rejected the authority of Paris. So low had the credit of the government fallen that in July 1793 the assignat stood at 23 per cent of its face value. The Committee of Public Safety nevertheless was determined to signify to the world that a new epoch had dawned. By a decree of the Convention of 24 November 1793 a new calendar was imposed upon France, reckoned from the autumn equinox of 1792, from which the year I began, with months each with names to indicate its character.[1] The very introduction of this calendar was an indication that the republican régime was confident that it could make itself the master of France and impose upon the country its own enlightenment.

In some manner governmental authority in France had to be restored. The assassination of the left-wing journalist, Marat, by Charlotte Corday pointed the way to a drastic political purge. The revolutionary Tribunal established in Paris began to increase the number of political trials. Under the Law of the Suspects of 17 September 1793 virtually any opponent of the régime could be arrested, and many were given a summary trial and executed upon the guillotine. The most famous victim was the queen, Marie Antoinette, but with her died many of the prominent figures of the early stage of the revolution, Brissot, Vergniaud, the Duke of Orleans, called Philippe Égalité for his support of the revolution, Madame Du Barry and the scientist Lavoisier. Others anticipated conviction and death by suicide, Roland, Condorcet, Clavière and Pétion. In the March of 1794 the extreme left in Paris, Hébert and his followers, most famous for their anti-clericalism and institution of the Cult of Reason, were executed, but in April Danton and the relatively moderate group around him met the same fate. In the end the Committee of Public Safety represented nothing except itself. It enjoyed no basis of popular support. While France was under threat of invasion the Committee, by the law of 4 Frimaire Year II (4 December 1793) in control of all subordinate authorities in France, achieved a degree of centralization beyond the dreams of the Bourbon monarchs and held France together by the exercise of the political purge which has come to have the name of the Terror. Perhaps as many as 300,000 persons were arrested, but far fewer

---

[1] Autumn (22 September–22 December) consisted of *Vendémiaire* (Vintage), *Brumaire* (Fog) and *Frimaire* (Frost); winter (22 December–22 March) of *Nivôse* (Snow), *Pluviôse* (Rain) and *Ventôse* (Wind); spring (22 March–22 June) of *Germinal* (Sprouting), *Floréal* (Flowers) and *Prairial* (Grass); and summer (22 June–22 September) of *Messidor* (Harvest), *Thermidor* (Heat) and *Fructidor* (Fruit).

were executed; in Paris less than 3,000 persons were condemned to death.

The horror of the Terror should not be allowed to detract from the very real achievements of the Committee of Public Safety. In October 1793 Lyons fell to the Republican Army and the internal discords vanished before the onslaught of the government. An army of 650,000 men was created, officered by young men who under the Old Régime could never have found expression for their ability. Pichegru, Masséna, Moreau, Davout, Lefèvre, Serrurier, Augerau, Brune and, not least, Bonaparte appeared to give force and renewed vigour to a system of warfare which had in the eighteenth century developed the finesse of a game of chess and lost sight of the fact that battles have a wider strategic purpose. The war which the French Revolution was prepared to fight was not one of set battles and compromise peace, but a struggle for total victory. Total victory, however, or even the partial victory of French arms spelled defeat for the dedicated Left, which ruled in Paris. On 26 June 1794 the French army defeated the allies at the battle of Fleurus and once more the Austrian Netherlands were overrun by French troops. The internal revolts were suppressed or rendered ineffective. The danger to France had passed and the need for severity had gone. Now the moderates raised their heads. The left wing in the Committee of Public Safety had rendered their service to France and public anxiety subsided. Robespierre and his followers wished to maintain the momentum of the Revolution. On 26 July 1794 Robespierre denounced the enemies of the Revolution in the convention and stirred his opponents into resistance. On 27 July the moderates summoned their courage and attacked Robespierre. By a vote of the Convention Robespierre and his supporters were arrested before they could summon their supporters from the streets of Paris. On the following day Robespierre, Saint Just, Couthon, Hanriot and seventeen others were executed. The Paris Commune was purged of its left-wing element and the capital freed from the violence and the high idealism of the proletarian revolution. These events which took place between the 8th and 10th of the revolutionary month of Thermidor are known as the Thermidorian Reaction. Undoubtedly the inhabitants of France could breathe a sigh of relief, but the rule of the Terror has served ever since as an example of what ruthless centralization can obtain for a revolution. In the future men were to look back to the France of 1793–4 for a model of what a revolution could achieve in the face of apparently overwhelming odds.

The Counter-revolution in France

The Thermidorian Reaction soon disposed of the machinery erected by the Jacobin Left. The Committee of Public Safety was reconstituted and with it the Revolutionary Tribunal. Deprived of its leaders, the Paris mob proved singularly ineffective to determine the course of events. On 1 April 1795 (12 Germinal) a riot was suppressed without difficulty; a new feature, however, now appeared in the law permitting the army to be called into Paris. On 20 May 1795 (1 Prairial) the mob again marched upon the Convention, but the National Guard turned out to save it. Three days of disturbance were brought to an end by the entry of the army into Paris. Increasingly the army was to become a political force. In the eighteenth century probably only in Russia was the army actively engaged in politics. Now this phenomenon was to appear in France.

The Thermidorians abandoned the economic controls of the Terror and confined the powers of the Committee of Public Safety to the spheres of War and Foreign Affairs. The National Guard was placed under the direct control of the Convention and its headquarters staff changed every ten days. The Paris Commune was suppressed and its place taken by commissions of Police and Taxation. The situation in France after the abandonment of the Terror reverted to that of 1792, when most deputies would willingly have accepted a constitutional monarchy. Unfortunately on 8 June 1795 the Dauphin died in custody and it was thus impossible to revive the Bourbon monarchy. The brothers of Louis XVI were too closely identified with the enemies of France. The legitimate heir to the throne, Louis, Comte de Provence, now technically Louis XVIII, breathed fire and slaughter. He threatened to punish the regicides and to restore the Old Régime in all its forms. France could not tolerate such a monarch.

Recourse was therefore had to another solution. The Crown was in effect put into commission. Under a new constitution, the work of Boissy d'Anglas, the executive was conferred upon a Directory of Five, which had powers to supervise the government. Universal suffrage was abolished and a new suffrage invented which bore a close resemblance to that adopted for the elections to the Legislative Assembly in 1792. The vote was given to all Frenchmen over the age of twenty-one who paid direct taxes, with the exception of domestic employees. Under the system of indirect election the electors of the primary assemblies, who had to be over the age of twenty-five and men of property, amounted to only 20,000. It was these men who elected the 750 members of the Legislative Body (Corps Législatif), divided into two houses, the *Ancients* (Les Anciens) composed of men over the age of forty-five and the *Five-Hundred* (Les Cinq Cents), who must have reached at least thirty years. From this body there was to be an annual retirement of one-third and fresh elections. The Convention had no illusions about its own position. It knew that if a general election were held very few of its members would be returned and that the weapon of political revenge would be turned upon them by the members of the new Legislative Body. It was therefore laid down that two-thirds of the Legislative Body were to be chosen from members of the Convention. This solution not unnaturally gave rise to discontents among the royalists and conservatives, who on 5 October 1795 (13 Vendémiaire) attempted to overthrow the new Constitution by a coup d'état in Paris. Barras, who in 1794 had mustered support in Paris for the overthrow of Robespierre, called in the young artillery officer, Napoleon Bonaparte, who for all his success in the recapture of Toulon was suffering a temporary eclipse for his previous associations with the Jacobins. Placed in command of 6,000 troops, Bonaparte did not hesitate to use artillery against the mob as it advanced upon the Convention. The myth that the mob could determine the course of French politics had been destroyed, but it was equally clear that the new régime was leaning heavily upon the support of the army. What the army could do for politicians it could equally well do for itself. Already it was clear that the army might one day itself seize political power.

The Directory, composed of Barras, La Reveillière, Reubell, le Tourneur and Carnot, a survivor in virtue of his organizing ability from the Committee of Public Safety, was installed on 3 November 1795. It presided over a seedy régime. All the *nouveaux riches* and the speculators, men who had done well out of the war, emerged to occupy the positions in society which their wealth could buy them.

With them appeared the courtesans, dressed in clothes of exaggerated styles. These men were symbolic of a certain moral degeneration and were accordingly held in contempt by the small groups of professional revolutionaries who remained faithful to the ideals of the Jacobins. Inflation and corruption kept alive a respect for the men of the Terror. One opponent of the new régime was Gracchus Babeuf, who began to plot for a fresh revolution. A revolutionary élite was to lead the masses of the capital to overthrow the Directory. There was nothing new in the technique of revolution proposed by Babeuf. Many of his followers merely wanted revenge, but Babeuf, whose own past was not without blemish, gave his 'Conspiracy of the Equals' a philosophy which contained the germ of a new thinking. For Babeuf the Directory was a mere usurpation and there was, therefore, no moral objection to a minority's using force in order to overthrow it. Such an action would merely be to give expression to the General Will of the people, an idea which he adopted from Rousseau's *Social Contract*, but what was original in Babeuf's thinking was that equality should extend not only to political and civil rights but also to goods. What was proposed in the *Analyse de la Doctrine de Babeuf* was equality of right to wealth, the duty of all to work and the coercion of the rich; the common good was now taken to mean community of goods, or the redistribution of the property of the rich in favour of the poor. Babeuf was arrested on 10 May 1796, but his trial of February–May 1797 left behind it a legend. The doctrines of Babeuf bridged the gap between the thinking of the *Philosophes* and the concepts of the nineteenth-century socialists. The conspiracy of the Equals is yet another example of how France, even in a moment of the corruption of the Thermidorian Reaction, was a seedbed of fresh ideas. It was not in the realm of ideas, however, but upon the field of battle that the France of the Directory was to make its most immediate impression.

The Collapse of the Resistance to France

I. THE PARTITIONS OF POLAND, 1793 AND 1795

The great French victory at Fleurus in June 1794 was a triumph which might never have been achieved if the great powers of Europe had fixed their attention solely upon France. By the treaty of Jassy in January 1792 Russia had brought her frontier to the Dniestr and sought a means to establish her influence over Poland once again, and even perhaps in Germany. Catherine II refused to recognize the Polish constitution of 3 May 1791 and received the representatives of the Polish reactionary opposition, Szczęsny Potocki, Rzewuski and Branicki, who drew up a plan for a Confederation, or legalized rebellion, to summon all those in Poland who objected to reform. Of these there were not a few in the eastern regions of Poland. On 14 May the opposition formed the Confederation of Targowica, a small town in the Polish Ukraine, and on 18 May Russian troops began to enter the country to restore the old system, which guaranteed noble privileges in Poland and preserved a weak state which could present no threat to Russia. The coincidence of events is important. On 20 April 1792 France had declared war upon Austria in her effort to occupy the Netherlands. Austria and Prussia were considering schemes of reorganization in western Germany. Prussia hoped to enlarge her dominions on the lower Rhine and Austria intended to make gains in Alsace; there was even talk of reviving the scheme for an exchange of the Austrian Netherlands for Bavaria. The Russian intervention in Poland created a double front. Prussia was torn between a desire to make gains in western Germany and the possibility of annexing Polish territory in order to round off her dominions in the east. In June 1792 Prussia declined to honour her treaty of alliance with Poland and the Poles were compelled to face the Russians alone. Austria looked askance at any territorial arrangement which might alter the balance of power on her northern frontier while she was committed to war in the west.

Disappointed by the progress of the intervention in France which was halted by the battle of Valmy in September 1792, Prussia on 25 October informed Austria that she intended to seek compensation for her losses in Poland; this Prussia made a condition of her renewed participation in the war in the next campaigning season. Catherine II was in possession of Poland by July 1792, but she judged it wise to associate one power at least with Russia in the maintenance of control in Poland. In order to bring the tension to an end in Poland Catherine consented to a partial dismemberment of the country with Prussia, and to the annoyance of Austria the treaty of partition was signed on 23 January 1793. To her satisfaction Prussia obtained the city of Danzig and a tract of Greater Poland which included the towns of Toruń, Gneizno, Poznań, Płock, Łęczyca, Sieradz and Wieluń, an area which was truly Polish, but which was now to be graced with the name of South Prussia; for her part Russia advanced her frontier to a line running almost due south from a point on the Dvina east of Dünaburg to the river Zbrucz, a tributary of the river Dneistr, territories which were not predominantly Polish in their ethnic composition and except in the Ukraine not particularly valuable. All that was left to Poland was a meaningless tract of land sandwiched between Prussia, Austria and Russia. To this solution the Polish Diet at Grodno was compelled to consent under the threat of Russian bayonets. The rump Poland was tied by an alliance to Russia.

The authors of the Confederation of Targowica were aghast at the destruction which their revolt had brought about. Instead of noble liberties being restored Poland had been reduced in size and virtually ceased to exist as a viable state. The second partition of Poland destroyed the prestige of the great families who had ruled Poland since the seventeenth century and led to a growth of radicalism among the lesser gentry. The petty *szlachta*, men technically of noble birth, but without property, had had much to win from the constitution of 1791, even though it was conservative in its provisions. It seemed that Poland would at last become a modern state. Some wished to restore the constitution of 1791; others were determined to go very much further and looked to the inspiration of the French Revolution. This latter group were to be known as the Jacobins. In the tense situation which followed the partition with the prospect of the small Polish army's being disbanded the government of Poland began to make precautionary arrests, which quickly provoked a rising. The leader of the Polish national movement was Kościuszko, himself a man of petty noble origin. Kościuszko undoubtedly was uncertain of success for a rising, but when once it had broken out he put himself at its head. On 4 April 1794 he defeated the Russian forces at the battle of Racławice, north of Cracow. The city of Warsaw rose in revolt, its first demonstration of a revolutionary zeal which in the future was to match that of Paris. On 7 May Kościuszko issued the manifesto of Połaniec, promising the peasants the protection of the law and a reduction of labour services by over a half.

Driven back upon Warsaw by Prussian troops, Kościuszko was able to counter-attack and compel the Prussians to withdraw, but he enjoyed less success when he was forced to meet the Russian army under its great commander, Suvorov. Kościuszko fell wounded at the battle of Maciejowice on 10 October and at the beginning of November the suburb of Praga on the right bank of the Vistula, opposite Warsaw, was stormed. On 8 November 1794 Warsaw itself fell. The Polish capacity to resist was destroyed and with it the Prussian enthusiasm for the war in the west. On 16 October the Prussian government decided that the situation in the east was so serious that peace must be made with France. Britain had been anxious to keep Prussia in the war in the west and concluded the treaty of the Hague on 19 April 1794, providing £300,000 to meet the costs of Prussian mobilization and £50,000 a month to keep 62,000 troops in the field, but it could be argued that this money had in effect been used to finance the campaign against Kościuszko. In anger the Younger Pitt abandoned the subsidy treaty and thus hastened the Prussian quest for an understanding with France.

Kościuszko's revolt removed the cornerstone from the European alliance against France. On 5 April 1795 Prussia concluded the treaty of Basel with France, granting her a free hand on the left bank of the Rhine against future compensation for Prussia elsewhere in Germany. This inglorious act left the United Provinces at the mercy of the French. The French armies had been able to move forward when the waterways were frozen in the winter and the small British forces opposing them were unable to offer significant resistance. The Dutch opponents of the Prince of Orange welcomed their advance and a new régime was established, the Batavian Republic, with which France concluded peace. By the Peace of the Hague of 16 May 1795, France already in possession of the Austrian Netherlands, took possession of Maastricht, Venloo and Dutch Flanders, obtained an indemnity of 100,000,000 guilden and secured support for 25,000 French troops from the new republic. French conquest was henceforth to be made to pay for itself. The Dutch did not reward the French with their gratitude. William V of Orange fled the country and took refuge in England, where the government promised him that British protection would be extended to the Dutch dominions beyond the seas (see below p. 369). The French were able to organize the occupied Netherlands south of the Rhine as departments of France, but a change of far greater significance took place. Since the seventeenth century Amsterdam had been the financial capital of Europe, but this position was destroyed by the French occupation. Britain was in a perilous position and without influence upon the continent of Europe, except in as far as she could provide subsidies, but the strength of the British economic system, in spite of periodic crises, was such that ultimately the financial centre of Europe was transferred to London. It would have been a wise man indeed who could have foreseen this development in 1795, but the truth remains that the French annexationist policy already decided the future pattern of the wars. France might proceed to the reorganization of Europe, but the world beyond Europe rested with the ability of Britain and her navy to control the colonial trade without which Europe itself could not live. The strategy of the Younger Pitt was defective and British statesmen were slow to appreciate the problem. If Britain had organized a national army to make a decisive intervention upon the continent of Europe the course of the great war against France might have been different. As it was, the struggle continued in the conventional terms and France was able to exploit her advantages to the full.

In eastern Europe attention was focused upon a regional equilibrium. Catherine II, to some extent alarmed by the appearance of radicalism in Poland, but concerned more with the egocentric policy of Prussia, determined to make an end of the rump Poland which emerged from the second partition of 1793. Now Austria must be strengthened and conciliated. Russia decided that her own frontier must be advanced to the line of the river Niemen and from Grodno stretched south to the river Bug, where it met the Austrian province in Poland, Galicia. The intervening territories were to be distributed between Austria and Prussia. Austria was to receive an expanse of territory, contained within the triangle of the rivers Pilica, Vistula and Bug, with the exception of Praga; the province subsequently received the name of Western Galicia. The remainder, a rayon of territory in the south called New Silesia and the territory north of the Bug, with an eastern frontier running through the primeval forest of Białowieża to the Niemen, which became New East Prussia, was surrendered to the rule of the Hohenzollern dynasty. Poland as a state ceased to exist. Once again Russia occupied territories which were not predominantly Polish in speech, though the upper classes were Polish by sentiment. The final treaty of partition of 1795, completed by the abdication of the Polish king, Stanisław August, placed Austria in possession of a large part of Lesser Poland, but Prussia, though treated with scant respect, momentarily became a state of great importance in Eastern Europe, possibly more Slav than German. The narrow self-seeking ambitions of Prussia kept her out of the war until 1806. Prussia ran with the hare and hunted with the hounds in prosecution of a policy which had small regard for the overwhelming danger of French domination. Undoubtedly Prussia benefited for the time being from her neutrality. The new territories could be organized. The price of grain rose in Europe and junkers and Polish landlords drew rich profits. When disaster ultimately came injudicious investment in land, purchased by loans, struck hard at the estate owners, but artificial prosperity encouraged Prussia to adhere to an inglorious and short-sighted role which was in the end to prove her own undoing.

II. SPAIN AND HER REVERSAL OF POLICY

Spain was a poor country, but she had the pretensions of a great power. She entered the war when France declared war upon her, having been little influenced by the Enlightenment and still confident that she would preserve her position as an independent state with world-wide possessions. The Bourbon kings of Spain had done what they could to restore the vitality of Spanish society, but startling progress was not possible. Ferdinand VI had divided Spain into provinces and strengthened central control in the interests of fiscal reform. By the concordat of 1753 the king had secured his right to appoint to benefices, but there was a residual opposition in the Jesuit Order and among the officials of the Inquisition. Charles III on his accession in 1759 had continued to strengthen the control of the state over the Church and secured the expulsion of the Jesuits in 1767, but the Church remained a very powerful factor in Spanish society. In 1788 there were 2,000 convents and monasteries for men and 1,000 for women. There were 68,000 monks and 33,000 nuns together with 88,000 secular clergy, which in spite of an estimated growth of the population from 4,500,000 in 1650 to 10,400,000 in

1787 represented a large proportion of the inhabitants of Spain engaged in unproductive occupations. Spain was a country in which natural riches were confined to the north and north-west coastal regions and the southern slopes of the Pyrenees and Catalonia. Where peasant proprietorship existed there was subdivision of holdings and sub-letting. Some freedom had been given to the trade with the colonial territories of South America, while royal encouragement had led to a slight expansion of industry. Progressive ideas were for the most part, however, confined to a small group of royal officials and to the embryonic capitalist class. It remained true that the conservatives and the religious orders sought to retain their control over the land and education. There was not an acute conflict in Spain. Charles III, for all his anti-clericalism, regarded the Church as a necessary and traditional instrument of royal control.

His successor, Charles IV, made no significant changes in royal policy. It seems to have been the aim of the Spanish monarchy to permit Spain to evolve upon her own lines without drastic reforms. In common with France, Spain had experienced a grain shortage in 1787 and 1788. There were grain riots in Barcelona in February 1789, but nothing occurred seriously to shake the authority of the state. It was the policy of the chief minister, Floridablanca, to insulate Spain from news of events in France. Some disquiet was experienced when the Galician peasants rioted against the taxation system in 1790–1 and fears were entertained lest the French merchant community should indoctrinate Spaniards with the ideas of the revolution. On 24 February 1791 all except official periodicals were suspended, which brought to an end the controlled intellectual development encouraged by Charles III. The weakness of Spain lay in the personality of Charles IV. He lacked the energy of Charles III and relied too much upon the advice of the queen, Maria Luisa. On 28 February 1792 Floridablanca was dismissed and replaced by the Conde de Aranda, a leader of the old nobility, but little change was in fact experienced in the system of government. The change seems to have been induced in part by the decision of Charles IV that it was in the interest of Louis XVI that Spain should not adopt an attitude of overt hostility to revolutionary France. The appointment of the Conde de Aranda was therefore an indication of willingness to seek an accommodation with France, but the execution of

Louis XVI caused Aranda to revert to the policy of Floridablanca. War in fact broke out with France when Charles IV made a plea that Louis XVI's life should be spared. France declared war on 7 March 1793, but hostilities were desultory. In April 1794 the French were able to overrun Roussillon and threaten the erection of a Catalan Republic, but Spain was not receptive of revolutionary ideas. There was in fact a national reaction against France, led and encouraged by the Spanish clergy. To the opposition of the priests was added the hatred which the looting of the French soldiers aroused.

The weakness of Spain lay in the unsavoury atmosphere of the Court. It was an accepted social custom among the aristocracy of Madrid that their wives should have a male companion (*cortejo*), a practice much disliked by the lower classes, but Charles IV tolerated the association of the Queen with Manuel Godoy. Annoyance gave way to scandal when on 15 November 1792 Godoy was made first secretary in place of Aranda. Aranda and his following, together with many high officials, were appalled that an apparently untalented courtier, whose sole qualification for advancement was the Queen's passion for him, should be promoted to the highest position in the state. Fear of rebellion caused the Spanish government to seek peace with France, which was signed in July 1795, but even this was an occasion for grumbling. Godoy was rewarded with the title of the Prince of the Peace, which appeared to give him precedence over all the Spanish nobility. The incident brought about an erosion of the dynasty's prestige. On the one hand, the high nobility were alienated. On the other, there was a growth of liberalism, encouraged though without conspicuous success by the handful of Spanish *émigrés* who had thrown in their lot with France. Spain was not influenced by the ideals of the revolution, but Godoy was henceforth compelled to twist and turn in the vicissitudes of international politics to uphold his position. Steady progress made under Charles III was replaced under Charles IV by tensions within Spanish society which have not to this day been resolved. Under the guidance of Godoy Spain concluded an alliance with France on 19 August 1796, like Prussia, to pursue her own egocentric aim, in this case the Spanish domination of the Iberian peninsula, but just as the United Provinces found themselves separated from their colonies, so Spain was separated from her vast dominions in South America. The Spanish declaration of war upon Britain on 5 October 1796 met with disappointment. On 14 February 1797 the British navy won a fine victory over a superior Spanish fleet at Cape St Vincent. The cheese-paring financial policy of the Younger Pitt by very neglect caused the British fleet to mutiny at Spithead in April 1797 and at the Nore in May in protest against rates of pay, which inflation rendered absurd, but the British sailors, when once their grievances had been met, were still in good enough heart to defeat the Dutch fleet at the battle of Camperdown on 11 October 1797. Even in her extremities Britain could retain her domination of the seas. What she could not do was to influence the great battles which were fought upon land.

III. THE FRENCH OFFENSIVE OF 1796

The main danger of an invasion of France passed with the battle of Fleurus in 1794. In 1795 first Prussia and then Spain withdrew from the war. A puppet régime had been erected in the United Provinces under the name of the Batavian Republic and the Directory established in France in spite of domestic opposition. The Low Countries up to the Rhine were incorporated in France. The year 1795 was one of solid achievement for France, which was not matched by further military success. The French offensive on the Rhine in the later summer and autumn of 1795 ended in stalemate. With the conclusion of an armistice operations ceased for the moment.

It was at this point that the Directory yielded to the advice of Napoleon Bonaparte that the war should be prosecuted with greater energy on the Italian front. Bonaparte had already won the gratitude of the Directory by his suppression of the insurrection of Vendémiaire (3–5 October 1795) and had a powerful ally in the beautiful creole, Joséphine de Beauharnais, who had influence with the Directors, especially Barras. On 2 March 1796 Bonaparte was appointed to command the army of Italy and, as if his future were assured, married Joséphine on 9 March, departing for his headquarters two days later. Bonaparte, as a Corsican, was familiar with Italian conditions, but he was equally well aware that political power was slipping already from the hands of the Directors into the hands of the French army, upon whom public order in Paris had come to rest. On a battlefield of his own choosing he could make a career for himself in France and serve France in as far as her interests coincided with his own. The Directors had greater hopes of the two armies on the Rhine, the armies of Sambre-et-Meuse and Rhin-et-Moselle, than of the army of Italy, which was a scratch force whose discipline was not good on account of shortage of supplies and arrears of pay and not at all impressed by Bonaparte, who seemed an adventurer owing his promotion to political services. Bonaparte was, nevertheless, a professional officer, who had the requisite qualifications in spite of his seedy antecedents. The result was surprising. The army of Italy was distributed along the coast from Nice to Savona. On 12 April 1796 he struck at the Austrian army at Montenotte and divided it from the Piedmontese army, which concluded with him the armistice of Cherasco on 28 April. Piedmont-Sardinia was compelled to sue for peace and on 15 May ceded Nice and Savoy to France. The troops of Bonaparte could now enter the northern Italian plain, living by pillage and crediting their commander with their good fortune. Milan soon fell before them, and the petty states of Italy demanded armistices in May and June: Parma, Modena, Naples and the Papal States. With his right flank secure, Bonaparte pushed his forces forward to the fortress of Mantua.

There was in Bonaparte's behaviour a self-confidence which gave him the air of being more than a general. The conclusion of the armistice of Cherasco was completed without the authority of the Directory. Drawing upon the resources of northern Italy, Napoleon could pay and feed his troops upon a scale to which they were unaccustomed. Unlike the other French commanders, he became a power in his own right. His success was such that the Archduke Charles denounced the armistice on 20 May and reopened hostilities on the Rhine, but with at first scant success for Austrian arms. Prussia on 5 August signed a new convention of neutrality, and the petty states, Baden and Württemberg, obtained first armistices and then treaties of peace. The Archduke Charles, however, was able to launch a counter-offensive and force the French commanders, Moreau and Jourdan, back beyond the Rhine. The key to the situation was Mantua, to which Bonaparte laid siege and which Austrian armies repeatedly attempted to relieve. After four battles Mantua capitulated to Bonaparte on 2 February 1797. With this fortress cleared from his path, Bonaparte resumed his offensive in March 1797 and sensing that the Austrians were in disarray took his forces as far as Judenberg in Styria, when at last on 7 April the Archduke Charles requested an armistice, lest Bonaparte penetrate deep into the Austrian dominions. On 18 April 1797 were signed the preliminaries of peace at Leoben.

IV. THE PRELIMINARIES OF LEOBEN (1797), THE PEACE OF CAMPO FORMIO AND THE RISE OF BONAPARTE

The preliminaries of Leoben were arranged by Bonaparte, an event in itself of great importance, because for the first time a general acted on behalf of the French Republic as if he were already a ruler of France. The basis of the agreement was that France should receive Lombardy and the Low countries, while Austria should receive compensation at the expense of the Venetian Republic. From the French conquests in Northern Italy was to be constructed the Cis-alpine Republic, a French puppet state organized upon French lines like its counterpart, the Ligurian Republic formed from the terri-tories of Genoa. The terms of the preliminaries were ratified by the Directory. Bonaparte took good care to make certain that the text of the Franco-Austrian agreement should reach the public before it became known to the Directors. In Paris the victory of Bonaparte proved so popular that it would have been very dangerous for the Directors to have refused ratification. Their own position was extremely precarious. It was easy enough to dispose of the Babeuf conspiracy, but there was a marked growth in royalist feeling, encouraged to some extent by the British agent in Switzerland, Wickham, but increased by the general disgust with the Directory's handling of affairs at home. In the elections of 1797 only eleven members of the former Convention were returned out of 216. All the conditions for the restoration of the monarchy existed, but as was so often to happen, the hard core of the *émigrés*, thinking still in terms of their privileged position under the Old Régime would make no concessions to the achievements of the Revolution. The republican directors, Reubell, La Reveillière and Barras, decided that the circum-stances did not permit a royalist restoration and called in the army under Augereau to carry out a purge of the royalists who had been returned in the elections. The Directors, Carnot and Barthélemy, were purged by the coup d'état of 18 Fructidor (4 September 1797) and many enemies of the régime were deported to Guiana. The army had finally emerged as the real power in politics. The most acceptable of the French generals, Hoche, died of consumption on 19 September 1797, and power therefore resided with the two main commanders, Augereau, who commanded the Army of Germany, created by the union of the two armies, Sambre-et-Meuse and Rhin-et-Moselle, and Bonaparte, the victor in Italy. The Directors' tenure of power seemed likely to be short. It was therefore more in the interest of preserving their own power than securing a general pacification that they consented to the opening of peace talks with Britain at Lille. Peace and demobilization would reduce the influence of the generals.

While Bonaparte was negotiating a definitive peace with the Austrians at Campo Formio, simultaneous negotiations were proceeding in Lille, at which the French tried to put pressure upon Britain to restore her conquests, but the British negotiators would not yield, and departed for London on 19 September, though Talleyrand, the minister of foreign affairs, continued to negotiate. On 11 October the Dutch fleet ventured out and was defeated by Admiral Duncan at the battle of Camperdown. No longer need Britain fear an invasion. The battle marks a turning point in the long struggle. Both in France and in Britain there was a growing determination to pursue the war to the end. While Britain in the west offered resistance, Bonaparte considered not only the Rhine but also his personal fortunes. France required the left bank of the Rhine, and the prospect of continued British resistance kept open the possibility of a renewed Anglo-Austrian understanding. Winter was approaching and the importance of Augereau in command of the army of Germany seemed to grow. If Bonaparte were to have any political future at all a peace was necessary. Agreement was reached upon a basis which was not entirely unsatisfactory to Austria. The Austrian Netherlands and the left bank of the Rhine, including the fortress of Mainz, went to France. The Cisalpine Republic was recognized as consisting of Lombardy, Modena and the papal legations of Bologna, Ferrara and the Romagna, and including also the towns of Brescia, Peschiera and Mantua. Nevertheless, Austria acquired the Archbishopric of Salzburg and the rayon of territory in Bavaria between Salzburg, the river Inn and the Tyrol. Any French gains at the expense of Germany were to be accompanied by compensation for Austria, while Austria's rival, Prussia, was to receive nothing. These arrangements were to be completed by a conference at Rastatt. Austria in reality emerged from a disastrous campaign with her own dominions rounded off and without any increase in Prussian territory. France acquired the left bank of the Rhine, but the revolutionary ardour was noticeably diminished. The Italians of Venetia were surrendered to Austria and all the Venetian dependencies, Istria, Dalmatia, and the Ionian islands of Corfu, Zante and Cephalonia, together with other minor Venetian possessions in this region. Gone was the determination to aid subject peoples against monarchs. France was now a great state with acquisitive instincts which she was prepared to satisfy by indulging the taste for annexation in Austria. The Directory was not entirely satisfied by Bonaparte's dispositions, but peace was very popular. He was now both a military and a political figure, a fact which received recognition in his appointment to command the army of England, which was being prepared to execute an invasion of Britain, and his nomination as leader of the delegation to conduct negotiations at Rastatt.

France was confronted by problems of considerable importance which demanded the maintenance of internal stability. She was required to incorporate the lands on the left bank of the Rhine and provide for the protection of the Cisalpine and Ligurian Republics. The Directors enjoyed the possession of power and were ready to manipulate the electoral system to secure the return of deputies favourable to themselves. The pretence of expressing the will of the people was dropped. By a law of 11 May 1798 (22 Floréal) a commission was appointed, which rejected 106 elected deputies, of whom only fifty-three were replaced. Secure in their majority, the Directors nevertheless were leaning heavily on the support of the army. Upon Bonaparte's advice unreliable political figures were removed from Paris by the simple device of appointing them to embassies in foreign capitals. Bonaparte's position proved by no means as strong as he had supposed. A coup d'état was not easy to promote without civilian support. For the moment he confined himself to the organization of the projected invasion of England. There was a temporary hiatus in the advance of France. The interval was occupied by the occupation of Switzerland and the creation in February 1798 of the

Helvetic Republic in order that it might no longer provide a refuge for spies and *émigrés*, and at the same time might give France control of the Alpine passes. The larger problem of British resistance remained unsolved. A prolonged debate occurred in French official circles at the beginning of 1798 upon the method of bringing Britain to submission.

V. THE EGYPTIAN EXPEDITION OF 1798

France from the beginning of the war had been preoccupied by questions affecting her own immediate security, but it had not escaped notice that the Near East offered a field for expansion. The Ottoman Empire was very weak. Egypt was under the control of the Mamelukes, a caste of mounted soldiery, initially of Circassian origin. In the Balkans and Albania the local pashas paid scant respect to the authority of the Sultan. The unsuccessful war against Russia led to the growth of banditry in European Turkey in which de-mobilized soldiers did what they wished in defiance of the Sultan. In this situation it was possible for France to consider the occupation of the delta of the Nile and Suez, not only to extend French influence in the Levant but also to establish a base for the invasion of India. The extension of French influence in India was not fanciful. There was enough native Indian resistance to British penetration (see below pp. 364–8) for France to envisage the destruction of the East India Company's power. Bonaparte and the minister of foreign affairs, Talleyrand, who saw in the advancement of Bonaparte's career a means of securing his own promotion, considered that an attack in the Near East would provide an alternative to the hazardous direct assault upon Britain. Bonaparte was attracted to the Mediterranean, having first made his name in Italy. At first he had wished to become a Director, though by the provisions of the constitution he was too young, but he was ready to forego this dignity if he might lead an expedition to Egypt. On 5 March 1798 the final decision was taken and an expedition of 54,000 men and 171 guns sailed for the east. Malta was occupied and garrisoned. On 1 July Alexandria fell and the French army marched upon Cairo, brushing aside the Mameluke cavalry charges at the Pyramids. The French for want of cavalry could not pursue the Mamelukes, but they were the masters of Egypt. The quick-won success was followed by an event of overwhelming political importance. The British fleet under the command of Nelson found the French fleet at anchor in Aboukir Bay near Alexandria on 1 August 1798 and destroyed it. Britain entered into command of the Mediterranean and for nearly a century remained the dominant naval power in that sea. It was not until September 1800 that Britain took Malta, but the inescapable fact remained that for once her naval power had succeeded in doing more than protect Britain from invasion. Bonaparte was isolated in Egypt and his communications with France cut completely.

VI. The Creation of a Fresh Coalition against France

The French occupation of Northern Italy was at first based upon an understanding with local families of importance, but it quickly became clear that French domination meant exploitation. Unrest was rife and there were frequent manifestations of opposition to France. French control was very insecure. On 5 February 1798 France took possession of the Papal States and erected the Roman Republic, forcing the Pope, Pius VI, to take refuge in Sienna. The Cisalpine Republic was compelled to conclude an alliance with France on 21 February 1798 and provide 25,000 troops in the event of war. Attempts at subversion in Piedmont failed, but a French garrison remained quartered in Turin. Tuscany sought to escape French control by a policy of compliance. In Naples Ferdinand I and his queen, Marie-Caroline, were determined to follow a policy of resistance. The British victory at Aboukir Bay and the return of Nelson's fleet to Naples seemed to offer the basis for an attempt to drive the French out of Italy.

Britain could not challenge the French unless she found allies. Austria was cautious of breaking a peace so recently concluded. Frederick William II of Prussia had died in November 1797, but his successor, Frederick William III, was equally concerned merely with local interests and would not undertake a war with France without certain knowledge of the form which territorial compensation for Prussia would assume. On the other hand, there had been a change of régime in Russia. Catherine II had died in November 1796 and her son, the eccentric Paul I, became tsar. An assessment of Paul's character is not easy. He was certainly capricious and gave the courtiers and ministers most closely connected with him cause for alarm, but he was not entirely devoid of reason, however much he might resemble his father, Peter III, in his self-willed arrogance. What occurred under Paul was a change in Russian policy. Catherine II had brought the Russian frontier to the line of the Dniestr. Instead of seeking to make further gains at the expense of the Ottoman Empire, Paul was ready to enter into an alliance with the Porte and Britain in order to exclude French influence from the Near East. It was Russian and British policy to bolster up Turkey; Britain was in alliance with Turkey from 9 August 1798. Paul signified his interest in the Mediterranean by accepting the Grand Mastership of the Knights of St John at Malta in October and in December concluded an alliance with Turkey and a subsidy treaty with Britain.

The change in Russian policy happened while important events were occurring in Italy. On 18 July 1798 Naples concluded a convention with Austria, by which the latter agreed to support Naples if the French should attack, but Austria was not willing herself to adopt a forward foreign policy. This situation was not to the satisfaction of the Queen of Naples, Marie-Caroline, who desired an immediate attack upon the Roman Republic. Austria was in full agreement that France should be driven back to her pre-war frontiers and that the former Austrian Netherlands ought to be joined to the defunct United Provinces in order to provide for a bastion of defence against France on the lower Rhine, an object dear to the hearts of British statesmen, but war could not be thought of before the spring of 1799.

In Naples, however, the urge for action was strong. On 22 November 1798 the Neapolitan army invaded the newly constructed Roman Republic and Rome fell; on 1 December 1798 Britain concluded an alliance with Naples, a factor important in deciding the mind of Paul I to agree to the subsidy treaty with Britain. The French had no doubt that a fresh coalition was being prepared and on 5 September 1798 had adopted conscription, a device which had hitherto been avoided and one which was intensely disliked in the provinces newly incorporated in France. The French began to mass under Jourdan the army of the Danube, which was to cross the Rhine on 1 March 1799. The Italian command was given to Joubert with instructions to hold the Austrians in Piedmont; its ruler, Charles Emmanuel, was escorted to his island of Sardinia and France took control of the country. The position in southern Italy was soon restored. Naples was quickly overrun by General Championnet, who took Naples in a battle of 20–23 January 1799 and compelled the King and Queen to flee to Sicily, though the operation was marred by a savage pillage of the city. Naples was transformed into the Parthenopean Republic. The French triumph did not last for long. The army of the Danube crossed the Rhine, but was checked by the Archduke Charles at the battle of Stockach on 25 March 1799. The French retreat in Germany was accompanied by an even worse reverse in Italy. A Russian auxiliary corps under the great general, Suvorov, arrived to strengthen the Austrians. The Russians had learned their generalship in wars with the Turks and fully understood the importance of rapid manoeuvre; the Russian soldier, moreover, has a self-confidence born of many victories and, though this factor may be exaggerated, a national consciousness uncommon in the cosmopolitan armies of the age. Marching his men in the cool of the night and resting them in the heat of the day, Suvorov dealt the French a series of crushing blows. In a three-day battle on 17–19 June he defeated the army of Naples and drove it over the Apennines. On 15 August the French army of Joubert was defeated at Novi by Suvorov and Joubert himself killed. The genius of an able general had revealed that the French were not invincible, and Suvorov's victories induced a sense of premature exhilaration.

Austrian policy was under the control of the minister, Thugut, who began to think in terms of a peace settlement favourable to Austria. With Piedmont overrun, he considered that Austria might dispose as she wished of Italy and refused to consider the reinstatement of Charles Emmanuel at his capital of Turin. A British and Russian expedition under the Duke of York was to be despatched to the Netherlands. The decision was therefore taken to send the army of the Archduke Charles to Mainz and thence to the Netherlands in order that Austria might strengthen her political claims in an area over which she had formerly ruled. Russia was treated as having no interest in the settlement of western Europe. The attitude adopted towards Suvorov and his men was that they were only mercenaries in the service of the allies. The Russians were withdrawn from Italy and ordered to join the other Russian army under Rimsky-Korsakov at Zurich. The Duke of York's expedition did not prosper in the Netherlands, and by the convention of Alkmaar of 18 October 1799 he was compelled to agree to evacuate his forces, but more serious was the dangerous position in which Rimsky-Korsakov was left. On 25–27 September 1799 the French commander in Switzerland, Masséna, threw his forces against Rimsky-Korsakov, who was compelled to cut his way out of the French encirclement with grievous losses. Suvorov, marching up from Italy, escaped from a very dangerous situation only at the cost of sacrificing his baggage and his guns. By playing politics Thugut had thrown away all the victories which had been won in 1799. Having treated Russia as if she were a petty German principality providing a military contingent and not as a great power with a policy of her own, Austria paid the price for her egocentricity. Livid with rage, Paul I on October 1799 withdrew the armies of Rimsky-Korsakov and Suvorov from the war and decided that for the future Russia would pursue her own interests. The first positive evidence was the demand that Britain should withdraw her ambassador in Russia, Whitworth. On 21 March 1800 a convention was concluded with Turkey by which a Russian force was to be installed in the former Venetian territories in the Ionian Islands. On 27 August 1800 Paul I made a proposal that the powers of the north should form an alliance of 'armed neutrality' in defence of their own interests. In this manner was created in December 1800 the Second Armed Neutrality of the North, composed of Russia, Denmark, Sweden and Prussia. If Austria could adopt a policy serving her own interests in defiance of the wishes of other powers Russia was equally capable herself of following such a course. French armies owed as much to the incompetence of their opponents' diplomacy as they did to their own skill. The need for collective resistance to the French aim of making France the dominant power on the continent of Europe, which had been understood in the reign of Louis XIV, had to be learned again before France could be defeated.

VII. The Coup d'État of 18 Brumaire and Military Rule in France

The lack of success of French arms in 1799 destroyed the prestige of the Directory. The strains of war upon French finances were creating discontents, while the generals, whom the war had by now converted into the leaders of a professional military caste, required that they should have a greater say in the affairs of state in recognition of the fact that the Directory existed only as a result of their support. The withdrawal of the Russians from the war and the temporary respite which Masséna's victory at Zurich gave permitted constitutional change in France before the reopening of hostilities in the spring of 1800. Bonaparte, cut off in Egypt, had pressed his advance into Palestine, but his progress was stopped at Acre, the siege of which he was compelled to raise in May 1799. In the same month all hope of exploiting discontent in India disappeared when Sir Arthur Wellesley destroyed for ever the power of Tippoo, the Sultan of Mysore. The Directory issued orders that Bonaparte should return from Egypt with all or part of his forces. Britain's position in the Mediterranean was too strong for the French in Egypt to be evacuated, but Bonaparte could escape alone. On 9 October 1799 he landed at Fréjus in Provence. Opinion wavered between accepting a peace in which France secured the gains she had made and appeal once again to revolutionary ardour to achieve renewed conquests. Bonaparte offered an alternative. What he proposed was an authoritarian régime and a policy of conquest. He was, however, a general without an army. All he had to rely upon was his immense prestige, which failure in Egypt had not dimmed, but he could serve as a man who could rally all the discontented elements who had lost faith in the Directors. There were the politicians excluded from office, the propertied classes who disliked the Directory's financial policy, which included forced loans, the generals itching to obtain control and the moderate republicans who feared the restoration of the monarchy. Three Directors, Siéyès, Ducos and Barras, were prepared to accept constitutional change which placed power in the hands of Bonaparte. The coup d'état was easy enough to arrange. Siéyès and his party induced the *Ancients* to decree their transference to Saint Cloud on the grounds that they were endangered by a Jacobin conspiracy. The *Five Hundred* followed them. On 18 Brumaire (9 November) Bonaparte's brother, Lucien, who presided over the *Five Hundred*, invited the deputies to appoint a new government, Siéyès, Ducos and Barras, having resigned their Directorships. Bonaparte, who had been entrusted with the command of the security forces, was brought in to explain the dangers of the alleged Jacobin plot to the *Ancients*, but he lost his nerve. His speech was a lamentable failure. The *Five Hundred* attempted to administer to him a beating-up. The coup d'état seemed likely to dissolve into a vulgar brawl, but Lucien Bonaparte saved his brother's cause with a lie. The troops guarding the Legislative Body were uncertain of what to do when Bonaparte appealed to them to act against the deputies, but Lucien declared that some deputies of the *Five Hundred* had attempted to stab his brother to death and were terrorizing the remainder. This decided the soldiers, who entered the assembly rooms and ejected the *Five Hundred*. It was not a moment which did Napoleon Bonaparte much credit, but it served his purposes.

The *Ancients* then decided to appoint three 'provisional consuls', Bonaparte, Siéyès and Ducos, and to appoint a legislative commission on the grounds that the *Five Hundred* had dissolved themselves, but Lucien Bonaparte gave the proceedings a certain respectability by assembling a second legislative commission from such members of the *Five Hundred* who would support the new régime. Real power lay with the military. The Constitution of the Year VIII established the Consulate, Bonaparte being First Consul with two others to assist him, Cambacerès and Lebrun, sound, safe men unlikely to challenge his authority. In theory universal suffrage was restored, but a system of indirect election nullified the will of the people. Each communal district chose electors, who in their turn chose electors for the department, who among themselves selected electors for the national list. The communal district (*arrondissement communal*) was not defined. The new legislative organs of the state imposed no checks upon the power of the First Consul. There was created a Tribunate which could discuss measures but might not vote upon them, and a Legislative Body which could vote but not discuss. The Senate, consisting of sixty members, appointed by Bonaparte and the two consuls in collaboration with Siéyès and Ducos, the two consuls appointed provisionally on 9 November, selected the Consuls, the Tribunes and the Legislators from the national list; the senators received a salary of 25,000 francs a year, the possession of which guaranteed their good behaviour. The most important body was the Council of State, the duties of which were the drafting of laws and decrees, the organization of the administration and the hearing of appeals. It was a committee of experts, divided into five sections, finance, civil and criminal law, home affairs, war and the navy. The Council of State took the burden of administrative work off the shoulders of the First Consul, but, being appointed by him, reserved to him the right of final decision. What Bonaparte had achieved was a constitution which permitted the notables of France, whether of the Old Régime or the new, to enjoy a recognized and official dignity and appear to be consulted, but at the same time gave the head of the administration an autocratic power far greater than that possessed by Louis XIV in the height of his reign. Of his ministers only Talleyrand was the recipient of Bonaparte's confidences, having from the first attached himself to his cause when he perceived chance of his own advancement in fidelity to a successful general; he was equally one of the first to desert his master when he realized that the régime would eventually collapse. In 1799 Bonaparte was full of energy. France obtained for a master an enlightened despot, a solution which before 1789 might have been satisfactory and even prevented revolution from breaking out at all. What Bonaparte did was to systematize and reform the administrative, financial and judicial institutions of France. The men whom Bonaparte appointed to carry out his work were at first able and conscientious. It nevertheless remained an undeniable fact that Bonaparte was an adventurer, elevated by success as a general and therefore equally likely to be cast down by defeat in battle. Napoleon Bonaparte might create a system, but he was not essential to it. In 1799 there was little to indicate whether the new régime might prove enduring. Money was scraped together for the campaign of 1800. If the régime were to survive at all it had to make victories pay for themselves and place the French armies upon the charge of conquered countries. The financial demands both of the Convention and the Directory had been the real reasons for acceptance of their overthrow. The future of Consulate rested with the outcome of the war. A decision had to be reached quickly.

VIII. THE CAMPAIGN OF 1800 AND THE PEACE WITH AUSTRIA

The collapse of the Austrian resistance was swift and sudden. The Austrian army under Melas in Italy was besieging Genoa and was caught in the rear by Bonaparte's unexpected decision to take his army, consisting only of 35,000 men and 5,000 horse, across the Great St Bernard Pass in May 1800. At the battle of Marengo on 14 June Bonaparte destroyed, though only with the greatest of good luck, Austrian military power in Italy and under the terms of the military convention of Alexandria was able to exact the evacuation of Liguria, Piedmont and Lombardy. The Austrians were no more successful on the German front. Moreau, the commander of the army of the Rhine, defeated them at Hochstädt on 19 June and on 19 July granted the armistice of Parsdorf. The basis which Bonaparte offered for the conclusion of a peace was the treaty of Campo Formio, which Francis II was ready to accept. This did not mean that Bonaparte did not intend to exploit his victory to achieve more than in 1797. By the convention of San Idelfonso of 1 October 1800 he promised Spain to enlarge the Duchy of Parma, which was ruled by the brother of the Queen of Spain, at the expense of Austria, in return for which Spain was to cede Louisiana to France. He intended, moreover, not to conclude a general peace, but rather to keep his negotiations with Austria and Britain separate. On 20 June, however, Lord Minto signed with Thugut a fresh Anglo-Austrian subsidy treaty upon the basis of neither party concluding a separate peace. Austria sought to gain time by negotiating with France at Lunéville, and Britain agreed herself to enter into peace discussions. Bonaparte demanded that the discussions should be accompanied by a cessation of hostilities and required that supplies should be permitted to go to the French garrison in Malta and the army in Egypt. This was a condition which was unacceptable to Britain; the French forces on Malta itself surrendered to Britain on 5 September. By making an unacceptable demand to Britain Bonaparte ensured that he could treat with Austria alone. Austria's will to resist was already weakening. Thugut was dismissed on 25 September under the pressure of the Austrian peace party. An Austrian plenipotentiary, Cobenzl, went to Paris to gain what he could from Bonaparte by diplomatic dexterity. The negotiations were opened at Lunéville in Lorraine, but on 28 November hostilities were resumed in Italy and Germany. On 2 December the French army under Moreau won a great victory at Hohenlinden which placed Vienna under the threat of French attack. In Germany Austria was compelled to sign the armistice of Steyer on 25 December. The renewed French advance in Italy completed the Austrian misfortunes. On 16 January 1801 the armistice of Treviso was concluded. With each battle and armistice Cobenzl negotiating at Lunéville found his position weaker. There could no longer be any thought of avoiding a separate peace. On 9 February 1801 he signed the peace of Lunéville and left Britain alone in Europe to face a hostile France and an unfriendly Russia.

Once more the triumph of Bonaparte appeared complete. French gains under the treaty of Campo Formio were confirmed. The Cisalpine Republic was enlarged in order that its eastern frontier might stretch almost the whole length of the Adige to the Adriatic. The Grand Duke of Tuscany was obliged to surrender his dominions in return for compensation in Germany; by the convention of Arunjuez of 21 March 1801 Louisiana was ceded to France and the Duke of Parma surrendered his Duchy in return for which he received Tuscany, converted for the purpose into the Kingdom of Etruria, which was virtually a puppet state of France. By the peace of Florence of 29 March France exacted from Naples the right to garrison Pescara, Brindisi and Otranto, which gave her a virtual domination of southern Italy. On 21 April Piedmont was annexed and turned into a French military province. The fortunes of Britain were indeed at a low ebb. In January Lucien Bonaparte concluded a convention with Spain to force Portugal out of the British alliance. Grenville, the British foreign secretary, could do no more than advise the Portuguese to make peace with Spain upon the best possible terms. After a short war Portugal was compelled to capitulate and agree to join the French camp. Everywhere the French influence could make itself felt. Under the terms of the treaty of Lunéville France had a right to be consulted in the indemnification of the German princes for their losses, the chief of which was to be the compensation to be found for the Grand Duke of Tuscany. One part of Europe alone eluded the grasp of Bonaparte, the Russia of Paul I.

IX. France, Russia and Britain, 1800–2

The humiliation of success in Italy and defeat in Germany had caused Paul I to withdraw from the war and create his Armed Neutrality of the North. Paul had aspirations of his own in the Mediterranean, which the British predominance seemed to threaten. Bonaparte thought that some effort ought to be made to seek an understanding with Russia and, as a gesture, was ready to release Russian prisoners taken in Switzerland. Paul was agreeable to an entente with France and considered a partition of European Turkey, which under the plan of Rostopchin would have given Moldavia, Bulgaria and Rumelia to

Russia; Wallachia, Serbia and Bosnia to Austria; and Egypt to France, while Prussia might take Münster, Paderborn and Hanover in Germany. Russia and Britain in 1801 began to adopt an attitude of hostility one to another. Paul actually issued an order for the formation of an expeditionary force to march upon India, which is indicative of a surprising ignorance of the enormous geographical difficulties involved.

The policy of Russia might have been different if it had received the approval of the Russian official class, but court circles viewed with suspicion a tsar whose whims appeared to place Russia in a position of opposition to Britain, a country from trade with which the Russian gentry drew substantial incomes. Nevertheless, there were other forces at work. The Russian autocracy itself was under the fire of criticism. There was a desire to obtain for the aristocracy a larger say in the affairs of state. It would be difficult to describe this feeling as liberal. It was rather a desire among the senior officials and the high aristocracy to place the powers of the Tsar in commission and erect a system in which the upper classes ruled the state. On 23 March 1801, with the approval of the heir to the throne, Alexander, a coup d'état was carried out, which, as Alexander must well have known, could not in Russian conditions have been executed without the murder of his father. Almost simultaneously Britain had recourse to an act of desperation. The British fleet, taking advantage of a dispute with Denmark concerning the right of search on the high seas, forced the passage of the Sound and on 2 April bombarded Copenhagen in order to destroy the Armed Neutrality of the North and keep the Baltic open to British shipping, though Prussia used the occasion to occupy the Electorate of Hanover. The new Russian government was weak and anxious to restore normal relations with Britain. The embargo on British goods was abandoned, and by the convention of 17 June 1801 regular relations with Britain were re-established.

In theory in an age when men counted for more than machines Russia was a powerful state. The population of the Russian Empire was probably 35,000,000 in 1800 and 45,000,000 in 1815, but the human resources of so large an Empire were difficult to concentrate. Russia was, moreover, a poor country, beset with financial difficulties. The coup d'état which removed Paul I from the throne and elevated Alexander I shook the whole fabric of the Petrine autocracy.

It is self-evident that Alexander I on his accession needed time in order to restore the traditional form of government in Russia. At first there were declarations that Russia would return to the system of Catherine II, which in effect meant that there would be concessions to the gentry, but Alexander was compelled to consider the forces within the governmental machine. The authors of the coup d'état of 1801 were disreputable and after a few months were removed without difficulty, but inside the bureacracy there were men who wished to limit the autocratic powers of the emperor. As a counter-weight to the officials of the system which prevailed under Catherine II, Alexander I turned to his personal friends, Stroganov, Novosiltsev, Kochubey and the Pole, Czartoryski, but Alexander I, often thought of as a liberal, had been reared in a court, where even princes of the imperial house might be done to death if an opposition group decided that their removal was necessary. Alexander I, before he could undertake an active policy, had first to establish himself as master in his own house. When he appointed the so-called Secret Committee of his friends he had no intention of exchanging one set of masters for another. For him it was a means only of dividing his domestic opposition and in their division to reserve to himself the effective power of decision. The older generation of officials wished to impose upon him a system under which the Senate obtained the right of remonstrance and thereby secured some control over his arbitrary powers, but within the administrative system Alexander I established his ascendancy by the creation on 20 September 1802 of the eight ministries of War, Admiralty, Foreign Affairs, Justice, Internal Affairs, Finance, Commerce and Education. The ministers appointed belonged to the older generation, but each was given a deputy minister from the younger generation associated with the Secret Committee. In this way was established a system of checks and balances, which reserved to the emperor the power of ultimate decision. Derzhavin, a leader of the old school, was told by Alexander: 'You always want to teach me. I am an absolute monarch and that is the way I want it to be!' While these administrative difficulties awaited their solution, there could be no thought of an active foreign policy, but when once they had been resolved Alexander I could take up the question of French expansionism. For three years Russia was relatively passive in European politics, but there was never any doubt that Russia must come to grips with the problem presented by the growing French domination of central Europe. Unable in the first instance to check France, Alexander decided to collaborate with Bonaparte. As a result of the Franco-Russian treaty of peace of 8 October 1801 and the secret convention which completed it on 10 October, Alexander I agreed to the principle that some reorganization of Germany must take place as a result of the French acquisition of the left bank of the Rhine, where German princes had lost territories. In this manner Alexander I obtained the right to be consulted in German affairs. It was, moreover, provided that France should observe the neutrality of Naples and evacuate Piedmont after French troops had been withdrawn from Egypt, in itself a good reason for Britain to hasten the conclusion of a peace with France. The temporary crisis of the Russian autocracy and the collapse of Austria left Britain without hope of obtaining any ally in Europe. There was no other course than to negotiate a peace.

X. Great Britain, France and the Peace of Amiens, 1802

Britain had by her command of the seas rendered it impossible for France to threaten her security. In December 1796 Hoche had sailed for Ireland with 15,000 men, where there was enough discontent to give France the support to drive out the British forces, but the weather had been bad and storms dispersed the French force. In general, Britain had been successful where her navy could be effective. She commanded the Mediterranean and in September 1800 had taken Malta. In June 1801 a British expeditionary force landed in Egypt and compelled the French to capitulate. The war placed Britain in control of the Atlantic and the trade from the East. Britain had almost a monopoly of the colonial trade. Economically Britain was winning the war, because the states of continental Europe were compelled to look to her for the goods of colonial countries. The expansion of her commerce, the stimulation of a moderate inflation and the ability to collect taxes from her citizens, among them the hated Income Tax instituted in 1798, gave Britain the capacity to finance the war effort, in spite of the poor harvests of 1799 and 1800, which compelled her to buy grain abroad. In 1801 the situation was serious, but not desperate, though complicated by the Younger Pitt's effort to conciliate Ireland by pushing through the Irish parliament an act of Union with Britain on the understanding that the Roman Catholics would receive emancipation from the disabling statutes which excluded them from public life. To this proposal the king, George III, would not agree, and Pitt was compelled to resign.

The ministry which replaced that of Pitt in March 1801 was headed by Addington, with Lord Hawkesbury at the foreign office. It was ready to conclude a peace with France, whereas Pitt had been committed to the continuation of the war. Peace was signed at Amiens on 27 March 1802. Britain made a restitution of her colonial conquests at the expense of France, Spain and the former United Provinces, with the exception of the Spanish island of Trinidad and the Dutch possessions in the island of Ceylon. There was little that Britain in fact lost, because with the renewal of the war she could always reoccupy the territories and islands which she now restored. The real difficulties which presented themselves to Britain lay in the Mediterranean. She was obliged to recognize the seven Ionian Islands as a republic, occupied though they were by Russian troops. The island of Malta was to be restored to the Knights of St John three months after the ratification of the treaty of peace and placed under the joint guarantee of France, Great Britain, Austria, Spain, Russia and Prussia. It mattered little that France undertook to evacuate Naples and the Papal States. Britain was required herself to evacuate the key to the Mediterranean, which, for all the French professions of willingness to observe Malta's neutrality, would lie exposed to a French occupation. There was war-weariness in Britain which permitted the government to secure the ratification of the peace of Amiens, but there were critics of the peace, among them Pitt, who regarded it merely as a truce which ought to be broken when the possibility of a fresh coalition presented itself. The dominant position which France had secured on the continent of Europe could not long remain unchallenged.

The French Consulate and Empire

I. THE DOMESTIC REFORMS OF BONAPARTE

Bonaparte had brought peace by his military efforts. Within France there was a war-weariness in spite of brilliant victories. He perceived that it would be necessary for him to prove to France that not only was he capable of defeating the enemy in the field but also that he could win the peace. He was aware that peace might bring with it a general relaxation and desired to make a renewed effort at home to reduce France to order. He used the prestige of victory to secure for himself the appointment of First Consul for life on 2 August 1802 as a result of a plebiscite, in which his cause obtained an overwhelming majority of 3,500,000 to a mere 8,000 against. In May 1804 even greater permanence for his régime was aspired to when he was proclaimed Emperor as Napoleon I and had the Pope come to attend his coronation in the cathedral of Notre Dame, though it was Napoleon who placed the crown upon his own head. This step had been preceded by a purge of elements which might have attempted to oppose him. Plots existed to assassinate him, especially that of Cadoudal, the royalist, and of the discontented generals. General Moreau, whose military ability had contributed so largely to the defeat of Austria, and Pichegru, who had like Cadoudal taken temporary refuge in England, had no regard for the Corsican upstart who controlled France, but a plot of 1803 misfired and Cadoudal and Pichegru were put to death, while Moreau went into exile. Bonaparte systematically purged all elements in France which might contest his authority.

The marks of a deterioration in the régime began to appear at an early stage. Bonaparte tolerated not the slightest opposition within France. The proclamation of the Empire, the Constitution of the Year XII, inflated his sense of self-importance. Even the original Consulate and its institutions proved unsatisfactory. The Senate was expanded to contain the Princes, whom the Emperor created, together with the high officers of state, and given the power of veto over the bills passed by the Legislative Body. The Tribunate had its powers curtailed in April 1802, even though these were only the authority to discuss Napoleon's measures, and eventually in 1807 ceased to exist. To keep control of the public at large Fouché was appointed minister of police with wide powers of arrest, which, when it suited him, he interpreted with a laxity which did him more credit than his master. Those who did not please the new autocrat were soon visited with his displeasure. Lucien Bonaparte, at first the minister of the Interior, who was the ablest of Napoleon's brothers, was discarded when it was shown that he had a will of his own. In time, as he sought to conciliate discordant elements in French society, Napoleon began to import into the administration persons of inferior quality in order that they might be fused with the parvenu nobility he was creating from among his own clientele. By a law of 26 April 1802 (6 Floréal) an amnesty was granted to the *émigrés*, with some exceptions, provided that they would take an oath of loyalty. When the Empire was created Princes, Dukes, Barons and Chevaliers of the Legion of Honour, all of them provided with salaries, cluttered the Court of the Bonapartes and constituted a caste dependent upon their master for all they possessed, aping the manners of the old nobility. The rough cameraderie of the battlefield gave way to a court etiquette, which gradually forced upon Napoleon isolation from French society and led to a situation in which he could no longer assess the degree of support he enjoyed. Having surrounded himself with his own creatures, he tended to receive only the advice he wished to hear.

The new autocracy worked through the Council of State, the business of which increased greatly as time went on. Already in 1800 the system of elected councils in the departments and communes was abolished in as far as it determined the appointment of local officials. All appointments were henceforth made direct from Paris and the prefect became the agent of the central government, watching over every aspect of local life, selecting the conscripts, making requisitions for the army and ensuring that Napoleon's will should be observed. Undoubtedly the most arduous task of the prefect was the imposition of conscription, effected under the law of 1798 by the drawing of lots, but permitting substitution if the conscript had enough money to buy himself out. Conscription was unpopular and French tactics wasteful in lives. Altogether about 2,500,000 Frenchmen were called upon to render military service from 1800 to 1814, of which perhaps 1,500,000 were embodied in the regiments of the line. As long as the countries conquered by France could be made to pay for the military effort the propertied classes upon which the régime was based were unlikely to complain, because it was only the poor who risked losing their lives and by recompense often achieved rapid promotion. While victory followed upon victory there was to be no serious difficulty in raising men from France.

Napoleon set about solving the social problems which beset France with the zeal of a reforming autocrat. The Bank of France was established in 1800 at first with a capital of 30,000,000 francs under the control of fifteen regents and three censors and in 1804 alone was permitted to issue bank notes. Its purpose was to handle the accounts of the government, but it was never able to promote large loans, because no one in France believed that the Napoleonic system would last for ever. Nevertheless, the Bank did put some order into the French financial system and was to prove like the Council of State more lasting than the régimes it was to serve. Equally enduring and to carry the emperor's name thereafter was the codification and simplification of the laws in the form of the *Code Napoléon*. In this little originality was shown, because most monarchs in Europe aspired to reducing the tangle of laws to a coherent shape. In 1800 a committee of lawyers was set up to produce a civil code with orders to make haste. Their proposals, representing a synthesis of Roman, Revolutionary and customary law, were ready by 1 January 1801, but it was not until 1804 after much discussion that the Code received approval in its final form. Very great control was given to the father as head of the family, even to the extent of his being able to imprison his children under sixteen years of age for one month and between the ages of sixteen and twenty-one for six months. The status of women was equally limited. The wife was subject to her husband's authority and had no right to a say in the disposal of family property. Marriage and divorce were subject to strict rules. Nevertheless, property was equally divisible among all legitimate children upon the father's death, except for a devisable portion which was limited to one-tenth. This provision had a profound social effect. Fathers could, if they wished, be tyrants, but most were not. Wishing to bequeath as much as possible to their heirs, Frenchmen of all classes took care to limit the size of their families. The expectancy of an inheritance led to pressure upon the father from children to act with caution in money matters (see below, p. 222). To the Civil Code there were added the Code of Civil Procedure, the Commercial Code and the Criminal Code. Everything was reduced to a system, though sometimes the system was harsh, especially in the case of the Criminal Code. The procedure of examination left much to be desired; suspects could be kept in prison while the government prosecutors gathered evidence from witnesses in the prisoner's absence. Nevertheless, the Code marked a complete break with the past, constructing the basis for a modern society with provision for personal liberty, equality before the law and liberty of conscience. Labour was regarded as a commodity, the price of which rose and fell with the fluctuations of the economy.

By a law of 12 April 1803 (22 Germinal XI) workmen's associations were forbidden, and it was subsequently ordered that an official booklet must be obtained before the workman could be employed at all. Nothing which restricted the power of the employer was admitted in a régime which sought, above all, to conciliate the upper classes of France. The general tendency of Napoleon's legislation was to reinforce social discipline, and therefore it inclined towards conservative solutions acceptable to the propertied classes. It was, moreover, an article of export. Wherever French influence or conquest made itself felt in Europe, the Codes could be accepted by other states struggling with legal confusion as ready-made solutions of their problems.

The conservatism which was exhibited in the laws found its counterpart in the peace which Bonaparte made with the most conservative of all institutions in Europe, the Roman Church. The Jacobins had attacked the church by instituting their own worship of Reason. The Directory had not openly attacked the principles of religion, but it had done nothing to encourage religious observance and had excluded religious instruction from schools. There were parts of the country, especially in the west and in Normandy, where the clergy were still powerful, while the acquisition of the Austrian Netherlands presented a special problem of relations with a clergy traditionally inclined to defend their claims. French kings had since the Concordat of Bologna in 1516 sought the alliance of the Church, and Bonaparte now reverted to the old policy, abandoning the anti-clericalism of the Left. Pius VII, formerly Cardinal Chiaramonti, was elected Pope in succession to Pius VI in March 1800 and desired to come to terms with Bonaparte, not only because dechristianization was making progress in France but also because France herself was an Italian power as a result of her hegemony in northern Italy. On 18 April 1802 a fresh concordat was published to regulate the affairs of church and state in France. France was to experience many troubles which stemmed from the Church, but the settlement of 1802 lasted until 1904–5 when at last anti-clericalism forced the separation of church and state. The Church was required to accept the alienation of its lands, in return for which the clergy were to be paid a state salary. A new episcopacy was appointed with a certain number of the constitutional bishops retaining their sees, but the Church in fact was to come under the control of the state. In return for submissiveness to the prefects the bishops obtained a greater measure of control over the parochial clergy. Roman Catholicism was recognized as the religion of the majority of Frenchmen, but the Concordat represented something more than an alliance between church and state. The bishops looked more and more to Rome, where the choice of bishops lay. In the long run Papal authority was to grow in France, especially when it was accompanied by a religious revival, of which Châteaubriand's *Génie du Christianisme*, published in 1802, was an early example. Gallicanism was discredited by its association with the Bonapartist régime, with a consequent growth of Ultramontanism.

The reaction against the indifference of the early days of the Revolution created a difficulty which was to plague France throughout the nineteenth century. Napoleon was willing to enlist the Church to bolster his régime, but he had no intention of permitting the Church to control more than primary education. The system of education under the Bonapartist system was to be one worthy of a great empire. The law of May 1802 provided for a hierarchy of schools, and 6,400 scholarships were granted to attract boys, necessary to the government's aim of enlisting an educated élite, to the so-called Lycées; it was from the Lycées that the officials of the new régime were to be found to administer the new France. It was at an early age that the patronage of the state began to exert its attractive power upon the Frenchman. In 1808 the Imperial University was founded, which was to provide all the teachers of France in the higher ranges of education, under a Grand Master imposing the orthodoxy in political and religious thought required by Napoleon.

Nothing escaped Napoleon Bonaparte's attention. Literature, the theatre, painting and architecture were submitted to a uniform and often philistine pattern, but the regimentation demanded by Napoleon's orderly mind produced an activity in quantity which was subsequently to produce a qualitative change attracting men to French ideas long after the ephemeral empire had dissolved. Napoleon Bonaparte left his mark upon French society, which was entirely independent of his own personality. It is difficult to admire Napoleon Bonaparte, closer acquaintance with whose career often produces a sense of revulsion. On the other hand, it must be recognized that he completed the destruction of the Old Régime in France and gave a permanence to the bases and essentials of a modern state, in which thought could flourish unhampered by the traditionalism which has transmitted to Britain slower but no less constructive habits of mind. The respect which may readily be accorded to France need not necessarily be granted to the Corsican adventurer, Bonaparte, whose pre-eminence reflected only the genius of which the country of his adoption was capable.

II. THE BRITISH DESIRE TO RENEW THE WAR

War had placed a great strain upon the British economy, but peace with France seemed likely to impose an even greater burden. Between 1789 and 1801 wages rose in France by 41 per cent, while between the years 1785–9 and 1797–1803 corn prices rose by 27 per cent. It seemed likely that Napoleon could add to his military achievements an economic prosperity which would place his rule upon a firm foundation. With the signing of the peace he turned his attention to the mechanization of the textile industry in order to imitate the British methods of production with the object of supplanting Britain in the continental market. If the workers of the cities could be kept contented and the peasants assured of stable and even buoyant prices for their grain and wine the social and economic foundations of the Consulate and Empire would be so firmly secured that the new régime would achieve a permanence which it would be hard to shake.

The peace of Lunéville presented France with an opportunity not only of securing allies in western Germany but also of opening markets to a France which might displace Britain as the dominant commercial power. Under the terms of the peace treaty with Austria it had been agreed that the German princes should receive compensation for the lands which they had lost on the left bank of the Rhine. This provision made it possible for France to win the gratitude of the south German princes by enlarging their states at the expense of the Church, the minor rulers, the imperial knights and the free cities. France had a long tradition of looking to Bavaria and, indeed, Bavaria had frequently allied herself with France. The Elector, Maximilian Joseph, and his Savoyard minister, Montgelas, adhered to the French camp in August 1801 and with them went the rulers of Württemberg, Hesse-Cassel and Baden; in May 1802 Prussia, as ever prepared to seek her own advantage with as little cost to herself as possible, was won over after some hesitation for the French scheme of reorganization which would give her the bishoprics of Paderborn, Hildesheim, Erfurt and part of Münster. The essence of the diplomatic problem was Russia, for not only had Alexander I an interest in Germany but his aid was necessary also to secure the isolation of Austria. Alexander I was much attracted by a scheme which would result in the enlargement of the petty princely houses with which the Romanovs were connected by marriage. Austria adopted an attitude of resistance, but by the convention of 26 December 1802 she yielded, receiving Trentino, which enabled her to guard Vienna and the bishoprics of Eichstädt and Salzburg as compensation for the dispossessed Grand Duke of Tuscany. Austria may have accepted the reorganization sourly, but the real victims were the ecclesiastical states. Under the terms of the Recess of 25 February 1803 the Catholic Church lost its territorial influence and revenues in Germany; swallowed up in the reorganization were two million inhabitants and revenues amounting to 21,000,000 florins. Three protestant states, Württemberg, Baden and Hesse-Cassel, were raised to the rank of electorates, which established a protestant majority in the college of electors. The Catholic universities were secularized and with them the convents. Out of fifty-one free towns forty-five passed into possession of the princes. The general result was the creation of much more compact states within Germany. Bavaria, Württemberg, Baden and Hesse-Cassel emerged enlarged in size and more easily managed and organized, though not large enough to offer a threat to France, yet with sufficient military resources to be useful allies in any future struggle and as allies to claim further rewards for their services. Napoleon Bonaparte and the French foreign minister, Talleyrand, who managed the reorganization in Paris and in the process acquired a fortune in bribes from the German princes, in 1803 set in motion the modernization of Germany. The German princes, certain of French military support, could proceed to the reorganization of their states with a speed and brutality which was impossible for the French authorities in the German lands on the left bank of the Rhine, who could make their incorporation into France acceptable only if they handled the local population with tact and understanding. Speed was essential to the German princes in order that they might consolidate their power and be able to change sides if ever the tide of success turned against France.

Elsewhere the French reorganization was more brutal. Piedmont, which in 1801 became a French military district, was reconstituted to form six French departments on 11 September 1802. The Ligurian Republic in June 1802 was given a constitution, but was subsequently reorganized as a French military district, while the Cisalpine Republic in January 1802 was renamed the Italian Republic, of which Bonaparte himself became president. The Batavian Republic in October 1802 received a new constitution, consisting of a Legislative Body and Regency consisting of twelve members; the overwhelming majority of the Dutch abstained from voting in the plebiscite and, whether they liked it or not, received the new institutions. In February 1803 Bonaparte compelled the warring Swiss factions to accept his mediation; the Helvetic Republic was given a federal constitution, which left virtual control in the hands of France.

The satellite states had heavy burdens to shoulder, both military and commercial. Batavia and the Cisalpine Republic were first compelled to support French garrisons from their budgets and then provide men. The Helvetic Republic was required to provide four regiments each of 4,000 men. The Cisalpine Republic raised 24,000 men by conscription. Piedmont was integrated economically with France, directing her silk to Lyons, but the Italian Republic was designated as a market for French manufactured goods under the tariff system of 1803.

The belief held generally in Britain that the signing of peace would lead to an expansion of British trade did not in fact prove correct. There was a decline in the volume of British trade, which could make little impression upon the areas of French influence. The French tariff of 1803 placed heavy duties upon sugar and penalized textiles. The progress of France in promoting her own trade was imposing. In her peace treaty with Portugal in September 1801 economic concessions were extorted. With the general pacification of Europe France began to re-establish contacts in Algiers, Tunis and Turkey. The young colonel, Sébastiani, attempted to assert French influence in the Levant and Egypt. The colonial territories of France in the West Indies and Louisiana were occupied. In December 1801 an enormous army for the task in hand was sent under Leclerc to San Domingo to suppress the Negro régime of Toussaint-Louverture, which gave rise to the suspicion that its real destination was the British sugar island of Jamaica. Happily for Britain and unhappily for the French troops, which were largely Poles, Leclerc's expedition came to nothing as a result of a yellow fever epidemic, but the episode was seen as yet one more illustration of the dangers which faced Britain. Pitt and his supporters began to argue that the peace had led only to colonial restitutions to France, who could then begin the organization of a fresh attack. There was a growing conviction that Britain would be more prosperous if she resumed the war. The British foreign secretary, Hawkesbury, could not stand by and be a passive spectator of Bonaparte's expansionism. As early as September and October 1802 Hawkesbury proposed an alliance of Austria, Russia and Britain against France, but Alexander I was then still too much interested in the reorganization of Germany lightly to throw away his entente with France.

III. The Origins of the War, 1803

The key position in the diplomacy of 1802–3 was held by Russia. The great fear of Russia was that the defeat of Britain would result in the extension of French influence in central and south-eastern Europe. While Russia had under Paul I been technically at war with Britain, it had been hoped to control the ambitions of France, but this policy had led to the hostility of Austria and Prussia. Alexander I believed that it was necessary to avoid a crisis in the Near East while Germany was being reorganized, though Bonaparte through his agent Duroc sought to keep Russia's interest alive in this area. An indication of future attitudes was the refusal of Alexander I to accept the Mastership of the Order of St John at Malta, lest Russia should be involved unnecessarily in a conflict with Britain, who held the island. There had been a debate within the Secret Committee established by Alexander I at a meeting on 13 July 1801, whether Russia should choose a French or a British alliance, but the question was unresolved. Peace had been established with Britain in June 1801 and was to follow with France in October 1801, which was supplemented by a secret convention for Franco-Russian co-operation in Germany in return for a promise from Bonaparte to respect the neutrality of Naples and provide compensation for Piedmont. Russia could clash with Britain in the Mediterranean or with France in Central Europe. The danger which Britain presented in the Near East was hypothetical. The threat which France seemed to offer in Central Europe was real and urgent. In the end the Russians decided upon a course of prudence and chose the British alliance.

At the beginning of February 1803 Hawkesbury ordered Warren, the British ambassador in St Petersburg, to propose an alliance to Russia to cover the Ottoman Empire only, but from the Russian side deeper fears were revealed when on 8 February 1803 Britain was advised not to evacuate Malta. As long as Britain held Malta and was menaced by France, European conflicts could hardly extend themselves to the Straits and the Near East. On 14 April 1803 the Russian reply to Warren's approach was received; Russia undertook to act in accord with Britain if Turkey were menaced. While this reply did not reveal an identity of interests, it showed at least that the views of the two powers coincided upon one important issue. In the meantime there was no improvement in Anglo-French relations. As a gesture of good will the Cape of Good Hope was restored to the Dutch, but it was obvious that it could be retaken at will. The king's speech of 23 November 1802 advised vigilance, which could mean only a public declaration of distrust. An article placed in the official newspaper, *Moniteur*, giving an account of Sébastiani's mission to the Near East, seemed to foreshadow a fresh Egyptian expedition by France. The receipt of the Russian advice on 8 February was decisive. On 9 February 1803 the British government informed France of its refusal to evacuate the island of Malta. After bitter exchanges the British ambassador, Whitworth, left Paris on 12 May 1803 and hostilities were resumed by France and Britain. There had been no sincere desire for peace from the British side and only a wish to prolong the peace for a while on the French.

The opening of the war followed the predetermined pattern. Britain quickly confined France to the continent of Europe. The French expedition to San Domingo had ended in ruin and Louisiana had been sold to the United States on 30 April 1803. Bonaparte had already turned his back upon the New World before the war began, but in Spain France had an ally who was an American power and therefore possessed a fleet. Spain had requested to be allowed to remain neutral and agreed to pay France a monthly subsidy in lieu of armed aid, but

Bonaparte conceived a plan by which the Spanish fleet, which had a nominal strength of fifty-seven ships of the line and thirty-eight frigates, should join with the French fleet to lure the British fleet in the direction of the West Indies. In the meantime a French army was to be massed at Boulogne and when the Franco-Spanish fleet had eluded the British battle fleet in mid-Atlantic it should move into the Channel in order to give the French a temporary command of the seas and permit them to land an expeditionary force in England. Spanish policy was still commanded by the Queen's favourite, Godoy, who had little support within the country and therefore believed that a splendid success in foreign policy would serve to bolster his position. He agreed to the French project, and on 12 December 1804 Spain declared war on Britain. In April 1805 the French admiral, Villeneuve, left Toulon and proceeded as if in the direction of the West Indies and was joined at Cadiz by a token Spanish force. In the meantime France hoped that Europe would remain quiet.

In 1803 Russia proposed to Britain an alliance to cover the event of a French landing in Egypt, but this had met with no response. In April 1804, however, the government of Addington in Britain fell and was replaced by the administration of the Younger Pitt, who proposed to Russia a treaty of alliance with a subsidy. The relations of Russia and France were gradually deteriorating. Bonaparte in August 1803 refused a Russian mediation in the war with Britain, knowing full well that Russia had encouraged its resumption. At the beginning of 1804 Russian foreign policy came under the control of Adam Czartoryski, a Pole full of plans for his own country's reconstruction and reshaping of the map of Europe in the interest of Russia. A series of diplomatic incidents poisoned Franco-Russian relations. The Russian ambassador, Markov, was required to leave France. The protest of the Tsar against the execution of the Bourbon duc d'Enghien in March 1804, after he had been seized in Baden for alleged participation in the Cadoudal plot, evoked from Bonaparte references to the murder of Paul I upon Alexander I's accession. Novosiltsev was sent from St Petersburg to London with extensive instructions from Czartoryski, which Pitt reduced to the simple aim of reducing France to her old limits and constructing a system of collective security. Buffer states were to be erected in the Low Countries, Prussia and Piedmont to prevent French aggression in the future. Eventually on 11 April

1805 was concluded the Anglo-Russian alliance, by which Britain guaranteed to pay £1,250,000 a year for every 100,000 regular troops Russia put into the field, provided that Austria joined in the coalition. Austria was cautious of entering this third coalition against France. Financial difficulties coupled with Francis II's inability to make quick decisions delayed Austria's adherence to the plan of collective opposition to France, but, not content with his recently acquired title of Emperor, Napoleon added to his dignities by having himself called to the throne of Italy on 17 March 1805 and crowned with the Iron Crown of the Lombards in the cathedral at Milan, while the Ligurian Republic was induced in June to request her annexation by France. The French action seemed to threaten the Austrian possessions in Italy precisely at a moment when the main French army was concentrated at Boulogne. On 16 June 1805 was signed the convention which secured Austria's adherence to the coalition.

In the face of the coming war Prussia as ever faltered. France was prepared to make concessions to Prussia at the expense of Hanover, which the French army had occupied in June 1803, whetting Prussian appetites even though it was fully realized that a French domination of Europe would be to Prussia's disadvantage. To the lesser states of Germany Napoleon could appeal with every chance of success. Treaties of alliance were secured with Bavaria, Württemberg and Baden in August and September 1805 which were of great strategic significance. The French armies could cross the Upper Rhine and pass through the Black Forest without encountering any opposition. Already on 24 August 1805 the order was given to the French Grand Army to strike its camp at Boulogne and march into Germany. Whatever might be the fate of the war on the sea, the invasion of England was called off. It was in fact in the midst of Napoleon's first successes in the new war in Europe that on 21 October 1805 the British fleet under Nelson destroyed the united Franco-Spanish fleet off Cape Trafalgar. Great Britain had finally won the war on the sea and separated France and Europe from the New World and the East, but Napoleon could be defeated in the end only upon the land.

IV. Napoleonic Methods of War

Napoleon Bonaparte has enjoyed great fame for his generalship, but inherent in the methods which he adopted in the organization of the

French army and in its strategy and tactics in the field were many weaknesses, which explain his ultimate defeat. In theory all French between the ages of twenty and twenty-five years were liable for service, but there were many exemptions. Between 1800 and 1812 1,500,000 men were levied from the French dominions of which three-quarters perhaps came from pre-1789 France. It was not French practice to give the recruits much basic training in barracks. Instead they were sent to the fighting units in small groups and embodied with the experienced soldiers. Discipline was poor and there was much insubordination. The private soldier was paid only 5 sous a day and then often irregularly. Reserves of weapons were often slender, while supplies of food in the rear of the army non-existent. The principal aim of the French commanders was to encourage an aggressive spirit in the troops and a desire for battle. The army was represented as a career with many openings for advancement. In fact, neither the men nor the officers were well trained, while there was virtually no general staff. The army consisted virtually of an élite which directed operations under the guidance of Napoleon and a mass of raw soldiery, diluted as time went on with more and more foreigners. As the military operations extended themselves the central control of Napoleon became weaker and French generalship less effective.

The success of French arms can best be explained in the light of these deficiencies. It was essential that the French army should be victorious and live upon the resources of the enemy. Already the military writers of the Old Régime had objected to the chessboard generalship for which the Prussian army was famed. From the revolution emerged a new conception of warfare. Masses of men were let loose in the theatre of operations in divisions and corps. The object of Napoleon was to effect a concentration of these units upon the field of battle as early in the campaign as possible in order to destroy the enemy. The opposing army was engaged at first with only the minimum of skilled troops, the sharpshooters and the artillery, and then a shock was administered by a mass attack in columns by the concentrated infantry formations, for whom therefore only a minimum training sufficed. The aim was to destroy utterly the opposing army and then to pursue it relentlessly, requisitioning or simply looting supplies to maintain the momentum of the French advance. These methods were undoubtedly effective, but they contained the reasons for Napoleon's ultimate downfall. The British army learned first the art of pouring fire into the massed columns of the French army, which blunted the force of its attack. Other armies were to stand their ground in a similar manner and inflict ever-increasing casualties upon the French. The general strategy of Napoleon was, moreover, applicable only in the relatively highly developed areas like Italy, where an invading army might expect to draw upon plentiful supplies. When the French army was employed in Spain, Northern Germany, Poland and Russia, it was less easy to live off the country. These were countries in which the population was sparser and supplies correspondingly more difficult to obtain. The energy and ingenuity of Napoleon, which won him victories in Italy, was coupled with a lack of inventiveness in unfamiliar lands. When a French army retreated the absence of proper preparation in its rear could lead only to chaos. The Napoleonic conquest of Europe was to be an improvisation. Perhaps the greatest advantage which Napoleon had was the willingness of his opponents to offer battle early in the campaign. In 1805 the Austrian army obliged the French by itself seeking an early decision of the war.

V. THE CAMPAIGN OF 1805: THE DEFEAT OF AUSTRIA

For the war against France three Austrian armies were assembled, one in northern Italy, which consisted of the best troops, another to cover Switzerland and a third of 80,000 men, under the nominal command of the Archduke Ferdinand, but under the actual orders of General Mack, to operate on the Danube. Behind them advanced two Russian armies, each of 50,000 men. The original plan of the Russian general, Kutusov, was that the allies should concentrate their forces and launch a simultaneous attack upon the French armies, but General Mack allowed the Austrian army on the Danubian front to be surrounded at Ulm and forced to capitulate on 20 October 1805. The result was disastrous. The leading Russian army under Kutusov had reached Braunau on the river Inn. In the face of what through Mack's folly had become overwhelming opposition, Kutusov was compelled to withdraw into Bohemia and Moravia to link forces with the second Russian army which was coming up. The best strategy to have adopted would have been continued withdrawal before the French, but this course meant the exposure of Vienna to capture on

13 November which entailed the loss of a large quantity of Austrian military stores. Kutusov,urged continued withdrawal, declaring 'In the depths of Galicia I will bury the bones of the French', but Alexander I was influenced by political considerations and bad military advice. Francis II did not wish to see his dominions overrun by the French, while fresh troops were coming in from Russia and the Archduke Charles still had 80,000 men under his command, which seemed to offer the opportunity of winning a decisive battle and reversing the fortunes of war. A great battle was fought at Austerlitz, a small town east of Brno, in Moravia, on 2 December. The defeat which Kutusov feared and for which he took the blame, in view of the fact that the two emperors would not take responsibility, resulted in the loss of 21,000 Russians with 155 guns and 6,000 Austrians with 25 guns. The best which the Russians could do for the moment was to conclude the truce of 4 December 1805, by which they undertook to evacuate Austrian territory.

For Austria loss of territory was inevitable. Under the terms of the peace concluded at Pressburg on 27 December 1805 Austria was excluded from Italy and lost control of the passes which connected Italy with Germany. In Italy she ceded to Napoleon in his capacity as king of Italy Venetia with its former dependencies of Istria and Dalmatia. Baden and Württemberg partitioned the Habsburg dominions in Swabia, but it was Bavaria which obtained the most important additions. In return for the cession of Berg and Wurzburg, Bavaria obtained the Vorarlberg and the Tyrol, together with Augsburg, Lindau and the principality of Ansbach and Eichstädt. These changes were not effected without Prussia's first being compelled to sign an offensive and defensive alliance with France at Vienna on 15 December 1805. Prussian policy in the crisis wavered between the views of Hardenberg, who favoured association with Russia, and Haugwitz, who wished to commit Prussia to France. After the battle of Austerlitz the bargaining power of Prussia was much reduced, and under the terms of the alliance she was obliged to cede Ansbach to Bavaria and Neuchâtel to France; Prussia's compensation was to be the acquisition of Hanover, which was agreed by the subsequent treaty of 15 February 1806 and coupled with the Prussian obligation to close the north German rivers, the Elbe, Weser and Ems to British trade. In March 1806 the annexation of Hanover was announced and

Prussia placed in a state of war with Britain, a situation which resulted only in the seizure of Prussian shipping without increasing her real power in Germany. In Germany, the Low Countries and Italy Napoleon was triumphant.

VI. THE NAPOLEONIC REORGANIZATION OF EUROPE, 1806

The battle of Austerlitz, which Napoleon regarded as his finest military achievement, gave him the power to do what he wished with those parts of Europe which French arms could dominate. The Bonaparte clan and their hangers-on were all endowed with titles to make them fit company for an emperor. In February 1806 French troops entered Naples to depose Ferdinand IV and in March Joseph Bonaparte was made King of the Two Sicilies. Louis Bonaparte was made King of Holland in June 1805. The marshal, Murat, who was married to Caroline Bonaparte, was made Grand Duke of Berg out of territories ceded to Napoleon by Prussia and Bavaria against compensation elsewhere; when events took a fresh turn Murat was transferred to Naples to be its king. Upon the marshals and ministers were conferred titles or petty principalities. There was, however, no doubt that real power resided with the emperor and not for one moment were even his brothers allowed to forget that their titles were a façade which barely covered a French dictatorship.

In no part of Europe was Napoleon to achieve such lasting effects as in Germany. France had not increased her territories beyond the Rhine in 1805, but Napoleon had every intention that western Germany should serve the purposes of France. It was his object that the petty states of Germany should be brought into an association and act as a buffer between France, on the one hand, and Austria, Prussia and Russia, on the other. By an act of confederation of 16 July 1806 the states under the domination of France formed the 'Confederation of the Rhine' and in August 1806 declared their separation from the Holy Roman Empire; Francis II resigned the imperial crown and took the title of Francis I, Emperor of Austria. In the first instance the Confederation included the three southern states, which had done so much to aid Napoleon, Bavaria, Baden and Württemberg; and the petty states to the north, Hesse-Darmstadt, Nassau, Berg and Frankfort together with units of insignificant size. The Confederation of the Rhine was in theory controlled by a Diet at Frankfort, with a college of Kings and a college of Princes under a president, Dalberg, Archbishop of Ratisbon and Archchancellor of the Empire, who was given the title of Prince-Primate. Napoleon disclaimed any intention himself of becoming emperor and took the relatively modest title of Protector, but the Confederation was bound by an alliance to France and provided an army of 63,000 in the event of war. The French domination was sweetened by the repetition of the events of 1803. The small German states were able to enlarge their territories at the expense of the even smaller states. The Confederation of the Rhine in one sense represented the reduction of western Germany to a state of dependence upon France, but in another it was a measure of unification, which in the long run could be only to the disadvantage of France. The rulers of Bavaria and Württemberg now became kings and were determined that the fortunes of war should not reduce them to anything less than sovereigns in their own right, but the creation of bigger units implanted in the minds of Germans a conception of a larger unity which would produce a German state capable of speaking with authority in international affairs.

VII. FRANCE, GREAT BRITAIN AND RUSSIA: PEACE NEGOTIATIONS

The victory of Austerlitz almost coincided with a political crisis in Britain. On 23 January 1806 the Younger Pitt died and there was appointed in his place Fox, committed by the perversities of his politics to seeking an accommodation with France. The 'Ministry of all the Talents', in the face of the Napoleonic victory on the continent of Europe, was ready to explore the possibilities of peace, and Lord Yarmouth was sent to France in June 1806 to negotiate with France. At the same time Alexander I of Russia was willing to treat with Napoleon, and the Russian envoy, Oubril, arrived in Paris on 6 July 1806. The negotiations proved abortive. Napoleon, intent upon preserving France's dominance in Europe and extending her influence in the Mediterranean, attempted to keep the conversations with Britain and Russia distinct one from another. Britain was to be required to surrender Sicily to the new régime in Naples, but to this proposal Fox was not willing to agree. For Russia Oubril was induced to sign a treaty of peace on 20 July by which Cattaro on the Adriatic was ceded to France and Ragusa with the Ionian Islands recognized as independent, in return for which French troops would be withdrawn from

Germany. Fox was disillusioned in his attempt to secure peace, and when he died on 13 September 1806 his successors were not seriously disposed to parley with Napoleon. Alexander I, after Austerlitz despairing of securing a solid basis for resistance to France, was at first ready to seek peace, but it was evident to him that France was not negotiating with sincerity. Once more he was prepared to take up arms against France, and therefore refused to ratify the treaty of peace negotiated by Oubril.

VIII. THE DEFEAT OF PRUSSIA, 1806

While negotiations were proceeding in France there was a change of heart in Prussia. Possession of Hanover had meant war with Britain, but there were rumours that France, in order to secure peace with Britain, was agreeable to the retrocession of Hanover to George III. The twists and changes in the negotiations gave the Prussian Court the impression that there was no hope of reaching a lasting settlement with Napoleon, and Frederick William III came to the conclusion under pressure of the war party that Prussia must take up arms against France. On 26 September 1806 Prussia despatched to Paris an ultimatum, demanding that French troops should withdraw behind the Rhine. There was an unwarranted self-confidence in the action of Frederick William III, which owed much to the belief that Prussia could repeat with ease the victories which she had won over the armies of France during the Seven Years War, but in this conviction lay an illusion. The Prussian army had not won a battle since the Seven Years War, and its military methods, based upon excellence in drill and barrack-square manoeuvre, demanded nothing of the soldier except obedience. This obedience was given to an officer corps which was wedded to the traditions of a past, which it had itself done much to create. Most of the general officers were old, and the soldiers of the army without deep consciousness of the importance of a war designed to prevent a French domination of Europe. Nevertheless, there was the certainty of Russian support, while Britain, in spite of Prussia's possession of Hanover, would join in the general resistance to France. The Prussian army could put into the field 193,000 men, which ought to have been enough to offer a stout resistance to France until the Russians arrived, but the same initial error which had marred the campaign by the Austrians in 1805 was made by the Prussian command. The Prussian army advanced into Saxony and permitted the French to attack it in the early stages of the campaign, before they had tired. On 14 October 1806 the Prussian army was defeated at Jena by Napoleon and at Auerstädt by Davout, for which the latter through Napoleon's jealous determination to take all the glory was not allowed full credit. With the French victory all Germany lay at Napoleon's command. Prussia was overrun as far as the Vistula. Saxony had joined Prussia in the war, and as a result was now compelled to join the Confederation of the Rhine and pay an indemnity, in return for which the elector was raised to the rank of king. The Elector of Hesse was deprived of his territories, which joined with the Prussian territories west of the Elbe were subsequently to form the Napoleonic Kingdom of Westphalia and bestowed upon the Emperor's frivolous brother, Jerome. France was now approaching the pinnacle of her power under Napoleon I. All northern Europe seemed likely to fall under French influence when Napoleon entered Berlin on 27 October. On 21 November was issued the Berlin Decree by which the United Kingdom was declared to be in a state of blockade and all states under the domination of France required to adhere to this system. British goods were henceforth to be excluded from the continental market, and Britain, though supreme upon the sea after the battle of Trafalgar, compelled to submit out of sheer economic necessity. The European economy was to be organized under a Napoleonic 'Continental System'. Blockade and embargo were not new weapons of war, but for the first time Napoleon could envisage a system which excluded Britain altogether.

IX. The Treaty of Tilsit, 1807

The confidence of Napoleon knew no bounds. Prussia prayed for peace, but he would not grant it. Even an armistice was refused. Battle was to be taken to the farthest limits of Prussia. For once the best rules of Napoleonic warfare did not hold good. When the French armies entered northern Europe to meet the Russian armies they were entering an unfamiliar country, poorer by far than central Europe and less able to provide supplies. The dreary plains of central Poland, which Prussia had occupied under the terms of the Second and Third Partitions, were not the best theatre of operations for an army accustomed to quick victories. The Prussian forces, such as remained, withdrew into East Prussia and were joined by two Russian armies, under Hanoverian Bennigsen and the Livonian Buchshöwden, with the aged and almost blind Field Marshal Kamenskoy in supreme command. The aim of Napoleon was to destroy the Russian army once and for all, but he was fighting in new conditions of cold and hunger against troops which in spite of the uninspired leadership of their generals did not melt before the fury of a French attack. A series of indecisive battles were fought which seriously weakened the French. The Russians held the French at Pułtusk on 26 December 1806 and again at Eylau on 8 February 1807, when severe losses on both sides and the onset of extreme cold forced both sides to go into winter quarters. For once Napoleon was forced to leave a campaign unfinished, and Prussia and Russia on 26 April 1807 concluded the convention of Bartenstein, under the terms of which they agreed to drive the French out of Germany. The confidence which this convention seemed to express was not accompanied by a capacity to give it effect. Britain might make peace with Prussia and make her usual offer of a subsidy, but it was not an easy matter to translate money quickly into weapons and armies. When Danzig fell in May 1807 Napoleon was able to re-open the offensive against the Russian army. On 14 June 1807 a great battle was fought at Friedland, which, though it was not an overwhelming victory for the French army, compelled the Russians to withdraw across the Niemen.

Alexander I recognized that Russia could not continue the struggle without effective support from another power. The Prussian army had ceased to be effective. The enlistment of Poles by the French meant that the wide area of western Russia, which had been gained by the Partitions of Poland, but still contained a large Polish population, would be unreliable. In December 1806 Turkey had made war upon Russia with French encouragement, while Persia remained a threat in the Caucasus. Russia was in danger of fighting a war on many fronts, and experience had taught Russian statesmen that such a situation would bring disaster. Britain, normally ready to offer a subsidy, was now holding back. There was nothing for Russia to do but to make peace as best she could. Napoleon for his part had so distended his resources that peace was doubly welcome from the French point of view. The French army in eastern Europe was reaching the point

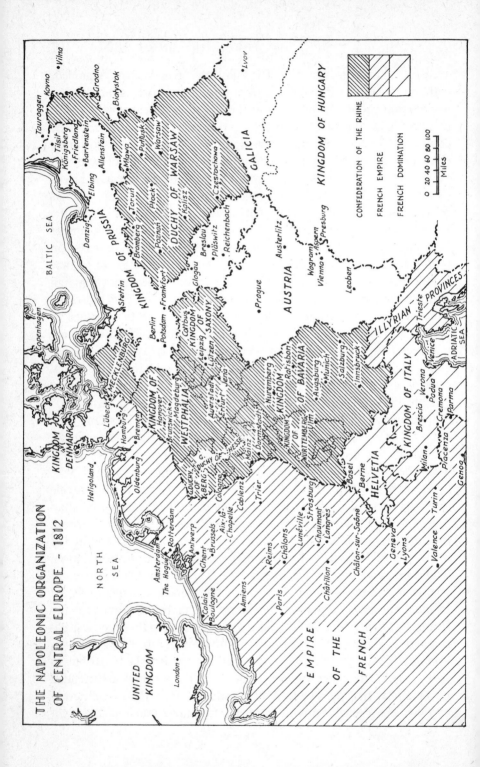

THE NAPOLEONIC ORGANIZATION OF CENTRAL EUROPE - 1812

CONFEDERATION OF THE RHINE
FRENCH EMPIRE
FRENCH DOMINATION

0 20 40 60 80 100
Miles

UNITED KINGDOM

London

NORTH SEA

BALTIC SEA

Copenhagen

KINGDOM OF DENMARK

Heligoland

Lübeck
Hamburg
Bremen
Amsterdam
The Hague
Rotterdam
Antwerp
Ghent
Brussels
Aix-la-Chapelle
Calais
Boulogne
Amiens
Paris
Reims
Châlons
Lunéville
Chaumont
Châtillon
Langres
Châlon-sur-Saône

MECKLENBURG

Stettin

KINGDOM OF PRUSSIA

Danzig
Elbing
Königsberg
Tilsit
Tauroggen
Kovno
Vilna
Friedland
Bartenstein
Allenstein
Grodno
Bialystok

Berlin
Potsdam
Magdeburg
Brunswick
Hanover
Oldenburg

KINGDOM OF WESTPHALIA

Cologne
G. DUCHY OF BERG
G. DUCHY OF HESSE
Mainz
Cassel
Coblenz
Trier
Strasburg
Basel
Berne

HELVETIA

Geneva
Lyons
Valence
Turin

Cottbus
Leipzig
Auerstädt
Jena
Erfurt
Lützen

KINGDOM OF SAXONY

Frankfort
Poznań
Bromberg
Toruń
Płock
Warsaw
Pułtusk
Milawa

DUCHY OF WARSAW

Kalisz
Częstochowa
Glogau
Breslau
Reichenbach
Pläswitz

Prague

GALICIA

Lvov

KINGDOM OF HUNGARY

AUSTRIA

Vienna
Wagram
Aspern
Austerlitz
Presburg
Leoben

KINGDOM OF BAVARIA

Nuremberg
Ratisbon
Augsburg
Munich
Salzburg
Innsbruck
KINGDOM OF WÜRTEMBERG
Ulm
Darmstadt

ILLYRIAN PROVINCES

Trieste
Venice

ADRIATIC SEA

KINGDOM OF ITALY

Milan
Brescia
Verona
Padua
Cremona
Piacenza
Parma
Genoa

EMPIRE OF THE FRENCH

of exhaustion, while peace opened the opportunity to giving effect to the Berlin Decree of November 1806 and organizing Europe against Britain.

On 25 June 1807 Alexander I and Napoleon met on a raft moored in the middle of the river Niemen at Tilsit, and without the participation of Prussia agreed upon the bases of peace, which was signed between France and Russia on 7 July and between France and Prussia on 9 July. Prussia lost all her provinces west of the Elbe and all her gains under the Partition of Poland in 1793 and part of West Prussia acquired in 1772. Danzig was restored to its status of an independent city. From the Polish territories of Prussia, with the exception of Białystok, which was surrendered to Russia, was created the Duchy of Warsaw. The Duchy was given a constitution and a ruler, the King of Saxony, and was compelled to join the Confederation of the Rhine. As ever the French had recourse to extortion. Napoleon granted the Polish territories to the King of Saxony, but insisted that Prussian crown assets, which consisted of the very considerable royal domains which had previously belonged to the Polish state, were his own and subsequently negotiated their sale to the Duchy for 40,000,000 francs at 4 per cent interest. In addition to having to pay for their liberation from Prussia, the Polish landlords now found themselves embraced by the Napoleonic economic system. They and with them the junkers of Brandenburg and Pomerania lost the markets for their grain which had existed in Britain. The consequence was an agricultural slump everywhere in northern Europe, which rendered the French connection intolerable. For the Polish nobility the erection of the Duchy of Warsaw seemed a nucleus for the re-establishment of a Polish state, and they remained loyal to Napoleon, but the ruling classes in Prussia recognized fully that the defeat of 1806 had been the result of unpreparedness.

X. Franco-Russian Co-operation, 1807: The British Reaction

In the open treaty of Tilsit Russia and France offered one another their good offices, France to assist in the conclusion of a peace between Russia and Turkey, which it was hoped would be easy to obtain because the Sultan Selim was assassinated on 29 May 1807, and Russia to intervene in London on behalf of France. In the secret articles, however, France and Russia agreed to an offensive and defensive alliance in the event of Britain's refusing peace upon France's terms. Russia agreed to break off diplomatic relations with Britain and join the continental blockade, while France expressed willingness to free the European provinces of the Ottoman Empire from the Turkish yoke, with the exception of Constantinople and Rumelia. There was some opposition in Russia to the treaty of Tilsit, which was looked upon as a capitulation, but it was in fact an escape from a very dangerous isolation. Russia could not find effective support in Europe, while the creation of a Polish régime in Warsaw threatened the security of the entire western frontier.

For Napoleon the advantage of peace was equally obvious. When Napoleon was at war he was obliged to concentrate his forces for battle, but during time of peace he could disperse his troops throughout the continent of Europe and use them to prevent the importation of British goods. Of the significance of Tilsit the British government had no doubt. If Russia had escaped from a dangerous isolation because no other power could assist her militarily on the continent, Britain no less stood in mortal danger on the high seas. When news reached London that the treaty of Tilsit contained secret provisions for the closing of Danish, Swedish and Portuguese ports to British ships and a general declaration of war on Britain, a British expedition was sent to Denmark. Copenhagen was bombarded and on 7 September 1807 Denmark surrendered her fleet to Britain. The ruthlessness of this measure shocked continental opinion and caused Denmark and Russia to declare war on Britain, but it at least kept the Baltic open to trade and eventual communication when the opposition to Napoleon could reassemble its forces. Almost as important was the British seizure of the island of Heligoland at the mouth of the Elbe, which proved a useful centre for British smugglers.

XI. THE CONTINENTAL SYSTEM: ECONOMIC WAR AGAINST BRITAIN

France's effort to exclude British goods from the continent of Europe in order to destroy Britain's capacity to resist did not begin with the Berlin Decree of 1806 and the supplementary Milan Decrees of November and December 1807, which laid down the principle that any neutral ship entering British ports was liable for seizure and became denationalized, for which reason it could be considered British property. Already from the beginning of the war after the rupture of the peace of Amiens efforts had been made to keep British goods out of Europe. Britain had retaliated in 1803–4 by blockading the Elbe and the Weser and all the French ports on the North Sea and the Channel. In 1807 Britain produced a series of Orders in Council which imposed a blockade upon all states under the influence of France and required neutral shipping to enter a British port to pay duty and obtain a licence, a step which ruined the neutral carrying trade and gave British shipping a corresponding advantage. It should not be imagined that Britain was held in much respect in continental Europe. The measures taken by the British navy upon the high seas were often arbitrary, while the bombardment of Copenhagen on 2 September 1807, which kept the Sound open, created a very bad impression when it was learned that the city burned for three days. The very cheapness of British goods aroused hostility among the continental manufacturers, and as early as 1800 Fichte had produced his *Der Geschlossene Handelstaat* (The Closed Commercial State), which advocated a system of tariff protection to encourage native industry. When Napoleon imposed his commercial measures upon the whole of Europe he was not necessarily appearing in the role of a tyrant. He was appealing to the continent of Europe to adopt an attitude of solidarity against a power which acted in a high-handed and arrogant manner.

The failure of Napoleon to make the Continental System effective had many reasons. Britain was by no means as vulnerable as he supposed. Britain was still fundamentally an agrarian country, and Napoleon was in practice attacking only one sector of the British national economy, the textile industry. If the textile industry had been seriously affected by the blockade it would not have led necessarily to any political disorders in Britain or weakened the government. The financial system of Britain was, moreover, strong where the French was weak The spiral of inflation was not steep enough to create ruin; on the contrary, it provided a stimulus to industrial production. The British investors, moreover, had confidence in the monetary system, and the flexibility of British credit in turn helped British industry out of its temporary crises. The London money market could make credit available in areas likely to suffer from depression. Cash payments had been suspended and notes could no longer be converted into gold. As a result, the government, though its own system of accounting was often literally medieval, found it easy to float loans and finance the war. The politically conscious classes in Britain accepted the war with a certain nonchalance. There were very few defeatists among them and they had no political influence. The Berlin Decree was certainly not a shock, because Britain had already survived thirteen years of war conditions. The reasons for this confidence are not hard to find. Britain's population was increasing. The growth from 10,943,000 in 1801 to 12,597,000 in 1811 in economic terms represented an expansion of the internal market, which was linked by an excellent system of waterways and canals. The rise in the price of grain encouraged agricultural production, and higher yields served to feed the growing population. The working classes were kept under strict control by the Combination Acts of 1799 and 1800 and there was little danger of mob violence. The British poor-law system may not be admired but it was an effort on the part of the ruling classes to meet the social problem of poverty. Britain was not threatened with danger of revolution from within. Her position was rather one of fundamental strength.

Having a monopoly of colonial goods, the most important of which were sugar and cotton, Britain could always trade with the states of continental Europe if her merchandise could penetrate the French cordon. It is true, however, that any complication in Britain's relations with the United States might lead to a crisis, because they were the principal source of cotton, a factor which did not escape the notice of Napoleon. This was initially not a factor with which to reckon. As long as Britain had the goods to offer, there was a lack of willingness in Europe not to buy them. It was only too clear that the object of the French commercial system was to favour French industry by keeping prices high when its products were sold abroad, in order that there might be money in plenty in the French towns to buy the produce of the French countryside. The French commercial hegemony suffered from one major disadvantage. It was based upon a land empire, and transport was invariably slow. The British commercial system depended upon sea transport, which was relatively cheap and quick. For this reason alone British prices for industrial goods were always lower than French prices. The superior mechanization of British industry was an added advantage in the struggle with

France. To maintain control over the coasts and ports of Europe Napoleon was obliged to employ an army of officials, who are said to have numbered 27,000 in 1809, but they could not be controlled. The result was smuggling on a large scale and the corruption of customs officials with bribes. In the end Napoleon decided to adopt a system of licensed imports and exports. Napoleon, who was not an expert economist, believed that the export of French goods and produce to Britain would aid French production and drain Britain of specie. Such was French lack of confidence in the permanence of his régime that shipmasters who were allowed to carry goods to Britain often failed to return to their home port, and for the remainder of the war swelled the volume of shipping at Britain's disposal.

The defects of the Napoleonic system are easy to perceive, but it was not necessarily doomed to failure. The economic war should not be divorced from political events. During the first period of the war up to the peace of Amiens there was a general increase in the volume of British trade. If the export index of 100 is accepted for the year 1806 the index figure for 1797 was 72, rising to 104 in 1800 and 113 in 1802. The conclusion of the peace saw a recession, the index for 1803 being 86 and for the following two years 94. The year 1806 was a year of prosperity though not of boom, because the theatre of war was in Northern Germany and there was a consequent expansion of trade with Sweden and Russia, but the Prussian political tergiversations led to a decline in the trade of Britain to northern Europe. In 1805 British exports to Prussia amounted to £8,000,000, but fell to £462,000 in 1806 as a result of the closure of Prussian ports upon the occupation of Hanover. It was at this point that there was a decline in British trade with the continent of Europe and a consequent turning to the New World both in the United States and in the South American colonies of Spain. The first nine months of the Napoleonic blockade following the Berlin Decree of 21 November 1806 did not produce a real crisis, because the French forces were still deployed in Poland to face the Russian threat, but with the conclusion of the treaty of Tilsit they could be used to enforce the exclusion of British goods. It was not until the autumn of 1807 at a moment before the normal seasonal decline in trade was about to begin that Britain's position began to appear desperate, which accounts for the seizure of the Danish fleet at Copenhagen. Denmark declared war upon Britain, and Russia followed her example. In November 1807 French troops entered Lisbon and completed the exclusion of British goods from the continent, except for their import into Sweden through Göteborg. This highly dangerous situation coincided with a crisis in Anglo-American relations. In June 1807 Vice-Admiral Berkeley gave orders that his flagship, the *Leopard*, should search the United States frigate *Chesapeake* for British deserters, but when the American captain refused to admit a search party the British vessel opened fire. The result was that President Jefferson put into force in December 1807 the non-importation law of April 1806, with the intention of cutting off supplies of cotton, cereals and timber both to Britain and to France and her dependencies in an effort to compel the belligerents to respect neutral rights. Normal relations with Britain were terminated, and finally on 18 June 1812 the United States declared war upon Britain. The years between 1807 and 1812 did not see the complete breakdown in Anglo-American trade, because in many cases British goods, including woollens, cottons, iron, steel and glass, were admitted into the United States, but the tension was so great that no great certainty could be placed in the North American market. The year 1808 was one of crisis for Britain. By 1807 the British export index fell to 95 by comparison with the index of 100 in 1806. The Baltic could be kept open by the annual appearance of a British naval squadron, and every device available to British ingenuity was used to maintain the volume of exports. Everything depended upon the political and military situation in Europe. The South American markets assumed an enormous importance in the thinking of the British government and the commercial classes. It was at this point that events in the Iberian peninsula took a turn in favour of Britain.

XII. THE COLLAPSE OF GODOY'S RÉGIME AND THE INSURRECTION IN SPAIN

The régime of Godoy in Spain was no more stable than it had ever been. As ever he was seeking the opportunity of a coup which would establish his reputation. His aim was to secure French aid for an expedition to Portugal, but Napoleon was unimpressed. Before and after the defeat of the Franco-Spanish fleet at Trafalgar Russian diplomacy was attempting to lure Godoy from his attachment to

France, a course which caution would have seemed to recommend when Britain began to attack the South American colonies of Spain, and in June 1806 actually took Buenos Ayres. Godoy was prepared to listen to these approaches, but the completeness of Napoleon's victory at Jena prevented him from taking action. The nearness with which he came to a decision was shown by his summons to the Spanish nation to arms on 5 October 1806, against whom it was not stated, but in Spain it was generally understood to be a preparation for war with France to free the country from what was commercially an onerous alliance. Napoleon had no doubt that Godoy would turn the Spanish forces against any enemy in a cause which would serve his own interest and by now had small interest in the Spanish alliance, because it provided him with no vessels of war to use against Britain. Godoy had played a double game, and Napoleon was equally capable of duplicity. As a result of renewed Spanish pressure Napoleon consented to the treaty of Fontainebleau of 29 October 1807 by which France and Spain were to partition Portugal, an area of the south to be given to Godoy and the area north of the Douro to the Queen of Etruria, while central Portugal was to await the provisions of a general peace. Godoy was delighted by the success of his project, but he did not realize that when once the French had introduced troops into Spain they would be masters of the peninsula. On 30 November 1807 French and Spanish troops in none too good a condition after their march entered Lisbon, but the British fleet under Sir Sidney Smith escorted the Prince Regent of Portugal, John, together with the entire Court, administration and the archives, away from the capital to Brazil.

The expedition to Portugal placed French troops in control of north-western Spain. On 27 October 1807 a quarrel which had long been smouldering in the Spanish Court burst into flame. As a result of a dispute between Godoy and their heir to the throne, Ferdinand, Charles IV gave orders for the latter to be arrested on charges of plotting a coup d'état. In this situation Napoleon, to whom both sides appealed, could enter into the intrigues of Spanish politics and placed troops in Pamplona and Barcelona. The Spanish Court took flight before the advance of the French, but on 17 March 1808 there broke out a Spanish insurrection at Aranjuez, where the Court had arrived, and Godoy was made prisoner by the army and Ferdinand proclaimed king. By this time Napoleon cared little what happened in the Spanish Court and clearly believed that he could append Spain to his empire. The Bourbons were persuaded to consult with Napoleon in May at Bayonne, where he compelled them to abdicate. Joseph Bonaparte was given the order to transfer himself from his Kingdom of Naples and occupy the throne, but the Spanish question was already a matter of more than kings and court intrigue. On 2 May 1808 an insurrection broke out at Madrid against the French troops in the city. Spain remained basically loyal to the Bourbons, and though an expedition led by Napoleon himself in December 1808 quickly broke Spanish military resistance and permitted the installation of Joseph in Madrid, there were few supporters of the French régime to be found in the peninsula.

Britain's first attempt to take advantage of the situation in Spain proved unsuccessful. Troops which had been sent to Sweden to assist in the war against Russia were withdrawn and despatched to Spain. The army under the command of Sir John Moore, which operated in the north of Spain, was soon disposed of by the French when Napoleon himself appeared to take command and obliged to seek the refuge of the British ships at Corunna in January 1809, where Moore was mortally wounded, but a second force of 12,000 men under Sir Arthur Wellesley, a commander with battle experience in India, landed at the mouth of the river Mondego in August 1808 and fared better. On 21 August 1808 Wellesley defeated the forces of the French marshal, Junot, at Vimiero. Under the terms of the convention of Cintra, which gave extreme annoyance in both Britain and France, the French army surrendered Lisbon and was transported to France in British ships, but the circumstances of the convention were in the long run unimportant. Britain had at last obtained a foothold in continental Europe upon its very fringe, where Napoleon's resources would be stretched to their utmost. The whole of the Iberian peninsula was hostile to France, and the régime which Napoleon established in Madrid under Joseph Bonaparte could be sustained only by the presence of French troops. No less than 320,000 French soldiers were put into Spain in 1808 and their numbers rarely fell below a quarter of a million. Many were afflicted with disease and not available for combat, while Britain with barely more than 40,000 men of her own, certain of a retreat to the sea and fitfully supported by Portuguese troops and the Spanish juntas and guerrillas, could tie down a large French army out of all proportion to the size of the opposition which confronted it. Wellesley was a sober and cautious commander, whose object was to keep open the second front which by luck had been created. On 27 July 1809 Wellesley held the French army under Marshal Victor at the battle of Talavera, for which he was raised to the dignity of Viscount Wellington, even though he was compelled to retreat in face of threatened encirclement. Wellington's object was to keep the field and win the war rather than undertake battles which would, if they went badly, exclude Britain from the Iberian peninsula. The mere conquest of territory for a naval power like Britain was unimportant. Typical of the strategy of Wellington was the method by which he dealt with Marshal Masséna in the campaign of 1810. Masséna met with Wellington's forces at Bussaco, north of the Portuguese town of Coimbra, on 27 September 1810 and after driving off the French attacks the British army withdrew to previously prepared lines at Torres Vedras. For the first time the methods of Napoleonic warfare were shown up in all their elementary defects. In the vigour of their attacks and their skill of manoeuvre the French marshals could at the cost of human lives defeat their opponents, but everything depended upon the quick victory. Masséna advanced and reconnoitred the lines at Torres Vedras, but the obstacles which had been placed in his path could not be taken by troops whose energies had been sapped by the long march and shortage of supplies. In November 1810 Masséna withdrew over the Portuguese frontier to Ciudad Rodrigo.

During the remainder of the war in the peninsula the troops under Wellington's command, in spite of frequent breakdowns of discipline, began to get the measure of the French. When the British forces met the French in the open field they lined themselves in two ranks and discharged into the French columns 800 shots to forty or at the best eighty of the French. Napoleon, ignorant of what was happening in Spain and confident in the methods which had won his own battles for him, did not perceive at first hand the errors of his subordinate commanders. It is true that the British military effort did not create at first serious embarrassments for the French. The battle of Fuentes d'Oñoro of 3–5 May 1811 merely prepared for the British sieges of

Ciudad Rodrigo and Badajoz which fell on 19 January and 6 April 1812 respectively, while the battle of Salamanca of 22 July 1812 permitted Wellington to advance through Valladolid to Burgos, which yielded to him on 18 October 1812. The largest battle of the war was fought at Vittoria only on 21 June 1813 and ended with the rout of the French army, which was compelled to retreat over the Pyrenees into France. By this time Napoleon was already seriously troubled in central Europe. At the most the best which can be said of the British military effort is that with an economy of effort it disposed of a disproportionate number of French troops. The political consequences of Wellington's campaigns were of far greater significance.

Britain fought to free the Iberian peninsula of the French, and by her efforts could claim a special voice in its affairs. Portugal in the absence of the regent, John, came under British influence, while the Spanish military effort was effective only when the British troops were present. Of far greater importance was the fact that both Spain and Portugal possessed colonial empires, which during the fighting in the home countries were necessarily deprived of political direction. While Spain was at war with Britain, penetration of the Spanish colonies was not easy. In 1806 a British force under Sir Home Popham had invaded the River Plate and occupied Buenos Ayres for three months, but could not hold its own against the local opposition. In 1807 Montevideo was taken, but the force sent to take Buenos Ayres was compelled to surrender. The Napoleonic invasion of Spain and the deposition of the Bourbons changed the situation in a dramatic fashion. The army, which Wellesley took to Portugal in 1808, had been raised in Ireland for the expressed purpose of operating in South America, but from being the enemies of Spain the British suddenly became her allies, supporting the cause of Ferdinand VII, for whom the Spanish American juntas declared their allegiance. The regency in Spain during the war against France could not extend its authority over the whole of the country and in the circumstances of confusion the Spanish left wing obtained the upper hand, promulgating the liberal single-chamber constitution of 1812. The Spaniards of the colonies were invited to send representatives to the Cortes, but it was obvious that metropolitan Spain even under a constitutional system intended to retain her control over them when the war had been won. What began as a movement in support of Ferdinand VII soon became an expression of the desire to rid the colonies of control from home. Everywhere power was taken out of the hands of the royal intendants. The presidency of Charcas and the presidency of Quito first sought to free themselves of royal control, only to be brought back to obedience as a result of a counter-revolutionary movement in Peru, but in 1810 the captain-generalcy of Venezuela fell to the control of the colonists, and the viceroyalties of La Plata and New Granada, together with the captain-generalcy of Chile, soon declared themselves to be self-governing, though there was at first no attempt to deny the sovereignty of the Spanish Crown. It was only a question of time, however, before all the territories which threw off metropolitan control declared their full independence. There was a close parallel between the events which led to the severance by the British mainland colonies in North America of their connection with the British Crown in the eighteenth century. There were loyalists who wished to preserve the Spanish imperial supremacy, and the insurgents only with difficulty were able to maintain themselves against what at first appeared to be overwhelming odds. When the war in Spain came to an end in 1813 the issue was by no means decided, but the Spanish closed colonial system was in practice destroyed, and in these troubled years Britain supplanted metropolitan Spain as the dominant commercial power, a factor which to some extent offset the restrictions upon British trade imposed by the Napoleonic Continental System. Under the terms of Article IV of the Franco-British treaty of alliance of 5 July 1814 Spain agreed to place Britain upon an equal footing with all other nations if trade with her colonies were declared open, but theory and practice were no longer in accord. Britain was already before the end of the war trading freely with the Spanish colonies, and this was a victory, the proceeds of which she was not at all disposed to forego.

XIII. FRANCO-RUSSIAN RELATIONS, 1808

The French invasion and occupation of Spain was prompted by the desire of Napoleon to complete his system, but Spain proved difficult to subdue, and it was necessary to draw off part of the French forces available for action in Central Europe to deal with the Iberian peninsula. For this reason Napoleon was anxious to come to an understanding with Alexander I of Russia, and in February 1808 expressed a desire for a personal meeting to place their relations upon a sound footing. There was great disquiet in Russian official circles because of the continued presence of French troops in Prussia, though their evacuation was promised for 1 October 1808. It was Napoleon's policy to buy off Russian hostility. He was not sorry to see Russia become engaged in other parts of Europe, whether in the Near East or in the North. In spite of their fundamental hostility, France and Russia could in fact combine to their mutual advantage. Sweden remained the ally of Britain in spite of the treaty of Tilsit, and Napoleon was ready to encourage hostilities by Russia in order to make a renewed understanding between Russia and Britain more difficult. Russia, on the other hand, was aware of the dangerous proximity of Finland to the capital at St Petersburg and feared lest the province become a base for an attack either by Napoleon or by Britain. In February 1808 with French approval and support Russia made war upon Sweden and seized Helsingfors (Helsinki) and by May had captured Sveaborg. British ships arrived with an expeditionary force of 14,000 men to assist Sweden, but the situation in Spain demanded their withdrawal, and the Russian campaign was allowed to proceed unmolested. Eventually by a convention of November 1808 the Swedes surrendered Uleaborg and withdrew beyond the river Kem, while the Russian occupation of the Aland Islands seemed to threaten Stockholm itself. The purpose of Russia in invading Swedish territory was revealed to be strategic rather than annexationist. Alexander I summoned the estates of the Grand Duchy of Finland, and on 27 March 1809 confirmed the privileges of the province under his own rule as Grand Duke. Under the terms of the treaty of Frederikshamn of 17 September Charles XIII of Sweden ceded the territories occupied by Russia, and as a token of friendship joined the French Continental System. The Swedish dynasty was running into difficulties. Gustavus IV had been compelled to abdicate in March 1809 as the result of a military coup, and Charles XIII, his uncle, was without children. The designated heir, Christian of Augustenburg, died in the same year, and the Swedish Diet in August 1810 appointed Marshal Bernadotte, Prince of Ponte Corvo, who had commanded the French forces in Denmark and Holstein supporting the Russian invasion of Finland. This was an untoward turn of events from the point of view of Napoleon, who distrusted Bernadotte, and with some justification. Even though he was married to the sister-in-law of Joseph Bonaparte, Bernadotte did not identify himself with the fortunes of Napoleon's clan, and when he became heir to the Swedish throne decided that he would make his own fortune by adherence to the cause of the subjects over whom he would eventually rule. For this reason Sweden did not become a satellite of France, but rather looked to the friendship of Russia for her advancement.

In September 1808 Napoleon met Alexander I at the conference of Erfurt in order to establish closer relations. Already Napoleon's difficulties were inducing in him a spirit of compromise, while from the Russian side there was a wariness of French intentions. To dispel suspicion Napoleon had undertaken to evacuate Prussia, but withdrawal was made conditional upon the payment of an indemnity. After much haggling it was agreed on 8 September 1808 that Prussia should pay a sum of 140,000,000 francs, upon the discharge of which France should surrender the towns of Glogau, Küstrin and Stettin; the Prussian army was to be limited to 42,000 men and Prussia to ally with France in the event of a war with Austria. In these circumstances it was obvious that Prussia was designated as a puppet state of France. All the pomp and ceremony which Napoleon imported to Erfurt failed to impress Alexander I. The agreement which the two powers reached on 12 October 1808 renewed the treaty of Tilsit. France conceded that Russia should have Finland, Moldavia and Wallachia, while the French régime in Spain was to be recognized; some limitation upon Russian expansion was imposed by the provision that the integrity of the Ottoman Empire south of the Danube should be preserved. The French were to mediate in the dispute between Russia and Turkey. In the wider questions of European politics the two powers agreed to a peace with Britain upon the basis of *uti possidetis*, that is, upon the criterion of the present possession, a solution not likely to meet with the approval of British statesmen. In the event of a fresh war between Austria and France, Russia was to declare war upon Austria. Napoleon, however, refused to relax his hold upon Prussia.

For the moment France had secured her position in Central Europe, which permitted Napoleon to depart for Spain to restore

French authority between November 1808 and January 1809. Russia obtained a breathing space in which to complete her conquest and subjection of Finland with the connivance of France. There was a general retraction of French influence in Central Europe as a result of the war in Spain. The Grand Army which had won the battles of 1805–7 was dissolved, and all that remained to oppose a hostile coalition was two corps under the command of Davout which went by the name of the army of the Rhine.

XIV. GERMANY AND THE FRENCH DOMINATION

The humiliation to which Austria was subjected by defeat in 1805 and Prussia in 1806–7 gave rise to a new conviction that the old system of petty states and individual foreign policies had permitted France to exploit Germany. There was in Germany a growth of national feeling which was encouraged by the presence and the exactions of French troops. Too much should not be made of the activity among German intellectuals. Fichte's *Reden an die deutsche Nation* (Addresses to the German Nation), a series of lectures delivered in Berlin under the eyes of the French in 1807, attacking the Germans' concept of loyalty to the state of which they were citizens and appealing for a wider loyalty to the German community, were purely academic and only symptomatic of a new feeling rather than influential. In Prussia it was the reforming party in the bureaucracy which carried greater weight, but even with regard to their activities some caution is necessary. The basic concept of Frederick William III, whose part in the movement is perhaps underestimated, was that the old régime should use its initiative in order to carry out reform before it was forced upon it by the people. The central organs of government were strengthened by the creation of a council of state and a cabinet of ministers, with the task of co-ordinating the policy of individual departments. On 9 October 1807 a decree of emancipation was issued abolishing the limited form of serfdom known as *Unterthänigkeit*, but the donation of freedom to the people was more theoretical than real. The landlords retained judicial authority upon their estates, which preserved to them the essentials of the power which they had enjoyed under the system of *Unterthänigkeit*. Perhaps the most important aspect of the reform was that it removed the caste distinctions which had existed in Prussia, dividing the nobility from the bourgeoisie, each with their own functions to perform, but this did not destroy the predominance of the junkers in the state. The decree of economic emancipation of 14 September 1811 separated noble and peasant lands and abolished labour services and supplementary dues, but the peasants obtained their freeholds only at the cost of surrendering one-third of their lands to the landlords; there were, moreover, categories of small peasants who were not embraced by this decree, who losing their lands altogether were reduced to the status of landless labourers. In any case, agrarian reform was not achieved quickly, and the details of reform had to wait until the conclusion of the war. The most important and most effective of the reforms carried out after the treaty of Tilsit was the reconstitution of the army. Under the convention of September 1808 the Prussian army was reduced to 42,000 men, but with the guidance of able officers such as Scharnhorst and Gneisenau this army was used as a training cadre. Elderly generals were retired. The old system of enlisting foreigners was abandoned and only Prussian subjects were recruited. When once the recruits had mastered the elements of military training they were released to form part of the reserve. On mobilization therefore the Prussian army was in future to be able to call upon far more soldiers than appeared upon its paper establishment.

The old régime in Prussia was determined to win the war in its own way with its social supremacy preserved. Freiherr vom Stein, who was appointed minister of the Interior in October 1807, had fanciful notions of a popular war in which Prussia should lead Germany. The revolt in Spain had revealed a force in the common people which could be exploited with success against the French, but the situation in Prussia was hardly that of Spain. The peasants and burghers of Prussia did not possess the same degree of initiative as the Spaniards. In canvassing his ideas Stein corresponded with members of the upper classes in Prussia and north Germany, and it was not long before one of his letters fell into the hands of Napoleon's police. On 16 December 1808 Napoleon placed Stein under a ban, declaring him to be the enemy of France and liable to execution if captured. There was no longer a place for Stein in Prussia, and he was never to exert much influence upon German opinion. The attitude of the junkers was that they would expel the French under the orders of the King by means of the Prussian army. The landed gentry were to obtain the honour and the fruits of victory.

The spirit of resistance was equally present in Austria, but the motives which moved the Austrian government were different. Francis I (see below: Chapter IV) had little reforming zeal in him, however much he was pressed by the Archduke Charles, but he was determined to reverse the defeat of 1805. The minister of foreign affairs, Stadion, was a partisan of war, but the chronic disorder of the Austrian finances and the heavy burden of debt did not make preparations for war easy. It followed that, if Austria were to make war at all, she would have to adopt the strategy of surprise when an opportune moment arose. The Austrian ambassador in Paris, Metternich, advised caution. The conclusion of the peace at Tilsit in 1807 made war impossible, and Austria meekly adhered to the Continental System. The Spanish war, however, put a different complexion upon the situation. Napoleon himself had departed for Spain with a large army, and it was evident that Germany was no longer held in strength. Austria hoped for Prussian aid, but this was declined. Russia likewise had no wish in 1809 to renew the war, especially when one of Austria's objects was to prevent the partition of the European dominions of the Ottoman Empire by Russia with French assistance. On 8 February 1809 the fateful decision to make war was taken, and at the beginning of March Austria attacked France without making a formal declaration of war. It was not without significance that almost immediately after Russia resumed hostilities against the Turks.

The result for Austria was disastrous, though the Austrian action could not have come at a worse time for Napoleon when the Spanish campaign was uncompleted. When he arrived in Paris from Spain he found that opposition was raising its head through France. Talleyrand, who had been removed from the ministry of foreign affairs after Tilsit, was obviously unreliable and deprived of his honorific office of Grand Chamberlain. Fouché likewise seemed to have lost confidence in Napoleon. Having dismissed Talleyrand, the most devoted of his supporters in the early stage of his career, Napoleon gave the impression that no one could be safe from his anger. On the eve of one of his greatest triumphs there were indications that Frenchmen were no longer confident in the permanence of the

Empire. It was therefore doubly necessary for Napoleon to triumph. By March 1809 he had gathered 300,000 men in Germany, which was a figure far in excess of the Austrian estimates of the army he could raise. The war followed the usual pattern, but the Austrian armies fought much better than they did in 1805. As a result of early defeats in April at Eckmühl and Ratisbon the Archduke Charles withdrew his army into Bohemia, but Napoleon marched straight on Vienna in order to divide the main Austrian force in Central Europe from the armies fighting in Italy under the command of the Archduke John. Vienna fell, but in a bloody battle on 21–22 May at Aspern and Essling to the north of the Danube, in which 20,000 French troops and 23,000 Austrians were killed and wounded, Napoleon himself was checked. For once the great general was proved not to be invincible. The people, moreover, were beginning to turn against him. In the Tyrol the local population rose against Bavarian rule under the leadership of Andreas Höfer, which was followed in July by uprisings in the valley of the Adige and in the Romagna. In Austria the war was renewed after a seven weeks' armistice, and Napoleon regained some at least of his reputation at the battle of Wagram, 6 July 1809, when after two days' fighting the Archduke Charles conceded him victory, after losing 24,000 killed and wounded against the French losses of 18,000. What was more important, he was able to withdraw his troops in good order from the battlefield. Austria could still put a formidable army into the field, but the Archduke Charles considered it wiser to conclude an armistice on 12 July. A miserably managed British expedition to Walcheren failed completely to make any impression upon the French. Once more France might redraw the map of Europe.

Peace was concluded with Austria in the palace of Schönbrunn at Vienna on 14 October 1809. Napoleon took for himself parts of Croatia, Istria, Carniola and Carinthia, which with Dalmatia were to form the Illyrian provinces. Bavaria, rewarded as ever, received Salzburg and the district of the Inn (Innviertel). Russia, who had been bound under the Erfurt agreement of 1808 to declare war against Austria, received the district of Tarnopol in Galicia; the Russian commander had been under secret instructions not to launch serious attacks upon Austria and had advanced only very slowly, in order not to give any assistance to the army of the Duchy of Warsaw.

The Poles under Poniatowski, however, had launched an offensive, and in spite of a defeat at Raszyn in April had succeeded in taking the city of Lvov, the capital of the Austrian province of Galicia. For this service they received the Austrian province of Western Galicia, Austria's share in the partition of 1795. Austria was not the only party to suffer from the war of 1809. Pope Pius VII had consented to be present at Napoleon's coronation, but a series of difficulties had arisen. Neither aş an Italian sovereign nor as the Supreme Pontiff did Pius VII show the deference to Napoleon that he obviously considered his due. In February 1808 the Papal States were occupied by French troops, and on 17 May 1809 Napoleon declared their formal annexation. Pius VII replied by excommunicating Napoleon, who in his turn arrested the Pope and deported him to Avignon. It was only in 1812 that Napoleon was able to bring himself to reconciliation with the Pope, but Pius VII was the head of an institution which had existed for centuries before the Napoleonic Empire and stood his ground, refusing to ratify the so-called concordat of Fontainebleau of 18 January 1813. Only upon the defeat of Napoleon in 1814 was he released.

The campaign of 1809 completed the reorganization of Germany, and the annexation of the Papal states gave some measure of unity to Italy, but even in the provisions of the treaty of Vienna there were the signs of a conflict with Russia. The grant of Western Galicia to the Duchy of Warsaw was the enlargement of a potential base for an invasion of Russia. Napoleon was anxious for a marriage alliance with a Russian princess in order to be certain of Russian friendship. This would have required the divorce of the Empress Joséphine, but no Russian princess was provided for Napoleon. The divorce was therefore put off, but in 1809 a different plan encouraged by Metternich, who had become chancellor in Austria, was formed for marrying Napoleon to an Habsburg archduchess. In December 1809 Joséphine formally proclaimed her agreement to a divorce, which was given civil and religious approval at Napoleon's command. In February 1810 a marriage was arranged between Napoleon and the eighteen-year-old Archduchess Marie-Louise, daughter of Francis I of Austria. A year after the marriage on 20 March 1811 Marie-Louise gave birth to a son, who was given the title of King of Rome.

The circumstances of the marriage were scandalous, but its

political meaning was obvious. The understanding which Napoleon had reached with Alexander I at Tilsit and afterwards at Erfurt was to be replaced by a Franco-Austrian entente. Napoleon, the heir of the Revolution, which had sent Marie Antoinette, the aunt of Francis I, to the guillotine, now married his daughter. It was as if respectability had at last been achieved and the old and the new régimes reconciled. The marriage was symbolic rather of a further deterioration in Napoleon himself. His government of France was becoming more arbitrary, and Napoleon himself more inclined to bring nobles of the Old Régime into his administration. The ministers and prefects of the early days were replaced by men of lesser calibre. Towards his own family Napoleon behaved with brusque disregard when it suited his purposes. First he annexed Zeeland and the southern provinces of Louis Bonaparte's kingdom of Holland at the beginning of 1810 and in July annexed the whole kingdom. In January 1811 he took all the German territories north of a line running from the river Lippe to the river Trave, including the towns of Lübeck and Hamburg and the Grand Duchy of Oldenburg, the ruling family of which was connected with the tsars of Russia, and formed from them departments of France. Napoleon could now control the whole coastline as far as the mouth of the Elbe and hold central Europe within the grasp of his economic system.

The stopping of the British trade which had filtered through the Dutch Netherlands and Northern Germany coincided with a crisis of great magnitude for Britain. The opening of the South American markets had given a temporary relief, but South America by itself could not take all British goods. By 1810 it was becoming difficult to sell in that quarter. At the same time Britain was herself experiencing a grain shortage. The harvest of 1809 was poor and that of 1810 disastrous. Napoleon, however, convinced that Britain's dire need would force her to purchase abroad and thus cause a drain of specie, permitted the export of grain from the area covered by his Continental System. Of the 1,567,000 quarters of grain imported into Britain in 1810 1,306,000 quarters were provided by France and her allies. This to some extent enabled Britain to build up her reserves, with the result that in 1811 she imported only 336,130 quarters. In pursuit of a theory Napoleon allowed Britain to acquire food at a time when she was faced with an industrial crisis. At the same time

Napoleon changed his tactics with regard to imports into his system. By the Trianon Tariff of 5 August 1810 he imposed taxes upon all colonial goods in the belief that these duties would be borne by the British merchants and the smugglers and the advantage reaped by the treasuries of France and her allies, whereas in fact the burden was borne by the consumer. The Fontainebleau decrees of 18 and 25 October 1810 ordered the seizure and destruction of all British manufactured goods and the creation of tribunals to try persons discovered to have introduced them. To the discontents of the consumers Napoleon now added the anger of the merchant classes. It was not the British economy only which suffered in 1811. There was evidence of an industrial malaise also in France. In the industrial cities unemployment appeared, while the two great commercial ports of Marseilles and Bordeaux were ruined. The disorganization of commerce for etatistic reasons was the cause which seemed most probable to the inhabitants of the continent of Europe, and they blamed Napoleon. Napoleon was compelled to permit some relaxation of control and issue trade-licences in the same manner as the British government. In the end what was meant to be a system had in it no order at all. Only with the defeat of France could stability be achieved, and undoubtedly the citizens of the French satellite states grew disillusioned. The venality of French officials and their extortions destroyed the good will which the Continental System built up among those small industrialists who welcomed the protection against cheap British goods with which they could not compete. In the end the French Empire was becoming too burdensome to tolerate.

The Fall of the Napoleonic Empire

I. THE BREACH WITH RUSSIA

Since the meeting at Erfurt there had been a gradual deterioration in the relations of Russia and France. Russia was the last important state in Europe to remain outside direct French control. After the battle of Trafalgar in 1805 the conquest of Britain had been impossible, which was a temptation to Napoleon to coerce Russia into complete submission. From the Russian side there was discontent caused by Alexander I's decision to join the Continental System. Between 1801 and 1805 Russia had exported 1,054,000 chetverts (the Russian equivalent of the English quarter or 5.77 bushels) of wheat, but in the years 1806–10 only 176,000 were exported. Comparable figures for oats reveal a decline from 1,153,000 to 419,000 chetverts. The Russian landed gentry and aristocracy were the principal exporters, and even in autocratic Russia it was possible to convey a sense of dissatisfaction to the Tsar. On 31 December 1810 Alexander I abandoned the prohibition upon the importation of colonial goods, which was the first significant breach in the Napoleonic Continental System, because colonial goods could not be paid for without the resumption of normal trading relations with Britain.

The political relations of France and Russia went from bad to worse. The French annexations in northern Germany are normally pointed to as a cause of the dispute with Russia, because Oldenburg, which was incorporated in France, was connected with Russia by dynastic ties. Similarly, much emphasis has been placed upon the failure of Napoleon to negotiate a marriage treaty by which he might find a bride from the Russian ruling house. These factors were important, but they were not decisive. Russia was concerned for her own security. The real menace to Russia lay in the Napoleonic Duchy of Warsaw. The major threats to the existence of Russia as a state of European significance had come from Poland. In 1610 the Poles had occupied the Kremlin in Moscow. In 1708–9 Charles XII of Sweden had threatened the very existence of Russia by advancing from his base in Poland. The Duchy of Warsaw represented the nucleus of a future Polish state, which might extend itself to the limits of the old Polish frontiers of 1772 and even beyond. The political class in western Russia was still Polish by speech and national feeling. Alexander I was anxious to conciliate the Polish nobility and gentry in his dominions, and a complicated series of negotiations was conducted to retain their loyalty. Two solutions were possible for the Poles. They might re-create their country in full independence either with the aid of France or in collaboration with Russia. Prince Adam Czartoryski was favourable to a Russian solution. Prince Michael Ogiński was willing to collaborate with Alexander I on the basis of reconstructing a Grand Duchy of Lithuania in which the Poles might enjoy an autonomy slightly more extensive than that of the Grand Duchy of Finland. The Polish followers of Napoleon in Warsaw, on the other hand, were in favour of a total reunification of Poland upon as wide a basis as possible. Alexander I was an astute ruler and played for time. All the solutions to the problem of Russia's frontier could lead to the reduction of Russia to the confines of medieval Muscovy. It was worthwhile to postpone a struggle, but it was clear that in the long run the decision would rest upon Russia's capacity to resist the armies of Napoleon in the field. If Russia could win the war she could impose her own solution in her disputed borderlands and restore the influence in central Europe which had been hers in the eighteenth century. One traditional rule held good. If Russia were to enjoy any chance of success she must avoid a war on two fronts. It was essential to settle her quarrel with the Ottoman Empire.

II. The Russian Elimination of Turkey

On 30 December 1806 Turkey had declared war upon Russia with the aim of regaining the Crimea, but the murder of the Sultan Selim and the peace of Tilsit led to a momentary cessation of hostilities. Alexander I agreed with Napoleon that there should be no resumption of hostilities before April 1808 and that in the meantime the Russian forces would not seek to dominate the principalities of Moldavia and Wallachia. The war in south-eastern Europe had resulted in the extension of Russian influence into Serbia, where a revolt against the Porte had broken out in 1804 under Karageorge, who made an appeal for aid to St Petersburg. After the Erfurt meeting, where Napoleon was reluctant to offer mediation between Russia and the Ottoman Empire, Russia opened hostilities in March 1809, but the Turks sensed that they might obtain the eventual aid of either France or England. As a result of the Russian declaration of war Britain had made peace with the Porte on 5 January 1809, which in Article XI of the treaty provided for the closing of the Dardanelles and Bosphorus to vessels of war of all nations in time of peace, which was an indication of British fears lest Russian vessels enter the Aegean and the Levant. Russia feared above all France. She wished to obtain the cession of Bessarabia, Moldavia and Wallachia, together with the independence of Serbia and a confirmation of her position in the Caucasus, but the complicating factor was the fact that she could not concentrate all her forces against Turkey because relations with France were so tenuous. By 1811 it was considered essential to administer a quick defeat upon the Turks. Kutusov, reinstated to active command in spite of his disgrace after Austerlitz, was sent with 46,000 Russian troops to seek a decision on the Danube. The Turkish plan was to attack Rushchuk, but instead they found themselves attacked by Kutusov, who then to their surprise withdrew, evacuated Rushchuk and crossed to the left bank of the Danube. The Turks were encouraged to cross to the left bank themselves, whereupon Kutusov sent a small force to the right bank to cut off their retreat. On 19 December 1811 some 12,000 Turkish survivors surrendered to the Russian army and their commander, Achmet Bey, fled. The Porte was compelled to conclude peace at Bucharest on 28 May 1812, ceding Bessarabia to Russia, granting an amnesty and local autonomy to Serbia and confirming the rights of Russia to protect the Christian subjects of the Sultan. Kutusov had achieved for Russia a moral and a political victory. Faith in the Russian army when properly led was now restored. At the same time he had removed the possibility of Russia's being forced to fight a war on two fronts, if Napoleonic France should ever attack her.

III. THE FRENCH PREPARATION FOR WAR ON RUSSIA

Napoleon was reasonably certain in 1812 that he could attack Russia without creating serious complications in Central Europe. Prussia had been so reduced in size that she was incapable of following an independent foreign policy. Austria was linked with France by the marriage compact. If Russia could be reduced to the proportions of the Muscovite state which Peter the Great had inherited France could reign supreme in Europe. The adherence of Prussia was easy to obtain. Under the agreement of 24 February 1812 Prussia guaranteed to provide a corps of 20,000 men to cover the French left flank, in return for which she would receive the provinces of Courland, Livonia and Estonia, where the upper classes were German by speech. The right flank was to be shielded as a result of a secret agreement with Austria on 14 March 1812; Austria would put into the field a corps of 30,000 and be compensated either by the retention of her Polish province of Galicia or, in the event of its union with Poland, by the extension of her dominions in Illyria. Napoleon tried to induce Sweden to join in the coalition with France by the promise of restoring Finland, but Russia was ready to concede Denmark's province of Norway to Sweden. Bernadotte, who was in command of Swedish policy, had no intention of becoming the vassal of Napoleon. Alliance with Russia was more attractive than alliance with France, because in the event of a Russian victory a coalition with Britain would follow automatically and Sweden would be freed from the yoke imposed by the Continental System. Bernadotte had a shrewd suspicion of Napoleon's limitations and decided to ally with Russia by the convention of alliance of 5 April 1812. While Napoleon prepared what seemed a formidable alliance system against Russia, the advantages were in reality not as one-sided as they appeared. Russia remained technically at war with Britain, and it was privately agreed that this situation should be preserved in order that the French might not be encouraged to begin their attack as the result of a premature alliance. The prospective allies could not have viewed the future with confidence in 1812, but there was a sagacity in their preparation to meet the attack which Napoleon was planning. The fate of Europe depended upon the military skill of the Russians or, conversely, upon the deficiencies of French military organization.

IV. The French Invasion of Russia, 1812

The French preparations for the invasion of Russia seem impressive. The Grand Army consisted of over 600,000 men with 1,242 field guns and 130 siege guns, but the very magnitude of the force presented a problem which the rudimentary supply system of the French army could scarcely solve. A serious question of morale was bound to present itself. The French army now consisted partly of men without the coherence which might be expected in a national army—Germans, Poles and Italians. The French forces were no longer fighting in a well-developed country. Russia, even if the Russian forces were defeated early in the campaign, did not offer ample supplies. In the first instance the French army enjoyed an overwhelming superiority against the maximum of 200,000 men which the Russians could put into the field, but the weakness of Russia was an advantage, because the difficulty of concentrating to fight an early battle and the numerical inferiority of the Russians induced a sense of caution.

The French attack opened on 24 June without a formal declaration of war, but the central Russian army under Barclay de Tolly with-drew before the Grand Army. Vilna fell, and in August Smolensk was taken. It was only on 20 August that the Russian army was brought to battle on the Borodino, where under the rehabilitated general, Kutusov, the Russians took their stand with the intention of fighting a battle to destroy at least part of Napoleon's forces. By this time the French effectives had dwindled to 130,000 against the Russians' 120,000. The grand strategy of Napoleon now began to reveal its weaknesses. In the battle the French lost 58,000 men as opposed to the 43,000 lost by the Russians. The Russian army had not won the battle, but it had at least retained the power to launch a counter-offensive. It was a bitter pill for the Russians to swallow when they took the decision to permit Napoleon to take Moscow, but Kutusov's appreciation was a simple one: 'If we defended Moscow, we should not defend Russia.' On 14 September 1812 the French army marched into Moscow. Napoleon believed that he had cut the country in two, but there was no disposition on the Russian side to ask for terms. Kutusov retreated southwest from Moscow and waited for his opportunity. The French army attempted to withdraw from Moscow along a route over which it had not previously passed, but Kutusov blocked the road to Kaluga. By now the French army was at the mercy of its own inefficient methods. Marching parallel to the French army, Kutusov in effect escorted the French out of Russia. On 9 November the French arrived at Smolensk with 60,000 men. The Russian army's strength rose as the French forces suffered wastage. From the north came the army of Wittgenstein and from the south the army of the Danube. The Russians suffered losses, but their total strength rose as the numbers of the French fell. On 5 December 1812 Napoleon left the Grand Army in order to reorganize his forces in central Europe. Much has been made of the sufferings of the French as a result of the Eastern European winter, but this factor has been greatly exaggerated. The essential cause of the French defeat was that the advance had been conceived in terms of living off the country after a decisive victory. There had been no decisive battle, and for the first time in a major campaign the French army retreated into a country devoid of supplies. By contrast, the Russian army was able to re-emerge in central Europe as an effective fighting force, whereas the French army had to be reconstituted.

V. THE LIBERATION OF GERMANY

At the beginning of 1813 the Russian forces appeared in central Poland in pursuit of the French. All those states which had curried favour with Napoleon now began to fear that they would fall under the domination of Russia. Austria, wise from her defeat of 1809, waited to see how events would turn out, but the course open to Prussia was decided by General Yorck in command of the Prussian corps which had covered the French left flank. On 30 December 1812 Yorck signed a convention with Russia at Tauroggen which withdrew his troops from the war against Russia. The Prussian patriots exerted every pressure they could to resolve the doubts of the hesitant Frederick William III. Scharnhorst and Gneisenau urged him to join with Russia in order to rid Germany of the French. On 27 February 1813 Frederick William signed a treaty of alliance with Alexander I at Kalisz. The Prussian army was so weak that Russia could have laid her hands upon the whole of Prussia's gains at the expense of Poland under the terms of the partitions, but instead it was agreed in the secret articles that Prussia's existing dominions should be guaranteed and that Prussia should be restored to a position of power equivalent to that she had had in 1806. The implication was that Alexander I intended to retain the Napoleonic Duchy of Warsaw for himself, while Prussia should find compensation in Germany itself. Upon these terms Frederick William III declared war on 16 March. Prussia's action met with small response in the rest of Germany. There was some reaction among the student class, but the princes were only too well aware that Napoleon was reassembling his forces. He was, moreover, able to hold his own in the field. Taking over the command of his troops in Germany in April 1813, he was able to defeat the allies at Lützen on 2 May and again at Bautzen on 20 May, which secured his control of Saxony, as ever the key to any campaign in Germany, but he could not exploit his victories nor could the allies for the moment themselves renew the offensive. On 4 June Napoleon agreed to the armistice signed at Pläswitz to expire on 10 July. Where arms had failed, recourse was had to diplomacy.

In this situation it was obvious that Austria had a decisive part to play. The Austrian chancellor, Metternich, hesitated. The Austrian auxiliary corps which had covered Napoleon's right flank during the campaign of 1812 withdrew from the war in January 1813, but it was necessary to lend a cloak of decency to any pressure upon France when Napoleon himself was married to a Habsburg princess. Great Britain, on the other hand, was determined that no arrangement should be made by the continental states in which she did not have a hand. On 14 and 15 June Sir Charles Stewart negotiated treaties of alliance with Russia and Prussia, which as ever included the provision of British subsidies and at the same time guaranteed the integrity of Hanover, while conceding that Prussia should be restored to her pre-war position. On 27 June Austria entered into the alliance upon the condition that Napoleon should first have refused her offer of mediation. Austria's conditions were hard. Napoleon was required to give up the Duchy of Warsaw and dissolve the Confederation of the Rhine, restore Prussia to her territories of 1806 and surrender the Illyrian provinces to Austria. The anger of Napoleon was great, but it says much for Austrian moderation that this was a solution which would have left France in possession of the left bank of the Rhine and the former United Provinces. The armistice was prolonged until 10 August in order to give Napoleon an opportunity of making his decision. Alexander I undoubtedly looked with some suspicion upon Austria, but his fears that Austria would back out of her alliance were proved unfounded when Napoleon rejected Austria's conditions and Austria declared war on 11 August, even before his reply was received, the time limit having expired.

In the August of 1813 Napoleon faced the allies with a nominal strength of 550,000 men, but after an initial success of 27 August at Dresden the French army was compelled to fight a ruinous battle at Leipzig on 16–18 October, the so-called 'Battle of the Nations', though most of the soldiers involved were the peasants enlisted in the armies of the old régimes. Napoleon was forced to retreat upon the Rhine with only 70,000 men. Behind the Rhine he could muster only 200,000. Typhus carried away part of his army, while the garrison troops in Germany were shut up in their fortresses and could take no active part in the campaign. At once the satellite states changed sides. Bavaria, Württemberg, Baden and Electoral Hesse swiftly joined the allies; the only state which could not extract itself from the debacle was Saxony. The former allies of Napoleon saved themselves from occupation and at the same time secured the gains at the expense of the mediatized states which association with France had brought them. The days of Napoleonic France appeared to be numbered. The armies of the allies in central Europe began to mass upon the Rhine. In October 1813 Wellington crossed the Bidassoa pass into France. On 8 January 1814 Murat, anxious to save Naples for himself from the general collapse, deserted Napoleon, prompted by his wife, Napoleon's sister, Caroline, an act of treachery which forced the French to evacuate Italy and placed Austria in command of the northern plain. Behind the French armies the Empire was collapsing. The Continental System had been organized to benefit France, but the markets upon which it was based now lay under the control of the allies. War, which hitherto had been made to pay for itself, was now to be paid for by France. The devastation, which formerly France had meted out to conquered countries, now touched France itself. All the dormant opposition roused itself to criticism of the Emperor. The hangers-on of the Napoleonic régime in France began to think in terms of saving their positions. Peace was demanded on all sides.

VI. THE VICTORY OF THE ALLIES, 1814

Already the allies were beginning to consider the peace before they had won their final victory. Only 60,000 men stood between them and the capture of Paris. Resolution and unity were restored in the allied camp by the appearance of the British foreign secretary, Castlereagh, in the headquarters of the army. At Langres on 29 January 1814 he obtained agreement to offer France the frontiers of 1792 and at Chaumont on 9 March forced the allies to agree to an alliance for five years. Negotiations were simultaneously being conducted with Napoleon at Châtillon, but it was clear that he was not negotiating in earnest. The allies then marched upon Paris, which fell on 30 March.

The Napoleonic régime had collapsed and the French government, now under the control of Talleyrand, was uncertain what to put in its place. The decision was taken for it by the citizens of Bordeaux, a city famous in France for its independence of thought and hostile to a régime which had ruined its prosperity. When a small party of British troops arrived in the city on 22 March it declared for the Bourbons. On 6 April 1814 the Senate, hitherto submissive to Napoleon, called upon Louis XVIII to resume the throne. The Bourbon restoration had practical advantages. France accepted the frontiers of 1792, and the allies for their part under the treaty of Paris of 30 May 1814 demanded no indemnities of France. The object of the allies was to establish in France a régime which was not discredited by the signature of a humiliating peace. France accepted the Bourbon restoration by the peace of Paris of 1814. Louis XVIII came back to Paris. Napoleon, having abdicated, departed for the island of Elba, which was assigned to him, not an ungenerous award for a petty Corsican nobleman, who had begun his career with nothing. The powers in the meantime decided to assemble in Vienna to rearrange the map of Europe, which he had altered by his conquests.

VII. THE HUNDRED DAYS

The new Bourbon régime could have made its peace with France if it had been prepared to forgive and forget, but life in emigration had not induced a sense of reality in the intransigent royalists. The followers of Louis XVIII came back expecting their reward for fidelity, where the officers and soldiers of Napoleonic France expected merely a transfer of authority. *Émigrés*, who had done nothing to serve the cause of France in the war years and who had not fought in battle, were set in authority over men who had carried the standards of France to splendid victories. The past was too recent to be forgotten by the French army. In these circumstances Napoleon made a last attempt to restore his fortunes. On 1 March 1815 he landed at Fréjus and found that France was prepared again to accept him. Louis XVIII fled to Ghent. Napoleon realized that he could not re-establish his autocracy and was prepared to make concessions to constitutional feeling, Louis XVIII having himself consented to a limited constitution. The basic fact, however, remained. France required peace, and Napoleon could restore his empire only by war. The familiar routine was followed. Troops were levied, but Napoleon could raise an army only of a size which permitted one decisive battle. An improved mixed force was assembled under Wellington in the Low Countries, while a Prussian army advanced to its support. On 18 June 1815 Napoleon flung his forces against Wellington, having repulsed the Prussians at Ligny. The battle of Waterloo was fought without skill. The troops under Wellington's command repulsed the French time and again, until, when they were on the point of exhaustion, the Prussians arrived to render assistance. In the face of overwhelming odds the French army melted away. The stern soldier Wellington commented:

> It has been a damned serious business. Blucher and I have lost 30,000 men. It has been a damned nice thing—the nearest run thing you ever saw in your life . . .

Napoleon, whose soldierly abilities were never combined with such compassion, thought that he might yet raise an army to carry on the war, but discovered that France would no longer support him. Throwing himself upon the mercy of Britain, he sought sanctuary with the power which had so long resisted him and found that he was transported to the island of St Helena, where he spent a querulous exile debating the past and blaming everyone but himself for his failure until he died in 1821. The penalty of his ambition was paid by France. The second treaty of Paris of November 1815 reduced France to the frontiers of 1789, imposed an indemnity of 700,000,000 francs, provided for an army of occupation and exacted the restoration of the art treasures which the French army had collected to grace Paris from the countries which it had overrun. Louis XVIII returned to resume his throne for the second time. The allied powers combined to preserve a peace which they had already decided in principle at Vienna in 1814–5. The Hundred Days of Napoleon I's last bid for power were an epilogue to the history of the French Revolution and Empire. The future for the moment lay at the disposal of the allies.

Europe at the End of the Napoleonic Wars

Wherever the French had gone they had regarded themselves as occupying territory. They were not interested in maintaining the historic system in Germany. Medieval divisions were ignored and the political map was periodically recast in order that larger units might make government and exploitation easier. In this process the French had imposed administrative reform and equality before the law. The Church was brought under control and in Germany disappeared as a territorial power. However much the Italians and Germans may have disliked French occupation and exploitation, the experience of the war cultivated in them a taste for further unification. Old prejudices were abandoned and old divisions lost their validity. There was a general feeling among the European middle classes that the monopoly of political power by the monarchies should be broken and that the citizen should enjoy a wider share in government. A typical example among many was Benjamin Constant, who had run foul of Napoleon Bonaparte in 1802. In his *Cours de politique constitutionelle* (A course of constitutional policy), published in 1817, he declared in favour of sovereignty of the people, but he did not believe it to be absolute. For him there were five types of power: the royal, the executive, the power that represents permanence, by which he meant a hereditary chamber, the power which gave expression to opinion, or an elected assembly, and, finally, the judiciary. The function of royal power was to maintain a balance between the contending forces in the state. This represented a common opinion among European liberals, who sought some measure of centralization, but with a share in political authority for themselves, though it was open to question how far the people at large might receive representation. What the European liberals required above all was the career open to men of talent, which could not be achieved if power were retained by the monarchies and their bureaucracies. In one way the Napoleonic conquest hastened and accelerated the work begun by the enlightened despots, but in another brought under the fire of criticism a system in which legislation was not submitted to the decision of at least a section of public opinion.

The economic advantages of the larger units created by Napoleon were apparent, even though France had made conquests pay for themselves. The Continental System had given a boost to industrial production, especially in Belgium, the French and German Rhineland and Saxony, which the resumption of peaceful conditions laid open to attack with the unimpeded influx of cheap British goods. The hostility of the areas outside France to the Napoleonic policy of favouring French industry was quickly transferred to Britain. Whereas the commercial and industrial classes in Britain favoured free trade which would give them leadership in Europe, the continental industrialists looked to the state to support them and the more powerful the tariff protection which it gave them, the better they were pleased. The reaction of the European merchants to the Napoleonic system was less favourable. The commercial cities of Europe wanted as free as possible a movement of goods, which had in part been frustrated by Napoleon's tariff system, but the wider economic unity which had been achieved in spite of French fiscalism encouraged the desire for the maintenance of larger state units in order to create larger markets. Only the agrarian interests of Europe had suffered. Whereas there was a general maintenance of prices within France, requisitioning and purchasing at fixed prices by the French intendants-general had created conditions of real hardship, especially in Ostalbingian Germany and in Poland. The temporary adherence of Russia to the Continental System gave cause for grave discontents. For the landlords the burden of debt was often ruinous. From this factor emerged a conflict of importance. The landlords, many of whom had enjoyed a share in power under the autocratic monarchies, which employed them in the civil administration or as officers in the army, looked askance at the middle classes, who sought admission to a position of privilege in the political order and at the same time demanded legislation in favour of industry in order to keep domestic prices high when agriculture was depressed and required capital expenditure for the introduction of improved methods of tillage. Where noble tax exemptions remained, middle-class participation in government would mean their abolition. The conflict of town and country, a struggle as old as civilized society, remained acute and the old régimes which emerged triumphant in 1814–15 were not without their allies in the face of middle-class demands.

In addition to changes in political and economic attitudes there was a transformation in the moral climate of European opinion. The inspiration of the eighteenth century had been classical. Classical patriotism had taken the form of devotion to the community. National differences had been disliked and men had preferred to adopt cosmopolitan views. The French Revolution and Napoleon leaned heavily upon classical thought and models. It was significant that France created the Batavian Republic, the Helvetic Republic, the Cisalpine Republic, Parthenopean Republic and the Kingdom of Etruria, titles which were redolent in their classical associations. The French Empire could be nothing else than a cosmopolitan community. There had been a reaction already in the eighteenth century which questioned the inspiration of the Ancient World. One aspect of this revolt had been the rejection of the classical inspiration in literature and the growth of a deeper consciousness in the beauty of nature. In breaking with the discipline imposed by classical example already in the eighteenth century men had turned their attention to the inspiration of the medieval world. In Britain by the mid-years of the eighteenth century the revolt was apparent and by the end had a renowned representative in Wordsworth, to be followed by Scott, Coleridge, Byron, Shelley and Keats. This movement had its parallels in almost every country of Europe. The appreciation of scenic beauty aroused interest in national and folk traditions. Rousseau, in his dislike of large states and the tyranny which he associated with them, pleaded for the simplicity of communities in which every man knew every other. Herder in Germany investigated the lore not only of the German people but also of the peoples upon the borders of Germany. Sympathy was felt for Corsica, when the island was annexed by France in 1768 in spite of the resistance of Paoli. It was demanded by what right Poland was partitioned by alien powers. Cosmopolitanism seemed to strike at the very roots of the patriotic ardour which existed in communities bound together by common speech. The state appeared an artificial society, whereas the nation appeared a natural one. For the rebels of the eighteenth-century nationalism was synonymous with love of one's country and public spirit. Herder believed that the Germans could achieve a new self-respect if they took a pride in their national culture; the more secluded a nation, the more its national character was preserved, in itself a good reason for tolerance of national minorities. Just as the Enlightenment broke down the old religious loyalties, it gave birth to a deeper concept of men's brotherhood. This was extremely important in Germany, where the Catholics and the Evangelicals had long been divided. If the people existed as an organic ethnic whole, then it might be reasonable to express the General Will of the people, as Rousseau proposed in his *Social Contract*. The growth of nationalism was synonymous with left-wing revolutionary feeling. The inspiration of Romantic literature seemed to prescribe a role to a new kind of knight-errant who would devote his life to a modern chivalry, the service of the people. The appeal of this thought had its greatest effect upon young men, who had not experienced the full force of war and subjection. With the defeat of Napoleon the horrors of war, which were real to the older generation, were ignored and the bloody battles of the great European struggle assumed in the minds of the younger a heroic quality which they had not possessed. The Romantic conception of the recent past produced a mythology of its own, which found no echo of sympathy with older men in closer touch with reality. In the continental states the student class was to prove turbulent, infected with a desire for change and freedom of expression and impatient of the controls which their fathers sought to impose after so much dislocation and upheaval.

The *émigrés* who came back to France and the conservative classes in Europe generally sought peace. For them Romanticism frequently meant the reinforcement of traditional values. The intellectualism of the eighteenth century, questioning the wisdom of centuries, had brought disruption. Bonald and Joseph de Maistre saw in the Papacy an institution which represented permanence in an age of rapid change, independent of the vicissitudes of ephemeral fancy. Religion appeared as a social cement, binding men together in a spiritual brotherhood. Emphasis upon the claims of the church went hand in hand with the progress of technological advancement. The deism of the Enlightenment gave place in conservative thought to reinforcement of the sacerdotal powers of the clergy. From this was born the conflict of Clericalism and Anti-Clericalism. The age of Reason did not end with the wars. The revealed truths of science and reason were subjected to the challenge of the inherited truths of experience. In a conflict in which there was no common ground there could be no compromise. It was a struggle for men's minds which has never entirely been resolved in European society. In essence it represented a dispute not over fundamental principles, but rather over the speed which social change might take. The statesmen, who were required to set Europe in order after the great wars, sought merely the bases of peace. The forces which war had unleashed had to be brought within the bonds of discipline. The statesmen of the allied powers and of defeated France were accused of being reactionary. Reaction did not triumph in 1814–15. The peace settlement accepted what had happened in Europe as a result of the Revolutionary and Napoleonic Wars. Within the terms of the settlement the contending forces struggled with one another, while material progress pursued its inexorable path. The end of the wars marked a new phase in European development. The divergence of opinion prescribed the terms of a fresh conflict, but the fundamental impetus of industrialization could not be halted.

3: Peace and Reconstruction

The Making of the Peace, 1814–15

The end of the great war against France and the overthrow of Napoleon I gave rise to a mythology of its own. It was supposed that the reactionary powers of the old Europe, ignoring all that the French Revolution had done, combined to restore the pre-war system and place the continent under the yoke of the obscurantist Metternich. Alexander I of Russia was supposed to have forsaken his earlier liberalism and drifted towards mysticism under the influence of Madame de Krüdener. According to this view for over three decades Europe lay subjugated by conservatism, until in 1848 Europe awoke and a new age began. The revolutions of 1848 have even been given the name of the 'Springtime of the Peoples'. Such interpretations clearly spring from the interpretations current among middle-class liberals and radicals of the first half of the nineteenth century. The truth is in fact much simpler. Europe had suffered devastation and disruption as the inevitable consequences of a long war. The European powers wanted nothing more than a period of peace in which they might restore their finances and carry out reconstruction.

One aspect of this question may at once be removed. The powers which had defeated France were anxious to contain her, but neither Britain nor Russia sought to impose a vindictive peace. The treaty of Paris of 1814 preserved the integrity of France within the frontiers of 1 January 1792; Great Britain even made restitution of certain colonial territories, which she had seized from France during the war. The peace which followed the battle of Waterloo and the second abdication of Napoleon in 1815 was more severe, but it presented France with no grievance which might make war certain for the future. The frontiers of France were fixed within the limits of 1790. France was required to pay the allies an indemnity of 700,000,000 francs and to have quartered in her territory an allied army of occupation as a guarantee against further Bonapartist adventures. In fact, the army occupation was reduced from 150,000 to 30,000 men in 1817 and withdrawn altogether in 1818. What had appeared at first to be a very heavy burden, in practice was easy enough for France to bear. France had made Europe pay for her wars and had no difficulty in raising money to meet the indemnity and costs of occupation. It was true that the Bourbon dynasty was restored, but it was not the system of 1789 which was restored with it. The legislative achievements of Napoleon I remained untouched in the form of the *Code Napoléon*. The Bourbons, moreover, had no wish to abolish the Imperial administrative system, which placed so much power in the hands of the monarchy. Indeed, means had to be found to limit the power of the French king. A check was imposed in the form of the Constitution of 1814. No more determined supporter of the French constitution was found than Alexander I of Russia, the Tsar-Autocrator, not because he had an ideological preference for constitutions, but because he believed that a constitution gave a voice in affairs to a section at least of the French upper classes, who would act as a check upon the militaristic ambitions of the Bourbons. It seemed that a constitution with a limited franchise would satisfy the ambitions of at least a portion of the French bourgeoisie. Even in 1830 Nicholas I of Russia, allegedly the most conservative monarch of the nineteenth century, was pressing Charles X to observe the spirit as well as the letter of the French constitution. In France certainly the allies did not seek to restore the régime of Louis XVI. They were content to leave the French people with the positive social gains which the crisis of the revolution of 1789 and the régime of Napoleon I had given them. For them the main danger was that France might once again take up the aggressive foreign policy of the *ancien régime* and the Empire. Care was taken therefore to avoid provocation of France by the imposition of a Carthaginian peace. In spite of occasional outbursts of chauvinism, in origin mainly Parisian, the people of France for the most part accepted the solution imposed by the two treaties of Paris.

France was not, however, the only problem. In Article XXXII of the Treaty of 1814 it was agreed that France, Britain, Austria, Russia and Prussia should send plenipotentiaries to Vienna 'in order in a general congress to make the arrangements which ought to complete the dispositions of the present treaty'. In other words, when once the affairs of France had been arranged, the powers repaired to Vienna to settle the questions which had arisen as a result of the total collapse of the Napoleonic Empire. The treaties of Paris were thus outside the cognizance of the Congress of Vienna.

The reorganization of Europe had been the subject of abortive discussions between Britain and Russia in 1804 and 1805. In an official communication to the Russian ambassador on 19 January 1805 the British government stated three principles of policy:

(1) To rescue from the dominion of France those countries which it has subjugated since the beginning of the Revolution, and to reduce France within its former limits, as they stood before that time.

(2) To make such an arrangement with respect to the territories recovered from France, as may provide for their security and happiness, and may at the same time constitute a more effectual barrier in future against encroachments on the part of France.

(3) To form, at the restoration of peace, a general agreement and guarantee for the mutual protection and security of different Powers, and for re-establishing a general system of public law in Europe.

The battle of Austerlitz in 1805 and the defeat of Russia prevented the immediate application of these principles, but when once the French armies began to retreat this policy was again taken up by the British foreign secretary, Castlereagh. The defeat of France and the two treaties of Paris secured the first of these aims. In British eyes and, indeed, in the view of Alexander I of Russia, the purpose of the Congress of Vienna was to achieve the second and third of these points. Britain and Russia were already world powers with immense strategic problems. For them 'the re-establishment of the general system of public law in Europe' was not an abstract concept, but rather an instrument for the removal of the system of egocentric diplomacy which had been the curse of the eighteenth century. Prussia and Austria, being only regional powers, clearly lacked the broader vision which was the characteristic of British and Russian policy.

In the final outcome the Congress of Vienna did to some extent provide a system of public law for Europe. There can be no simpler way of understanding the achievement of the European statesmen than reading the actual text of the treaty of Vienna, signed on 9 June 1815. It consists of a final act, signed by the plenipotentiaries of Austria, France, Great Britain, Portugal, Prussia, Russia, Sweden, and Spain, to which are appended a series of subsidiary treaties relating to regional problems, seventeen in all, which were therefore to be considered integral parts of the general treaty. The treaty of Vienna embraced the whole of Europe affected by the French conquests. The signatory powers had for the future a right to be consulted if any of these arrangements should be modified or changed. What was conceded was the principle that where the interests of all the major powers were affected, they had a right to be consulted. The treaty of Vienna was thus a great international statute to which appeal might be made. In questions of major importance the interested powers could meet and concert measures to settle differences which might otherwise lead to armed conflict. The concert of Europe was by design an instrument for the maintenance of peace. Wars did occur in the nineteenth century, but never upon the scale of the Revolutionary and Napoleonic Wars. A major war occurred in 1914 for the simple reason that Austria-Hungary took unilateral action where the interests of all the major powers were involved. This was to revert to the policies of the eighteenth-century states. By comparison the concept adopted by the powers at Vienna in 1814–15 appears to be a step forward towards more harmonious international relations.

While the general utility of the arrangements made in Vienna is easily to be understood, the conflicts and stresses which preceded the signature of the treaties do not submit to as simple an explanation. In effect, the powers which had defeated France, namely, Britain, Russia, Austria and Prussia, though often at loggerheads among themselves, never lost sight of the fundamental principle, that their purpose was to produce a settlement which made further French aggression impossible. They might admit other powers to discussions, but they were determined to retain the power of ultimate decision in their own hands. It should, moreover, be recognized that within the victorious group of powers the more important were Britain and Russia. Britain had swept the French from the seas and liberated the Iberian peninsula, while at Waterloo she had won the final battle against Napoleon with some Prussian aid. She was, moreover, incomparably richer than any other continental state. Russia had raised the largest armies and by her military skill defeated the main forces of France. The part which Austria and Prussia had played in the wars had by comparison been inglorious, however much German panegyrists may subsequently have spoken of a 'War of Liberation'. The battles of Ulm and Jena were the measure of the importance of

Austria and Prussia. In reality the discussions at Vienna amounted to a conflict of views between Britain represented by Castlereagh, on the one hand, and, on the other, Russia, represented in person by the Tsar Alexander I.

The fault of many of our histories is their ignorance of Alexander I's aims. The primary aim of Russian policy was that of Peter I and his successors, to close the western frontier against invasion of the kind which had been experienced in 1812. Alexander I was therefore determined to retain the Napoleonic Duchy of Warsaw, with perhaps some minor cessions, and to ensure that Germany herself remained sufficiently divided not to constitute a threat to Russia; he was initially willing enough to find dominions for the ex-Viceroy of Italy, Eugène de Beauharnais, and the ex-Queen of Westphalia, from among the former ecclesiastical states of western Germany, while Prussia might receive portions of Saxony, the only German state which for its own special reasons had remained faithful to Napoleon. For the rest Alexander thought that increases of territory might be granted to the Duke of Oldenburg, the King of Württemburg and the Grand Dukes of Baden and Darmstadt. Italy for her part was to be surrendered to the hegemony of Austria. What Alexander I in effect proposed was that Germany should be a power vacuum consisting of relatively small states, not powerful enough to challenge Russia, but strong enough to resist France until Russia, always slow by her very size, could mobilize her resources and launch her armies into central Europe to restore the equilibrium. From the point of view of Russia this was an intelligible policy, but to Britain it seemed that the Napoleonic Confederation of the Rhine was to be replaced by a system of Russian domination. Castlereagh was conscious that such a system not only gave Russia excessive influence but also failed to give adequate security on the Rhine against French aggression. Castlereagh would have preferred to see a reconstituted Poland separating Russia from central Europe, but fundamental to his policy was the desire to erect a bastion against France on the Rhine. Austria, nervous of too powerful a Russian influence in Germany, veered towards the British view. Prussia, intent upon rounding off her dominions in northern Germany by annexations at the expense of Saxony, which Alexander I supported, looked towards Russia. The fate of Saxony appeared to be the crux of the situation, upon which no agree-

THE TERRITORIAL
SETTLEMENT
THE TREATIES OF PARIS, 1814-15,
& THE VIENNA TREATIES, 1815

SCHLESWIG

HOLSTEIN

Kovno

Königsberg

OLDENBURG

MECKLENBURG

P R U S S I A

HANOVER

Berlin

Warsaw

K. of the NETHERLANDS

WESTPHALIA

KINGDOM of
POLAND

Brussels

SAXONY

NASSAU

Prague

Cracow

GALICIA

Paris

BOHEMIA

Brünn

Lunéville

BADEN

WÜRTTEMBERG

BAVARIA

Pressburg

Chaumont

Vienna

FRANCE

Neuchâtel

Buda • Pest

SWITZERLAND

TIROL

AUSTRIA

HUNGARY

Geneva

LOMBARDY

VENETIA

Agram (Zagreb)

KINGDOM

Milan

Verona

Venice

of • Turin

PARMA

SARDINIA

Genoa

MODENA

Bologna

SERBIA

Marseilles

Nice

TUSCANY

Ancona

Ragusa • MONTENEGRO

CORSICA

PAPAL
STATES

OTTOMAN

Rome

EMPIRE

Gaeta

SARDINIA

Naples

KINGDOM of the
TWO SICILIES

IONIAN
ISLANDS
(British
Protectorate)

Palermo

Messina

KINGDOM OF PRUSSIA
HABSBURG EMPIRE
BOUNDARY OF THE
GERMAN FEDERATION

0   100   200
Miles

ment could be reached. Castlereagh's solution was to call upon the assistance of France. The plenipotentiary of France, Talleyrand, was dissatisfied with a situation in which the victorious powers alone took the major decisions and welcomed an overture which might restore France to the position of a great power and offer an opportunity of saving Saxony from total partition. On 3 January 1815 Austria, Britain and France joined in alliance to resist Russia and Prussia. Alexander I perceived that a compromise was necessary if open conflict were to be avoided.

In the end the solution was one which satisfied Castlereagh. The new Kingdom of the Netherlands, for which Castlereagh had demanded larger dimensions, included the former United Provinces, the former Austrian Netherlands and Luxemburg, which was to admit a Prussian garrison. Prussia herself was given only two-fifths of Saxony, but obtained the western portion of the Duchy of Warsaw, the so-called Grand Duchy of Posen and extensive territories on the left bank of the Rhine and in the Napoleonic Kingdom of Westphalia. In this manner two powerful territorial units were established upon the lower and middle Rhine to bar the way to French invasion of Germany. The German states, including Austria proper and the Kingdom of Bohemia, were given some cohesion by being joined in a Confederation capable in theory of combining to meet a French attack. In the centre the Swiss Confederation was declared neutral. In Italy Austria was placed in possession of Lombardy and Venetia, which gave her a base to resist French aggression. In Italy the situation was initially more complicated because of the presence of Joachim Murat as King of Naples, but Murat attempted to take advantage of Napoleon I's return to France in 1815 in order to rally Italy. The Muratist régime, however, collapsed and the Bourbon, Ferdinand I, returned in close alliance with Austria. Austria's provinces of Lombardy and Venetia were shielded from direct contact with France by the restoration of the Kingdom of Sardinia-Savoy and its enlargement by the addition of Genoa. Cadet branches of the Habsburg family ruled in Tuscany and Modena, while Parma was given to the former Empress of France, Marie-Louise. In the centre of Italy the Pope was restored to his dominions. Austria as the one substantial power in Italy obviously accepted responsibility for the prevention of French incursions and attempts to subvert the weak Italian States. By this system the map of Europe was reshaped in a manner designed to contain France. No longer would it be possible for France to further her territorial ambitions by playing upon the divisions of her smaller neighbours. Now they were backed by states capable of offering formidable resistance. Talleyrand's entry into the alliance of 3 January 1815, therefore, gave France little more than the show of appearing to be a great power.

While Castlereagh achieved the essence of his policy, none of the essentials of Alexander I's aims had been sacrificed. The planting of Prussia upon the middle Rhine in fact can be argued to have suited Russian purposes better than the initial proposals of Alexander. Prussia was capable of presenting strong resistance to France, but the acquisition of territories which contained a population influenced by French ideas and which were totally dissimilar in their social composition from the Ostalbingian provinces in the first instance created a grave problem for the Hohenzollern monarchy and inclined it to look more than ever for moral support to Russia; the statesmen of 1815 could not have foreseen that the inclusion of the Ruhr within Prussia gave her with Silesia the control over the greater part of Germany's future industrial resources. For the moment Alexander I was satisfied. For him the great task was to achieve internal stability in order that those parts of Europe which had been infected with the revolutionary fever might find some repose under the aegis of limited constitutions. In his view France was still the great enemy of European peace, and all efforts must be exerted to control her, for she would be no less restless under the Bourbons than she was under Napoleon. The concessions he had made at Vienna he represented as an attempt to dispel the 'chimerical apprehension' fomented by Great Britain and Austria that the domination achieved by Napoleon would shortly be exercised by Russia. In one sense the return of Napoleon in 1815 had restored a sense of reality. The destruction of Napoleon was in itself not enough. What Alexander looked forward to was the neutralization of the spirit which had restored Napoleon for a hundred days to his throne. The people were liable to be infected with revolution and could be won over to acceptance of the new system only by an enlightened and liberal policy. It was therefore essential to present an appearance of moderation and to work in concert with the allies.

The problems of post-war reconstruction and the fear lest the peace treaties should be overthrown were evident to each of the four victorious powers. The Quadruple Alliance was therefore renewed on 20 November 1815 as an instrument for upholding the settlement of 1815. The great powers now assumed responsibility for watching over the peace. Article VI of the treaty stated:

> To facilitate and to secure the execution of the present treaty, and to consolidate the connections which at the present moment so closely unite the four Sovereigns for the happiness of the world, the High Contracting Parties have agreed to renew their meetings at fixed periods, either under the immediate auspices of the Sovereigns themselves or by their respective ministers, for the purpose of consulting upon their common interests, and for the consideration of the measures which at each of these periods shall be considered the most salutary for the repose and prosperity of nations and for the maintenance of the peace of Europe.

The proposal for period reunions was novel. In this system may be perceived the origin of a permanent organization for the maintenance of the peace. Some confusion was introduced by the signature by the sovereigns of Russia, Austria and Prussia on 26 September 1815 of the so-called Treaty of Holy Alliance, by which they undertook to regulate their public acts in accordance with the principles of the Christian religion, a proposal which met with general approval in Europe except with constitutional Britain and the Pope; the Sultan could not sign for the obvious reason that he was a Moslem. The Treaty of Holy Alliance was an aspiration, not an instrument of policy, expressing the hopes of Article VI of the Quadruple Alliance without making formal provisions for action. Nevertheless, it created some suspicions, especially when Britain refused to adhere to it. It surrounded the treaties with an aura of mystery, which in fact they did not possess.

Europe had been dominated by a single power, France, and the Congress set itself the task of restoring the balance of power. Talleyrand, who could scarcely have admitted that he had been a party to the reduction of French influence, attempted to prove that legitimacy was the governing principle of the Congress, but in fact many of the changes instituted by France were accepted by the Congress and even turned against her. The French dislike of the Vienna treaties which persisted until 1870 was ideological. The new map of Europe was a monument to the defeat of France's great efforts. It was not an instrument for the oppression of France herself. Distrust of France survived in Europe, especially when the revolutions of 1830 and 1848 caused Frenchmen to remember the glories of the past. Napoleon III and his advisers were later to plead for the revision of the Vienna treaties. From 1815 onwards Europe was strong enough to induce caution in French foreign policy. All except a minority of Frenchmen were conscious that a general European war would place burdens and hardships upon them which hypothetical prospects of gains would not justify. Changes were to occur, but they were brought about by factors external to French history.

The Conference of Aix-la-Chapelle

France had little to complain of in the treatment which she received from the victorious allies. When the powers assembled in November 1818 at Aix-la-Chapelle for the first of the conferences proposed by the Quadruple Alliance they recognized the facts of the European system. Confidence in France was sufficiently restored by the administration of the Duc de Richelieu, who had discharged the indemnity imposed in 1815, for the powers to withdraw their army of occupation from France. The commander-in-chief, Wellington, was of the opinion that the continued presence of these forces in France, so far from contributing towards the maintenance of political stability, tended by 1818 to be provocative and that their withdrawal was in the interest of peace. The evacuation of this army meant, in other words, the restoration to France of complete liberty in foreign policy. For this reason France was admitted to the conference of the allies and thus took her rightful place in the Concert of Europe. Though France was admitted as being a great power, the allies none the less strengthened themselves against possible French aggression. The Quadruple Alliance remained in force and fresh provisions were made for the occupation of the barrier fortresses in the Netherlands by British and Prussian troops in the event of a crisis. The allied powers were determined that the entry of France into their counsels should not mean the abolition of the alliance which was meant to contain her. Their policy was a combination of firmness and conciliation.

The Challenge of Revolution

The restoration of France to a position of equality by the conference of Aix-la-Chapelle was quickly followed by a series of events which subjected the Quadruple Alliance to a severe test. The South American colonies of Spain had begun to challenge the authority of the home government in 1809. In January 1820 a military revolt broke out in Spain itself and the king, Ferdinand VII, was until 1823 a prisoner of the revolution. In July 1820 a revolution in Naples overthrew the Bourbon absolutism. In August 1820 a revolution broke out in Portugal. While the western half of the Mediterranean was in a ferment in March 1821 a revolt of the Greeks in Moldavia caused a revolt in sympathy in the Morea which spread throughout the Greek islands of the Aegean.

In the face of this crisis the attitude of the powers varied. Great Britain's interests were largely maritime and commercial. She objected to the interference of the continental powers in her fields of influence. They were to have no influence upon the conditions which determined the maritime prosperity of Britain. Prussia, Austria and Russia, however, were determined to maintain the political stability of Europe in order that they might recover from the stresses and strains of the war. All four powers looked askance at any revival of French aggressive intent. While the Quadruple Alliance remained as the instrument for the coercion of France, the continental states' policy clashed with that of Britain, especially in Spain. Britain basically had no objection to constitutional changes in Spain, because the paralysis of government in Madrid would make permanent the breakdown of the Spanish American empire and make it possible for Great Britain to supplant Spain as the major commercial power in Latin America. Britain's attitude was bound to be equivocal. As early as 1812 Castlereagh had been prepared to offer his mediation in the dispute between Spain and her colonies, but was not ready to offer Spain military support. Under the terms of the Hispano-British treaty of 1814 the trade of the colonies was thrown open and Britain placed on an equal footing with other powers, but the government of metropolitan Spain was determined to regain the substance of power in the New World. The neutrality of Britain, restated on 1 January 1816, revealed that Spain could not hope to receive any real aid from

Britain, who under the guise of friendship was in fact pursuing an anti-Spanish policy. Spain therefore began to look to the support of Russia. The Russian ambassador, Tatishchev, was inclined to lend his ear to Spanish pleas, but Alexander I adhered to a policy of moderation. Spain then tried to obtain the support of the Russian ambassador in Paris, Pozzo di Borgo, who carried greater weight than Tatishchev. The intrigues reached such proportions that Castlereagh decided to make a direct appeal to the Tsar himself over the heads of his ministers and from him obtained a recognition of the British principle that the powers could not arbitrate between a king and his subjects. According to Castlereagh they could 'mediate or facilitate, but not compel or menace'. The position of France, however, was different. The restoration of Ferdinand VII in 1814 meant that the close relations of the Spanish and French Courts could be resumed. France was not moved by any desire to preserve unity in the Quadruple Alliance, of which she was not a member. Already in 1818 French officials in the ministry of foreign affairs were exploring the possibility of interference in Buenos Ayres. Though Decazes disclaimed all knowledge of this intrigue, Castlereagh became wary of European support for Spain in America. A straw in the wind was his statement to the Columbian agent that Britain would recognize any colonial territory which adopted monarchical institutions. In the last resort he was prepared to recognize the severance from Spain of her colonies. Nothing was to overthrow the commercial gains which Britain had made in Latin America as a result of the war.

The Spanish Revolution of 1820 and the Crisis in the Iberian Peninsula

When Ferdinand VII was restored in March 1814 he had promised to maintain the constitution of 8 May 1812, which provided for a single-chamber parliament elected by universal manhood suffrage, but the strongly rooted absolutist tendencies of the Bourbon dynasty in Spain and the equally firm sympathies among the mass of the population for the traditional form of government combined to prevent the liberal minority from securing a constitutional system. The constitutionalists for their part themselves clung to the old system by which the colonies were subordinated to the home government. In these circumstances the separation of the colonies could only be complete if it were to be achieved at all. The Juntas which had established themselves in the areas now known as Bolivia, Peru, Chile, Venezuela, Argentina, Paraguay, Uruguay fought hard to maintain their independence of Spain, but with varying degrees of success. The issue was in doubt until January 1820, when a military revolution broke out in Spain which brought about the collapse of Ferdinand VII's régime and his acceptance of the Constitution of 1812. Quickly the revolt spread to Mexico, Guatemala, Costa Rica, Honduras, Nicaragua and Salvador.

The Portuguese dominions in South America had had a less tempestuous history than the colonies of Spain, because in 1807–8 the Portuguese royal family transferred itself to Brazil, which in 1815 was declared to be a kingdom and therefore granted equality with metropolitan Portugal. In 1821 John VI returned to Portugal, but at home the Portuguese resented the British domination and wished to reduce Brazil to its former dependence, with the result that on 7 September 1822, the king's son, Pedro, who had been left in South America, took command of the secession movement and proclaimed himself as constitutional emperor of Brazil.

The Spanish revolution of 1820 added confusion to a situation which was already complicated. Britain had fought to drive the French out of Portugal and Spain during the war, but if now the absolutist régime were restored in Spain with European aid it would follow that Spain would be able to make a great effort to restore her old colonial system and Portugal would in all probability follow suit. While Britain was in a general sense committed to friendship with Spain, this policy had to be combined with due regard to self-interest. Wellington, always conservatively inclined, advised against any form of interference in Spain, which his experience of the Peninsular War warned him was an intractable country, but Castlereagh elevated the whole question to one of major principle in his State Paper of 5 May 1820, subsequently published by his successor, Canning, in 1823. This appreciation contained a memorable phrase:

> When the territorial balance of Europe is disturbed she [Great Britain] can interfere with effect, but she is the last government in Europe which can be expected or can venture to commit herself on any question of abstract principle.

Castlereagh's argument was that the King of Spain had granted a constitution and that Spain herself presented no threat to the general peace. There was no question of establishing a republic, and therefore there was no threat to monarchical principles. Castlereagh's memorandum, drawn up in reply to a Russian memorandum of 30 April 1820, which suggested a five-power remonstrance in Madrid, was for all its elevated tone a declaration of British determination, though with the maximum of decorum and diplomatic tact, to permit Spain to wallow in her own civil disputes, while the Spanish leaders in South America carved out for themselves new republics which would pass under the domination of Britain. For the moment, however, the new liberal régime in Spain was left undisturbed by the continental powers. A revolution at this juncture broke out in Naples. Italy had been the theatre of operations in which Bonaparte had made his reputation. Here there arose the more pressing danger that the actual territorial settlement of 1815 would be overthrown. In this instance no abstract principles were involved.

Italy after 1815: the Desire for Unification

When the war came to an end in 1814 the Italians were heartily thankful that the period of French exploitation was over, but as in Germany so in Italy the French had left their mark. The Kingdom of Italy had created a vision of a larger political unit which created a taste for Italian unification. Within a united Italy industry and trade might flourish, with attendant profit for the Italian middle class. The ponderous structure of the Napoleonic state, moreover, was impressive, because it would provide careers for the educated classes. There was therefore among the Italian middle class a feeling that some change was necessary, but this sentiment conflicted with the principle adopted by the Congress of Vienna that Italy was a power vacuum in which stability was to be maintained by Austria. No longer strong enough to defend the Rhine against French aggression, she was to have the duty of protecting Italy. For this reason she was given Lombardy and Venetia, and Habsburg cadet branches established in Tuscany, Modena and Parma. Under a secret convention of 12 June 1815, after the expulsion of Murat from Naples where he sided with Napoleon during the Hundred Days, and the consequent reunion of Naples and Sicily, Austria obtained a right to intervene if constitutional changes were instituted; the Austrian general, Nugent, was appointed to command the Neapolitan army. Thus in effect Austria dominated most of the Italian peninsula. Virtually only Piedmont-Sardinia and the Papal states were outside her direct control.

A myth has arisen that Austrian rule was tyrannical. In fact, justice was relatively good and the clergy were kept under control. Education was compulsory up to the age of twelve years and is said, in fact, to have reached 68 per cent of boys and 42 per cent of girls. The censorship was extremely light, and some concessions were made to local self-government. In Parma under the former Empress Marie-Louise French law was retained, judges were given independence of the executive and alone in Europe Jews were admitted to the civil service. Tuscany under its Grand Duke Leopold enjoyed a mild paternalistic régime. The surveillance of the secret police in Tuscany was often ineffectual to the point of being ludicrous; only one death resulted from their activities, when as a joke they forwarded an intercepted letter of revolutionary tone to its addressee with their official stamp and so frightened him that he committed suicide. In Piedmont-Sardinia there existed a paternalistic military absolutism which protected the peasants and curtailed the privileges of the nobles and the clergy; if it had not been that the Congress of Vienna had added the town of Genoa to it there could have been no serious discords in the Kingdom of Sardinia. Piedmont and its ruling dynasty, the House of Savoy, was Provençal rather than Italian in outlook, and the fact that three-quarters of the revenue was devoted to the army indicates that it had an expansionist foreign policy which was anti-Austrian in the sense that it aimed at annexing portions of the Po valley.

The real objection to the system of government in Italy came from the middle classes. They disliked the parish-pump politics imposed upon them by partition into petty states. The Viceroyalty in Milan was slow to give decisions because too much central control was exercised by Vienna. Within the smaller states petty local issues contrasted sadly with the grandeur which might be achieved in a united Italy.

In the towns of Genoa and Leghorn there were radical movements which had little respect for the placid and unexciting governments of the states to which they belonged. At Leghorn the lawyer Guerrazzi was to win some influence among the working class before 1848. At the university of Pisa there arose a centre of Liberalism, encouraged by the professors who imparted nationalist ideas to their students. The Italian aristocracy looked askance at the activity of persons who would challenge their own social supremacy and were to seek for some alternative to the heady radicalism of the cities. In the north, however, it is broadly true to say that the Italians were not under any great pressure to break into revolt.

In central and southern Italy, however, discontent was greater. The papal dominions were restored to the Pope in 1814, and Pius VII and the Cardinal-Secretary of State, Consalvi, restored the old régime in May 1814. French law was abolished, the Jews were confined to the ghetto and all those who had worked with the French were victimized, but the French centralized administrative system was retained with the consequence that clerical government pressed more heavily than ever upon the population. Some vestiges of French rule remained, in the form of provincial councils, in which some lay members sat, preserving the separation of judicial and executive functions and a uniform taxation system, but on 5 October 1824 a complete reaction was instituted by Leo XII, who abolished the provincial councils, appointed the ecclesiastical tribunals and restored aristocratic privileges in the communes. In 1826 the land tax was reduced. Thus the aristocratic reaction in the Papal States was complete. Clerical rule was inefficient and arbitrary and in consequence led to a breakdown of public order. The so-called Carbonari, or Charcoal Burners, part of the wartime resistance to the French, conducted almost open warfare with the clerical faction, the Sanfedists.

In the Bourbon Kingdom of Naples and Sicily there were two distinct problems. The island of Sicily never looked with pleasure upon the mainland and had distinct separatist inclinations rooted in its Aragonese institutions and fostered by the French occupation of Naples. With the restoration of Bourbon rule in Naples the Austrians insisted under the terms of the convention of 20 April 1815 that the king, Ferdinand I, should respect the work of the French. The public debt was to be accepted and land grants confirmed. The army of Murat, moreover, was taken over. The Austrians were anxious to avoid repetition of the policy of vengeance adopted by the Bourbons when they had been restored in 1799. The Bourbons, however, did not follow a policy of conciliation. On the one hand, there were the 'Muratists', those Neapolitans who had collaborated with the French and who controlled the administration and the army. In matters of promotion the Bourbons tended to pass them over and give posts to the loyalists, the 'Fedeloni', who had followed the dynasty into exile. The Muratists, therefore, began to look towards a constitution as a means of controlling the actions of the King; this was to be a constitution of the French pattern which excluded possibility of democratic control and gave power into the hands of the upper classes. On the other hand, there were the Carbonari, the members of the wartime resistance who had worked for the expulsion of the French. They had been indifferent whether the Bourbons were restored or whether Murat remained, if only the country could be freed from the French yoke. In general, they favoured the Bourbons after suffering some persecution at the hands of the Muratists in 1813, but in 1815 they found themselves disowned by Ferdinand.

Inevitably the administration began to suffer. A counter-terrorism was organized by Prince Canosa in January–June 1816 against the Carbonari, which led to such dislocation that it was called off by the government and order restored with Austrian aid. Under the ministry of Luigi dei Medici the government adopted a moderate policy, and in 1817 the Austrians were able to withdraw. In July 1817 in order to maintain public order Medici organized a militia, composed of volunteers officered by the local proprietors. This measure, designed to prevent further Austrian occupation, the costs of which would be borne by the Neapolitan treasury, in fact placed arms in the hands of the enemies of the régime. The landed proprietors were hard hit by the competition of cheap Russian grain from Odessa, against which Medici refused to afford tariff protection. Demands arose for constitutional reform, especially in Sicily where an experimental constitution had been adopted under the British occupation during the war. In 1820 the revolt broke out in Spain and excited the fears of the government. Medici therefore determined to kill the opposition in its early stages. Precautionary arrests were made in order to avoid an Austrian intervention, but all that Medici succeeded in doing was to provoke an uprising in July 1820. By 6 July the Bourbon régime was overthrown and a constitutional system put in its place upon the basis of the Spanish system of 1812.

The Intervention in Naples

The revolt in Naples filled Austria with alarm. The British state paper of 1820 stated that intervention in the internal affairs of European states ought to be avoided, but it was undeniably true that the revolution in Naples threatened to upset the Vienna settlement in Italy. Privately it was the view of the British government that action might be undertaken, but that it should be the task of Austria alone and not of the Quadruple Alliance. It was a principle of Austrian foreign policy, however, never to act alone, because isolated action by Austria had in the past proved disastrous. On 26 July 1820 Austria appealed to Russia for aid. Alexander I accepted Austria's plea, because it presented him with an opportunity to establish the principle of a European intervention for the maintenance of the *status quo*, which might be applied elsewhere. Metternich, however, viewed with suspicion Alexander's proposal of a conference of the powers. Metternich did not wish to move without Britain, but Britain was troubled with domestic difficulties arising from the dispute of the King with his wife, Queen Caroline, and could not add to her difficulties at home by open participation in an intervention which might prove unpopular. When on 12 October 1820 Britain refused to send a plenipotentiary to the conference of the powers, but merely agreed to allow the ambassador in Vienna to attend as an observer, Metternich finally accepted Russia's offer of aid. Britain's policy was obviously at variance with that of Russia, but Castlereagh was prepared to avoid bringing this difference out into the open in order to preserve the outward unity of the Quadruple Alliance. The new Neapolitan government showed a clear understanding of its position, and on 1 October 1820 declared it intended to respect the integrity of neighbouring states. In theory the case for intervention, according to the British argument, no longer existed. For the European states there was a clash of principle, whether or not to intervene.

The Conference of Troppau, October 1820

When the representatives of the powers arrived in Troppau for their discussions in October 1820, the Tsar, Alexander I, had not clearly defined his policy. It was open to the powers either to preserve the rule of the Bourbons or to carry out some reform in Naples and Sicily which would satisfy the opposition. The Russian minister, the Greek Capodistrias, wanted reform on the lines of the French constitution, but this was opposed by Metternich lest it serve as a precedent for the rest of Italy. Capodistrias and Metternich struggled for the ear of the Tsar. The mind of the Tsar was made up by an untoward event, the mutiny of the Semënovsky Guards in Russia. Alexander at first inclined towards the view of Capodistrias, but any tsar who surveyed the history of Russia since the death of Peter the Great might feel nervous when a revolt occurred among the Guards, who in the eighteenth century had been responsible for so many coups d'état; in fact, the Semënovsky mutiny was little more than a protest against excessive spit-and-polish and drill, but it was enough to induce Alexander I to adopt a more conservative attitude and accept Metternich's view. In these circumstances there was drawn up the Preliminary Protocol of 19 November 1820, which established principles of action. It was declared that the states forming part of the European alliance system, if changed by revolution and constituting a menace to other states, should cease to form part of the alliance. The allies might refuse, if they wished, to recognize internal changes and bring such states back into the alliance by representations and in the last resort by coercion. The King of Naples was therefore invited to consult with the powers at Laibach (Lubliana). To these principles Great Britain refused her assent.

The Conference at Laibach, January 1821

Once removed from the control of the revolution by his attendance at Laibach, King Ferdinand obtained liberty of action. The moderates in Naples under Carascosa were willing to modify the Spanish constitution of 1812, which had initially been adopted, to the extent of creating two chambers, imposing a property franchise and granting extensive powers to the king in the hope of inducing Austria to accept the revolution, but the extremists forced the king to swear fidelity to the Spanish constitution as a condition of his leaving for Laibach. At the conference Austria, Prussia and Russia were prepared to accept the King's plea for intervention, but the British representative declared his opposition to an intervention which was announced to have the authority of 'les souverains alliés'. On 19 January 1821 Britain made a formal public protest against an action which was represented as having no authority in international law. Castlereagh objected to the abstract principles of Metternich and Alexander I, but he had no wish to overthrow the Vienna settlement in Italy. George IV and Wellington, however, gave their private approval for Austrian action which seemed to show that Castlereagh's public objections carried very little weight. As the intervention was launched against Naples the situation in Italy was unexpectedly complicated on 10 March by a revolution in Piedmont. Piedmont was outside the Austrian field of influence and the patriotic nobility, with the prince of Carignano, Charles Albert, at their head, raised the standard of revolt in their annoyance at the intervention. Victor Emmanuel I abdicated and in the absence of his successor, Charles Felix, Charles Albert, as head of the junior line of the Savoyard dynasty, exercised the powers of regent. This untoward event gave rise to fears of French intervention, because like Britain, France had refused to be associated with intervention, though for the reason that France could not give her endorsement to a step which seemed to restore the system of 1815. In his anxiety Alexander I offered Metternich a Russian army.

The Austrian intervention proceeded almost without incident. On 24 March 1821 Naples was occupied by Austrian troops and the old régime restored. Charles Felix of Piedmont-Sardinia refused to endorse the action of Charles Albert of Carignano. Austrian troops were called in to restore order in Piedmont and the *status quo* in Italy was re-established. Internationally the intervention in Naples was of great importance. A precedent had been made for intervention in the internal affairs of sovereign states. A fresh conference was to be called for 1822 to reconsider the Italian question, and it was obvious that the problem of Spain would then be discussed. Metternich, glad to have the aid of Russia in Italy, looked with much less favour upon an intervention in Spain, which he considered to fall within the British field of interest. He was therefore less disposed to join with Russia in proposing intervention, because he would need the support of Britain in the event of Russia's intervening in the Balkans.

From the Italian point of view the suppression of the insurrection meant the revelation of Austria's role in Italy with brutal clarity. From the point of view of Italian nationalists nothing could be achieved until Austria was driven out of Italy. Charles Albert of Carignano, who was to occupy the throne of Piedmont-Sardinia from 1831 to 1849, gained from the episode an unwarranted reputation for being a true Italian patriot. Beneath his apparent concern for Italy lay the traditional Savoyard desire for the expansion of Piedmont in the Po valley, which could obviously take place only at the expense of Austria. The coincidence of Italian middle-class aspirations and the expansionist policy of Piedmont was for the moment not of great importance, but in the future it was to contain the elements of tragedy. The House of Savoy was no more liberal than the House of Habsburg.

The Greek Revolt of 1821

While the powers sat in conference at Laibach news arrived of an outbreak of revolt among the Greeks against the Turks. The position of the Greek nation had been transformed by the Napoleonic Wars. They and the Italian shipmasters had gained control of the lucrative grain trade between the Russian ports on the Black Sea and the Mediterranean. It was they who filled the vacuum created by the disappearance of French commerce in the Levant while Britain held mastery of the seas. In 1789 there were eighty-one rich commercial houses at Marseilles, but in 1816 only twenty-three were still in existence. The French were not unnaturally anxious to re-establish their position, but they now found a new rival in Britain, who possessed the island of Malta and exercised tutelary powers in the Ionian Islands. A rising in Greece was equally disturbing to Alexander I and to Metternich, neither of whom in 1821 wished for complications in south-eastern Europe.

The basis of the Greek revolt was the patriotic association of merchants, the Philike Hetairia. The revolt began in two stages. In the March of 1821 Prince Alexander Ypsilanti raised the standard of revolt in Moldavia, to the intense disgust of Alexander I, whom as a Russian officer he served as an adjutant. His action seemed to give the revolt almost official Russian approval, but this was obviously not given. Alexander I would never have permitted independent action in an area in which vital Russian interests were involved. In fact, Ypsilanti's adventure was ill-considered and ill-starred. Moldavia was dominated by the local Rumanian boyars and a host of Phanariot Greeks, whom the native population disliked with considerable intensity as agents of the Turks. Nevertheless, the Rumanian leader, Tudor Vladimirescu, was willing to consider collaboration with the Greeks, but Ypsilanti underestimated the possibilities which a Rumanian peasant movement might open up to him and did not respond to Vladimirescu's approaches. In consequence, the Greek revolt in Moldavia collapsed for want of mass support in June and

Ypsilanti fled to be interned in an Austrian fortress, disavowed by Alexander I. His action, however, caused a revolt in sympathy in the Morea. The Turkish order of 14 May 1821 for the pre-emption of foreign produce within the straits in order to obtain supplies for the army hit the Greek shipowners, and the ferment then extended itself to all Greece and the islands of the Aegean. The Russian ambassador, Stroganov, had tried to induce the Greeks not to revolt and persuaded the Patriarch to declare against the national movement, but riots broke out in Constantinople among the Greek population which led to the Turks executing the Patriarch. A campaign of Turkish reprisals was begun in the Morea which seemed likely to assume the proportions of a wholesale massacre. With very great reluctance Russia was compelled to intervene. In July 1821 Stroganov presented a four-point ultimatum, demanding the strict fulfilment of the treaties; this in effect, meant that Turkey was required to uphold the co-existence of the Christian and Islamic religions, but on 18 July Turkey rejected the Russian demands. Stroganov therefore withdrew from Constantinople, and with this rupture of diplomatic relations war between Russia and the Ottoman Empire seemed imminent. In the pro-Turkish attitude of Lord Strangford, the British ambassador, the Porte sensed the beginning of a crisis in Anglo-Russian relations. The basis of British policy was Article XI of the Anglo-Turkish treaty of 5 January 1809 which reaffirmed the principle that no foreign vessels of war might enter either the Dardanelles or the Bosphorus in time of peace; the object of British policy was to prevent Russian warships from the Black Sea entering the Aegean and Mediterranean. Russian policy was equally well defined by the treaties of Kutchuk Kajnardji (1774), Jassy (1792) and Bucharest (1812), the instruments of peace which had brought the Russian frontier to the line of the Pruth and the mouth of the Danube; in these treaties Russia had extra-territorial rights, which made the Tsar the protector of the Christian subjects of the Porte and gave him specific interests in the Principalities and in Serbia. In this situation Prussia was neutral, but Austria, normally in agreement with Russia in Central Europe, did not wish to see the extension of Russian influence on her eastern and southern frontiers. Metternich's advice to the Sultan was that he should withdraw his troops from the Principalities and concentrate upon the suppression of the revolt in the Morea. Castlereagh, alarmed by

Russian bellicosity, advocated that Russia should adopt a policy of caution, for fear of disrupting the alliance; this was little less than a proposal that the Russians should allow the Greek revolt to be extinguished. There was a coincidence of aims in Austrian and British policy, which resulted in an informal entente, cemented by the meeting in Hanover between Metternich and Castlereagh, under which the two powers decided to work for the maintenance of peace between Russia and Turkey and at the same time to place pressure upon the Porte to moderate its behaviour. Faced with the possibility of isolation in the Near East, Alexander I took the decision to defer action until after the proposed conference of the powers in the autumn of 1822. The Tsar thus inclined towards the policy of caution advocated by Nesselrode rather than the forward policy represented by Capodistrias, who was in favour of breaking up the Ottoman Empire in the Balkans.

Spain and the Congress of Verona

When the representatives of the powers met at Verona in October 1822 the situation in Spain was becoming more acute. In the struggles between the king, Ferdinand VII, and the moderates extremists of all sides began to gain in influence and the condition of the country degenerated into anarchy. The Villèle ministry in France and the foreign minister, Montmorency, perceived an opportunity for France to intervene to crush liberalism and gain influence. In order to give assistance to the royalists the French government began to build up in the south an army of intervention under the pretext that it was necessary to establish a *cordon sanitaire* against the spread of disease into France. In May 1822 the Spanish liberal government protested, but the king appealed to the allied sovereigns. The response of the Tsar was a proposal for the creation of a European army to re-establish peace in the country, which would create a precedent for intervention in the Greek question, but Britain knew that a European army of intervention would inevitably be a French one. The French government, however, desired no European commission, but for reasons of prestige intended rather to secure independence of action. The situation became very tense when the king's Guards unsuccessfully attempted a coup d'état. The de la Rosa ministry was replaced with a fresh ministry which was much more extreme in its outlook.

Castlereagh in drawing up instructions for the Congress of Verona divided the question into two aspects. With regard to European Spain he was prepared to act to secure the personal safety of the King, but in Portugal he excluded all interference. On the other hand, he held the view that the South American situation, in which Britain had vital interests, was completely separate. In the United States opinion was strongly in favour of recognizing the Spanish American colonies and the Secretary of State, John Quincy Adams, came under attack for alleged subservience to Spain. In May 1820 Henry Clay carried a motion in favour of recognition, but Adams was compelled to restrain the United States cabinet. His main concern was with Florida, of which the United States wished to complete the purchase from Spain and which was at length ratified in February 1821. Adams wished to act with caution, and in April 1821 he had approached the British ambassador, Stratford Canning, with an inquiry whether Britain could join with the United States in a common policy. In March 1822, however, a presidential message to Congress recommended recognition and the president received authority to send, at his discretion, diplomatic missions to South America. On 19 June 1822 the representative of Colombia was received and the Colombian leader, Zea, therefore threatened to close Colombian ports to states which did not recognize Colombia. The action of the United States placed Britain in a curious position. The European situation required caution, but the forward policy of the United States demanded initiative on the part of Britain. The case for commercial recognition was strong. In a note of 3 May 1822 to Spain Castlereagh stated that some recognized and established relations with South America were required and was clearly tending himself towards a policy of recognition. Undoubtedly he could have carried out this policy, possessing as he did the confidence of George IV and the cabinet, but a personal tragedy engulfed him. On 12 August 1822 he committed suicide. His successor, Canning, was distrusted by both the king and the cabinet. Britain's recognition, therefore, of the insurgent South American colonies of Spain was postponed, but a change now appeared in European diplomacy. Much has been made of the differences in the policies of Castlereagh and Canning. The policies were in fact identical, but the methods of Canning were not the same. He was less concerned with conciliating the European powers and acting in concert with them. Thus under Canning British policy became more adventurous.

The Congress of Verona, October 1822

The British representative, Wellington, attended the Congress carrying with him the instructions of. Castlereagh. With regard to the Greek question he was to attempt to preserve peace between Russia and Turkey and soften the rigour of the war between the Greeks and the Turks, but he was instructed to say that 'it may be difficult if a *de facto* government shall be established . . . to refuse it the ordinary privileges of a belligerent'; Castlereagh had therefore been moving towards a policy of recognition in the Greek question as well as in the question of the Spanish colonies. With regard to Spain, if the King could not restore his authority in South America Britain was to have 'an independent discretion to act according to the circumstances'; with regard to metropolitan Spain Wellington was to uphold the principle of non-intervention, which in effect meant that Ferdinand VII would be unable to deal with his domestic opposition and therefore lack the power to reimpose his authority in the New World.

It was France who created difficulties at Verona. Louis XVIII was now past his best, and the authority of the Crown tended to be exercised by the king's brother and heir to the throne, the Comte d'Artois, and his son, the Duc d'Angoulême. In September 1822 the Villèle ministry, which was to remain in power for six years, was determined to end the confusion which these circumstances created and to adopt a strong policy in Spain, which would appease the domestic critics of the government. Villèle and Montmorency were clear in their determination to avoid any kind of European intervention, which was a weapon which could be employed against France. On 20˙ October 1822 Montmorency posed three questions to the powers. Would they take similar action if France recalled her ambassador from Spain? Would the powers give moral support to France if she intervened in Spain? Would the powers give France assistance if she required it? Austria and Prussia agreed to sever diplomatic relations and give France moral support, but would give armed aid only if the other powers concerted with France. Russia offered full support, including an army of 150,000 to cover the rear of the French army against possible Jacobin revolution while the intervention was taking place, which was a suggestion most unwelcome to the French because it seemed to point to a basic political weakness in France and make Russia the protector of the dynasty precisely at a moment when it was seeking prestige. Only Wellington protested against intervention, which he declared to be an unnecessary assumption of responsibility, because the Spanish revolution was not likely to extend itself beyond the frontiers of Spain. The continental powers, however, decided to act without Britain. Russia, Austria and Prussia defined the *casus foederis* as arising if Spain attacked France, or deposed the King or carried on propaganda activities in France. On 30 November 1822 Wellington, refusing to be associated with this view, left Verona. The split in the Quadruple Alliance was complete.

The French Intervention in Spain

France now had the authority to manufacture a crisis in Spain, but at the same time she aroused the hostility of the British public and strengthened Canning's hand against the King. In a public speech in Harwich on 11 February 1823, an event in itself, because British ministers did not normally make speeches on foreign policy in provincial towns, Canning roundly condemned the French attitude, but he had already decided that Britain would go to war only if France tried to recover South America for Spain or invaded Portugal. In a despatch to Sir Charles Stuart in Paris of 31 March 1823, which was published on 5 April, Canning declared that there must be no permanent French military occupation of Spain, no appropriation of part of the Spanish colonies and no violation of Portuguese territory. This was a virtual ultimatum, and it received no French reply. On 6 April 1823 the French army invaded Spain.

The French army did not find much difficulty in disposing of the Spanish opposition. Liberalism was a feature virtually of two towns only, Madrid and Cadiz. Not for the first time, however, was France to become enmeshed in a web of her own weaving. The French army entered Spain with the intention of securing from Ferdinand VII an amnesty for political offences and the grant of a modified constitution. This, it was thought, would be enough to satisfy the moderate left wing at home in France, but anti-liberal feeling in Spain had a popular basis. When Ferdinand was restored to power he indulged in a policy of political terror on a scale so large that the Russian ambassador, Pozzo di Borgo, who was not squeamish, described it as 'a royal anarchy'. The French commander-in-chief, Angoulême, departed for France rather than be associated with a régime so fanatically vengeful. The French troops remained in Spain until 1827, but France obtained no influence at the Spanish Court. For France her invention proved fruitless, while Britain lost nothing by her policy of non-intervention.

The Polignac Memorandum and the Monroe Doctrine

Upon the death of Castlereagh the position of Britain with regard to the American colonies of Spain which had seceded from the mother country was that she recognized their flags only. Castlereagh had attempted as far as possible to maintain friendly relations with Spain. Canning, his successor, however, was prepared to adopt a more positive policy. With regard to the dispute within Spain he assumed an attitude of neutrality, even when the constitutionalists attempted to purchase his assistance with trading concessions. When the French army invaded the peninsula Canning offered them nothing more than his moral support, but when on 10 October 1823 he was informed of the fall of Cadiz he decided that the influence of France might extend itself to the New World and that he therefore ought to take active steps towards the recognition of the new republics. Consuls were therefore sent to Spanish America and special commissions of inquiry were appointed to investigate conditions in Colombia and Mexico as preliminaries to granting them recognition as sovereign states.

Wellington had learned from Villèle in December 1822 that France would lend aid to Spain if she tried to recover Mexico and Peru. On 1 October 1823 Canning sought a clarification of the position from the French ambassador in London, Polignac. The result of their meetings was the 'Polignac Memorandum' of 9–12 October. This was a record of their conversations, in which Polignac for France gave what amounted to a French disclaimer of intention to intervene by force in South America or to annex territory there for herself, while Canning made a similar disclaimer and promised not to resort to recognition as long as there was a possibility that Spain might find some means of reconciling herself with her colonies. The Polignac Memorandum was the turning point in the history of Latin America.

It amounted to a warning to the European powers that Britain considered her vital interests involved and would not tolerate the interference of the European states. The memorandum was circularized to the powers and published in March 1824.

While Canning was placing pressure upon France he was extending the hand of friendship to the United States. Having no intention of bringing the Spanish American colonies under the oversight of the Concert of Europe, he turned to the United States ambassador, Rush, to strengthen his position. Rush was asked in August 1823 if there were any possibility of a common understanding. Rush was without instructions and could give no definite reply to Canning's inquiry whether he could sign a convention to maintain a policy of nonintervention. On 31 August 1823 Canning informed Rush that he could not tie Britain's hands for the moment and asked him to consider the proposals that he had made to be those which he should have liked to make if he were at liberty to do so. Rush's reports were clear enough to give his government in Washington the impression that the British government was veering towards a policy of recognition and that in the last resort Britain would appeal to force in order to prevent European intervention in South America. In other words, the whole power of the British fleet would be interposed between Europe and the New World. An unsolicited expression of thanks by the Russian ambassador in Washington, Baron Tuyll, revealed the existence of differences in Europe; the Tsar, who was unwilling to receive ministers and agents of the new states, expressed his satisfaction at United States neutrality. President Monroe was worried by the prospect of conflict, but the Secretary of State, John Quincy Adams, professed unconcern. His view was that if the British fleet stood between America and Europe no power in Europe would dare to intervene and that this situation should not be allowed to pass without some expression of United States policy. He declared on 7 November that 'it would be more candid as well as more dignified to avow our principles explicitly to Russia and France than to come in as a cockboat in the wake of the British man of war'.

Monroe accepted Adams' point of view and on 2 December 1823 delivered his celebrated message to Congress, which enunciated what has since come to be known as the Monroe Doctrine. The message contained two main principles: the American continent was not to be regarded as a place of colonization by any European state; and interference with the liberty of the South American colonies would be regarded as 'a manifestation of unfriendly disposition towards the United States'. There is no evidence for the nineteenth-century legend that Monroe acted upon the prompting of Canning, who was in fact very angry that the United States anticipated British policy in order to gain credit for herself with the Spanish American states. It was made plain to Rush in London that the doctrine expounded by Monroe was not one which had any practical application. Rush was asked on 24 January 1824 what the United States' attitude would be if Great Britain planted a colony on the North or the South American mainland, a question to which neither Rush nor Monroe could give an answer. In 1823 the Monroe doctrine had no significance. Forty years later it was to have considerable significance when the United States had grown in power and could back her policy with armed force. The publication of the Polignac Memorandum in March 1824 left the South American states in no doubt that they owed more to Canning than to Monroe.

By the summer of 1824 Canning was coming under the pressure of the British merchant classes for recognition of the new states. Canning's view was that early recognition of Colombia and Mexico was necessary in order to prevent the growth of the United States' influence and proposed, moreover, that a consul-general should be sent to Buenos Ayres. At length, on 14 December 1824, the British cabinet decided to deal with the question of recognition without the concurrence of the continental powers, a decision which was taken only after a threat by Lord Liverpool, the prime minister, and Canning that they would resign if their recommendation to this effect were not accepted. The king, George IV, tried to prevent a policy which seemed to him the encouragement of republicanism, but the British cabinet, divided as they were, stood no truck from him. Canning took immediate steps to recognize the governments in Buenos Ayres, Mexico and Peru, which had achieved some stability and already had won *de facto* independence of Spain, but left open the question of recognition where fighting was still in progress. The formal announcement of Britain's recognition was not completed without comic incident. The King's speech on 7 February 1825 was to be made the vehicle for announcing recognition, but the King, irritated because he had been overridden, declared that he could not make the speech on the grounds that he had lost his false teeth; the speech was therefore read by the lord chancellor, Eldon, the principal opponent of Canning within the British cabinet. Russia, Prussia and Austria might protest, but at the conferences of Troppau, Laibach and Verona they had ignored British views and therefore could not stand very well in their protests against Britain's action in South America.

Canning was to boast in his speech of 12 December 1826: 'I called the New World into existence to redress the balance of the Old.' There was an element of exaggeration in this statement, but he had undoubtedly gained a great diplomatic victory for Britain. Metropolitan Spain was separated from her colonies, and a claim upon the good will of the political class in South America had been made. South America became part of what may be termed 'the invisible empire' of Britain, in the sense that Britain became the dominant commercial power without having to bear any of the costs of administering fresh territories. The brilliance of Canning's success, however, should not be allowed to conceal the fact that the emancipation of Latin America in the form it is known today was not an unmixed blessing. It was not the peoples of these countries who won their independence, but the Spanish upper classes, who were thus able to rule the roost without any check from the government of metropolitan Spain. British capital investment might assist in the development of the richer parts of South America, but the common people did not always reap much benefit from it.

Britain, Russia and the Eastern Question

In the crisis of international relations caused by the revolution in Spain and the anxiety of Britain to prevent the European powers from intervening in the New World the problem of Greece temporarily receded into the background. This question was virtually ignored by the congress of Verona in 1822. Before his death Castlereagh had admitted that it would be difficult to refuse *de facto* recognition to the Greeks, and in March 1823 Canning granted them belligerent rights to the annoyance of Russia and Austria. Canning's motive, on the one hand, was to protect British commerce from Greek piracy and, on the other hand, to please the British middle classes, who were infected with a pro-Greek feeling which saw in the revolt against

Turkey the regeneration of an ancient civilization. Unilateral action by Canning, however, did not mean that he intended to adopt an attitude of hostility towards Russia. His aim was to induce Russia to restore normal relations with Turkey by the restitution of the Russian embassy at Constantinople. Alexander I was as ever cautious and hesitated to adopt an independent policy which might cause a breakdown in Russia's relations with Austria. Metternich was conscious that the collapse of Turkish rule in the Balkans would lead to the construction of independent Slav states on Austria's southern frontier, which was pregnant with alarming possibilities; the southern regions of the Austrian Empire were inhabited predominantly with Slavs. The expansion of Serbia, in particular, might lead to the creation of a new and dangerous situation in which the Serbs, Croats and Slovenes of the Empire might seek unity with their fellow Slavs south of the frontier. It would be unwise to over-emphasize this factor in the 1820s, but it was clear that some feeling of brotherhood already existed. The breakdown of the Ottoman Empire in Europe, therefore, might lead to the emergence of a problem akin to that which had made its appearance in Italy in 1820–1. In September 1823 Alexander I met the Emperor Francis I at Czernowitz and as a conciliatory measure agreed to send a commercial attaché to Constantinople, but he could not entirely ignore Russian feeling. Within Russian official circles there was a fellow-feeling for the Orthodox Christians of Turkey which had very deep roots. Alexander I therefore in January 1824 submitted to the powers a *mémoire* in which he proposed the creation of three Greek principalities, paying tribute to the Porte and garrisoned by Turkish troops. This at least was a concrete proposal, but it satisfied neither Greeks nor Turks. It disposed of more territory than was actually under Greek control, while the Greeks by the constitution of Epidauros of 1822 claimed independence for all Greece. A conference of the powers' representatives in St Petersburg failed to produce results. Austria wished to spin out discussions until the Greek revolt was crushed. Canning had little enthusiasm for a solution imposed by a congress of the powers, which might place him in the position of appearing to co-operate with the autocratic states; if all else failed, he was ready to collaborate with Russia in a policy of intervention in order that by formal association with her he might obtain some control over her actions. As late as November 1824, however, he was pressing Russia to send an ambassador to Constantinople and renounce the use of force.

In December 1824 the situation was transformed. The Sultan, Mahmoud, unable to make progress against the Greeks, decided to call upon the aid of the pasha of Egypt, Mehemet Ali. In the Ottoman Empire the pashas, who governed the provinces, enjoyed considerable independence of the central government in Constantinople, and Mehemet Ali had pressed this independence to the point where he was virtually a sovereign ruler in his own right. Certainly he possessed the most efficient army in the Turkish Empire. Promised rewards by the Sultan for aid in Greece, Mehemet Ali expanded the horizons of his ambitions. From 1801 he had been building up his resources in Egypt. With the aid of Sudanese troops he had taken possession of the Moslem holy cities of Mecca and Medina, and in the south had established Egyptian power in the Sudan with the foundation of Khartoum. The Sultan now offered him the Morea if he could reconquer it. Not unnaturally Mehemet Ali began to entertain visions of founding a great empire in the Levant. His son, Ibrahim Pasha, was sent with a force of 10,000 men first to Crete and then to the Morea, where they landed in February 1825. The Greeks were no match for the battle-seasoned troops of the Egyptians and there was no prospect of their surviving if the great powers did not give them immediate assistance. The British cabinet hesitated. Wellington had no love for Russia, whom he suspected of expansionist ambitions, but Canning was willing to evolve a plan of joint action with Russia. It was difficult to reach an agreement with Russia which would satisfy both parties. The dilatoriness of Britain was swept away once and for all on 1 December 1825 when the Tsar Alexander I died unexpectedly at Taganrog and was succeeded by Nicholas I, his youngest brother, the second son of Paul I, Constantine, having foregone his claims to the throne in order to contract a morganatic marriage. A new tsar meant a new policy, which was not long left in doubt.

Nicholas I of Russia and the Eastern Question

On the death of Alexander I Russia was for the moment thrown into confusion. A military revolt was being planned during Alexander I's reign, which had as its aim the modernization of Russia. The conspirators belonged to the progressive element among the Russian gentry and aristocracy, whose eyes had been opened by personal observation of what had happened in Europe as a result of the French Revolution. These were the men who had served in the Russian army which had driven Napoleon out of Russia and pursued him to Paris. They were acutely aware that Russia in her social organization was less advanced than the countries of the west. Among them grew a desire for the complete reform of Russia, the liberation of the serfs, the introduction of civil equality, freedom of the press and religion, the reform of the army upon the basis of universal military service, the abolition of tax exemptions and the establishment of a just judicial system. The unexpected death of Alexander I and the obscurities which surrounded Constantine's renunciation of the throne caught the conspirators unawares. At first it was thought that Constantine would succeed, but he confirmed his renunciation, and it was only on 26 December 1825 that Nicholas I was formally acknowledged as the Tsar-Autocrator. The military conspirators acted with great haste, and on the night of 25–26 December 1925 a coup d'état was attempted in St Petersburg, in which the soldiers of the garrison were called upon to declare for Constantine and refuse allegiance to Nicholas I. The whole day of 26 December was one of disorder in St Petersburg, and with some luck Nicholas I was able to impose his authority. A movement in sympathy by one regiment in the Ukraine in January 1826 was quickly crushed. The so-called Decembrist movement was a flash in the pan, but it revealed to Nicholas I that Tsarism could survive in Russia only if the Tsar himself ruled with energy. By temperament Nicholas I was fitted for this role. Resolution at home and a forward foreign policy abroad were the means by which he was determined to preserve the prestige of the dynasty. Even before his accession his characteristics were well known in the west. Popularly he has often supposed to have been a black reactionary. It is difficult to compare an autocratic monarch with a constitutional sovereign. The real comparison is between Nicholas I and the monarchs of the eighteenth century, who both ruled and reigned with the aid of a loyal bureaucratic class and the support of the army. In spite of an accession marred by a military insurrection, Nicholas I quickly established his authority in the army. Not until 1917 did a tsar lose the loyalty of a considerable section of his armed forces.

The circumstances of Nicholas I's accession explain a momentary wavering in the foreign policy of Russia. On 26 December 1825 Nesselrode informed the powers that the new government would follow the principles adopted by Alexander I, which gave satisfaction to Austria and Prussia, but on 1 January 1826 Nicholas I received the diplomatic corps and informed them that he was not 'in a position to give any sort of guarantee concerning the future line of activity, in spite of the purity of his intentions and determination to follow in the steps of his predecessor'. A new uncertainty now enveloped Russian policy. It appeared that a fresh definition was about to be given to the Holy Alliance, by which the monarchs were to be called upon to assist in the liberation of the Christians from the Turks. The Duke of Wellington and the Archduke Ferdinand d'Este were despatched to congratulate the Tsar upon his accession, but with the important task also of seeking clarification concerning his attitude towards the Greek Question. Wellington was empowered to conclude an agreement with Russia for interference by force, if it should be required, to bring about a settlement of the war in Greece. To this proposal Nicholas I readily agreed, and the St Petersburg Protocol of 4 April 1826 was signed by which Russia and Britain undertook to mediate in the dispute between the Greeks and the Ottoman Empire. The Greeks were to be allowed to form a state, which would be tributary to the Sultan, but should have full internal self-government; the Porte was to have a share in the nomination of the ruler. Apparently Britain and Russia had concerted to find a solution, but Russian policy had a subtlety which circumvented the normal procedures of a concert of two powers.

On 5 April 1826 Russia presented an ultimatum to the Porte, which demanded the evacuation of the Principalities of Moldavia and Wallachia, the release of Serbian representatives who had been imprisoned by the Turks and the agreement to meet in conference to discuss the implementation of the Russo-Turkish treaty of Bucharest of 1812. Russia thus separated the Greek and Balkan questions. In Greece and the Aegean she was willing to act with Britain, but north of the Balkan range she was ready to act alone. Britain and Austria placed pressure upon the Porte to acquiesce lest a war should break out, and as a result conversations between Russia and Turkey were opened at Akkerman in July 1826. At first the Turks showed little disposition to come to any agreement. The crisis was enlarged on 28 July 1826, when the Persians launched an attack upon the Russian posts in the Caucasus.

Hostilities between Russia and Persia had gone intermittently from 1804 to 1813, when they were brought to an end by the peace of Teheran. The Persians realized that they could not defeat Russia without the aid of another European power and had turned to Britain, or rather to the Governor-General of India, within whose province British foreign policy in Middle Eastern affairs then lay. The Persian army was reformed with an annual subsidy of £150,000 and the introduction of European methods of warfare. When the troubles began in the Balkans the Persians saw an excellent opportunity to seek a solution of their frontier disputes with Russia. The Persian attack opened in the area of the khanate of Erivan against the small force of Russian soldiers, amounting to some 3,000 men, who held the Russian frontier. In April 1827 General Ivan Paskevich was sent to the Caucasian front, and after a long siege in October captured the Persian fortress town of Erivan. In February 1828 the Persians signed the peace of Turkmanchay, by which they agreed to cede to Russia the khanates of Erivan and Nakhichevan and to pay an indemnity of 20,000,000 silver roubles. They agreed also to receive a Russian embassy in Teheran. Griboyedov, the first Russian minister, was in fact murdered in February 1829 in Teheran, but fresh war did not result. Russia was now firmly established south of the Caucasus. Her problem was henceforth to gain control over the highlanders rather than look for opportunities of further gains from Persia.

For some weeks the Turks watched the progress of events in the Caucasus, but they soon became convinced that the Persians would not seriously embarrass the Russians, and accordingly on 7 October 1826 the Turkish representatives agreed to the convention of Akkerman, by which they confirmed the treaty of 1812, which contained all the provisions of the treaties of 1774 and 1795, agreed to make new arrangements to satisfy the Serbs and promised to restore the Principalities to the situation they had been in in 1802. The first essay of Nicholas I in the field of European diplomacy was therefore crowned with success. Russia's position in the Balkans was confirmed. The next move of Nicholas I was to induce Britain to offer armed aid to solve the Greek question, but here he met with difficulties. Canning visited Paris during September and October 1826, where he found Charles X, who had succeeded to the throne in 1824, anxious to associate France with Britain and Russia in the Near East as part of a policy of restoring French influence in the eastern Mediterranean. Co-operation between the three powers might have been agreed earlier, had it not been for the fluctuating conditions of British politics. In February 1827 the prime minister, Liverpool, suffered a stroke which totally incapacitated him. It was not until 10 April 1827 that Canning himself became prime minister at the head of a much weakened Tory administration. Only on 27 July 1827 was the treaty of London signed. The terms of the treaty were almost identical with those of the St Petersburg protocol, except that it was laid down that, if the Turks did not accept the mediation of the powers, consuls would be sent to Greece and, if an armistice were not accepted, the fleets of the three powers would be sent to blockade the Morea and to intercept Turkish and Egyptian supplies. It was understood that the powers would, if possible, avoid hostilities, but the conclusion of the treaty revived the flagging spirits of the Greeks, who elected as their president Capodistrias, now no longer in Russian employ. The Greeks, however, did not increase their military pressure upon the Turks and Egyptians, who therefore felt under no compulsion to accept the allied mediation. The British, French and Russian admirals consequently were given instructions to blockade the Morea. Canning died on 8 August 1827 and did not live to see the consequences of his policy. On 12 September the allies found the Turkish and Egyptian fleets at anchor at Navarino in the Morea. Ibrahim Pasha refused to evacuate the Morea, and on 20 October the allies decided to intimidate him by entering the bay as if prepared for battle. The Egyptians fired upon a boat approaching them under a flag of truce, and a general engagement ensued in which the Egyptian and Turkish fleets were destroyed. It had been the policy of Britain only to compel the Turks to accept mediation. The battle of Navarino not only seriously weakened Turkey but also deepened the whole crisis. The Greeks could not defeat Ibrahim Pasha, who was now unable to leave the Morea. The Turks for their part unwisely repudiated the convention of Akkerman in protest against the participation of the Russian fleet in the battle. Wellington, who became prime minister in Britain in January 1828, had been out of sympathy with

Canning's policy and had refused to serve under him when he had formed his ministry in April 1827, but he had no alternative except to continue with the course which Canning had set for him. To his annoyance he discovered in March 1828 that the Russians now intended to make war on their own account north of the Balkan range on the grounds that the Turks had repudiated the convention of Akkerman. The attitude of the Tsar was that the Greek and Balkan questions were completely separate.

The Establishment of Greek Independence

On 24 April 1828 Russia declared war upon the Ottoman Empire. While this war was being fought, Wellington was compelled to find a way out of the entanglement in Greece. On 19 July it was agreed that France should send troops to land in the Morea to compel Ibrahim Pasha to submit. The confused situation excited the sarcasm of Metternich. Russia was at war with the Ottoman Empire. France was waging war on land, but maintaining an attitude of neutrality upon the sea. Britain was the ally of both France and Russia, but up to February 1828 had been supporting Persia in her struggle with Russia in the Caucasus. The solution of the Greek problem indeed proceeded on its desultory way. Admiral Codrington concluded the convention of Alexandria with Mehemet Ali on 6 August 1828, by which he agreed to withdraw his forces from the Morea, leaving only a token force of 1,200 men, but the French assaulted the Egyptian positions in the Morea and arranged their own armistice with Ibrahim Pasha, which the Turkish *reis effendi* agreed to accept unofficially, because Turkish troops were being sent north to fight the Russians in the Balkans. France and Britain found it difficult to agree upon the extent of the new Greek state. The ambassadors in Constantinople on 12 December 1828 proposed a line from the Gulf of Arta to the Gulf of Volo as the northern frontier of Greece, together with the islands of Negropont (Euboea) and Samos; it was recommended also that Crete (Candia) should be given to Greece. The Greek state should pay a tribute of 1,500,000 piastres a year to the Porte. This was far more territory than Wellington wished to grant. It was only after the Turkish defeat in the war against Russia that the Turks themselves were willing to accept the mediation proposed in the treaty of London. In February 1830 a final agreement was reached. The new state was granted the Arta–Volo frontier, but this left Thessaly and Janina under Turkish rule; the islands of Crete and Samos likewise remained under Turkish rule. The Greeks were required to content themselves with possession of the Cyclades. In fact, the Greeks were content with nothing. The Greek president, Capodistrias, tried to rule the new state in accordance with the methods of the Russian bureaucracy and excited criticism for his nepotism. In October 1831 he was assassinated, and the Prince Otto of Bavaria was by the international agreement of the three protecting powers, Britain, Russia and France, made king of Greece in May 1832. King Otto was no better than Capodistrias. Into Greece he imported the ideas of a German princeling and his own Bavarian officials to carry them out. It was surprising indeed that he should have held his throne so long. In 1843 he submitted to the indignity of drawing up a constitution, and it was not until 1862 that he was compelled to abdicate.

The Russo-Turkish War 1828–9

North of the Balkan range the Russians were determined to secure a victory to force the Turks to confirm their rights under the treaties of 1774, 1795 and 1812. The campaign of 1828 did not make much progress, but in July 1829 General Diebitsch succeeded in crossing the Balkan range and marched in the direction of the Straits. The Sultan requested an armistice, which the Russians were glad to grant him. The Russian expedition was not more than a flying column. Out of the 40,000 men who began the march, only 12,000 were under arms by the time the column arrived at Adrianople, so heavy were the losses from sickness. On 14 September 1829 Russia and the Porte concluded the peace of Adrianople. The treaties were confirmed. In Europe the Ottoman Empire ceded the territory between the Kilia and St George mouths of the Danube, a gain for Russia of both economic and strategic importance. In Asia the Porte confirmed Russia's gains under the treaty of Turkmanchay with Persia and agreed to the cession of Akhaltsikh and Akhalkaki, which rounded off the annexations at the expense of Persia. The Turks, moreover, surrendered Guria and the possession of the long coastline from the south of the Kuban river, which the Porte had held. This latter gain was of great importance because the wild Circassians were now cut off from the sea and could henceforth be dealt with at leisure by the

Russian army. Equally important was the Turkish agreement to a Russian occupation of the Principalities for five years. Russia had every reason to be satisfied with these gains. The prospect of victory had already led Nicholas I and his advisers to a reappraisal of their policy towards Turkey. On 16 September 1829 a committee of ministers made its submission to the Tsar. Its recommendation was that in future Russian policy should attempt to bolster up the Ottoman Empire:

> The advantages of maintaining the Ottoman Empire are greater than the inconveniences it causes.

A weak state in a condition of partial decomposition, as the Ottoman Empire was, represented no danger to Russia, but the partition of Turkey might lead to some more efficient state being created in its place. Henceforth it was to be Russian policy to uphold the authority of the Sultan. Talk of the historic drive of Russia towards Constantinople might be current in Britain and even have its supporters in Russia, but the seizure of the Straits was a desperate remedy which Russia considered desirable only in the event of a complete disintegration of the Ottoman Empire. Just as Russia sought to maintain the *status quo* in Central Europe, so now in south-eastern Europe it was her intention to sustain it, even though Christian peoples remained under Moslem rule. Russian policy as ever was guided by reason of state rather than by ideologies.

The Revolutions of 1830

I. FRANCE UNDER THE BOURBON RESTORATION AND THE JULY REVOLUTION

The restored Bourbons survived as the rulers of France only until July 1830. After the Hundred Days Louis XVIII returned to Paris and resumed his throne. The basic difficulty which confronted him was his own past. While he might comfort himself with the thought that he had never been anything else than King of France, the truth remained that during the years in which France had been transformed by the Revolution and the Empire he had been the leader of the *émigrés* who had done everything in their power to harm their own country. With the return of Louis XVIII and the establishment of stability, the *émigrés*, whose leader was the Comte d'Artois, the king's brother and heir to the throne, appeared with the attitudes of mind which had caused the *Révolte Nobiliaire* before the revolution of 1789. The year 1814 had seen the possibility of reconciliation in France, but the Hundred Days of 1815 and Napoleon's second abdication brought about a White Terror, especially in the South of France. Revenge was taken upon the supporters of Napoleon. Ney, who had deserted to Napoleon, was executed. Royalism was from the outset tainted with terrorism. The one firm and solid grouping in French politics were the Ultras, the extreme royalists, under Artois, Polignac, Montmorency, Chateaubriand and Villèle, supported by the clericals Lamennais, de Maistre and Bonald, whose revivalism endowed the French church with an ultramontanism designed at freeing the clergy from the bondage which the Napoleonic Concordat had imposed upon them. The *émigrés* and the extreme right wing were intellectually out of tune with the new French society. Politically their programme from the outset contained an element of weakness which had little to do with ideology. With the Restoration the land settlement of the Revolution was upheld and the *émigrés* who had lost their estates were required to content themselves with the re-establishment of the monarchy, but the *émigrés* had chosen exile in the first instance because they had taken their stand upon the preservation of the privileges they had enjoyed under the Old Régime. Equality before the law and the failure of the new government to restore their estates led them into a state of exasperation which deprived them in many instances of the capacity for intelligible political thought.

The French Constitution of 1814, with its House of Peers and Chamber of Deputies, in theory ought to have given the extreme right wing political power, but it was combined with the Napoleonic administrative system in which the prefects ensured that candidates favourable to the régime could be returned. The franchise was exercised by persons who paid over 300 francs in direct taxes, which in effect meant that less than 100,000 persons had the vote. The voters chose electors for electoral colleges, who were required to choose deputies to the Chamber from persons who were over forty years of age and paid over 1,000 francs in direct taxes, of whom in France there were about 15,000. Obviously this was a system heavily weighted in favour of the propertied classes. In 1815, unfortunately, the chief ministers, Talleyrand and Fouché, were unable to exercise adequate control over the elections, with the consequence that a violently right-wing, reactionary and royalist Chamber of Deputies was elected, the *Chambre Introuvable*. Talleyrand and Fouché fell from power, and the Duc de Richelieu took office as President of the Council of Ministers. Richelieu was a hard-working official, who had served an apprenticeship in Russia as governor of Odessa, for which reason he was eminently acceptable to Alexander I. For all the difficulties which the Chamber gave him, Richelieu managed to pay off the indemnity and secure the evacuation of the foreign troops in occupation of French fortresses. Even more important for France was the dissolution of the Chamber in September 1818. The new Chamber of Deputies was much easier to manage, though Richelieu's administration, based upon a right-centrist grouping, gave way in December 1818 to the left-centrist government of Decazes. The policy of Decazes was based upon satisfying the moderates and those leftists who were satisfied with the gains which the Revolution and Empire had brought them. The extreme left never had significant representation under the restored Bourbons. The largest grouping in the Chamber was always the substantial landed proprietors, but they were almost equalled by officials who were open to pressure from the government. Trade, finance, industry and the professions were underrepresented in the French Chamber.

The political class, or *pays légal*, which enjoyed the vote and provided deputies to Parliament, was so small a section of the French nation that it could not represent all the national aspirations of France. A substantial section of the bourgeoisie remained outside the pale of the constitution. The traditional left-wing radicalism of the Jacobins was as yet scarcely a factor in French politics, and Bonapartism virtually non-existent except perhaps in the army. The astonishing feature of Restoration France was the fact that, though the method of election was indirect and the country controlled by the prefects, opposition did make its appearance in the Chamber. The elections of 1819 resulted in a victory of the left, but the assassination of the Duc de Berry, the son of the Comte d'Artois, in February 1820 brought down the government of Decazes, who was replaced by Richelieu. He imposed a severe censorship, doubled the vote of the men of substantial property and provided legislation for the arrest of suspected persons. From this moment the disenchantment with the Bourbon régime began, especially when the wife of the Duc de Berry gave birth in September 1820 to a son, which offered the prospect that the dynasty would continue to rule France for a long time. The child was sarcastically known as *l'enfant du miracle*. Only revolution could dispose of the Bourbons. Under the surface of French society an international revolutionary movement began to appear. The restoration of the Neapolitan Bourbons caused many Carbonarists to move to France and England, who established contacts in France with students, minor officials and young officers. Under the leadership of the student, Bazard, and the writer, Buchez, a Carbonarist movement grew up, based upon a series of *Ventes*, a French adaptation of the Italian *Venti*, or *Twenties*. The basic organization was composed of twenty members, the *Vente Particulière*, of which twenty were organized in a *Vente Centrale*. In their turn the *Ventes Centrales* were controlled by a *Vente Haute*, which owed allegiance to the *Vente Suprême*. In this way was set up a pyramid of associations. This underground movement, which is said to have gathered some 40,000 members, sought to establish contacts with other groups. Within the army some support was found, while La Fayette and Dupont de l'Eure flirted with the idea of an alliance with Carbonarism, but Richelieu soon found traces of this activity. The upper-class element deserted the movement, when they were warned by Richelieu that he knew that a plot was being hatched. In 1822 what was intended to be a rising throughout France was a failure. The army failed to respond to revolutionary appeals and the movement collapsed. This incident was of considerable significance. For the extreme left the dynasty was discredited and with it the moderate bourgeoisie under La Fayette. There followed a quiet period in left-wing circles in which study turned to the writings of Rousseau, Kant, Bentham and, above all, Saint-Simon. It was Saint-Simon who led the intellectuals of the French left into their first tentative association with the working class.

The French intellectuals were conscious that the nobility admired only their family trees. The big bourgeoisie tended to marry among themselves, secure in the fortunes made from the war. Isolated from the upper ranks of society, the intellectuals came to despise lineage and wealth and turned to the arts, science, history, painting and music, in which distinction was independent of birth and money. In the realm of political theory the writer who most attracted them was Henri Comte de Saint-Simon, a name redolent with the associations of the Old Régime, but whose writings set in motion a train of thought which was never to be suppressed. The fundamental concept of Saint-Simon's ideas was that 'politics based upon ethics and institutions of a people are nothing, but the application of its ideas'. In his view the eighteenth century had been destructive, whereas the new era should produce constructive thought in order to rebuild the organic society which the Revolution had destroyed. In the new society the certainties of the priest were to be replaced by the more soundly based assurances of the scientist. Humanity was now required to abandon the quest for original truth and look to the effective laws of social development. In Saint-Simon's *Réorganisation de la société européenne* science replaced the dogma which had inspired men in previous epochs. Property existed, but effective control must pass into the hands of the scientist. For this purpose an industrial parliament must be created in which there were to be three chambers, the Inventive, which provided a plan of development; the Examining Body, which scrutinized the plan; and the Executive Body, which carried the plan into effect. In modern terms this means no more than a state planning commission, a legislature and an executive; such a system would restrain the anti-social tendencies of the rich and condemn the individual search after wealth. The new industrial system was to be *Le Nouveau Christianisme*, or New Christianity, after the title of Saint-Simon's last book published in 1825, in which the pursuit of wealth was to be based upon a concept of brotherly love. It would be easy to criticize Saint-Simon for Utopianism, but long before the reality had made its appearance Saint-Simon had perceived the inevitable clash of capital and labour in the new industrial society and foresaw the need for planned production to avoid disorder. The writings of Saint-Simon assume a larger importance than they were generally given in their own day. Buchez, Louis Blanc, Fourier and Proudhon in their various ways took up the theme of Saint-Simon and developed Socialist theories of their own. As influential as Saint-Simon's work was the interest aroused by Buonarroti's *L'Histoire de la conspiration pour l'Egalité dite de Babeuf*, published in Brussels in 1828. Buonarroti opened the eyes of the French left to the forgotten conspiracy of Gracchus Babeuf of 1796, which amounted to nothing less than an attempt by an intellectual élite to lead the workers of Paris to the capture of political power and the imposition of social justice in place of the shallow corrupt system of the Directory. Already before 1830 there existed in Paris the germ of the idea that the French intellectuals of the city could seize power and exercise it for the good of mankind.

Outwardly the régime of the Bourbons appeared to be fixed upon firm foundations. In 1822 Richelieu once more resigned and was replaced by Villèle, who pursued a policy of financial reform in order to balance the budgets, but in 1824 Louis XVIII died and was succeeded by the Comte d'Artois as Charles X. Villèle, unlike Decazes and Richelieu, who saw their duty as Presidents of the Council of Ministers to be the co-ordination of the ministries, tended to work with the king alone. This was a system which suited Charles X, who desired in effect to be his own chief minister. The realities of politics no longer seemed to penetrate into the mind of the King. Gradually the clericals were extending their control over education. In 1821 the bishops were given control of secondary education, and in 1824 they obtained the right to nominate primary school teachers. In the same year Charles X had himself crowned with all the trappings of medieval splendour at Rheims. With his accession the appetites of the émigrés were whetted by the prospect that the king, their leader, would restore them to their confiscated property, but some 70,000 claimants were compelled to be satisfied with a fund which was to pay 3 per cent a year upon a total claim of 1,000,000,000 francs. This provided too little to satisfy the émigrés, but in view of the propertied classes, who saw themselves as being the section of the community which was required to provide the money, far too much for nobles who had made no contribution to France's struggles. The result was further disenchantment with the dynasty, which under Charles X was far too closely identified with government policy. In March 1827 the respectable middle-class Parisian National Guard greeted the king, who had come to review it, with cries of protest against clerical government and the censorship. The king could not accept such an affront and was compelled to dissolve the National Guard. The elections of November 1827, however, heaped more humiliation upon him, when the liberal opposition, in spite of the usual methods of administrative pressure, increased its strength in the Chamber to the point where it equalled the number of government supporters. Villèle was compelled to resign. For the moment Charles contented himself with a ministry without a president, but in August 1829 he appointed the Prince de Polignac, his favourite, as President of the Council of Ministers, which shocked French opinion, including as it did a minister of the interior, La Bourbonnaye, whose name was for ever associated with the White Terror of 1815; at the ministry of war, Bourmont, whose reputation was tarnished by his desertion of Napoleon before Waterloo; and a minister of justice, Courvoisier, a barely coherent clerical.

Already the forces of resistance were massing. The press was becoming increasingly hostile to the régime, whether in Paris or in the provinces. On 3 January 1830 was founded the bourgeois monarchical paper, *Le National*, supported by the banker Laffitte and edited by Thiers and Mignet. The society *Aide toi, le Ciel t'aidera* (God helps those who help themselves) was in existence to organize the electorate. Even the propertied classes could no longer tolerate Charles X. In June and July 1830 fresh elections to the Chamber were held, which gave the opposition an overwhelming majority. Before Charles X lay the alternatives of abandoning his policy or attempting a coup d'état. It was the latter course which recommended itself to him when on 9 July 1830 he heard that Bourmont had succeeded in capturing Algiers. In the flush of success he believed that public opinion would support him in a coup d'état. On 25 July 1830 the celebrated Ordinances were issued, imposing a ban upon the publication of any printed journal or pamphlet containing more than twenty-five pages, dissolving the Chamber of Deputies, restricting the vote in the electoral colleges to the 25 per cent of the richest electors and summoning the colleges to elect a new Chamber. In 1789 the Crown was more than once guilty of provocation. Once again in 1830 the Bourbon monarchy procured its own ruin. The country was in no mood to be provoked without seeking remedy. In 1826 an economic crisis had begun as a result of repercussions of a crisis in Britain. This depression was to continue to 1832. The pressures were perhaps not as great as in 1789, but crisis prices did exist in July 1830. In the Paris building trades it is estimated that wages fell by 30 per cent. In the textile industry there was a fall of 40 per cent. When the *National* under the editorship of Thiers published its manifesto calling upon France to resist the coup d'état there was plenty of raw material for a mass rising to develop in Paris. Charles X was at first nonchalant, but it soon became apparent that he had set in motion a revolution which he could not control. By 29 July Marmont was compelled to pull his troops out of Paris; the most effective units of the army were in any case on the other side of the Mediterranean in Algiers. The *National* demanded the calling of Louis Philippe, the Duke of Orleans, to the throne, and the provisional government of the insurgents called upon him to assume the office of lieutenant-general of the realm. Since the beginning of the eighteenth century the House of Orleans had waited for its opportunity and Louis Philippe acquiesced. Charles X abdicated in favour of his grandson, the *enfant du miracle*, but the child's claims were brushed aside. The Chamber of Deputies was called and the political class now took the leadership of the revolution out of the hands of the workers and students who had fought against the coup d'état. The choice was between a republic and a monarchy. The solution adopted was to call upon the Duke of Orleans to lend respectability to the revolution by becoming king. By a compromise solution he became Louis Philippe, the King of the French, and accepted the Tricolour instead of the White Flag of the Bourbons as the standard of France. A purge of the supporters of the deposed régime was made and the new government settled down to curb the revolution which had brought it to power. Almost immediately a revolution broke out in Brussels, which seemed to offer France an opportunity of resuming a forward policy in the Netherlands. Faced with a left-wing domestic opposition which believed that the new régime had cheated the radicals and workers of their efforts, the government of Louis Philippe had now to meet with the criticism that it lacked energy in the field of foreign affairs.

II. THE BELGIAN REVOLUTION OF AUGUST 1830

The Kingdom of the Netherlands had been created as a barrier to French expansion in the Low Countries, but the amalgamation of the former United Provinces and the Austrian Netherlands could not remove problems which had arisen from the long historical process by which different attitudes of mind had developed. Religion certainly divided the predominantly Calvinist north from the solidly Catholic south, but the south was in part Flemish and therefore linguistically akin to the former United Provinces, for which reason the French-speaking Walloons of the industrial areas were conscious that they might find themselves a minority in a Flemish–Dutch state. William I intended to rule with firmness and hoped to link the commercial north with the industrial south in the best interests of both sections of the community, but his government was based inevitably upon Dutch officials. A Belgian consciousness existed among the Flemings and the Walloons, but at first it was not easy to reconcile the views of the Flemish clergy and the liberal Walloon bourgeoisie with regard to education. By 1828 some common ground had been found between the two parties. A portion of the Flemish clergy accepted a more liberal policy with regard to education, while the Walloon liberals were prepared to adopt a more understanding attitude towards the Flemish clergy, if a common front could be established with regard to the Dutch domination. Ideological questions, however, gave way before the economic crisis. From 1824 there was a rise of prices in the southern Netherlands, which led to a decline in the real wages of the workers in the industrial areas. The textile crisis of 1830 struck hard at Verviers, Liège and Tournai. Overproduction brought about unemployment in a period of high prices caused by poor harvests. Hardship transformed itself into criticism of the union between the two parts of the Kingdom. On 25 August 1830 riots broke out in Brussels, and the Belgian bourgeoisie emerged to take control of the situation. The Dutch army attempted to re-occupy the city in fighting of 23–26 September 1830, but it was repulsed. A provisional government was established on 4 October, and on 22 November the new authorities declared in favour of a constitutional monarchy. In the meantime the Dutch army took possession of Antwerp. The international system of 1815 favoured re-occupation by the Dutch, but the people of the southern Netherlands were united at least in the desire not to see the Dutch régime restored. Superficially the situation favoured French intervention, but the complex conditions of the country did not favour union with France. If a Belgian state were to be created, its existence must meet with the approval of the great powers.

III. Europe and the French Revolution of 1830

When the revolution broke out in France in July 1830 anxiety arose lest the new France should take up the expansionist policy of the Old Régime, Revolution and Empire. France had been admitted to the concert of the great powers after 1815, but the other powers had not ceased to regard her as the main danger to the European peace. The Quadruple Alliance had been brought into existence to restrain her from making advances into Belgium and Italy. The rights of the great powers to hold France in check were clear enough, but they possessed no authority to intervene in France itself in order to restore Charles X. The real danger would arise if the French left wing obtained control and forced France to undertake a forward foreign policy.

Metternich and Nesselrode conferred at Carlsbad, and on 6 August 1830 agreed upon a common policy. They were agreed that there should be no interference with France provided that France herself did not infringe the treaties. According to their agreement in the so-called 'Chiffon de Carlsbad' their principle of action was:

> To adopt for the general basis of our conduct not in any way to interfere in the internal disputes of France, but, on the other hand, to permit no violation on the part of the French Government either of the material interests of Europe, as established and guaranteed by general transactions, or of the internal peace of the various states composing it.

Early assurances of non-aggressive intent in France seemed less certain and sure when revolution broke out in the Netherlands, especially when moves were made by Prussia to uphold the Orangist government. It was then France which proclaimed the doctrine of non-intervention. On 31 August 1831 the French foreign minister, Molé, saw the Prussian ambassador, Werther, and declared that France would intervene in Belgium if Prussia were to send troops into the country. This was exactly the situation which the European powers wished to avoid, and there was a general disposition to recognize the new régime in France, but there were many unsolved questions. If the Italians were to throw off the tutelage of Austria the doctrine of non-intervention might be used to prevent the Austrian army from restoring the *status quo*. Quite clearly, the formulation of the doctrine of non-intervention by France was merely another means of keeping the Low Countries and Italy open for French interference and expansion. Nicholas I of Russia was determined that he would make a demonstration of strength when a new French ministry was formed on 2 November 1830. The original ministry was conservative in its complexion, containing the moderates, Guizot, Broglie, Molé and Casimir Périer, but as a result of pressure from the left a more radical ministry was formed under Laffitte, with the Corsican, General Sébastiani, as minister of foreign affairs. The Russian announcement of calling men to the colours met with a re-iteration of the doctrine of non-intervention by the French and the calling of 80,000 men to arms for the spring of 1831.

It was at this point that the international influence of Russia was severely reduced by the outbreak of a revolution in Warsaw on 29 November 1830. Until October 1831 Russia was engaged in the difficult task of overcoming the resistance offered by the regular army of the Kingdom of Poland. During this time the diplomatic influence of Russia in western Europe was potential rather than actual.

IV. THE POLISH REVOLUTION OF 1830

Russian government in the Kingdom of Poland since 1815 was not tyrannical, but it was narrow in its concepts. The constitution of 1815 gave a voice in political affairs only to the propertied classes, which in effect meant the Polish aristocracy and substantial *szlachta*. There was opposition in the Polish Diet, the intellectual content of which was not high, but which nevertheless gave cause for annoyance to Alexander I. The policy pursued by Alexander I in Congress Poland was the conciliation of the upper classes, and under Prince Lubecki some progress was made towards improving the economic position of the country, which had suffered grievously in the Napoleonic Wars. The real difficulty of Russia was that Warsaw remained the capital in the eyes of the Poles of a future Polish state and therefore the centre of a social system, which in spite of partition continued to exist in their minds, but the resources of the petty Kingdom of Poland were limited and the opportunities presented by it for advancement too small to satisfy the social aspirations of the Polish educated class. Conspiracies arose first among the students and then among the officers of the army. Undoubtedly the viceroy, the Grand Duke Constantine, was a martinet, but the real problem within the army was the absence of promotion for the junior officers in a period of peace. An obscure conspiracy in the army, led by the junior officers, Wysocki and Zaliwski, came to the notice of the authorities and arrest seemed imminent, but the conspirators decided to stake all on a rising. The revolt broke out on 29 November 1830 and succeeded beyond its wildest dreams. A handful of cadets and intellectuals gave the signal for a rising, which was immediately joined by the civilian working class of Warsaw, whose aid had hardly been solicited. Like many townspeople in Europe, they were discontented by the rise in prices attendant upon a bad harvest. Units of the Polish regular army refused to fire on their fellow countrymen and went over to the side of the revolt. The few Russian troops under the Grand Duke Constantine could not risk a pitched battle, and consequently were led by him out of the country into the Russian empire proper. The Polish upper classes were appalled by the prospect of a proletarian revolution and resolved to take over leadership of the movement in order to prevent attacks upon property. Prince Adam Czartoryski, formerly minister of foreign affairs of Alexander I, and the popular general, Chłopicki, managed to set themselves up as a temporary authority in Warsaw, and within a few days a semblance of order was restored.

The difficulty of the new Polish government was that it in theory acted in the name of the King, who was also the Tsar Nicholas I of Russia. The Polish intention was to maintain the fiction that in this conflict of two countries the Tsar-King could reach a compromise with himself and thus be able to make concessions to the Poles, but the Tsar could hardly have permitted so great a loss of prestige, though it is clear that privately he was prepared to overlook much of what had been done during the revolution when once his rule was restored. The Poles were required to submit, but the Polish Diet on 25 January 1831 in a meeting, where emotionalism and stupidity took the place of common sense, by acclamation proclaimed the deposition of Nicholas I and in effect declared war upon Russia. The Russian army under Field Marshal Diebitsch-Zabalkansky quickly drove into Poland, and in three days' fighting on 23–25 February at Grochów, east of Warsaw, the Poles were defeated and compelled to withdraw upon the city, but the Russians could not make more progress, because the poor harvest made it difficult for them to concentrate their troops. There were thoughts among the Polish radicals of calling upon the aid of the people, and agrarian reform was considered in the rump parliament, which remained in Warsaw. It was proposed that the private landlords be set an example by the government's undertaking the grant of freeholds to the peasants on the crown estate, but at the beginning of April 1831 the Polish army was able to make a raid from Warsaw which temporarily drove back the Russian army. In triumph the conservative *szlachta* returned to Warsaw and rejected out of hand the modicum of reform which the radicals had proposed.

It was easy enough to drive in the Russian forward positions, but the harvest failure of the previous year now began to have an adverse effect upon the Polish offensive. The farther the Polish army reached out from its base, the longer its supply lines. On 26 May 1831 a battle was fought at Ostrołęka which split the Polish army. The main body under Skrzynecki was compelled to find cover behind the Vistula, while a second force under Giełgud, cut off by the Russians, marched into Lithuania, where it was quickly compelled to seek refuge in East Prussia. Quarrels and difficulties in the Polish leadership began seriously to affect discipline. Diebitsch having died, his place at the head of the Russian forces was taken by Field Marshal Paskevich, the victor of Erivan. Rather than undertake a direct assault upon Warsaw, Paskevich decided to cross the Vistula in the lower reaches near the Prussian frontier and attack Warsaw from the west, a move which he effected with some assistance from the Prussian government, which wished to see the rising in Poland brought to a speedy end. On the night of 15–16 August 1831 there were disturbances in Warsaw among the unemployed officers and radicals which caused Adam Czartoryski to flee to the army for safety. General Krukowiecki, who replaced him at the head of the government, knew that there was no alternative but to submit to Russia. Submission, however, carried with it a sense of national humiliation. Part of the Polish army withdrew over the Galician frontier into Austria, while the main body crossed into East Prussia and laid down its arms.

In this manner Polish resistance came to an end. What had begun as a revolution of the people of Warsaw ended by being a conventional military campaign against Russia, which could scarcely have succeeded without foreign aid. An alternative, the summons to the people to rise against Russia, was considered and attempts were made to put it into effect, but the peasants of Congress Poland had small love for their landlords and still had no consciousness of the national cause. In Congress Poland the *Code Napoléon* was the basis of law, recognizing only two conditions of land tenure, ownership and tenancy, whereas the Polish peasants regarded that both the landlord and the tenant had rights to the soil. The tendency among Polish landlords was to use the right of eviction which they possessed under the *Code*. For the peasants to fight for the Polish noble class something more substantial than national freedom had to be offered them. This was the lesson which the Polish radicals drew from this episode. A large number of Polish officers and intellectuals went into exile, where the social problems of Poland were debated. In 1836 the left-wing Polish Democratic Society in France drew up a Manifesto in which it was proposed that in the future struggle for independence the Polish insurgent government should make a call to the people by promising them unconditionally their freeholds; the landlords were to be compensated from a state fund. The cause of national independence and agrarian reform were declared to be inseparable. This event was not without significance. Agrarian reform had been the weapon of the enlightened despots of the eighteenth century. For the first time on any significant scale agrarian reform appeared as the tool of a left-wing organization.

V. THE ITALIAN CRISIS OF 1830-1

The food shortages which had led the Warsaw workmen to rise in November 1830 were equally present in Italy. Here, too, there were conspiracies directed against foreign domination. Since the suppression of the Neapolitan revolution it had been recognized that Italian unification could not be achieved unless some means could be found of containing the Austrian army. Under the leadership of Menotti a plan was formulated by the Carbonarists to gain control of a small Italian state and use its army as the nucleus for a national uprising. The plan of revolution was made with the hope of winning over Francis IV of Modena, a ruler who considered the small size of his dominions inconsistent with his own dignity. Francis IV, however, knew that if Austria reacted strongly and France failed to intervene this scheme had no chance of success. His attitude was therefore in part that of an agent provocateur. The repetition by French ministers that France would not permit the principle of non-intervention to be violated encouraged the conspirators and alarmed the Austrian government.

There was some justification for this alarm. The raw material existed for revolution, especially in the Papal Legations, the territories of Bologna, Ferrara and Ravenna. These towns had once enjoyed a privileged position within the Papal States under which they exercised internal self-government and sent ambassadors to Rome to represent their interests, but this curious system, a relic of the medieval organization of Italy with its autonomous city states, had been abolished by Bonaparte in 1797. With the restoration of the Papal power the centralist system of Bonaparte was retained and local autonomy of these towns was not revived. The papal administration was inefficient and justice was bad. There was thus middle-class leadership for revolution. Harvest failures and high prices gave rise to mass discontents and placed at the disposal of the revolutionaries the power of the mob. Francis IV knew that revolution was planned for Modena on 5-6 February 1831, and therefore made precautionary arrests of conspirators, but the Austrian army in Italy was without orders and decided in accordance with best military procedure to permit the revolution to break out in the Papal States in order more easily to be able to suppress it. At Bologna the Pope was deposed, but the provisional government did not for long enjoy popular support when it was perceived that it intended to restore the hated French system. There was no movement in sympathy either in Tuscany or in Naples. The Italian revolution was too weak to survive by itself, and hopes were therefore turned towards France, whose aid alone could bring salvation.

France was, however, already showing caution. Metternich sounded France on her attitude before the revolutions broke out and received from Sébastiani a conciliatory reply in which he denied that France was moved by any hostile spirit. Metternich skilfully played upon the dangers of encouraging Bonapartism in Italy, while at the same time appearing to offer France support for her policy in Belgium. On 23 February 1831 Sébastiani defined the area in which the principle of non-intervention was to apply; it included Belgium, Piedmont, Spain and the Rhineland, which represented a retreat from the earlier French view. This in itself was evidence of the growing influence of the clericals and the peace party in France. On 13 March

1831 a new and more moderate government was formed under Casimir Périer, who declared that his policy was determined by the principle of 'Au dedans l'ordre, au dehors la paix, sans qu'il coûte rien à l'honneur'. In short, he was prepared to follow a policy of no war in Italy, provided that France was subject to no humiliation. The powers were assured that France was not ready to support the revolution, and on 8 April 1831 instructions were given to French embassies not to support the Italian revolutionary movement.

Austria had already acted upon the supposition that France would not aid the revolution. On 4 March 1831 Modena was occupied and Bologna was pacified on 21 March by Austrian troops. Bologna was the test case of Franco-Austrian relations. Modena could be represented as the dominions of an Austrian cadet house, but Bologna was in papal territory. Casimir Périer adopted the attitude that he was prepared to support the Pope, but that reform ought to be introduced in the Papal States. Britain had no desire to see the extension of French influence in the Italian peninsula and tended to play with both sides. French plans for reform received British backing, but Palmerston went out of his way to be polite to Austria. He worked for a solution in which no encouragement was given to France to think that honour was involved, while no promise of automatic British support was given in the event of Austrian independent action. On 21 May 1831 a five-power conference submitted a memorandum on reform in the Papal States, providing for the secularization of the administration in the hands of the cardinals and the bishops. The Pope finally agreed to a system by which municipal and provincial councils might contain laymen to assist the clerical rulers, and the Austrian army withdrew on 17 July. Clerical rule, however, proved unsatisfactory in the Papal States, which led to disturbances and a fresh intervention by Austrian troops in January 1832. France, who wished to put future intervention upon a joint footing between Austria and herself, retaliated by sending troops by sea to occupy Ancona without papal authority. In fact, the papacy under the new Pope, Gregory XVI, elected in the height of the crisis in 1831, wished to preserve his absolutist rule and leaned heavily upon Austria. In the view of the British diplomatist, Seymour, 'the Vatican door is locked and the key is in Vienna'. The British government had enough difficulties of its own in Ireland without wishing to increase its burden by annoying Irish Roman Catholic opinion in an effort to force the Pope to modify his views. Italy resigned itself for the moment to the restoration of the *status quo*. France remained in occupation of Ancona until 1838. Papal administration with all its shortcomings was restored in the Papal States. As in Poland, Italy experienced no significant changes as a result of the European upheaval of 1830–1. Foreign rule remained and the Papacy enjoyed a renewed tenure of its territories. It remained beyond doubt that the old régime in Italy was under the fire of public criticism and could not for ever maintain itself against the desire for radical change.

VI. THE BELGIAN QUESTION

The principal concern of France, deeply conscious of the fact that Belgium was in part French by speech, and of Britain, traditionally fearful for the fate of the Low Countries, was to secure a peaceful settlement of the rift which had occurred in the Kingdom of the Netherlands in 1830. Poland and Italy were important questions, but the treaty of 1815 with regard to the Netherlands transcended all other problems in its gravity. A conference of the five powers in London on 4 November 1830 advised a cessation of the hostilities between the Belgians and the Dutch, and on 17 November recommended a withdrawal of both sides to the old frontiers which divided the United Provinces and the former Austrian Netherlands. With the change of government in Britain in 1830 the policy of Canning was resumed. The foreign minister of the Whig government, Palmerston, wished to restrain France and saw the best means to this end in acting with France, especially because Britain herself was about to experience the crisis which culminated in the Reform Act of 1832.

Three basic problems confronted the powers: the actual division of the Kingdom of the Netherlands; the subsidiary question of Luxemburg, which was technically part of the Germanic Confederation; and the future constitutional forms of the Belgian state, whose existence no one was seriously willing to contest. In December 1830 it was decided that the union of the northern and southern Netherlands could no longer be maintained. After some discussion among the powers it was recommended that the Kingdom of the Netherlands should have the frontiers of 1790, while William I should remain Grand Duke of Luxemburg; one-half of the public debt was to be shouldered by the new state of Belgium. To these proposals France on 1 February 1831 refused her adherence. Sébastiani, supporting the Belgian National Congress in Brussels, which found these terms burdensome, declared that the powers had no right to impose upon Belgium conditions which she did not wish to accept. Sébastiani upheld the doctrine of non-intervention while he thought some advantage might be obtained for France. There were two candidates for the Belgian throne: the duc de Nemours, the second son of Louis Philippe, and therefore unacceptable to Britain, and the Duke of Leuchtenberg, the son of Eugène de Beauharnais, who was rejected by France for his Bonapartist connections. The difficulties were in part solved by the moderation of Louis Philippe, who at length on 17 February declined the Belgian throne for his son; on 17 April France eventually agreed to the protocols of separation proposed in the winter. An alternative candidate was therefore presented in the person of Leopold of Saxe-Coburg-Gotha, who agreed to become king if the Belgians accepted him.

The Belgians only belatedly accepted Leopold, but continued to raise difficulties concerning the articles of separation. Some effort was made to accommodate the Belgians in the eighteen articles of separation signed by the powers on 26 June 1831, by which Luxemburg was to be left open to a separate negotiation and the public debt more equitably divided. After some debate the Belgians accepted these conditions, but the Dutch for their part now showed intransigence, insisting upon the original articles of separation and refusing to recognize the election of Leopold as king. In a protest of 12 July the Dutch government declared that it would regard Leopold as an enemy if he took possession on any other than the terms originally proposed. William I was playing with fire. The French government was in difficulties at home for its apparent inactivity in foreign affairs. Little had been done to assist the Polish revolt, and Italy had been surrendered to Austrian domination. The determination of the Dutch to teach the Belgians a lesson forced the French government to intervene. On 1 August 1831 the Dutch denounced the armistice and announced that from 4 August hostilities would begin. The Belgians were easily defeated at Louvain, but a French army under Marshal Gérard entered the country, and by 20 August drove the Dutch out of Belgium.

A situation arose which throughout the negotiations the British government had tried to avoid. The French were now in possession of Belgium. Talleyrand, the French ambassador in London, declared that the French occupation would end when once the Dutch had evacuated the country, but the foreign minister, Sébastiani, insisted that occupation must continue until a definitive treaty was obtained. A complete breakdown seemed likely amid the designs of the French, the chagrin of the Dutch and the claims of the Belgians, but in October 1831 the Russian government's authority was restored with the defeat of the Poles, and the strength of the French position correspondingly weakened. Fresh articles of separation were drawn up on 14 October 1831. The great powers were now determined to force upon the two small powers a settlement of this question, which was now threatening the peace of Europe. Leopold declared that he would abdicate if the Belgians refused to accept the terms offered, while the Dutch were warned that war would follow if they renewed hostilities against Belgium. It was necessary to make some concessions to French feeling. Sébastiani required the removal of the barrier fortresses in the southern Netherlands, which he declared to be a menace to France. The other powers were not anxious to hand them over to a state as weak as Belgium, which would be unable to keep them in good condition or even garrison them; their mere existence would be an encouragement to France to intervene in the future. Nevertheless, for form's sake the powers did insist upon the retention of the fortresses of Charleroi and Tournay. At this point the French government refused its adherence to the separation, but the British government stood its ground. The alternative to the government of Lord Grey in England would be a Tory government under the Duke of Wellington, whose attitude towards France was likely to be very much stronger. At the same time an international dispute threatened the stability of the French government at home. One section of the chamber supported the Casimir Périer government only on condition that it cooperated with the British Whig government. On 31 January 1832 the French government gave its consent to the articles of separation. Russia proved a little more difficult and attempted to sustain the Dutch cause, but this was not on a matter of principle. Under the arrangements of 1815 a loan of £20,000,000 borrowed by Russia in Amsterdam was taken over, half by the Kingdom of the Netherlands

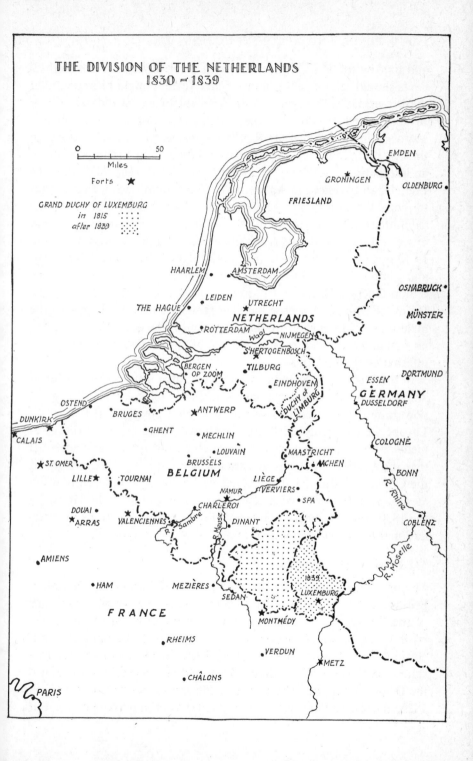

THE DIVISION OF THE NETHERLANDS
1830 - 1839

0   50
Miles

Forts ★

GRAND DUCHY OF LUXEMBURG
     in 1815
     after 1839

EMDEN

GRONINGEN ★
OLDENBURG

FRIESLAND

OSNABRUCK

HAARLEM   AMSTERDAM
                              MÜNSTER
        LEIDEN
THE HAGUE   UTRECHT ★
          NETHERLANDS
    ROTTERDAM
                    Waal
                         NIJMEGEN
            S'HERTOGENBOSCH
                                ESSEN   DORTMUND
BERGEN   TILBURG   GERMANY
OP ZOOM   DÜSSELDORF
              EINDHOVEN
                        DUCHY of
                        LIMBURG
OSTEND
DUNKIRK   BRUGES   ★ANTWERP
CALAIS   ●GHENT   ●MECHLIN
                         ●LOUVAIN   MAASTRICHT COLOGNE
★ST. OMER   BRUSSELS   ●AACHEN
LILLE★   ●TOURNAI   BELGIUM   BONN
                         LIÈGE
                    NAMUR   ●VERVIERS
                 ●CHARLEROI   ●SPA   R. Rhine
DOUAI ●   R. Sambre   DINANT
★ARRAS VALENCIENNES   COBLENZ
                              R. Meuse
●AMIENS   R. Moselle
                                    1839
●HAM   MEZIÈRES●   LUXEMBURG
              SEDAN
FRANCE   ★MONTMÉDY

●RHEIMS

            ●VERDUN
                    ★METZ

     ●CHÂLONS
PARIS

and half by the British government; if the Kingdom of the Netherlands should cease to exist in its original form it might be argued that
the provisions with regard to the loan might be invalidated. Great
Britain agreed to take over the Dutch portion of the loan, and the
way was thus smoothed for Russian agreement to the separation. In
the last resort only the Dutch proved difficult and France was given
an international authority to coerce them. On 21 May 1833 after the
French had advanced to Antwerp William I submitted and agreed not
to renew hostilities until the conclusion of a definitive treaty. Having
submitted with grace, William I then withheld his signature to a treaty
of separation, but at length the financial strain proved too great. On
19 May 1839 the definitive treaty was signed, by which Maastricht
and Limburg were joined with the Kingdom of the Netherlands, the
Grand Duchy of Luxemburg, somewhat reduced in size, given to the
House of Orange, in whose hands it remained until the expiry of the
male line in 1890, when by the operation of the Salic Law it passed
into other hands, and, most important of all, Belgian neutrality given
international recognition.

In this story of Belgian intransigence, Dutch intransigence, French
ambition and Russian obstinacy one clear fact emerged. The great
powers were prepared to override the small powers if the peace of
Europe were endangered by their actions. There might be disagreements among the great powers themselves, but it was now accepted
that the Belgian crisis was a matter which required the oversight of
the Concert of Europe. The France of 1793 replied differently when
an opportunity presented itself for expansion in the Netherlands. By
the 1830s the machinery and the will for peaceful solutions of international problems existed and a general war was avoided.

The Crisis in the Near East

The preoccupations of the powers in the Low Countries, the Italian
peninsula and Poland, problems which were covered by the provisions
of the Congress of Vienna, excluded for the moment the unsettled
crisis in the Levant. The construction of a Greek state and the con
clusion of the Russo-Turkish war still left the Ottoman Empire in a
state of confusion. The Sultan, Mahmoud II, was seeking to reform
the Ottoman Empire. The power of the Janissaries was destroyed in
1826, and the Sultan was to some extent master in his own house, but

the reconstruction of the Ottoman Empire would take a long time. French foreign policy, moderately successful in Belgium and demonstrative, rather than effective in Italy, still hankered after a substantial success in Egypt, where the pasha, Mehemet Ali, looked to French support and financial aid to give him complete independence of the Porte. Any alteration of the *status quo* in the Levant, however, was bound to raise the suspicion of both Britain and Russia.

I. THE OTTOMAN EMPIRE AND THE TREATY OF UNKIAR SKELESSI

The pasha of Egypt, Mehemet Ali, nursed a grievance because the Sultan had failed to pay him for the effort which he had made in the Morea to re-establish Ottoman rule there. The attitude of Mahmoud II was that Egyptian aid had been of no avail and that Mehemet Ali had not fulfilled the terms of his contract. The aims of Mehemet Ali were, however, much wider than the desire to obtain compensation. In 1831 Mehemet Ali's son, Ibrahim Pasha, invaded Syria and drove out the Turks. In December 1832 the Turks were utterly defeated at the battle of Konieh and it seemed that all Asia Minor was at the mercy of the Egyptians.

The Turks appealed first to Britain for aid, but no aid could be given in view of the situation in western Europe. Reluctantly the Sultan appealed to Russia. In the different circumstances of 1829 Nicholas I and his advisers had decided that it was not in the best interests of Russia to partition Turkey. Partition would lead only to the growth of influence of France and Britain in the Near East, which would give Russia powerful and hostile neighbours. It was the policy of Russia therefore to bolster up a weak and inefficient Turkey which presented no threat to Russia herself. The appearance of Mehemet Ali in Asia Minor in 1832 seemed to foreshadow the collapse of the Ottoman Empire and its replacement by a strong régime under Mehemet Ali. A revival of the fortunes of Turkey was the last event Russia wished to occur. In the February of 1833 Russia responded to the Turkish appeal and Russian troops were sent to occupy the eastern shores of the Bosphorus. For all his energy Mehemet Ali could hardly challenge the power of Russia, and the Ottoman Empire was thus saved for the moment. By the peace of Kutiah of April–May 1833 a compromise was reached for the moment by the Sultan and Mehemet Ali.

The Sultan ceded Adana to Ibrahim Pasha and the possession of the pashaliks of Syria and Tarsus for Mehemet Ali's lifetime. On 8 July 1833 the Ottoman Empire and Russia concluded at Unkiar-Skelessi a treaty of mutual assistance and alliance for eight years, which gave Russia the right to enter Turkish territory in the event of fresh Egyptian aggression. Stability was assured, but the addition of a separate and secret article gave grave cause for concern to Britain and France. Its text was apparently innocent:

> The Sublime Ottoman Porte in place of the assistance which it must lend in case of need, in accordance with the principle of reciprocity in the open treaty, shall limit its action in favour of the Imperial Court of Russia, to closing the Straits of the Dardanelles, that is, to not allowing any foreign vessel of war to enter under any pretext whatsoever.

The wording of the secret article differed in a sense not easy to define from Article XI of the Anglo-Turkish treaty of 1809, which closed the Straits to the passage of foreign warships in time of peace. It was the view of Nesselrode that the secret article merely confirmed an ancient principle, but this argument did not convince British and French ministers. Guizot considered that the Black Sea was now closed to foreign vessels of war, but that Russian warships might now pass into the Mediterranean. Palmerston's attitude was that, if no new interpretation were necessary, then equally a secret article in the treaty of alliance was not required by Russia. Palmerston's view was that some mischief was intended, and he began to adopt an unconciliatory attitude towards the Straits Question. In fact, Nicholas I's policy was much broader in its scope than it appeared. He was in the process of completing a vast security system.

Austria was not anxious to see the extension of Russian influence in European Turkey, but she was equally unwilling to strengthen the Ottoman Empire. After the treaty of Unkiar Skelessi there was an apparent identity of purpose between Austria and Russia. In central Europe they neither wished to encourage the spread of revolutionary doctrines, while in the Russian view the maximum which might have been achieved in Turkey had been obtained. In this way was established the system of Münchengrätz, where two conventions were signed by Austria and Russia. Under the terms of the convention of 6–18 September 1833 Austria and Russia agreed to maintain the *status quo* in the Ottoman Empire and, in the event of an attack by Mehemet Ali, decided that he should in no circumstances be allowed to extend his rule to the European provinces of Turkey. By a second convention of 7–19 September 1833 Austria and Russia agreed to collaborate in the preservation of the *status quo* in their Polish dominions. To this system Prussia acceded by the convention of 3–15 October 1833, which was signed in Berlin. The year 1833 saw the culminating point of Russian influence under the old régime. There was nevertheless a certain duality in the Russian system. Whereas in central Europe Nicholas I wished to uphold the princely states of Germany, in the Balkans there was a tendency for Russian officials to look to the support of the common people. Under the terms of the treaty of Adrianople the Principalities came under a temporary Russian occupation. In the Principalities the administration was placed temporarily in the hands of General Kiselev, who was required to draw up an 'Organic Statute' and supervise the appointment of new hospodars. The hospodars were to be chosen for life by an extraordinary assembly composed of the clergy, the boyars and the principal property owners, while an ordinary assembly was to meet as a rudimentary parliament. The political aspects of the Organic Statute gave little difficulty, but the definition of the rights of the landlords and the obligations of the peasants caused much ill-feeling between the local landlords and the Russian administration. Kiselev considered that it was necessary to limit the peasants' burdens in the interest of law and order, because civil disturbance would give the Turks a pretext for the introduction of their forces. Kiselev's proposals were in fact very limited; he suggested that the numerous categories of dependence should be abolished and the peasants required to work twenty-four days a year, but the landlords considered that he was infringing their interests. The opposition of the boyars was such that Kiselev decided that he must force his proposals through, an act which caused the Rumanian upper classes in future to look to Austria rather than Russia. In 1834 a uniform rent was established for the peasants of Wallachia and Moldavia and the Russian forces evacuated the country, but the Principalities still remained dependent upon the Sultan, which gave much cause for disappointment. Half measures were equally applied to Serbia, the position of which had been established by the treaty of Bucharest

(1812) and confirmed by the convention of Akkerman (1828) and the peace of Adrianople (1829). The prince ruled with the aid of a council of elders, and in September 1830 the rule of Miloš Obrenović was confirmed, but very soon popular discontent was apparent. In 1835 a law was published defining the power of the Prince; increased powers were given to the legislature and to the executive of the council, whose members were selected by the prince, but were irremovable, while it was laid down that the imposition of taxes could not take place without the confirmation of the Assembly (Skupshchina). Some fears were expressed in Vienna and St Petersburg lest a system of popular government be established in Serbia. In 1836 it was proposed by Russia that the Skupshchina should be abolished, but Miloš dared not follow the advice given to him. It may therefore be said that there was a tendency for Russian influence in European Turkey to decline in the 1830s and 1840s.

It was equally true that in the Caucasus Russian power was far from firmly established. Russia was in theoretical occupation of the area in virtue of her treaties with Persia and Turkey, but in fact her authority often was only nominal. A constant war was waged by the Russian army against the highlanders, and punitive expeditions were the order of the day under Nicholas I. Especially strong opposition was met from the Moslem Muridist movement. In 1830 Ghazi Mahomet was elected Iman in Gimri, only to be killed by the Russians in 1832. His successor, Hamsat Bey, was killed in 1834, but the new Iman, Shamil, succeeded in holding off the Russians for over twenty-five years. The Muridist movement was essentially a reaction of the Moslem highlands against the incessant Russian military expeditions; it had, moreover, certain social doctrines based upon the conception that all Moslems are free and equal, though there was a certain deterioration as time passed and the egalitarian element tended to disappear under Shamil's theocratic dictatorship. Very little progress was made by the Russians in establishing their authority in the Caucasus during the 1830s and 1840s. The area thus became an area for British intrigue, much of it privately inspired. In November 1836 the schooner *Vixen* laden with contraband arms was seized in Russian territorial waters, which led to an acid exchange of notes between London and St Petersburg.

Russia was still very far from establishing herself as a power in the

Middle East. An illustration of her basic weakness was the expedition to Khiva in 1839. Russia wished to establish her control over the Kazakh nomads of the central Asian steppe. Of the three hordes the Russians controlled only the Middle and the Younger, while the Older Horde was controlled by the Khanate of Kokand, while Kazakhs subject to the Khanate of Khiva frequently raided into Russian territory. In November 1839 the military governor of Orenburg, Perovsky, set out with 5,000 men and 19,500 camels to capture the city of Khiva. The plan was to use the winter months in order to avoid the intense heat of the summer; for this reason the expedition was brought to a standstill by the intense cold, in which the men were frostbitten and all the camels died. In consequence, the expedition was called off and operations against Khiva suspended. Russia was a world power in her extent, but her resources scarcely met her aspirations.

II. FRANCE, BRITAIN AND THE IBERIAN PENINSULA

The politics of Spain were never peaceful. Confusion was created by the fourth marriage of Ferdinand VII to his niece, María Cristina, daughter of Francis I of the Two Sicilies. On 10 October 1830 the Queen gave birth to a daughter, to the annoyance of the King's brother, Don Carlos, and the clerical party. In 1789 the ancient law of succession had been restored in place of the law of 1713, for which reason a woman could succeed to the throne. In September 1832 the law of 1789 was annulled during an illness of the King, but restored again when he recovered. On 29 September 1833 Ferdinand died and his daughter, Isabella, was proclaimed queen under the regency of the Queen-Mother. The supporters of Don Carlos, the so-called Carlists, refused to recognize Isabella, and a rising broke out in the Basque provinces with the revealing slogan of 'Long Live Carlos V! Long live the Inquisition!' Both Britain and France recognized Isabella, though they suspected one another's intentions.

Portugal as well as Spain was torn by faction when John VI died in 1826. Dom Pedro, his elder son, who in 1822 had established himself as a 'constitutional emperor' in Brazil, claimed the throne, but was challenged by his brother, Miguel, who had strong absolutist leanings. Pedro sought a way out of the crisis by resigning his claims in favour of his daughter, Maria, whose cause was upheld by a

British expeditionary force despatched in 1827, but in the following year Dom Miguel was offered the throne and Queen Maria withdrew to Brazil. In 1832 Pedro once more appeared to establish his daughter's rights, and in 1833, with the aid of a British force, he was eventually able to enter Lisbon.

Both in Spain and in Portugal Britain supported the apparently constitutional cause, but British action was determined more by a desire to prevent the Iberian peninsula from becoming a field for French intrigue. Out of this situation of mutual distrust was born the Quadruple Alliance of Spain, France, Britain and Portugal of 22 April 1834 for the exclusion of Miguel from Portugal and Carlos from Spain. Miguel gave little trouble and left Portugal, but the Carlist forces did not submit. A civil war continued to rage until at length in August 1839 by the convention of Vergara the Carlists were compelled to capitulate to the constitutionalist forces under General Espartero. To some extent therefore the alliance achieved its ends, but the suspicion which Britain and France entertained of one another's aims meant that the alliance did not rest upon a sure foundation. The supporters of Isabella were divided into two groups the *moderados*, who had authoritarian views, and the *progressitas* under the leadership of Espartero, who in October 1840 compelled the Queen-Mother to resign the regency under the threat of a revelation of her own scandalous private life. On 18 May 1841 the Cortes elected Espartero regent, but he and Narvaez, who displaced him in 1843, inherited the thorny problem of seeking marriages for the young Queen Isabella and her sister, the Infanta Luisa Fernanda, a question which plagued the relations of Britain and the France of Louis Philippe in the 1840s. The best that can be said of the Quadruple Alliance is that it prevented a major clash in Spain and thus to some extent permitted Palmerston to represent himself as having created a system of alliance among constitutional states as an answer to the close association of Russia, Austria and Prussia.

III. ANGLO-RUSSIAN HOSTILITY AND THE EASTERN QUESTION

The 1830s witnessed the growth of russophobia in Britain which was to render relations between the two countries difficult throughout the nineteenth century. As Russian and British influence began to extend throughout the world, so their interests were to overlap and the possibilities of clash multiply. The response of Palmerston to the secret article of the treaty of Unkiar-Skelessi was the so-called Discretionary Order of 10 March 1834. It was enclosed in a despatch to the British ambassador in Constantinople, Ponsonby. It was nothing less than an order to the commander-in-chief of the British Mediterranean fleet to comply with any request of the Turkish government, transmitted through the ambassador, to take action 'against any threatened attack of the Russians'; the one qualification was that the naval commander should assess whether his force was adequate for the task. In the brief Conservative government of 1834–5 Wellington discovered the existence of this order, which he realized was a very dangerous instrument indeed, especially in the hands of a man as unstable as Ponsonby, and likely to lead to rash moves by the Turks if ever they got to know of its existence. Upon consideration therefore Wellington decided to cancel the order. When the Whigs returned to power under Lord Melbourne and Palmerston again became foreign secretary in April 1835, the question of British naval policy was reconsidered and eventually the order to the fleet was restored in May 1836, though Palmerston now warned Ponsonby that he thought that the moment of danger had passed.

Palmerston's policy was determined by a dislike of the treaty of Unkiar-Skelessi, which seemed to him to place the Ottoman Empire and the Straits under the exclusive influence of Russia. His object was to merge the treaty in a compact of a general nature which would bring the Straits under the cognizance of the Concert of Europe. In the meantime he decided that he would do nothing which might lead to fresh Russian intervention. His aim was, on the one hand, to restrain Mehemet Ali from further adventures and at the same time to prevent the Sultan from launching an attack upon Mehemet Ali. In the course of 1838 the Russians themselves were considering their own attitude towards the question of the Straits. A plan was under discussion for the reinforcement of the Russian Black Sea fleet by the movement of ships from the Baltic through the Dardanelles. The Minister of Marine, Menshikov, and Nicholas I believed that it was in order for Russia to take this course, but the foreign minister, Nesselrode, raised grave objections in a memorandum of January 1838. He pointed to the existence of the ancient rule of the Straits, expressed in the treaty of 1809, which was in Russia's favour, but which was not expressed in the form of a direct obligation on the part of Turkey towards Russia. For this reason the secret article of the treaty of Unkiar-Skelessi had been drawn up. Nesselrode argued that if Russian ships passed the Straits through the Dardanelles Britain and France would be able to claim similar privileges, which it was the object of Russian policy to avoid. Nicholas I for the moment clung to the system he had created by the treaty of Unkiar-Skelessi and the Münchengrätz convention, which in effect excluded the question of the Ottoman Empire from the oversight of the Concert of Europe, but he perceived the logic of Nesselrode's argument, which revealed the unsoundness of Russia's policy.

The crisis which shook Russian confidence began in May 1838, when Mehemet Ali informed the foreign consuls in Egypt that he intended to declare the independence of Egypt and Syria. This announcement seemed likely to provoke a crisis. The first reaction of Nicholas I was to confer with his allies, Austria and Prussia, but Palmerston did not wish the question of the Levant to be solved without the participation of Britain, and therefore sought an association of Britain, Austria and France. In 1838 it appeared for the moment that Britain would adopt a hostile attitude towards Russia. The Anglo-Turkish commercial treaty of 16 August 1838 seemed to be the beginning of British penetration of the Ottoman Empire. The military preparations which the Sultan Mahmoud began to make in January 1839 for an attack upon Mehemet Ali gave Russia grave cause for concern, because she could hardly restrain her ally from making an effort to recover control of Syria. The situation was so fraught with danger that Nicholas I decided that the safest course was to seek a compromise with Britain, by which he would give up his exclusive right to intervene at the Straits in return for an international guarantee which secured their neutralization.

Diplomatic reconciliation had scarcely begun, when Mahmoud II in April 1839 opened his attack upon Mehemet Ali. On 24 June the Turkish army was destroyed by the Egyptians at the battle of Nezib. On 30 June the Sultan himself died. On 7 July the Turkish admiral, the *capitan pasha*, deserted to the Egyptians. Complete chaos reigned. This was a confusion far worse than that produced by the events of 1833. In the midst of this crisis Palmerston proposed joint action to France in order to keep the Russians out of Constantinople and restrain Mehemet Ali from further attack, but France had designated Egypt and Syria as a field of future French penetration and therefore declined to coerce Mehemet Ali, whom she regarded as a French protégé. It quickly appeared that the divisions of France and Britain were deeper than those which troubled the relations of Russia and Britain. France was willing to bolster Turkey against Russia, but in Egypt her policy was basically anti-British. On 27 July 1839 the five great powers informed the Porte that no step with regard to the future of the Ottoman Empire might be made without their consent; this move was made when the Porte was about to concede the demands of Mehemet Ali and was intended to sustain Turkish morale. It meant in effect that Turkey had now come under the supervision of the Concert of Europe. Nevertheless, at a meeting of the French cabinet on 6 August 1839 it was decided that France could take no part in the coercion of Mehemet Ali. The crisis in effect forced Nicholas I to make his final decision. Nicholas I at last accepted the advice of Nesselrode that the treaty of Unkiar Skelessi would in any case lapse in two years and that new arrangements would be required. An international régime at the Straits could give Russia all the security she required without imposing upon her the obligations of an alliance, but if Russia refused this solution Austria might look towards Britain for assistance. On 15 September 1839 the Russian ambassador at Stuttgart, Brunnow, arrived in London with proposals for a compromise solution. Palmerston was taken aback by the Russian approach, but he saw in it a means of achieving his basic policy, the imposition of a general European guarantee upon the Straits. In January 1840 Palmerston proposed that the five great powers should send troops to Constantinople to defend the city against Mehemet Ali and that the Sultan's right to close the Straits to warships of all foreign powers should be affirmed for the future. With regard to the Egyptian question Palmerston offered France as a basis of settlement the hereditary tenure of Egypt and the pashalik of Acre for Mehemet Ali; the Porte was, however, to recover Syria. This solution was rejected by France. On 21 February 1840 the Soult ministry fell and was succeeded by that of Thiers, which favoured a direct settlement between Egypt and the Porte upon the criterion of the existing possessions of Mehemet Ali. Palmerston was reluctant to leave France out of the general settlement, but at last on 8 July 1840 the British cabinet decided that, if France would not join the other powers, then Britain, Austria, Prussia and Russia must concert among themselves to bring about a solution. Austria and Britain were commissioned to coerce Mehemet Ali, who was to be given Egypt in hereditary right and Palestine for life, if he submitted, but if he refused to comply with the powers' demands he should then be confined to the hereditary pashalik of Egypt. The convention, signed on 15 July 1840, led to a war scare in the west, and Nicholas I received with surprised pleasure the request of Palmerston that the Russian fleet should be made ready to protect the British coast against French attack.

The forces of Mehemet Ali collapsed before the attack of Britain and Austria. When Acre fell on 3 November the resistance of Mehemet Ali was crushed and Ibrahim Pasha was obliged to evacuate Damascus. Syria, Crete and Arabia were restored to Turkey, and Mehemet Ali was confined to the hereditary pashalik of Egypt, a situation which he accepted with surly reluctance. These actions were disapproved of by the government of Thiers, who sent a hotly worded despatch to London on 3 October 1840, protesting against coercion, but strong words were mixed with irresolution. Louis Philippe refused to permit his government to carry out a policy which might bring about a war in which France would be isolated. On 21 October 1840 Thiers resigned and was succeeded by a ministry under the leadership of Soult and Guizot. French anger cooled only slowly, but the other powers made every effort to bring France back into the Concert of Europe, because they needed her guarantee of the new régime at the Straits.

IV. THE STRAITS CONVENTION OF 1841

On 13 July 1841 the Straits Convention was signed, an instrument as brief as its implications were wide. It was an agreement between the five European great powers and the Porte, by which the Sultan undertook to admit no foreign vessels of war within the Straits while he was at peace, except for light vessels on embassy service. This was not a guarantee of the integrity of Turkey, which Metternich would have been glad to obtain, but it was a surrender of the hegemony over the Ottoman Empire which Nicholas I had established by the treaty of Unkiar-Skelessi. The Straits Convention amounted to an international agreement by which no one single power would seek to dominate the Ottoman Empire. In the opinion of Nicholas I 'the Treaty of Unkiar-Skelessi, though annulled to all appearance, has been really perpetuated under another form. The new act, which has replaced it and been recognized by all the powers, forbids foreign warships to enter the Dardanelles and assures us henceforth against all naval attack'.

In fact, Palmerston believed that the terms of the convention could be evaded if the Turkish government called upon Britain for naval aid to maintain order in Constantinople, but restraint was required lest this serve as a precedent for other powers to act in a similar manner. Lord Aberdeen, who in 1841 succeeded Palmerston at the Foreign Office, adopted a more conciliatory attitude towards Russia, and in 1844 in talks at Windsor with Nicholas I and Nesselrode, agreed verbally that Turkey should be held to her obligations and that both powers ought to use their influence to prevent the Turks from provoking a crisis in the Balkans; it was, moreover, understood that both Britain and Russia would call upon Austria to assist them if there appeared to be a chance of the Ottoman Empire's breaking up. Nicholas I, moreover, gave Austria repeated assurances that he had no intention of seizing Constantinople and disclaimed any intention of interfering in the Balkans. In short, Nicholas I was content to let matters rest as they were, a policy to some extent determined by his fear that western and central Europe were about to be scenes of civil disturbances, which would require the vigilance of Russia elsewhere than in the Near East.

The settlement of 1841 reduced Anglo-Russian tension, but the coercion of Mehemet Ali rankled in the minds of the French government. Aberdeen sought to mollify France, and it has even been alleged that an 'Entente Cordiale' came into existence between France and Britain under his guidance, but there was in fact an undercurrent of acidity and spite in French policy which threatened to find fresh expression in Spain. The question of the Spanish marriages offered an opening for French intrigue. Aberdeen wished to postpone the marriage of Queen Isabella, which under Spanish law was possible when she reached the age of twelve, but it was French policy to bring it forward. The question was complicated by the multitude of candidates and embroidered with many malicious comments upon their capacities from the side of the Spanish Court. Aberdeen was anxious to avoid the marriage of Isabella to a son of Louis Philippe, but such a marriage might be open to her sister, the Infanta Luisa Fernanda. Aberdeen moved cautiously towards an agreement with France whereby Isabella should marry Francisco of Cadiz, her cousin, and the Infanta Luisa Louis Philippe's son, the Duke of Montpensier, but, when Peel's cabinet fell in 1846 and Palmerston returned to the foreign office he found no trace of these purely private negotiations, it was argued that Great Britain had not been committed to any particular course. The question was complicated by the scandalous suggestion that Francisco of Cadiz could not or would not be a father of children to Isabella and that France therefore hoped the succession would fall to the offspring of Montpensier and Luisa, a view which did not take into account Queen Isabella's own amorous temperament. Palmerston at once upset the patient negotiations of Aberdeen and suggested that Isabella should be married to Francisco's brother, Enrique of Seville, and Luisa to Leopold of Saxe-Coburg-Gotha, which was nothing less than to exclude a French prince altogether. In anger Louis Philippe, under pressure from Guizot, agreed to the Queen Mother's proposal to carry out the original intention of marrying Francisco to Isabella and the Infanta to Montpensier. This was a storm in a teacup, but it was sufficient to bring about a momentary revival of the tense relations which had existed between France and Britain in 1840–1.

V. The Relations of the Powers Before 1848

In 1848 Europe was to be swept by revolutions. The conflicts of the powers which had preceded the revolutions had done little to change the system imposed upon Europe in 1815. The Concert of Europe had in fact extended its grasp to the question of the Straits. The great powers had resolved their major difficulties. Already in 1830–1, however, social forces had made their appearance to challenge the international stability. It was not the validity of the treaties themselves which were called into question, but the very existence of the governments which had signed them. Revolutions broke out in Paris, Berlin and Vienna in 1848. With the revolutions came new policies and new problems.

4: The Age of Revolutions, 1830–50

Between 1815 and 1830 revolutions occurred in Spain, Naples, Piedmont, Northern Italy, France, Belgium and Poland, but none of them seriously threatened the peace of Europe. Basically they were repercussions of the great war which had preceded them. By 1848 a new situation had arisen. Almost simultaneous revolutions affected the whole of Italy, France, Germany and the Austrian Empire. Even in the principalities of Moldavia and Wallachia there were repercussions.

The basic cause of the revolutions of 1848 lay in the metallurgical revolution and its subsidiary effects, which resulted from the building of railways. In 1840 only Britain had an extensive railway network, which supplemented relatively easy transport by water, whether by sea or canal. In the continental states demands arose for the construction of railways, and the 1840s saw remarkable progress. In Britain there were 6,400 km of line, in Prussia 3,100, in France 1,930, in Austria 1,555 and in Belgium 670 km. Russia lagged behind, with only 438 km connecting Warsaw and Cracow, not St Petersburg and Moscow. An omen for the future was that in the United States of America 14,000 km of line had been laid. To some extent the length of railway line was indicative of the relative industrial power of the individual states, but the burst of railway construction placed stresses and strains upon the economy of each country. Hitherto the expansion of European industry had been based largely upon textile production, but now the metallurgical industries assumed a vast importance. Iron and steel were needed for the railways, and when once the lines were laid down there was a boom in the excavation of coal. Iron, steel, coal and textiles now assumed an equal importance in the European economy. In France the Nord and Alsace, in Germany the Ruhr, the Saar and Silesia, in the Habsburg Empire Bohemia, Lower Austria, Styria and Carinthia, in Italy Piedmont, Tuscany, Naples and Campania, all in a greater or lesser degree experienced the impact of an increasing industrial tempo. To meet

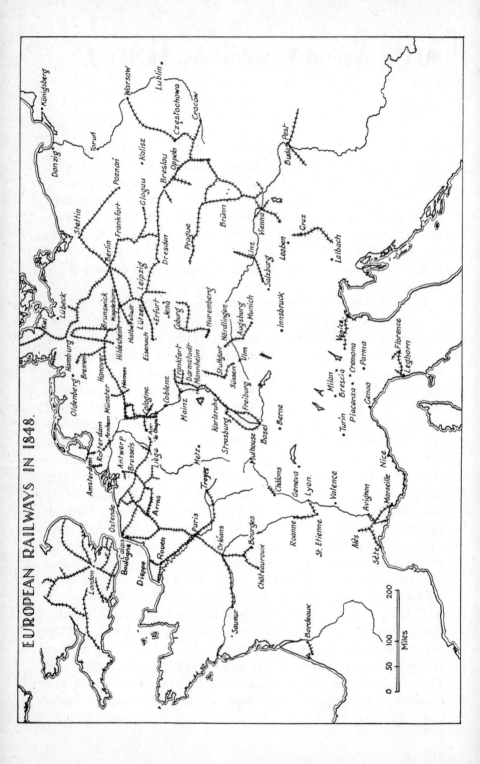

EUROPEAN RAILWAYS IN 1848.

this expansion there was a need to develop a financial system to raise money. International finance capital became a factor which added a fresh complication, because financiers were often slow to realize the effects of their operations upon other countries than their own.

Industrial expansion could not have failed to have had a disturbing influence upon the political situations in countries which even after the Napoleonic Wars had remained relatively stable. New problems arose which by their very novelty threw Europe into confusion. Before the old régime was taken by storm it was undermined by sap.

The Crisis in Europe 1830–48

The main feature of the revolutions of 1848 was that the populations of capital cities, swollen by the influx of workers, were able to paralyze the security forces of the state and thus permit new governments to be appointed. The political classes of Europe had witnessed the French Revolution of 1789 and the troubles of 1815–30 and had long been defining their attitudes towards the impending struggle. The nobility of the eighteenth century had absorbed the literature of the Enlightenment and had on the whole been indifferent to religion, but after 1815 it was noticeable that there was among the upper classes an emphasis upon Christianity as a form of social discipline which would serve to inculcate respect for persons and property in the masses. This movement was most pronounced in France, where the claims of the clericals were pressed to extremes, but elsewhere in Europe it is possible to observe the same tendency. The desire of the moderates among the propertied classes was to achieve the transition from one form of economic order to another with the minimum of disturbance and with the preservation of the existing social hierarchy intact. Whereas some placed stress upon social rigidity and the reinforcement of traditional concepts, there were others who thought that the best way to meet the coming crisis was to make concessions before it was too late. The country in Europe which was subjected to the most considerable strain was Britain, where the rate of industrial growth was quickest. The ruling classes bowed before each storm and survived the attacks of Chartism, the most powerful working class movement in Europe during the 1830s and 1840s. The collapse of Chartism in 1848 was comic by comparison with the bloody events which took place in Europe. In Europe barricades were erected and men fought and died in street battles, but in Britain on 10 April 1848 the great Chartist gathering at Kennington Common was forbidden to cross to the north side of the river Thames in order to present its petition; the leader, O'Connor, asked his followers to obey the police orders, and the Chartist petition was conveyed to Parliament in a cab. The incident has great significance. In Britain the lower middle classes were admitted to the franchise by the Reform Act of 1832 and even before had not been entirely unrepresented. In 1846 Peel had conceded the abolition of the Corn Laws rather than face the opposition of the middle class. As Morley, the biographer of Cobden, the leader of the opposition to the Corn Laws, wrote,

> The conflict . . . was not merely a battle about a customs duty; it was a struggle for political influence and social equality between the landed aristocracy and the great industrialists.

What the British statesmen of the old régime did was to admit a new class to a share in the framing of legislation. On the continent of Europe the situation was different. The aristocracy was inclined to be more exclusive in its outlook, whereas in England merchants had since the Middle Ages married into the aristocracy. In Europe there was an instinctive dislike of admitting new men to the secrets of government and a disposition often to have recourse to force. Where British statesmen yielded in time, continental statesmen tended to provoke. The European governments were in a way stronger to deal with opposition, because they had at their command large armies, where Britain traditionally relied for her security upon the navy and kept her army small.

The strength of the European governments induced in the liberal opposition a sense of moderation. There were radicals of the extreme left who would have established workers' republics, but their views were not to the taste of most liberals. In the 1830s and 1840s the word 'communism' was in general use to describe extremism and was for most men synonymous with total anarchy and the breakdown of society. Most liberals would have been satisfied with a modicum of popular representation. A constitution held in high esteem was that granted to Belgium in 1831, under which the king was responsible to a parliament consisting of two chambers, both elected by the people;

the judiciary was independent and the clergy, though in receipt of salaries from the state, were independent of it. The system which emerged from the French Revolution of 1830 was also considered satisfactory. The British reformed constitution of 1832 likewise seemed a model, though it was recognized that in Britain different conditions prevailed. The facts of the case were, however, that apart from Britain, France, Belgium, the Kingdom of the Netherlands and a few minor states constitutionalism in the proper sense of the term did not exist. Russia, Austria and Prussia remained autocratic states. Elsewhere there were façades of constitutionalism, but initiative invariably remained with the head of state. What the middle class in most of these states required was to be admitted to partnership. A minimum of representation which did not admit the extreme left to a voice in affairs would have satisfied them. Everywhere there was a consciousness of economic growth and a desire to advance the progress of civilization without recourse to political violence. The crisis of industrialism was imposing enough for the French clerical, Lamennais, to adjust his thinking to the problems of the times. Lamennais offered the view that the Roman Church was the most universal of all human institutions and therefore the most popular and that it should act as the friend of humanity and freedom, a point of view which earned him the condemnation of Pope Gregory XVI in the encyclical *Mirari Vos* of 15 August 1832. Lamennais proceeded to the logical end of this thinking and produced *Les Paroles d'un Croyant* (The Words of a Believer) in 1834, which announced his conversion to democracy and brought down upon his head a further papal condemnation. His friends, Lacordaire and Montalembert, remained faithful to the Church, but Lamennais left it in the hope of imparting a moral tone to the new political forces which were beginning to express themselves.

To the left of the moderate liberals were the revolutionary extremists. In their eyes there could be no solution which did not express the revolutionary purism of Robespierre. For them the people, or rather their chosen or self-appointed representatives, should rule. Carbonarism, at first only a resistance movement against the French in Napoleonic Italy, had allied itself with the Babeuvist doctrine of a revolutionary élite leading the people to victory, but now the revolution was to spread across Europe and free humanity from the chains of the old order. Allied with this philosophy was a conception borrowed from the Romantic movement in literature, that the people were the repository of all virtues and would lend their support to any movement for their improvement. Unfortunately the people frequently proved false. The industrial workers tended to be quiet when money was easy to earn and restive when the periodic recessions set in. The capitalist economy in the 1830s and 1840s was subject to frequent fluctuations. It was no coincidence that the two major crises of 1830 and 1848 produced major political upheavals. It was hunger which brought the town mobs out on to the streets and overthrew governments. When times improved the workers returned to their employment and left their would-be political leaders to themselves. No less ungrateful were the peasants. When in February 1846 a Polish rising was called for an onslaught upon the partitioning powers there was no response in Poznania, where the movement was betrayed, but in the western portions of Galicia, where the population was Polish, the peasants rose and killed 2,000 of the Polish gentry who were professing their zeal for the complete emancipation of the rural population. The revolutionaries of the intellectual classes could establish contact only with a small section of the lower orders of society. While it would be dangerous to declare that the majority of the European population was illiterate, it must be admitted that the common man before 1848 had only a limited political consciousness. The great game of politics was played out by a minority of the European population.

The revolutionary situation would be easy enough to understand if it depended entirely upon a class structure of the new society, the landed aristocracy, the industrialists, the merchants, the radical intellectual élite with revolutionary tendencies, the workers and finally, most numerous of all, the peasantry. European society was infected with a new concept, which had an influence on all except, perhaps, the peasantry. This was the doctrine of nationalism. The eighteenth century had been cosmopolitan in its outlook. Men had conceived it to be their duty to work for the good of humanity irrespective of race or language. For the educated classes French was the language both of diplomacy and thought. Nevertheless, the ideal of cosmopolitanism was questioned even in the eighteenth century. Rousseau had challenged the French acquisition of the Italian island of Corsica and the first partition of Poland. The German author, Johann Gottfried Herder, had emphasized that there were other cultures than French in his *Ideen zur Philosophie der Geschichte der Menscheit* (Ideas on the Philosophy of the History of Mankind), published in 1785. The Napoleonic Wars, which took armies across Europe, awakened men's minds to the reality that there were linguistic groups in Europe which did not correspond to the political boundaries which had been drawn by historical processes. After 1815 there grew a conviction that the state should be founded upon a linguistic unity, but it was unfortunate that men of different nationalities were often inextricably intermixed, especially in the Austrian Empire. Nationalism in itself is not an evil concept, but it assumes a diabolical character when one nationality seeks to impose itself upon another. Where nationalities are represented by different classes in society, nationalism gives an added acerbity to class conflicts. Nationalism is a phenomenon which is not easy to define. Where the state already corresponded approximately to linguistic boundaries nationalism tended on the whole to be moderate in its tone, but in mixed nationality areas it was often strident. An added complication appeared in areas like Germany, where a national consciousness was apparent but the national state did not exist. In Germany the concept of constitutional freedom and liberty was interwoven with a desire to procure the unity of the nation. The German liberals, whether moderate or radical, were pulled in two directions. Freedom contained two meanings, freedom from autocracy and freedom for the German people. In the event it turned out to be a question of whether the individual German might enjoy personal liberty or whether the German people as a collective whole should be represented by its own government, even though it encroached upon the liberty of the individual. The problem would have been less acute if each individual nationality in Europe had not by 1848 conceived notions of its own importance.

Nowhere was the problem more difficult than among left-wing circles. One of the most influential writers of the nineteenth century was the Italian, Guiseppe Mazzini, who for all his political failures in Italy transmitted his own conception of nationalism to Europe. Mazzini was not a great thinker and perhaps for that reason was influential. The achievement of Mazzini was to give the idea of a *nation* a moral significance which it had hitherto lacked. He accepted the notion that Christianity was the final form of religion and all classes enjoyed an equality before God; fundamentally Mazzini wished to work for the interest of humanity at large, but it was precisely in his emphasis upon collective humanity that he produced the elements of discord. Christianity he conceived as an individualist religion in which an individual Christ saved the world, but in the future it would be the 'initiator people' which would provide salvation. At some moment in history a people would arise to give leadership and it would be national apostasy for a people to refuse the call. Upon each people was laid the duty of action to lead the world in the cause of the oppressed. He allotted to each nation a role. Britain was to excel in industry. Poland was to give leadership to the Slavs. Russia was to civilize Asia. The realm of France lay in action and Germany in thought. Each people was at some time or another to act as a Messiah in the cause of humanity. Mazzini's thought contained an attractive hotchpotch of ideas, which permitted nationalists to act upon their own appreciation of a situation. So far from serving the interests of mankind, Mazzini encouraged the growth of competitive nationalism and sowed the seeds of discord. His appeal was primarily to the youth of each nation, politically the least experienced element in any society. He founded 'Young Italy' in 1831, and 'Young Europe' and 'Young Poland' soon followed. Similar organizations were founded elsewhere, but they were without serious political effect. What they did do was to establish a climate of opinion which reinforced current trends in political opinion which were already present in each class of European society. Devotion to the national cause by the 1830s was a plank of all political groupings which were in any way responsive to public opinion. The old régimes which retained the cosmopolitan feelings of the eighteenth century were unsympathetic, but they, too, were to recognize the force of national feeling. It would be dangerous to accord Mazzini an influence upon the entire continent of Europe, because nationalism had appeared before his own impact upon European thought in the 1830s. The plain truth is that nationalist thought had already permeated European society, where literacy could convey its meaning, but in the years between 1830 and 1848 it acquired a force and violence which would have shocked the humanitarian Herder, to whose initial researches it in a great measure owed its origin.

France under the Orleans Monarchy

Of all countries in Europe France was the most revolutionary. When Louis Philippe became King of the French in 1830 there was certainly nothing which resembled a solid Orleanist party to bolster his régime, but the strength of the French administrative system was such that within a short time it was found possible to create a party to uphold it. Among the first acts of the new government was to carry out a wholesale purge of the administration and appoint new men, who by their very association with the government and the acceptance of its favours would be compromised into becoming its supporters. A great show was made of the new king's being Louis Philippe, King of the French, and the acceptance of the Tricolour in place of the White Flag of the Bourbons, while the abolition of the censorship and the declaration that Catholicism was the religion of the majority of Frenchmen seemed to give the new order a refreshing freedom from the obscurantist views present in the court of Charles X. The appearance of liberalism, however, should not be allowed to disguise the fact that the régime was fundamentally conservative. In March 1831 the National Guard was reconstructed on the basis of enlisting men who paid direct taxes and was supposed to act as an internal security force against the restless workers of the towns. In December 1831 came constitutional changes. The upper house of parliament was reconstructed not upon the basis of hereditary peerages, but by the virtual nomination to it of supporters of Louis Philippe. The new régime ostracized the supporters of Charles X, and many members of the French nobility who could not reconcile themselves with change retired to their estates and divorced themselves from public affairs. The kernel of the new system was the alliance between the king and the chamber of deputies, held together by the astute distribution of patronage and favours to their constituencies. Under the new constitution to be elected a deputy must have reached the age of thirty years, whereas under the restored Bourbons the age had been forty years, while the franchise was granted to every man over the age of twenty-one years who paid 200 francs in direct taxation. This was a scheme which was less liberal even than the

English Reform Act of 1832; it gave only some 250,000 Frenchmen the right to vote. Similarly a narrow franchise kept local government in the hands of local oligarchies, except for the fact that the mayors were selected by the central government or the prefects. The Orleanist régime placed power in the hands of notables of every social origin, but in the main of the families which had achieved prominence during the Revolution and the Empire; there was certainly no predominance of the bourgeoisie under Louis Philippe. It was rather that property of every kind was represented in the legislature, whether landed, industrial or commercial. In this lay the reason for the discontent of the Parisian working class, which felt that it had been cheated by the upper classes, much as the English working class was disillusioned in 1832.

The disturbed economic conditions which had brought the people of Paris out on to the streets in July 1830 continued to trouble France in the first years of the new régime. In left-wing circles in France, which had come under the influence of Carbonarist thinking, it was believed not only that the techniques of Babeuf might be employed to seize control at the centre but also that a revolution in France would lead in its turn to a wave of revolutions in sympathy throughout Europe. It was argued by German Carbonarists, for example, that a coup d'état might be carried out at Frankfort and the revolutionaries take control of the Germanic Confederation's funds as the prelude to a revolution in western Germany. Allied with the French left were the groups of Polish émigrés, ready to turn their hand to any revolutionary enterprise. By the summer of 1832 the general opinion was that the time was ripe for revolution, not only in France but also in Germany, Italy and Poland. Demonstrations in Lyons in October 1831 had been fired upon by the army and barricades had been raised which it took a military operation to destroy, but there the revolutionary spirit was only cowed. The Lyons riots were symptomatic of the left-wing desire for direct action. Equally the government was prepared for a tougher policy. The Laffitte government of 1830 seemed to retreat before every pressure of the left, but in March 1831 the ministry of Casimir Périer was formed, determined that the government should be master of the situation. In July 1831 elections were held in which every method bequeathed to French governments by the Napoleonic régime was used to return a chamber of deputies prepared to authorize the use of force against the left. Shortly after the death of Casimir Périer in May 1832 the Parisian left raised its head again. On 5 June 1832 at the funeral of General Lamarque, a Napoleonic veteran, there was an attempt at a revolution, where for the first time in Paris the red flag was raised as the symbol of revolution. The army was brought in to quash the revolt in an action in which there were some 800 killed and wounded. After this sorry experience there was some confusion in left-wing circles. The society which was called *Amis du Peuple* (Friends of the People) ceased to be effective. Authority on the left passed into the hands of the *Société des droits de l'Homme et du Citoyen* (Society of the Rights of Man and the Citizen), which itself split into two groups, the moderates or *Girondins*, who preferred legal action to secure the rights of the workers, and the revolutionaries or *Montagnards*, who favoured the continuation of direct action. In this confusion there was doubt whether in fact Paris could serve as the centre of the European revolution. The possibility of a successful action being begun first in Germany was not ruled out, while the appearance of Mazzini in exile in Marseilles in 1831–2 seemed to point to a shift of the revolutionary centre of gravity to Italy, a hope which was not substantiated by the miserably led expedition of Mazzini to Savoy at the beginning of 1834 (see below p. 275). Under a law of 16 March 1834 the French government announced its intention of dealing harshly with members of secret societies. Most of the Parisian revolutionaries were prepared to concede that there was little hope of success, but the situation in Lyons was different. In the local committee of the *Société des Droits de l'Homme et du Citoyen* the left-wing carbonarists were in control, and they were matched by an employer class which was prepared to provoke the workers. A reduction of the weavers' wages caused a general strike on 13 February 1834, the failure of which prompted the Parisian leaders, Godefroy Cavaignac, Buonarroti and Cabet to urge caution, but the promise was made that in future Paris would follow Lyons if Lyons were to rise in revolt. On 9 April 1834 Lyons as a result of arrests of left-wing leaders once more rose in revolt and took Paris by surprise. A four-day rising took place in the streets of Lyons which was suppressed by the army, well prepared to deal with insurrection. On 13 April 1834 there was a spontaneous rising of workers and students in Paris, which was likewise put down by the army. Minor outbreaks at Lunéville, Saint-Etienne, Châlons-sur-Saône, Clermont-Ferrand and Marseilles proved ineffective. The failure of 1834 was a turning point both in the history of the Orleanist monarchy and of the European revolutionary movement.

The moderates of the French left wing were thereafter suspicious of the elements which had been responsible for the outbreaks in Lyons and Paris. The international revolutionaries lost faith in the concept that Paris was the inevitable centre of the European uprising and began to turn their attention to the doctrine of Mazzini, that every nation had a mission to fulfil and that each revolutionary movement should work within its only national area rather than submit to central control from Paris. Internationalism and materialism were replaced by the mystic nationalism of Mazzini. Nevertheless, the revolutionary tradition lived on in France. There were the *Montagnards*, who, having failed to raise the people, suggested the assassination of Louis Philippe. On the other hand, there were the professional revolutionaries, Blanqui and Barbès, for whom the coup d'état was an art demanding skill and precision. It was they who kept the Babeuvist egalitarian tradition alive, in and out of prison. In June 1837 Blanqui formed the *Société des Saisons* (The Society of the Seasons), a body with a hierarchical carbonarist organization and composed exclusively of Parisian working men. The *Montagnards* under Mathieu d'Epinal objected to this class exclusiveness and tried to lend point to their argument by attempting the assassination of Louis Philippe on 15 October 1840. Blanqui had already by then shot his bolt. On 12 May 1839, in order to take advantage of an economic crisis and the simultaneous cabinet disagreement which led to the resignation of the Molé government, Blanqui and Barbès attempted a fresh coup d'état, with as little success as before. The authors of this venture were both imprisoned for life, after death sentences upon them had been commuted. In this way ended the last serious attempt at a proletarian revolution under the Orleanist monarchy. If the Orleans régime subsequently found itself in difficulties, they could only have been of its own making.

Louis Philippe was self-opinionated and garrulous. He acquiesced in the strong government of Casimir Périer, but with the end of the depression and the collapse of serious left-wing activity after 1834 he wished to exercise not only his powers but also the talents which he prided himself he possessed. In 1832 was formed a ministry with Marshal Soult at its head, technically a non-political appointment, but within it real power was exercised by the duc de Broglie, Thiers and Guizot. This combination proved too strong a solution for Louis Philippe, who sought to split his ministers one from another in order that final decisions should rest with himself. In 1838 Louis Philippe, after some changing and reshuffling of ministries, finally secured the appointment of the Molé ministry, which was more amenable to his control, but in 1839 Molé held fresh elections, which in spite of the usual administrative pressure resulted only in strengthening the opposition. This constitutional crisis coincided with the crisis in foreign affairs of 1839–40, in which the Soult ministry was replaced by that of the bellicose Thiers, who led France to the point of war, but was compelled to resign by Louis Philippe, who had the common sense to realize that France was on the whole by no means as warlike as Thiers. Once more in October 1840 Soult was again appointed president of the council of ministers with Guizot, as the real power in the government, at the ministry of foreign affairs. Guizot was a man with whom Louis Philippe could work in partnership.

The Guizot ministry depended for its existence upon the extensive and unscrupulous manipulation of the electoral system through the administrative pressure which could be exerted by the prefects and the mayors. Undoubtedly Guizot aimed at stability, but by emasculating the opposition he produced a lack of vitality in French politics which made it difficult for him to assess the true state of opinion in the country. There was general dissatisfaction with his conduct of foreign policy, but this is a factor which should not be over-emphasized. Between 1839 and 1847 Algeria was brought under French control with the final defeat of the Arab leader, Abd-el-Kadir, a campaign distinguished upon both sides by remarkable ferocity. A not very successful Entente Cordiale was maintained with Britain until it broke down upon the trivial and not very creditable question of the Spanish Marriages. It was not, however, in the field of foreign affairs that Guizot aroused dislike. It was rather in domestic politics that he ran into difficulties.

One of the main drawbacks of France in the nineteenth century was her slow rate of industrial growth. Under the inheritance laws of the *Code Napoléon* property was equally divisible among co-heirs. The French entrepreneur therefore was always careful in his investments lest he should endanger the family fortunes, whereas the British industrialist, feeling less obligation to his children, might take risks and accepted bankruptcy as part of the harsh code of ethics prevailing in an era of industrial expansion. Under the French social system it was the custom to provide a son or a daughter with a settlement upon marriage equal to that granted by the parents of the other partner in the marriage. If an industrialist were to lose money he might be held responsible for his children's fall in the social world, they then being able to marry only persons with less money to bring into a marriage partnership. The French industrialist therefore tended to seek safe investments and, if he accumulated capital, to secure it by the purchase of land or of government stock. It is true that in the 1830s and 1840s France did make progress, but by comparison with Britain and Germany it was not dramatic. There was only a slow development of coal mining between 1789 and 1815, the annual tonnage rising from 700,000 to 800,000 in the areas which constituted France after the two treaties of Paris; by 1847 production had risen to 5,153,000 tons, but this was less than the total production of Belgium and certainly did not meet all France's needs. Not only was Belgian coal imported but British coal also. The same picture appears with the production of pig iron. Production rose between 1821 and 1847 from 221,000 tons to 591,000 tons, but it is estimated that in the same period British production rose from 400,000 tons to 2,000,000 tons. Equally the mechanization of the textile industry was less highly developed than in Britain. Most disastrous of all was France's suspicion and wariness of investment in railways. Railways were not merely means of developing markets but were also the vehicle of transporting troops. Guizot's railway scheme was produced only in 1842. It was a plan to link Paris with the great provincial centres; under this system the state acquired the land, but the railway companies were left to construct and operate the railways. In the years 1844–6 France was like other European countries to suffer the so-called 'Railway Mania', when the building of railways and investment in them was regarded as the panacea for all economic ills. The slowness of French progress was marked. By 1848 1,930 km of railway track had been laid in France, but 3,100 existed in Prussia.

The maps of 1848, moreover, reveal that in Prussia Berlin was already the centre of a railway network, connected with all the provincial capitals except Königsberg. In France, on the other hand, there was rail connection between Paris and Calais, Lille, Orleans and some miles beyond it to Saumur, Châteauroux and Bourges, and Troyes, but there was no direct connection with such cities as Bordeaux, Marseilles, Lyons, Mulhouse and Strasbourg. Whereas in Prussia railway construction had achieved some degree of transport unification (see below p. 249), by 1848 France remained fragmented, at least by the standards of the 1840s.

Industrialism nevertheless created acute social problems. The familiar difficulty experienced by handicraft industries in the face of goods manufactured by machinery, a factor present in all European countries, led to the depression in the standards of living of traditionally prosperous crafts. On the other hand, the lot of the industrial workers was uncertain. There existed a working class, or proletariat, which relied wholly upon its labour for its existence, but the growing industry attracted peasants to the towns, who supplemented their incomes from the land by wage labour. Because they had an alternative source of income, they were willing to accept lower wages than the genuine proletariat, and in moments of economic crisis could return to their homes, where they could be assured of finding enough to eat. French labour in the 1830s and 1840s was therefore diluted, and the genuine industrial workers in the new factories even in the best of times did not enjoy a high standard of living, and during periods of unemployment were given no relief, a factor which accounts for the readiness of the city populations to have recourse to violence in moments of depression. It accounts also for the readiness of the French workers to listen to the doctrines of socialism which were current in France in this period of unrest. Saint-Simon had given an impetus to socialist thinking, which had found fresh expression in the doctrines of Blanqui, Buchez, Louis Blanc, Fourier and Proudhon. Louis Blanc desired a parliament elected by universal suffrage to carry out a programme of social reform for the establishment of a Ministry of Progress controlling the main sectors of the national economy and the foundation of state workshops to provide employment under government supervision. Fourier and Proudhon, however, were not prepared to give the control of economic activity to the state. For them the solution lay in some form of co-operative production in which economic justice might be combined with liberty. It was Proudhon who coined the phrase which struck at the very roots of all the ideas current among the moderates in France—'Property is theft!' The French factory owners differed sharply from the bourgeoisie of 1789, who had been egalitarian in their outlook and thought that all men ought to be given the opportunity of acquiring property. By the 1830s and 1840s employers looked upon the workers with hostility. They believed in *laissez-faire* as a sound economic doctrine, but, whereas in Britain it meant that the government should not interfere with the natural workings of the economy, in France it was taken to mean that the government should not interfere in the relations of employer and worker; most French business men, on the other hand, were in fact strongly protectionist in their outlook and considered that the state had a duty to intervene and safeguard them from foreign competition.

Discontent rose in the 1840s as a result of the investment in railway construction. There persisted the old factors which caused the breakdown of the town–country exchange. By 1847 France was hit by the potato blight and poor grain harvests. In the north and north-west grain prices rose by 100–150 per cent, though in the east and the south-west and south there was a diminishing picture of hardship. In earlier times this would have resulted in a slackening of rural demand for the textiles of the towns, but now was added the factor of the metallurgical revolution, which had expanded the working class of the cities. About 1,000,000,000 francs had been invested in railways and a crisis of overproduction arose. Criticism was directed against the grain policy of the government and against the tariffs, which were declared to be insufficient to exclude foreign textiles and steel.

While elemental murmurings were heard among the workers, the educated classes enfranchised by the constitution were making demands which bore small relation to the basic problems of poverty and hunger. The clericals had certainly sought to make the most of Charles X's short reign and were disappointed by the lack of sympathy shown by the government of Louis Philippe. Under the leadership of Montalembert they took up the question of state education. By a decree of 1816 it had been laid down that there should be a school in every commune, and in 1833 a fresh law authorized the institution of a training college for elementary school teachers, or *École Normale*, in each department. Secondary schools, moreover, were to be set up in the main towns. The schoolteacher (*instituteur*) was required to have a certificate from the state training college, though it was admitted that a member of a religious order could be a schoolteacher. This meant that the state schools would be better staffed than the church schools and that France would fall under the influence of secular thought. It was the object of Montalembert and his newspaper, *L'Univers*, to which he appointed as editor the Catholic zealot, Louis Veuillot, to obtain complete freedom for church education in the hope that the educated class in France might come under the guidance of religious thought and be weaned away from dangerous political doctrines. Guizot, himself a Calvinist, was prepared to make some concessions to the Church and even offered a new education law in 1844, but anti-clericalism was strong in France, and his proposals were rejected by an otherwise disciplined chamber in May 1847. By the beginning of 1848 Guizot could not count upon the support of at least one section of the propertied classes upon which the Orleanist régime sought to base itself.

On the left there was equal discontent. The newspaper *Le National*, under Armand Marrast, was critical of the government. In 1843 was founded *La Réforme*, of which the leading figure was Ledru-Rollin, equally hostile to the government. These manifestations of opposition would have been insignificant if there had not been discontent among the politicians, who ought to have been among the very pillars of Louis Philippe's system. Odilon Barrot and Thiers grew discontented with Guizot's system, which excluded them from office; the frequent changes of government made by Louis Philippe in the first years of his reign multiplied the number of candidates for office. On 25 December 1845 Odilon Barrot and Thiers made a pact by which they undertook to combine to secure constitutional reform. These were not democrats who desired universal suffrage. The limit of their proposals was that the franchise should be extended to persons who paid 100 francs in direct taxes, as opposed to 200 francs in the existing system. Such a reform, they calculated, would be sufficient to secure for them a larger following in the Chamber and enable them to force themselves into office. Guizot challenged this alliance by holding fresh elections in 1846, which returned a handsome government majority but also underlined the fact that the electoral system, which almost invariably enabled the ministry to maintain its hold upon parliament, was in itself bad. In July 1847 the opposition took the decision to organize a series of banquets to agitate for reform. The opposition politicians thus tried to manufacture a crisis within the Orleanist political system, when its very existence was threatened from without. In January 1848 the government decided to put an end to the banquet agitation, and its organizers were prepared not to force the issue. It was merely a question of withdrawing with good grace and no loss of prestige, but the opposition newspapers, *National* and *Réforme*, began to call upon the people to take up the cause of constitutional reform. What had begun as a movement of the professional politicians, by the beginning of 1848 took upon itself the dimensions of a mass agitation.

The French Revolution of 1848

On 22 February 1848, the day of the cancelled banquet, a procession of protest was organized in Paris and the King, believing that a policy of intimidation would be sufficient to frighten the demonstrators, called out the bourgeois National Guard for review for the first time since 1840, but even the National Guard declared for reform. Only then did Louis Philippe realize that a crisis had arisen. Guizot was dismissed and Molé was appointed president of the council of ministers, and the strong man with a reputation made in the fighting in Algeria, Bugeaud, to command the army. As so often happened in the European capitals in 1848, the army clashed with the crowd. On 23 February troops guarding the Ministry of Foreign Affairs fired into the crowd and killed eighty persons. At once barricades were raised all over the city and the mob seized the Hôtel de Ville. Louis Philippe might have withdrawn from the city and permitted the revolution to declare itself. The army was still loyal and could have upheld the régime from the provinces. Instead Louis Philippe decided on 24 February to abdicate in favour of his grandson, the comte de Paris.

Louis Philippe's belief was that by sacrificing himself he might at least preserve his dynasty, but he was to reckon without the mass discontents of Paris, now swollen to a city of 1,250,000 inhabitants.

All those elements which had been compelled to accept the régime of Guizot could now emerge under the cover of the mass violence which was now unleashed. The solidly Orleanist Chamber was invaded by the mob and amid scenes of disorder compelled to nominate a republican government with Lamartine as foreign minister and Ledru-Rollin at the ministry of the interior, assisted by a host of republicans, including Louis Blanc. Universal suffrage was proclaimed and slavery abolished. On 25 February Louis Blanc was appointed to the 'Ministry of Progress and Work', from which he was expected to organize his national workshops, in his view as part of a new socialist order of society, but in the view of his colleagues merely as a form of relief to keep the workers of the city quiet for the moment. Those republicans who were not socialists had a respect for all the dogmas of orthodox finance, balanced budgets and the maintenance of public credit. Not for them could there be a socialist system, nor were many of them entirely in favour of universal manhood suffrage. In reply to a demonstration of the well-to-do Grenadiers of the National Guard, protesting against the disbandment of some of the richer battalions, 100,000 workers of Paris assembled for a manifestation of their own on 17 March 1848 in which two demands were made to the provisional government of the Republic: the regular army was to be excluded from Paris and the elections were to be postponed. Quite clear in these demands was the conception that Paris should be the bastion of a revolution and give leadership to the nation, whether it liked it or not.

The republicans had declared for universal suffrage, but its consequences were easy enough to see. In the elections to the constituent assembly the masses would not support the Republic. Sovereignty would be placed in the hands of the peasants, irritated that the provisional government had increased direct taxation to 45 centimes in the franc in order to restore the public finances of France, the bulk of which would fall upon themselves. Ledru-Rollin did his best to make the administrative system of France serve the interests of the Republic. *Commissaires* were sent to the prefectures, and republicans were appointed in place of Orleanists, but the government enjoyed small success in its attempt to secure a majority for itself. The clericals under Montalembert began to organize their support in the country. The provisional government in its folly appointed Easter Sunday, 24 April 1848, as the day of the election, when the clericals would be certain that they could concentrate every one of their supporters at the polls; pressure by the prefects, easy enough when the electorate was small, was virtually impossible in the conditions pertaining under direct universal manhood suffrage. It was not to be wondered that a conservative majority was returned. In an election in which 84 per cent of the electorate voted local men of substance were chosen in the majority of the provincial seats, and out of a total of 900 members of the Constituent Assembly there were 300 who might be recognized as Orleanists and 150 Legitimists, upholding the cause of the deposed Bourbons. In this way it was demonstrated that representation of the will of people, to which the left wing so often appealed, was not necessarily synonymous with the election of those most desirous of giving that will left-wing or socialist expression. The workers of Paris had brought universal manhood suffrage into existence. There was for them no other course than by a coup d'état to undo the effect of their work.

In the chaotic conditions of the first quarter of 1848, when revolution was spreading throughout Italy and the Rhineland and was to overthrow even the governments of Austria and Prussia, there were those who thought that France would take up again the forward policy of the Revolution and Empire. Indeed, there were Frenchmen of the left who still thought in terms of the European revolution which France would lead, and statesmen in other countries who were prepared to look upon the new government in France with hostile eyes if she gave encouragement to attempts to alter the *status quo* established by the treaties of 1815. As foreign minister Lamartine was determined to allay the suspicions of the powers and on 4 March issued a manifesto, on the one hand, denouncing the provisions of the Vienna treaties, but, on the other hand, accepting them as existing; even before the manifesto was issued the powers were warned that the energetic sentences in it were designed to impress the domestic left-wing opposition. In fact, the French left was not deceived. The revolution of 1848 had released from prison Barbès and Blanqui, who believed that they had at last come into their Babeuvist inheritance. A peaceful foreign policy, among other things, meant that France would give no support to Poland. In March 1848 a short-lived National Committee was established in Poznania, and it was axiomatic in left-wing circles that France, having created the Duchy of Warsaw, should continue now to uphold the Polish cause. On 15 May 1848 a motion in favour of aid to Poland was tabled by the deputy, Wolowski, and Barbès and Blanqui organized in Paris a demonstration in support of Poland, the one point in the left-wing programme upon which all sections of radical Paris were agreed. The purpose of the leaders was to turn the demonstration into an assault upon the government and to place power in the hands of a revolutionary committee. The Chamber of Deputies was invaded by the mob, and for a moment Barbès was able to establish his own provisional government in the Hôtel de Ville, threatening war upon the German and Russian governments if they did not restore Polish independence. This fantasy could not long endure. The bourgeois battalions of the National Guard were called out and with the army restored the authority of the government. Barbès and Blanqui were once more confined to prison and with them their principal associates. The episode was one of considerable significance. The leaders of the extreme left were removed from the scene and the working class of the city deprived of direction.

The men of property who sat in the Constituent Assembly did not look with pleasure upon the working class or upon the national workshops, which they considered an impious imposition upon the taxpayer. At the head of the Labour Committee of the Assembly was the comte de Falloux, who secured the order of 22 June 1848 that all unmarried workers in the national workshops should join the army and the remainder should depart to the provinces. What then occurred was certainly not of the left wing's making. Barricades were erected in the poorer quarters of the city in a spontaneous insurrection of the people against the order. The minister of war, Cavaignac, who had returned from Algiers to take up his post in the government, was determined to teach the people of Paris a lesson. On 24 June the Assembly voted Cavaignac full powers and declared a state of siege in Paris. In six days of savage fighting street by street the forces of the government exacted a savage revenge upon the people, in which there were signs of a systematic massacre of the insurgents. No one knows how many of them were killed and wounded. The losses of the government troops were 1,600, but the Parisian working class may have lost over 10,000 men killed and wounded in the fighting. The prisoners taken amounted to 14,000, of whom the majority were transported to the colonies, especially Algeria. Cavaignac surrendered his dictatorial powers on 28 June, but his action had already set the stamp upon the character of the new régime. Organizations considered dangerous were suppressed, the national workshops abolished, the press circumscribed with renewed restrictions, the administration purged of persons suspected of holding advanced views and courts-martial established to deal with persons involved in these so-called 'June Days'. The victory of the men of property was complete, but the very savagery with which they exploited it created a deep fissure in French society. The population of Paris had no love for the bourgeoisie of the National Guard and the peasant soldiers who had executed the orders of the Assembly and Cavaignac with such unnecessary thoroughness. The Constituent Assembly of 1848 only widened the gap between the propertied classes and the workers of Paris and other industrial cities.

With the government under the virtual control of Cavaignac and with a satisfactory harvest some semblance of normality was restored in France in the second half of 1848. The constitution promulgated on 12 November 1848 reflected both the events which brought the Republic into existence in February and the fears which were excited by the June Days. Provisions were made for a single-chamber parliament consisting of 750 deputies, elected for three years by universal suffrage, but at the same time for a president with executive power, elected also by universal suffrage, whose task was to appoint the ministers, command the army and control the central organs of the administration. The one limitation upon the power of the president was that his office was tenable only for four years and he was not eligible for re-election. In one sense it was a liberal constitution, but in another it concentrated too much power in the president, who was both head of state and head of the administration. The new parliament represented the people, but so equally did the president. In their desire for strong government the authors of the constitution had made a rod for their own back. In any conflict between the assembly and the president the latter might appear to have a moral right himself to appeal to the people.

The election of the president was appointed for 10 December 1848. Cavaignac offered his own candidature as a right-wing republican, and with him stood Ledru-Rollin and, representing the republican left, Raspail, who could rally the socialist vote. A newcomer, scarcely involved in the events which had preceded the promulgation of the constitution, was Louis Napoleon Bonaparte, son of Louis Bonaparte, formerly King of Holland, and Hortense de Beauharnais. Louis Napoleon Bonaparte superficially had nothing to recommend him. With the death of Napoleon I's son, the Duke of Reichstadt, in 1832 there was no apparent reason for which the cause of the Bonapartes should revive. In 1840 Napoleon I's body was brought back from St Helena and entombed in the Invalides without causing more than a stir of mild nostalgia for the glories of the past. His nephew, Louis Napoleon, had engaged in a number of scrapes and twice invaded France, first in 1836 at Strasbourg, and second at Boulogne in 1840, without evoking any response to his cause. From 1840 to 1846 he was imprisoned in Ham, whence he escaped to London. What he saw when he returned to France in February 1848 did not please him and he withdrew to England, to appear again in France after the June Days to get himself elected in a Paris by-election to the Constituent Assembly. The hostility expressed by the Assembly towards him caused him again to withdraw, but on 17 September 1848, without any significant canvassing, he was again elected for a Paris constituency, this time at the head of the poll. There can be no doubt that among the candidates who offered themselves for election to the presidency Louis Napoleon was the least impressive. Having been educated in Germany, he spoke with a German accent and with such lack of fluency that he was dismissed as a nonentity. So stumbling were his speeches that there were politicians, ignoring the evidence of two separate by-elections which indicated that he could command popular support in his own right, who thought that he would be incompetent and therefore a tool in their hands. The politicians of the Orleanist opposition, Odilon Barrot and Thiers, with their followers among the professional political class, thought that they could use Louis Napoleon to give them the ministerial posts which they had coveted in the years immediately before 1848. There were the clericals, who had no love for the conservative, but staunchly anti-clerical Cavaignac, and who under the leadership of Montalembert and Falloux were ready to give even a Bonaparte their votes if he in return would permit them to expand the system of church schools.

The monarchists were in the majority, but had not yet resolved the rival claims of the houses of Bourbon and Orleans; the presidency of a Bonaparte for four years seemed to offer them a breathing space during which they could compose their differences. Louis Napoleon had flirted with most things in his time, including Carbonarism and Socialism. The most serious of his literary efforts was *Des Idées Napoléoniennes* (Napoleonic Ideas), published in 1839, a specious plea that the Bonaparte dynasty stood for social justice. His vague socialist ideas were enough to win him some support in the towns where the big bourgeoisie and Cavaignac were discredited after the horrors of the June Days. He was therefore not without appeal to the politically conscious elements in France. Sovereignty under the system of universal suffrage, however, lay with the peasants, naïve in their political judgments and wishing for a return to stability. Without much appreciation of the realities of politics in Paris, they at least recognized the name Bonaparte when they heard it. Cavaignac, Ledru-Rollin and Raspail meant nothing to them.

When the results of the elections were declared Louis Napoleon Bonaparte was elected with 5,400,000 votes against the 1,400,000 for Cavaignac, 300,000 for Ledru-Rollin and a mere 37,000 for Raspail. On 20 December Louis Napoleon was sworn in and at once did what the professional politicians expected of him. Odilon Barrot was appointed president of the council of ministers, with Drouyn de Lhuys, a man with considerable diplomatic experience under Louis Philippe, as minister for foreign affairs. On the other hand, Falloux was appointed minister of education as a gesture to the clericals, who were shortly to receive a promise from the president that French troops would be sent to extricate Pope Pius IX from his difficulties in Italy, where in Rome a republican government had been established. Louis Napoleon left it to the ministry to deal with the remnants of the republican left. On 29 January 1849 the society of *Solidarité Républicaine* was suppressed and twenty-seven active republicans arrested in spite of the refusal of the Assembly to give authority for this action. For the moment Louis Napoleon Bonaparte was prepared to tread warily. It was not immediately apparent that he harboured ambitions and he was content to remain all things to all men until he could build up for himself a Bonapartist party in France. In the meantime he could leave politics to the politicians to play as they saw fit. His problem was to convert himself from being a name into being a national figure. By touring the provinces and establishing connections Louis Napoleon set out to draw a distinction between himself and the politicians of the Legislative Assembly. For all the apparent victory of the propertied classes in 1848 the constitution invited a struggle between the Assembly and the President to determine which of the two should exercise executive power.

Central Europe Before 1848

I. Constitutionalism in Germany before 1848

The Germanic Confederation consisted of thirty-nine states, bound together in a union which was extremely loose. It is true that the Confederation was an improvement upon the situation which had existed before the wars. A Federal Council (*Bundestag*) existed at Frankfort under the presidency of Austria. Power, if it rested at all, was in the hands of Austria, Prussia, Bavaria, Württemberg, Saxony, Baden, Electoral Hesse, the Grand Duchy of Hesse, the King of Denmark as sovereign in Holstein and the King of the Netherlands in his capacity as Grand Duke of Luxemburg; the smaller principalities and the free cities counted for nothing. In fact, predominance rested with Austria, subject to the condition that due consideration was given to Prussian views. The Confederation was a creation of the Congress of Vienna to prevent French expansionism, but it did not correspond to a modern state.

After the defeat of France the petty states of the north, west and south were granted constitutions by their rulers, or to use the contemporary term were given *octroyé* constitutions, in the sense that they owed nothing to popular will. Frederick William III of Prussia in a moment of ill-considered enthusiasm before the battle of Waterloo promised on 22 May 1815 to concede a system of national representation to his dominions, but he never honoured his promise. Prussia and Austria remained, by comparison with the other states of Germany, countries in which constitutional life, if it existed at all, was based upon provincial assemblies which gave a not very large say in affairs to the nobility in the individual provinces, able to make addresses to the throne, but incapable of determining official policy. For the rest of Germany the parliaments did not enjoy the prestige even of glorified county councils. The best that can be said of the German constitutions after 1814 was that they acquainted Germans with the formalities of constitutionalism without conceding to the representatives real power. On the one hand, Germans looked for the advantages of a wider unity, but too often they were conscious of the advantages which they derived from princely particularism. Honorific posts and the dignity conferred by the possession of titles in the last resort often outrode higher considerations of national welfare. Particularism had deep roots in Germany, both among the princes and among the educated class. With some truth it may be said that, though the German state did not exist, no population has received such close attention from the state as the Germans. The German princes were conscious of their position as sovereigns, and their subjects rewarded them with deference and frequently sycophancy upon a scale unknown in, for example, the more robust political conditions of Britain, where, in spite of court etiquette, the monarch fully understood that the revolution of 1688-9 was based upon a compromise between king, lords and commons. Civic initiative in Germany, for the moderates, at least, was conditioned by a traditional respect for the rulers of the individual states. Nevertheless, the western regions of Germany had come under the influence of the French Revolution, and the left bank of the Rhine and parts of north-western Germany had for a time actually been part of France. The contrast between passive acceptance of the existing régimes and the potentialities of a united Germany created a radicalism outside the ranks of the officials, representatives and notables of the princely states. Karl Marx, born at Trier in 1818 and editor of the *Rhenische Zeitung* from 1842 to 1843, was the most famous, but only one of a new generation of Germans who wished to make a clean sweep of the petty principalities and convert Germany into a modern state with modern institutions. The radicals were, however, weak, and like the Babeuvists of France awaited the uprising of the people to bring them to power.

II. THE AUSTRIAN EMPIRE

In the past it was customary to regard Metternich as being the most important figure in Europe before 1848, but there was never even a *prima facie* case for this supposition. Metternich was to claim that

'J'ai gouverné l'Europe quelque fois, l'Autriche jamais'. In the first part of this statement there was little truth, because Austria was fundamentally a weak power, beset with financial difficulties, which rendered her cautious in foreign policy after 1815. In the second half of this sentence there is complete truth, because Metternich, though he was chancellor of Austria for thirty-nine years, never succeeded in imposing his will upon the Emperor Francis I (1792–1835), who remained until his death the real master of the state. At first Francis had shown some immaturity and an inclination to allow his ministers to rule his dominions for him, but between 1807 and 1809 he began to develop an interest in government and to exert his own autocratic powers. Francis I was not a genius. He was a man capable of hard work, and his very industry led him into a stiff pedantic routine, in which the smooth functioning of the bureaucracy became more important for him than the policy which the Austrian state was pursuing. Francis surrounded himself with men of a similar frame of mind, distinguished neither by their grasp of affairs nor by their intelligence. In fact, Francis suspected capable men, an unattractive feature of his personality which found expression in his jealousy of his brothers, the Archdukes Charles, John and Joseph, the Palatine of Hungary. Instead he turned to the shallow Archduke Ludwig, to whom on his death of 1835 he entrusted the oversight of affairs in the Empire. Francis was equally suspicious of the generals who had made reputations during the war, Schwarzenberg and Radetzky. In this system Metternich was compelled always to follow the general line of policy mapped out by Francis I, who kept a firm hand upon all branches of the state. Especially in internal affairs was the maximum security sought. In 1817 the interior came under the control of the police chief, Sedlnitzky, popularly supposed to be a tool of Metternich, but in fact the right-hand man of the Emperor, who did not hesitate to open the letters of even Metternich's assistant, Gentz. The letters of the Austrian foreign ministry to the Hospodars of Wallachia were regularly tampered with and, since Metternich was aware of this, serve as a valuable source of information on what Metternich wished his master, Francis, to think was the policy being pursued in international affairs. A strict censorship was imposed in Austria, which reached ridiculous proportions. No stories or plays which dealt with the subject of regicide or revolt might be made available to the public. German patriotic literature was excluded from the Empire. A strict control was maintained over the writing of history. After the upsets of 1830 Austrian students were prohibited from studying in foreign universities. Syllabuses were carefully prescribed in order that nothing disapproved of by the state or the Church might find its way into the ears of the students. The press was allowed to publish nothing which the state might consider inconvenient.

The stifling intellectual atmosphere of Austria under Francis I had its counterpart in the perennial financial difficulties of the state, which prevented Austria from speaking with full authority in international affairs. In 1812 Austria was bankrupt, and one of the tasks of Philip von Stadion, appointed minister of finance in 1814, was to put Austria's financial affairs in order. Some progress was made in the financial edicts of 1816 and 1818. A national bank was established, the issue of paper money kept under control and a sinking fund set up, but Stadion did not succeed in balancing the budget before he died in 1824. In 1829 once more a financial crisis set in. The view of the Bohemian nobleman, Kolowrat, was that among the causes of Austria's chronic insolvency was the excessive interest paid on the state debt, the repayment of foreign subsidies contracted in time of war, the fact that Hungary made all too small a contribution to the central treasury and the circumstance that far too much money was expended upon the upkeep of the army and upon Metternich's foreign policy. Kolowrat was himself a feudal aristocrat, but with regard to Austrian internal policy he was a Josephine centralist, for which reason he obtained the confidence of Francis I when he became a minister in 1826. Kolowrat knew that the system of Francis I, with its endless delays, lay at the root of Austria's troubles and was on occasion tempted to resign, but in the end he remained a member of the administration and the dominant voice in internal affairs, for ever demanding a modest foreign policy which would reduce military expenditure. Francis I, who was determined to maintain ultimate control in his own hands, was not loth to see the advancement of a man whom he could play off against Metternich. Autocratic monarchs customarily preserved their power by keeping their leading officials divided against one another.

The conflict between Metternich and Kolowrat revolved around a matter of principle. From Metternich's point of view the main need of Austria was co-ordination of the various departments of state. From time to time in Austrian history there had been efforts to shift the burden of routine work from the shoulders of the Emperor. Under Maria Theresa there was a council of state, formed by Kaunitz, to deal with all matters not relating to war, finance and foreign affairs. In 1802 there was created under the pressure of the Archduke Charles a *Staats- und Konferenzministerium* of six members, including the Emperor, which was to seek effective co-ordination of the state departments, but Francis rendered this reform ineffective by excluding matters of general policy and including questions of detail. Metternich realized the dangers of the system and sought some measure of decentralization. He was willing to base the future of the Empire upon the diets of the individual provinces and the Hungarian parliament; in short, this was a conservative solution which looked to the support of the historic nobility of the Habsburg lands. From 1811 onwards Metternich pressed for the revival of the Council of State to undertake general discussion upon policy, but invariably he found Francis I unwilling to consider any reform which infringed his own rights as an autocratic ruler. When he fell ill in 1826 Francis promised reform, but on his recovery soon reverted to his old policy of inactivity. In 1834 a similar situation occurred and Francis I undertook to mend his ways, but he recovered, only to die in 1835 having done nothing to meet Metternich's demands. Metternich's proposals virtually amounted to putting the powers of the Crown in commission, which was a solution which Francis I could not stomach. Thus under his rule stability in Austria became synonymous with inertia.

Francis was succeeded by the Emperor Ferdinand, his son, who suffered from rickets and epilepsy and could not therefore exert the same control over the administration as his father. Francis I in his will appointed the Archduke Ludwig as tutor to Ferdinand in domestic affairs and Metternich to advise him in foreign affairs. Kolowrat was not included in the provisions of Francis I's will, but the Archduke Ludwig soon took up the traditional policy of keeping Metternich and Kolowrat divided. The incapacity of the Emperor in theory ought to have presented a strong case for the creation of a council of state, but the system of paralysis which had grown up under Francis continued. When in 1836 a project for a council of state was once more put forward, Kolowrat rejected any measure which would lead to the reduction of his own importance in the conduct of internal affairs. Metternich was virtually excluded from all voice in the domestic affairs of the Empire.

Metternich could not, however, ignore the problems created by the multi-national nature of the Austria dominions. The core of the Austrian state lay in its German population concentrated in Austria proper, but representing a substantial minority everywhere, especially in the towns, but national aspirations were entertained by the Magyars of Hungary and by the Slavs of the Empire. The Slavonic peoples, who included the Poles, the Ruthenians of Galicia and north-eastern Hungary, the Czechs of Bohemia, the Slovaks of the northern parts of Hungary, and the Slovenes, Croats and Serbs of the south, were the largest single group with common ethnic affinities, but there were equally the Italians and the Rumans to be reckoned with. If once the constituent peoples of the empire became infected with revolutionary nationalism the Habsburg dominions would fall apart. Reform, which proved that the Habsburg dynasty had a role to fulfil and in performing it could contribute to a better life for the mass of the population, might have developed a loyalty to Vienna which would have counteracted separatist leanings, but the inertia imposed upon Austria by Francis I prevented the administration from adopting a progressive policy. Even Metternich's policy of giving greater control to the regional aristocracies would have been sufficient, because everywhere in the provinces the social domination of the great estate owners was being challenged by the middle classes. In consequence of his own powerlessness within Austria Metternich was thrown back upon the one field of Austrian policy in which he enjoyed some freedom of movement, namely, foreign affairs. In the face of the impending crisis he considered that it was essential to insulate Austria from the doctrines of nationalism, above all, from German nationalism, because, if a unitary German state were created, the Germans of Austria would be attracted to it and, if they seceded from the Austrian dominions, the other portions of the empire would naturally themselves seek separation.

Austria was endowed by the treaty of Vienna with the presidency of the Germanic Confederation, which gave Metternich the power to interfere in German affairs. German nationalism had certainly become a political factor as a result of the Napoleonic conquest. The simplification and reduction of the mass of petty states to an intelligible union under the Confederation of the Rhine and the creation of the Germanic Confederation in 1815 had encouraged a taste for unity. There grew up student associations, *Burschenschaften*, which were little more than drinking clubs with vaguely patriotic aims, but no particular political significance. On 18 October 1817 there was a meeting at Wartburg to celebrate the 300th anniversary of the Lutheran Reformation, a fraternal gathering of students with a religious rather than a political significance, but a minority of the participants took the occasion to burn books of which they disapproved, a corporal's cane and a military corselet, all of which were regarded as being symbolic of reaction. During the winter of 1817–18 discussions were held at Jena in order to formulate a political programme. The Jena students stated that they required the normal civic liberties, free speech, trial by jury, a free press, the abolition of serfdom and the secret police, and, above all, the erection of a constitutional federal state ruled by a German emperor, but equally it was recommended that they should abstain from joining secret societies and should serve in offices of state, provided that they were not connected with the secret police or the censorship. Their demands were therefore moderate, but only seven students could be found to sign the manifesto. The majority were too frightened for their careers to risk annoying the authorities to whom they look for employment. There was some radicalism in the Grand Duchy of Hesse-Darmstadt, where a certain Carl Follen emerged as an ideological leader of the students, demanding the unification of all Germans, including the Swiss, Alsatians, the Frisians and the Dutch, but excluding the Jews. Though there were peasant disturbances in Hesse in the winter of 1818, caused by a drought, which rendered heavy taxation more than usually burdensome, there were few students to throw in their lot with the peasants. The German intelligentsia was not revolutionary, but among them were men who talked airily of action. Such idle talk was taken seriously by Carl Ludwig Sand, a Jena student, who without informing his comrades travelled to Mannheim and murdered a right-wing journalist, Kotzebue, on 23 March 1819. Kotzebue was not a person of much importance, and his murder could hardly have been the signal for a great rising of the people.

Sand was undoubtedly a man of unbalanced mind whose act certainly did not have the authorization of any German student group, but it provided Metternich with the opportunity which he sought to nip German nationalism in the bud. Convincing Frederick William III of Prussia that a dangerous situation was arising, Metternich was able to issue the so-called Carlsbad Decrees, which were given the approval of the Germanic Confederation on 20 September 1819. They provided for the investigation of secret societies, the censorship of the press and laid down the principle that a student expelled from one German university might not thereafter be admitted to another. In this manner the German princes combined to suppress vocal discontent even of the most mild kind and, in doing so, endowed the *Burschenschaften* with a halo of martyrdom, which gave them a prestige which they scarcely deserved. The German intellectuals of the years immediately after the war against France were in fact timid and subservient to authority.

III. The Economic Problems of Germany after 1815

The creation of the Germanic Confederation offered some political strength to what had formerly been a power vacuum, but the divisions of Germany were still inconvenient. The restoration of normal trading conditions led to the influx of cheap British manufactures, where once the Napoleonic Continental System had protected the native producer. Some progress had been made towards greater economic freedom before 1815. Bavaria, Württemberg and Baden had abandoned their internal customs barriers, but Prussia had no general customs frontier. On 26 May 1818 a new Prussian tariff came into force with the object of protecting the Rhineland and Prussian Saxony from British competition. Colonial goods, wines and manufactured goods were made liable to tariffs, but raw materials were in general admitted free; all internal customs dues and prohibitions upon imports and exports were abandoned. This was a measure designed to lead to the unification of Prussia, but it gave some annoyance to the German states outside the Prussian system. Under Article XIX of the Act of Confederation provision had been made for discussions on economic affairs and there grew up a powerful agitation, led by Frederick List and others, for a general German tariff against British goods. Prussia, however, pursued her own course, determined by practical difficulties, rather than by any conscious policy of prompting German unity. There were within Prussia a number of small states which formed enclaves, with which she concluded customs unions, the first being Schwarzburg-Sonder-hausen, a petty state of 30,000 inhabitants, which joined the Prussian system in 1819. By 1830 this problem had been solved as far as Prussia was concerned. Bavaria likewise followed this policy. On 18 January 1828 Bavaria and Württemberg entered into a customs union. On 14 February 1829 Hesse-Darmstadt, experiencing grave difficulties because she was cut off from the Prussian market, entered the Prussian system. This growing economic unity was not to the liking of Austria, and under her influence a Middle German Commercial Union of Hanover, Hesse-Cassel, Saxony, Brunswick, Nassau, Frankfort-on-the-Main, Bremen and the Thuringian states were created on 24 September 1828, which proved a channel for British trade and smuggling and therefore incurred the hostility of Prussia. In 1831, however, Hesse-Cassel decided to join the Prussian system, thus splitting the Middle German Commercial Union and at the same time providing a link between the eastern and western portions of the Kingdom of Prussia.

In August 1832 Hanover proposed to the Diet of the Confederation that a general customs union should be created, a *Zollverein*, which would include all the German states, but the negotiations broke down. Prussia took the attitude that the individual states of the Confederation might conclude customs treaties with her, but that she would not be party to a general system. In the course of 1833 Bavaria, Württemberg, the Thuringian states and Saxony joined with Prussia, and from 1 January 1834 came into force the *Zollverein* under the leadership of Prussia, to be joined by Baden and Nassau in 1835 and Frankfort-on-the-Main in 1836. The union was not complete, but at least there came into existence a commercial unit of about 25,000,000 inhabitants which could speak with authority in matters of trade to the other states of Europe. It was ironical that the *Zollverein* should have been led by the least constitutional of the German states. Prussia's position in Germany was such that she served as the focus of attraction for those Germans who desired unification. Prussia was the largest German state, and it seemed logical that she should be the nucleus of the new Germany.

IV. GERMAN LIBERALISM ON THE OUTBREAK OF THE REVOLUTIONS OF 1848

The German liberals of 1848 have often been despised for the attitude which they adopted towards the Prussian state when they had the opportunity of taking power into their own hands, but this is altogether too simple a view. It must not be supposed that they in fact did wish to assume power. The core of the problem lay in the Rhineland. Traditionally the state intervened to assist the poor in times of hardship. In 1845 there was a failure of the potato crop. In 1846 there was a grain failure. Between July and October 1845 there was a 50 per cent rise in the price of potatoes, but by July 1846 it was 300 per cent. By July 1847 the price had again risen and reached the figure of 425 per cent. The price of wheat rose by about 250 per cent over the same period, while a slightly lower rise is recorded for rye. The price of barley had risen by 300 per cent. This was a crisis which the finances even of the Prussian state could do little to offset. The magnitude of the problem was too great. In the advanced industrial areas of the Rhineland the Zollverein tariffs did not in fact protect native industry against British and Belgian competition. There was added the problem of a conflict between the old handicraft industries which could not compete with the new machinery. Labour was without defence against exploitation by the factory owners. As in France, the capitalists exhibited apathy and lack of interest in the welfare of the workers, for which they felt no sense of responsibility. In the crisis of high food prices and unemployment, accentuated by the exceptionally cold winter months of January and February 1848, the situation grew very tense. The workers who had the money in many cases emigrated to the United States, where afterwards, quite erroneously, it was supposed that they had been driven out by political oppression. In fact, they fled from the political consequences of the depression. The majority of the working men of the Rhineland could not afford the money for a passage to the United States. For them in the face of the government's inability to alleviate their lot there was only the alternative of revolution, and by the 1840s there were Rhenish German intellectuals, of whom Karl Marx was among the most active, who would have given leadership to a proletarian revolution.

The upper classes in the towns of the Rhineland knew exactly the dangers which faced them. Men like Ludolf Camphausen of Cologne and David Hansemann of Aachen, who were to enter the Prussian government as ministers in 1848, were well aware of the risk of a proletarian revolution. They knew that there were Prussian bureaucrats who even sought an alliance with the proletariat in order to avoid power passing into the hands of the Rhenish bourgeoisie. The Rhenish liberals therefore wanted, on the one hand, the development of constitutional freedoms and the introduction of reforms which would favour themselves, but they desired, on the other hand, to control the proletarian revolution which threatened them from below. It was therefore axiomatic that they should seek to maintain the structure especially of the Prussian state and the efficiency of the Prussian army as a safeguard against attacks upon property. The moderate liberals required only an alliance between themselves and the King under a parliamentary system modelled upon the Belgian constitution. Far from being revolutionary, the Rhenish bourgeoisie feared the masses and were ready to be content with an *octroyé* constitution. There were, moreover, external dangers.

The German liberals of the 1840s were fired with a patriotism which had little in common with the humanitarian idealism of Herder in the eighteenth century. In common with other European peoples the Germans were infected with competitive nationalism to which they lent a vulgarity all of their own. Ernst Moritz Arndt (1769–1860) was giving German nationalism a racialist twist, which was in the long run to have unfortunate consequences both for Germany and Europe. For him the Germans enjoyed a superiority over all other European peoples:

> The Germans are not bastardized by alien peoples. They have not become mongrels, they have remained more than other peoples in their original purity and have been able to develop slowly and quietly from this purity of their kind and nature according to the lasting laws of time; the fortunate Germans are an original people.

Whereas the muddle-headed Mazzini at least appealed to God and Humanity, there was a mystical quality in German nationalism which could not be reconciled with the obvious fact that in the mixed nationality areas of Central Europe Germans would have to live side by side with other peoples, mainly Slavs. Already the good will non-

German peoples had towards Germany was subject to reservations. German liberalism was in fact aggressive. The crisis of 1840, when Thiers showed signs of making war against the rest of Europe rather than permit the French protégé, Mehemet Ali, to be coerced, gave rise to German claims to the German-speaking areas of Alsace and Lorraine, but German hostility was directed mainly against Russia. The defeat of the Polish revolution of 1830-1 and the passage of Polish refugees across Germany to France was an event of great importance in the political thinking of German liberals. For the first time the nearness of Russian power was appreciated. It was realized that the great enemy of German unification was Russia, which bolstered the morale of the petty princes and upheld the system of particularism which prevented Germany from becoming a great power in the political sense. While for internal reasons the German bourgeoisie in the Rhineland wished to maintain the Prussian army against the dangers of proletarian revolution, in the realm of foreign policy the Prussian army was required for a war against Russia. Russia was to be driven back out of Central Europe. The process by which she had been advanced towards the west under the terms of the treaty of Vienna in 1815 was to be reversed. Poland was to be re-created as a buffer state between Germany and Russia. In this lay the inherent weakness of German liberalism. The restoration of a Polish state would raise the awkward question of what should be done with the Polish provinces of Prussia. In Poznania, West Prussia and Upper Silesia there was a substantial Polish population, which, if it claimed the same rights of nationality as the Germans claimed for themselves, had a right to be included in the projected Polish state. At the same time the instrument of driving Russia out of Germany, the Prussian army, was officered almost entirely by the gentry of the Ostalbingian provinces, who, so far from believing that Russia was the enemy of Germany, recalled the Russian liberation of Germany in 1813 and looked with favour upon the conservative views of Nicholas I, which seemed a guarantee of maintaining the landed proprietor's social and political power in central Europe. The first act of war by Germany against Russia was likely to cause the Prussian army to range itself on the side of the Russian forces in a common effort to restore the old régime where it could not meet the challenge of liberalism. Severe as the crisis was, which Prussia was to undergo in 1848, the dynasty and the bureaucracy, which bolstered it up against the pressure of the liberal opposition, were not without advantages, which they were able to exploit as the realities of internal and external affairs were more closely considered by the bourgeoisie.

The Revolution of 1848 in Germany and Austria

The revolution which broke out in France in February 1848 in part had its origins in a political agitation for reform. Reform was equally in the air in Germany. By the beginning of 1847 the government of Prussia found itself in serious financial difficulties, and on 3 February 1847 Frederick William IV called a 'United Diet' of the eight constituent portions of the Prussian Kingdom. The liberals of Prussia remembered that Frederick William III in a moment of generosity in 1815 had promised to call a States General of his dominions and had never honoured his word. The terms upon which the United Diet were to meet proved a grave disappointment. The assembly was to have a consultative function only, though the right of submitting petitions was conceded. The Diet was, moreover, divided into a house of lords (*Herrenkurie*) and a lower chamber representing large property, the towns and the countryside; only on questions of finance would the two chambers hold joint meetings. This was a solution which was highly unpopular and attributed to the reactionary Prince of Prussia, William, the king's brother and heir presumptive to the throne. The Rhenish liberal, Camphausen, desired to make the most of the limited opportunities which presented themselves and convinced the doubtful liberals from East Prussia that they should enter into an alliance with him rather than refuse to attend. In this manner a liberal majority was secured in the lower house and the King, instead of solving his difficulties, found himself with a constitutional crisis on his hands. On 11 April 1847 he refused to grant a written constitution, which he contemptuously called 'a scrap of paper', while for their part the liberal majority refused to the government the loan it required for the construction of a railway from Berlin to Königsberg.

It appeared likely that a constitutional impasse would occur, but Camphausen was determined not to permit an open break with the monarchy. On 26 June 1847 the United Diet was dissolved and no decision was taken upon its next meeting, but Camphausen, in spite of severe criticism, agreed to the election of a 'Permanent Commission' of the United Diet to act in a consultative capacity. In its way the Diet and the commission gave Prussia a sense of unity which would have been impossible if the state had continued to exist as eight separate provinces. The actual calling of the Diet confirmed the liberal opinion in Germany that Prussia was the best choice of a state to head a union. Conferences were held in Offenburg on 12 September 1847 and at Heppenheim on 10 October 1847 to swing opinion in the states of the west and south-west in favour of Prussian leadership. By chance Bavaria, so often the stumbling block in German politics, was experiencing a crisis in which the clerical party and the liberals were united in their opposition to the King, Ludwig I, who had conceived a passion for the English demimondaine, who passed by the name of Lola Montez, under which she appeared on the stage as a rather indifferent dancer. In February 1847 the President of the Council, Abel, resigned, rather than be a party to the improprieties attendant upon the scandal, and in his place was appointed the Rhenish protestant, Maurer, who promised to make an end of 'the party of the Jesuits'. As a result of student demonstrations on 8 February 1848 the king decided to close the university and was in his turn requested by the president of the Bavarian chamber of peers, Karl von Leiningen, a half-brother of Queen Victoria, to exile Lola Montez. In this way even the most backward of the South-German states found itself in a state of crisis.

While constitutionalism and reform were under discussion the elemental disasters began to have their effect. In March 1848 in Baden, Württemberg, Hesse-Darmstadt and parts of Franconia the peasants began to rise in revolt against the landlords. Poor harvests had made intolerable the multitudinous feudal dues which remained to burden them. The peasants wished to be rid of seigneurial rights, hunting rights and arbitrary tithes. They required the lords to surrender their right to appoint mayors to the rural communes and demanded that they as well as the peasants pay communal taxes. There was repeated in southern and western Germany the same phenomenon as in France in 1789. The castles were attacked and the manorial records were destroyed in order that the landlords might have nothing in future to appeal to. Foresters and bailiffs were attacked everywhere and violence was given to the Jews, western and southern Germany being a seedbed of anti-Semitism. Equally the movement extended itself to the towns with attacks upon the municipal governments and upon the administrations of the petty states. Baden, Württemberg, Hesse-Darmstadt and Nassau fell before the revolutions and conceded the liberal demands. In Bavaria Karl von Leiningen took control and in the face of overwhelming unpopularity Ludwig I abdicated on 19 March in favour of his son, Maximilian. The surly Ernest-Augustus of Hanover submitted to the demand for a constitution on 17 March. The King of Saxony could not hold out against the hostility of the cities of Dresden and Leipzig. Even the Imperial Free Cities found their oligarchical governments challenged.

This was success indeed for liberalism and so complete that it could not have been unaccompanied by fear. The urban liberals did not look with pleasure upon the peasant jacqueries, nor could they feel entirely certain of the town mobs. In their anxiety they looked first to the large power, Prussia, to protect them. On 4 March 1848 occurred an event which in part resolved their difficulties. Lamartine, criticized at home for his lack of vigour in the conduct of French foreign policy, but at the same time anxious to reassure the powers of French pacific intent, on 4 March issued a manifesto which defined his government's position in European affairs, in which the vital phrase was:

> ... The treaties of 1815 legally no longer exist in the eyes of the French Republic; ... still their territorial clauses are a fact admitted by her as basis and starting point in relations with other nations.

This could mean nothing else than that France had no intention of resuming her forward foreign policy and that Germany was safe from any external danger in the west. On 5 March 1848 a meeting of fifty-one liberal notables was held in Heidelberg at which it was decided that the liberal opposition itself might take the initiative and summon for 31 March 1848 a Pre-Parliament in Frankfort to lay down the conditions for electing an all-German National Assembly. Initiative was taken out of the hands of the princes by the liberal bourgeoisie, though even at this meeting there was a division between the partisans of a republic and the supporters of an empire. In these circumstances it appeared necessary for the princes of Germany themselves to take the initiative. Max von Gagern, an official in the service of the Duke of Nassau, induced his master to send him upon a mission to the German Courts in order to obtain the adherence of the German princes to a policy of strengthening the Confederation.

At the beginning of March 1848 only the smaller states of Germany felt the full impact of the revolutionary movement. Prussia and Austria were apparently immune from the virus of revolution. In spite of the fact that Austria was shielded from all the influences of radicalism by the vigilance of the censorship and the police, Vienna also felt sympathy for the prevailing demands for reform. Like all cities, it, too, had a working class which was subject to the pressures imposed upon it by the general economic crisis. To the surprise of all Germany an insurrection broke out in Vienna on 13 March 1848. The middle class of Vienna had no love for the humdrum government of a state in which dynamic leadership was conspicuously lacking. The teachers and students of the university were suffocated by a system which reduced learning to the repetition of stale truths. By themselves the students and the middle class would have been insufficient to threaten the stability of the Habsburg Empire, but beyond them were the mass of the working class seething with discontent. The leading figures of the administration were not unaware that a revolutionary situation might arise. The popular governor of Styria, the Archduke John, the Archduchess Sophia and Kolowrat were prepared to yield before the need arose, but Metternich and the Archduke Ludwig were inclined to belittle the dangers which approached. Discussions in the council of state revealed that there was a desire among the leading figures of the empire to summon a parliament from representatives of the provincial diets, but, as had often happened before, no definite decision was taken. Metternich was confident that this was one more crisis which he could surmount and opposed concessions. On 13 March there were spontaneous gatherings in the streets which merged into a vast crowd before the building in which the Estates of Lower Austria were meeting. The Estates were invaded by the mob and compelled to transmit to the Emperor a demand for a constitution embracing all the territories of the empire. As so often occurred in 1848, the military fired into the crowd, and everywhere barricades were set up in the narrow streets of the old city. Metternich would have offered resistance, but he had

Louis XVI in the hands of the mob, 1792.

2 The execution of Louis XVI.

3 The coup d'état o
1799. A propagand
picture.

4 Napoleon I in 1814.

5 The Congress of Vienna 1814–15: The plenipotentiaries of the powers.

1. Wellington	Britain	13. Baron von Wessenberg	Austria
2. Lobo da Silveira	Portugal	14. Prince Razumovsky	Russia
3. Antonio de Saldahna da Gama	Portugal	15. Lord Stewart	Britain
4. Count Löwenhielm	Sweden	16. Don Pedro Gomez Labrador	Spain
5. Prince Hardenberg	Prussia	17. Lord Clancarty	Britain
6. Count Alexis de Noailles	France	18. M. Nikolaus von Wacken	Secretary
7. Metternich	Austria	19. Friedrich von Gentz	Bureau
8. Count de La Tour du Pin	France	20. Baron von Humboldt	Prussia
9. Nesselrode	Russia	21. Lord Cathcart	Britain
10. Pedro de Sousa Holstein		22. Talleyrand	France
de Palmella	Portugal	23. Count Gustav Stackelberg	Russia
11. Castlereagh	Britain		
12. Duc de Dalberg	France		

6 Prince Clemens Wenzel Lothar Metternich-Winneburg (1773–1859).

7 ALEXANDER I OF RUSSIA
(1777–1825).

8 NICHOLAS I OF RUSSIA
(1796–1855).

9 ALEXANDER II OF RUSSIA
(1818–81).

10 Boulton and Watt beam rotative engine 1827.

11 A British locomotive of 1843 (exhibited at the Festival of Britain, 1951).

12 The *Great Eastern*, 1858.

13 A battleship of 1861, H.M.S. *Warrior*.

14 Karl Marx (1818–83).

15 Charles Darwin (1809–82).

16 A barricade in the Rue St Martin, Paris, 1848.

17 A clash between the army and the populace
before the Royal Palace at Berlin, 1848.

18 A sitting of the German National Assembly, 1848.

19 Pope Pius IX (1792–1878), elected 1846.

20 GIUSEPPE GARIBALDI (1807–82) on the Isle of Caprera.

21 CAMILLO CAVOUR (1810–

22 The Battle of Gettysburg, 1863.

4 Otto von Bismarck-
chönhausen (1815–98).

25 Louis Napoleon Bonaparte
(1808–73)
(Napoleon III, Emperor of the
French). A photograph of 1871.

26

(a) A musket

(b) A musket modified to be used as a breech loader.

(c) A Martini-Henry rifle of 1869.

his enemies in the Court who were only too ready to use this opportunity of securing his resignation. Metternich was compelled to go,
and a new ministry was established under Ficquelmont as minister
of foreign affairs and the bourgeois, Pillersdorf, as minister of the
interior. The city of Vienna was brought under the control of a
middle-class committee, but the creation of an Academic Legion
and a committee of students revealed that there were other forces at
work which might not be satisfied with the minimum of concessions
which the new government was prepared to grant. For the moment
the Austrian government was gravely embarrassed, but it was only
in Vienna that the German population of the empire was prepared
to show substantial hostility to the régime.

Berlin in 1848 was no longer the capital of an agrarian state.
It was now the centre of a railway network and possessed an industrial
proletariat of its own. The population of the city had risen to
420,000, which placed it among the larger urban centres of Europe.
When the news of the revolt in Vienna reached Berlin it was greeted
with incredulous stupefaction, as if the old régime had suddenly
collapsed overnight. Frederick William IV had had a foretaste of
trouble in 1847, and on 14 March announced that he had decided to
call the United Diet for 27 April in the hope that timely concession
would calm the excitement, but during the evening the military
clashed with the people in the streets, which led to tension on the
following day. On 16 March it was learned that Metternich had fallen
in Vienna and the populace gained confidence in its own strength. In
its anxiety the Prussian government brought forward the meeting of
the United Diet to 2 April. As a result of further brushes between
the people and the army Berlin was in a state of insurrection on
18 March. There were royal advisers who counselled resistance, but
the King promised a constitution, and on 21 March declared that
'Prussia is henceforth merged in Germany'. It appeared that one of
the two larger German states was prepared to take the opportunity
of establishing a united Germany. In his extremity Frederick William
IV appointed Camphausen Minister-President and Hansemann
minister of finance. The alliance of the dynasty with Rhenish
liberalism was in fact hedged in by the reservations of the King and
the anxieties of the Rhenish liberals themselves, who looked with
fear upon the democrats of the industrial cities ready to call upon

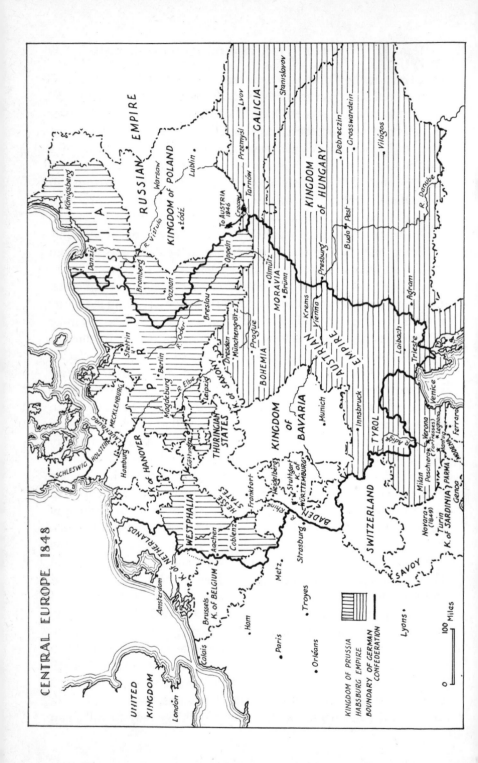

CENTRAL EUROPE 1848

RUSSIAN EMPIRE

UNITED KINGDOM
London

Amsterdam
NETHERLANDS

Calais
Ham
Paris
Troyes
Orléans
Lyons
Metz
Strasburg
K. of BELGIUM
Brussels
WESTPHALIA
Aachen
Coblenz
HESSE STATES
Frankfort
Heidelberg
Stuttgart
K. of WÜRTEMBURG
BADEN

Königsberg
Danzig
Bromberg
Poznań
Stettin
Berlin
Magdeburg
Leipzig
R. Elbe
R. Oder
Breslau
Oppeln
Dresden
K. of SAXONY
THURINGIAN STATES
Göttingen
Hamburg
K. of HANOVER
MECKLENBURG
OLDENBURG
HOLSTEIN
SCHLESWIG

P R U S S I A

KINGDOM of POLAND
Warsaw
Vistula
Łódź
Lublin
To Austria 1846
Cracow
Tarnów
Przemyśl
Lvov
GALICIA
Stanislavov

Münchengrätz I.
Prague
BOHEMIA
Olmütz
Brünn
MORAVIA
Krems
Vienna
Presburg
Buda Pest
KINGDOM of HUNGARY
Debreczin
Grosswardein
Világos

AUSTRIAN EMPIRE

KINGDOM OF BAVARIA
Munich
Innsbruck
TYROL
Laibach
Agram
Trieste
R. Danube

SWITZERLAND
SAVOY
Novara (1849)
Turin
Milan
Peschiera (Fortresses)
Verona
Mantua
Legnano
Venice
R. Adige
Genoa
K. of SARDINIA
PARMA
MODENA
Ferrara

KINGDOM OF PRUSSIA
HABSBURG EMPIRE
BOUNDARY OF GERMAN CONFEDERATION

0   100 Miles

the armed populace. The United Diet was prepared to accept the principle of universal suffrage for men over the age of twenty-four years, but election was to be indirect; the secondary electors were to appoint deputies who had attained at least the age of thirty. The aim of the Camphausen–Hansemann ministry from the first was to avoid the creation of a Prussian parliament which gave the people a direct voice in the affairs of the kingdom. Reform was to be controlled from above rather than forced from below.

The German Revolution and Foreign Affairs

From the very outset of the revolution in Germany the question of foreign policy was raised. Max von Gagern, the official in the service of the Duke of Nassau, commissioned to convince the princes of Germany that they must show initiative in the crisis, was proceeding on his journey to the various courts of Germany. Gagern was a partisan of a Germany created under the sovereignty of the King of Prussia, but he was not in favour of the Prussianization of Germany, which he knew would meet with strong objections in the west and south-west. In his view the unification of the country should take place as a result of an agreement between the states. In Hesse-Darmstadt, Baden and Württemberg he received approval for his ideas, but characteristically there were reservations in Bavaria. On 21 March he arrived in Berlin, where he saw the new minister for foreign affairs, Heinrich von Arnim. Gagern pressed upon him the necessity of making war on Russia, a course which would meet with the approval of the Germans of the west and south-west, who considered that the expulsion of Russian influence from the Confederation was vitally necessary. On 8 March 1848 Nicholas I had ordered a partial mobilization of his forces to meet the emergency. In the Kingdom of Poland were to be stationed 350,000 men with 100,000–150,000 held in reserve to reinforce them. Nicholas I had no interest in the internal affairs of France, however much he might fume, but he was concerned to see that France was kept to her existing frontiers, and he was prepared if necessary to intervene in Germany. What he was not prepared to do was to offer provocation to the Germans. Nevertheless, the concentration of a Russian field force on the eastern frontier did give cause for anxiety in Germany and lent a certain specious justification to the demands for a preventive war against Russia. Arnim sympathized with the point of view of Max von Gagern, but when Gagern saw Frederick William IV on 23 March he discovered that he was very far from being willing to make war on Russia. The court camarilla in fact regarded Russia as a potential ally in the struggle with liberalism. In this way a dual policy appeared in Prussia. Arnim began to sound out France upon her attitude to war with Russia. Through the French ambassador, Circourt, he inquired of Lamartine what France would do if Russia were to go to war with Germany, but the reply which was drafted for him was not encouraging. Circourt was instructed to inform Arnim that:

'If Russia attacked Prussia and invaded her territory seizing Poznania, France would give Prussia armed support.' You may use this phrase confidentially and in conversation, but you must go no further.

Since Russia did not intend to invade Prussia, this was equivalent to offering no support at all. Equally discouraging was the attitude of Britain. Sir Stratford Canning, on his way back to Constantinople, where he was ambassador, was commissioned by Palmerston to visit the European capitals to acquaint himself with the situation. When he saw Frederick William IV on 30 March he discovered him in a state of some anxiety lest Arnim should lead Prussia into a conflict with Russia and was obliquely invited by him to put pressure upon Arnim. It was British policy to preserve the *status quo*, and on 6 April Palmerston wrote to Stratford Canning that he was 'earnestly to recommend to the Prussian government to abstain from any proceeding which could justly be considered by Russia as aggressive and to avoid as far as possible any measure which might in their consequences lead to aggression on the Russian territory'.

The danger of aggression against Russia arose in Poznania, where as soon as the revolution had broken out in Berlin the Poles began to claim national freedom. In their last session the Prussian Provincial Estates of 6 April agreed that the Grand Duchy of Posen ought not to form part of the Confederation. In order to find some common ground with the Poles, who after the disappointments attendant upon the unsuccessful rising of 1846 were not prepared of their own accord to assume the initiative again, but preferred to wait for what they considered would be the inevitable war of Germany and Russia,

General von Willisen was sent to Poznania, and on 11 April at the farm of Jarosławiec, near Środa, came to an agreement, under the terms of which the Poles might maintain four units of 500–600 men under arms in preparation for their transformation into a Poznanian division. The Grand Duchy was to be divided into German and Polish districts, the German to form part of the new Germany. This measure, which was designed to prevent the Poles from themselves attacking Russia and provoking a war, was in contradiction to another policy transmitted to the military commander, von Colomb, who was ordered to disperse the Polish levies. Treating Willisen with scant respect, von Colomb dissolved all Polish institutions, and by 9 May, though with some difficulty, the Polish levies were disbanded. From that moment the danger that a spontaneous war with Russia might occur in the east disappeared. If war were to be made upon Russia, it would have to be the result of a deliberate act of the German state, and a German state did not in fact exist. The brief taste of Polish rule in Poznań gave the Germans second thoughts on the Polish question. Polish rule could mean only subjection for those Germans who lived among them, whereas the heady nationalism of western and south-western German liberals demanded that Germans everywhere should be free, even in the Baltic provinces, where they represented the upper classes superimposed upon the Lettish and Estonian peasantry.

The Polish question in 1848 threatened the general peace of Europe. Of lesser importance was the Schleswig-Holstein question. The problem of the duchies had become acute in July 1846 when Christian VIII of Denmark declared that female succession might be applied in them, though they were traditionally subject to the Salic Law, by which the succession could be transmitted only in the male line. If the Salic Law applied the succession would fall to the Duke of Augustenburg and the territories detached from the Danish Crown and joined with the new Germany. On the death of Christian VIII and the accession of Frederick VII the *status quo* was restored by which the two duchies were granted a common constitution. The facts of the case were that Schleswig was largely Danish in speech, while in Holstein there were substantial Danish minorities; both sides claimed the Frisian population of the western portions of Holstein for themselves. The Danish nationalists wished to incorporate at least Schleswig into Denmark, but the articulate German upper class wished to bring both duchies into Germany. With the general success of the revolution in Germany a provisional German government was formed at Kiel for the administration of the duchies with the general approval of the German nationalists throughout the Confederation. On 4 April the Diet of the German Confederation invited the Prussian government, which had recognized the German régime in the Duchies on 24 March, to maintain the *status quo*. The Danes were more than a match for the Schleswig-Holsteiners, but the Diet then requested Prussia to intervene by force. In this sorry expedition the government of Frederick William IV could appear to be serving the best interests of the German nation. In the authorizing of this task there was added a complication to the burdens of the National Parliament which was to assemble at Frankfort, the complexity of which German liberalism in its buoyant nationalism barely understood in the confusion attending the early days of the revolution.

The Frankfort Parliament of 1848

On 5 March 1848 there had been the meeting of liberals at Heidelberg, which decided that the existing Federal Diet was incapable of expressing the aspirations of Germany and that it would be necessary to call an assembly of notables, or Pre-Parliament (*Vorparlament*), to prepare for the election of an all-German Assembly to draw up a new constitution. When the Pre-Parliament assembled in Frankfort on 31 March 1848 it proved hardly to be representative of Germany; three-quarters of the notables present were from west Germany and the Rhineland, the area most influenced by the Napoleonic reorganization and differing in its social organization and outlook from the Ostalbingian provinces of Germany. There was in its deliberations much theory and little experience of political problems. It was indeed difficult to define Germany at all. Emotionally it was felt that Germany existed wherever there were Germans, but there were practical difficulties. Thus it was agreed, for example, that the provinces of West and East Prussia should be considered German, but that the Grand Duchy of Posen should remain outside the new Germany for the moment. Bohemia, Moravia and Austrian Silesia were considered German in spite of the Czech populations. As many as 190 seats were to be reserved for the hereditary dominions of

Austria in the National Assembly, but the steering committee of Fifty which invited the Czech leader, Palacký, to come to Frankfort received a foretaste of Slav hostility. In a letter of 11 April 1848 Palacký refused to attend on the grounds that, though Bohemia had long been associated with Germany, it was part of a historic unit of Slav origin and that the Czechs would look to Vienna for the solution of their particular problems. Palacký wrote:

> If the Austrian Empire did not exist, in the interest of Europe, nay, of humanity, it would be necessary to make haste and create it.

This was the basic conception of 'Austro-Slavism' by which the Slavs of the Habsburg Empire might find regional self-government in association with Austria. If this solution were to be adopted, then a Germany based upon the territories of a reduced Confederation only could be created, because Austria would necessarily survive as an independent political unit.

Not only did the Pre-Parliament have difficulties with Slav nationalism. The system it proposed was that there should be a head of state with a ministry responsible to a senate representing the individual states and a chamber elected by universal manhood suffrage. In the meantime a Committee of Fifty should remain in session until the new National Assembly met. This did not meet with the approval of the German left wing, who thought that the *Vorparlament* should proceed at once to consideration of social questions. In April 1848 the radicals organized a revolt in the Baden with the aim of imposing upon Germany a republican solution. On 12 April the revolt began at Mannheim, Donaueschingen and in the region of Lake Constance, but the troops of Baden, the Hesses and Württemberg combined to bring the upper Rhineland under control. It was therefore from the very beginning the armies of the existing states which stood between German liberalism and German republicanism.

When the National Assembly congregated at Frankfort on 13 May the affairs of Germany appeared to rest upon its shoulders, but it represented no more than an aspiration if it were not supported by deeds. In its social composition the Assembly scarcely corresponded to the structure of German society. There are varying estimates of the numbers of each class of the population in the Assembly. According to one view the Parliament contained out of nearly 600 members 38 landed proprietors, 20 members of the merchant and industrial élite, 49 university professors, 32 teachers from high schools, 78 magistrates, 64 lawyers, 73 senior civil servants and 20 heads of district administrations (*Landräte*). In general, the elections were unfavourable both to the very rich and, above all, to the very poor, because not a single worker was returned; they were a victory for the upper middle classes. Nevertheless, in the excitement of Frankfort they were often to be carried away with a sense of emotion.

The first question which the Parliament had to decide was whether it in fact was a sovereign body and, when once it had assumed that it was, it established a government for the Empire. Eventually it was decided to create a Vicar of the Empire (*Reichsverweser*) who was to exercise sovereign powers until the headship of state had been determined; by this device the way was left open for the candidature of Frederick William IV. The choice for the Vicar of the Empire, however, fell upon the popular Archduke John of Austria, who was appointed on 24 June 1848. On 8 August, in place of a temporary government established in July, he appointed as president of the Council, Prince Karl von Leiningen, with a minister of foreign affairs, Heckscher; a minister of war, the Prussian general von Peucker; a minister of internal affairs, Anton von Schmerling, an Austrian; and ministers of Justice, Finance and Trade. Within this ministry Prussia in fact had small influence. The Archduke John and Schmerling would watch over Austria's interests and seek to preserve her position within the Confederation. The measure of the ministry's power was shown in the response to the order of von Peucker of 16 July that on 6 August the troops of the constituent states of the new Germany should be paraded to take the oath of allegiance to the Vicar General. To this action Austria, Prussia, Bavaria and Hanover refused their assent. The shadowy authority of the Frankfort parliament extended in practice only to the smaller states.

The deputies were infected with a noisome nationalism. Germany for them was wherever there were Germans settled, irrespective of whether they constituted a majority of the population or not. The debate on the Polish question on 24 July was an occasion for much condemnation of the Poles for their backwardness and praise for German enterprise in the east. There were even deputies who praised

Field Marshal Radetzky for his victory over the Italians at Custozza on 25 July, as if this were a victory for German arms. Suspicion was entertained of the Czechs. When in May and June 1848 the Slavs of the Austrian Empire gathered in Prague to formulate a common policy and were even for a moment considered by the local authorities in Bohemia as a possible counterweight against Vienna, it was obvious that there were other forces at work than German nationalism. When on 12 June there was a peaceful demonstration of both Germans and Czechs in Prague and the troops of the G.O.C., Windischgrätz, fired into the crowd and provoked a rising, which was brought under control on 17 June by the bombardment of the city, there were Germans who thought that Windischgrätz had saved their fellow countrymen from Czech domination. There were violent speeches against the Czechs and demands that Bavarian and Saxon troops should be sent to save the Germans, which were, however, resisted by the few deputies who arrived from Bohemia, Moravia and Austrian Silesia and pointed out that the Austrian military were in control. The committee of inquiry sent by the Vienna Council of Public Safety was arrested by the Austrian soldiers. Germanism had not won in Bohemia, only reaction. The Frankfort deputies thought first as Germans and respected the rights of other nations only where there were no Germans to contest them. There was in the Parliament talk of extending Germany to include Alsace, Lorraine, German Switzerland, Dutch Limburg, Courland and Livonia. The attitude of the parliament was expansionist and corresponded with the ideal of the big bourgeoisie, which foresaw the creation of a great commercial empire in which Germans were the dominant race.

No question exercised the anxiety of the deputies more than that of Schleswig-Holstein. Britain had no wish to see Denmark under the domination of Germany, nor did Russia look kindly upon the control of the Sound at Copenhagen falling into German hands. It is true that the Baltic trade did not assume the importance in British minds that it had a century earlier, but there was no desire that the conflicts of the Danes and Germans in the Duchies should lead to the weakening of Denmark to the point where she became a German puppet state. Britain therefore put pressure upon Prussia to bring the war to a halt, and to this pressure was added Russian diplomatic support. Therefore on 26 August, rather than risk the hostility of two

great powers, Prussia concluded with Denmark the armistice of
Malmö, which was to last for seven months. The Danes were given
the whole winter in which to recuperate their forces. The armistice,
however, was concluded without the approval of the Vicar of the
Empire, which caused the Frankfort Parliament to declare that
Prussia had exceeded her powers. Behind the controversy concerning
the armistice of Malmö lay an important question. Was Prussia to
be part of the new Empire, or was she to dominate it? Characteristically it was the left wing in the assembly which offered its opposition.
Lord Cowley, the British ambassador in Frankfort, uttered the warning that refusal to recognize the armistice would lead to Britain's
breaking off diplomatic relations with the new Germany, but the
Assembly was undeterred by this threat, and on 5 September condemned the armistice by 238 votes to 221, whereupon Karl von
Leiningen resigned from his post as president of the Council. This
show of determination to assert the authority of the Assembly over
Prussia produced a crisis which was not easy to solve. It was not a
simple matter in these circumstances to find a replacement for von
Leiningen as president of the council. The Assembly was therefore
compelled to compromise. By a fresh resolution of 16 September
1848 the armistice of Malmö was approved by 258 votes to 237,
subject to modifications of its terms which would make it acceptable
both to the Parliament and to the Germans of Schleswig-Holstein.
The resolution was the admission that the Parliament could not
impose its authority upon Prussia. This was the moment of crisis in
the existence of the Frankfort Parliament. The moderates now feared
that the left wing would have recourse to direct action. The Archduke
John reconstructed the ministry with the Austrian, Schmerling, as
president of the council. On the night of 17–18 September Schmerling
brought in 2,000 troops, both Prussian and Austrian, from the
fortress of Mainz and stationed them around the Church of Saint
Paul, where the Assembly was meeting. At the sight of the military
the inhabitants of Frankfort began to raise barricades, raising the
slogan, which was indeed strange in a country which was demanding
unity—'The Prussians must leave the Town!' Such was the affront
which the Prussian troops gave to the inhabitants of a proud Imperial
Free City. The city was nevertheless brought under control and this
elemental rising, which none of the left-wing leaders had advised,

was suppressed. Once more it was proved that barricades were not effective and that the army could always deal with the mob. The bourgeoisie saw for themselves the dangers of social revolution. Point was lent to the Frankfort rising by the insurrection called by the left-winger, Struve, in Baden on 21 September. The German Republic was proclaimed at Lörrach and the revolutionaries proposed to finance it by taxation of the local oligarchs and the Jews, but Struve's movement collapsed ignobly on 24 September 1848. The German bourgeoisie perceived that they had a choice between red revolution and reaction. In relying upon the protection of the army they wittingly chose the cause of reaction.

The Austrian Revolution of 1848

The fall of Metternich led to the creation of an allegedly liberal ministry, of which the most powerful figure was Pillersdorf. In the meantime as a result of disturbances in Pressburg (Bratislava) and Pest a separate Hungarian Constitution for the lands of the Crown of St Stephen was granted on 22 March. At length on 25 April Austria was granted a constitution based upon the hereditary lands of the dynasty. The constitution provided for a chamber of peers and a lower chamber, but the property franchise was so high that it excluded the petty bourgeoisie, the shopkeepers and the peasants. The situation which these half measures created was so dangerous that on 9 May a new franchise was offered which admitted the petty bourgeoisie and the peasants, but excluded the working class of the towns. Pillersdorf believed that he could handle the situation by appeal to force, but as often in the revolutions of 1848 force merely provoked a stronger reaction. On 15 May he attempted to dissolve the revolutionary 'Central Committee' in Vienna, but renewed disturbances compelled the government at last to concede a constitution in which a single-chamber parliament was elected by universal manhood suffrage. In such a situation it was unwise that the head of state should remain in Vienna, even if he were only the incapacitated Emperor Ferdinand. On 17 May the Emperor left Vienna for the loyal town of Innsbruck, but in his manifesto of 20 May, though he condemned the excesses of the revolution, he undertook to uphold the concessions which had been granted in his name.

Pillersdorf did not forego his attempts to bring Vienna to order.

On 25 May he tried to dissolve the Academic Legion formed from among the students, but the students were regarded by the workers as their leaders and at once barricades were raised. On the following day Pillersdorf was compelled to yield and a Committee of Public Safety was established in the city. Vienna came under the control of a federation of the democratic clubs, the students' committee and the workers' organizations. The problem of unemployment demanded a policy of public works, but relief of this kind pressed heavily upon the resources of the state. A reconstituted ministry on 19 August attempted to reduce the wage-rates paid to workers employed upon these tasks, with the result that on 23 August there were fresh disorders, which were put down by the bourgeois National Guard. On this occasion the Academic Legion stood aside rather than have any part in the coercion of the working class. The Committee of Public Safety dissolved itself. Already it was plain that in Vienna the propertied element entertained second thoughts concerning the wisdom of supporting the revolution.

Beyond the capital there was little revolutionary feeling in the strictly German areas of the empire. Austria in 1848 was sustained by the insubordination of the regional military commanders and civil governors. The Poles of Galicia, their morale weakened by the disastrous revolt of 1846, were not prepared to challenge the dynasty directly. On the one hand, they saw the concentration of Russian forces in the Kingdom of Poland, while on the other, the peasants were by no means content with the concessions which the government had made them in 1846. The reluctant decision of the Polish leaders, under the pressure of their own left wing, was that the landlords should make a resignation of the labour dues which the peasants paid them; the surrender of these dues was to take place on Good Friday. The provincial governor, Franz von Stadion, on 22 April issued an imperial patent, back-dated to 17 April in order that it should appear to have no connection with the Polish decision, under which the labour services of the peasants were abolished without their being required to pay compensation to the landlords. This decree, promulgated without imperial authority, had the effect of cementing the loyalty of the peasants to the government. Cracow, which after the Polish insurrection of 1846 had, in defiance of the Treaty of Vienna, which had made it a Free City, been incorporated into the Austrian Empire, proved to be a troublesome centre of Polish radicalism; connected with western Europe by the railway, it was now filled with Polish *émigrés* of left-wing democratic opinions. On 26 April the local commander at Cracow, General Castiglione, decided to disarm the populace, and when he met with resistance bombarded the town from the castle, upon which the local conservatives offered their unconditional submission.

At Lvov in the eastern regions of Galicia a Polish national council remained in existence, challenged, it is true, by a Ruthenian council. Polish nationalism was harmless enough and the authorities tolerated a Polish national guard. The workers of the city, however, resented the inactivity of the upper classes, and at the beginning of November 1848 raised barricades in the streets. The local Austrian commander, Hammerstein, on 2 November bombarded the city into surrender, and a state of siege was proclaimed in the whole province. The Poles gave Austria little trouble in 1848, and their experiences at the hands of the military were typical of the sufferings of other nationalities.

The Czechs had no love for the Austrian revolution if it were to seek to incorporate Bohemia, Moravia and Austrian Silesia in the new Germany. At various points in the Slavonic portions of the Empire the idea arose that the Slavs should seek to speak with a common voice and assert their numerical supremacy in the Austrian dominions. The concept of a Slav Congress was especially attractive to the Czechs, who with the Slovaks were entirely encompassed by the Austrian dominions. The journalist, Karol Havliček, the historian, Palacký, and Šafařik, believed that a congress would serve as a platform for a policy of 'Austro-Slavism'. Because the Ottoman Empire was not involved in the disturbances which had swept Europe, the South Slavs, the Slovenes, the Croats and the Serbs, were not indisposed to take part in such a meeting, but the Poles as ever had reservations. The Poles in general sought the reconstitution of a Poland divided among Austria, Russia and Prussia, while the Poles from Galicia were cautious of adhering to racial equality among the Slavs, among whom were counted the Ruthenians in the eastern portion of the province. Appeal to the Slavs was in any case dangerous, because there were Slavs beyond the Austrian Empire. If the Slavs were to be called upon to unite it was possible that they might call in allies, the Rumans of Hungary, and, if non-Slavonic nationalities were to be invited to join in the common effort, appeal might be made to the Germans. In the end it was decided to limit the congress to the Austrian Slavs, who were divided into three sections, the Czecho-Slovak, the South Slav and the Polish-Ruthene. Lest there be any misunderstanding about the nature of the meeting, Palacký on 5 May 1848 proposed that a declaration of loyalty to Austria should be made, but such a suggestion met with ideological objections from the Poles. Only the Czechs therefore declared their unconditional loyalty. On 2 June 1848 the congress opened in Prague, presided over by Palacký and attended by 237 Czechs and Slovaks, 61 Poles, Ruthenians and Russians and 42 South Slavs. The concept of Austro-Slavism was conservative by the very fact that it did not challenge the dynasty, but there were expressions of doubt from those members of the congress who wished to give the congress a more radical twist. While these developments were taking place, the authorities in Prague looked with misgiving upon the turn of events in Vienna. At first the governor of Bohemia, Leo Thun, and the G.O.C., Windischgrätz, welcomed the Czech initiative, because it seemed that they might take advantage of Czech opposition to German radicalism in order to restore the authority of the crown. On 17 May Thun called the Bohemian Estates and refused to take orders any longer from Vienna. A provincial council was formed in Prague, containing two aristocrats, two Germans and the Czechs, Palacký and Rieger. This seemed to be a step towards Palacký's ideal of re-creating the Crown of St Wenceslas as an independent unit within the Habsburg dominions. Palacký reckoned without the radicalism of the younger generation, whether German or Czech. On Whit Monday, 12 June, there was a peaceful demonstration in Prague in which both nationalities took part. Windischgrätz wished to bring matters to a speedy conclusion and permitted his troops to attack the crowd, whereupon barricades were erected and the army withdrawn on 15 June. On 17 June Windischgrätz, as Castiglione had done earlier in Cracow, opened a bombardment of the city, and Prague was compelled to submit. Bohemia and the Czech lands were now brought under military control and thereafter presented no serious threat to the Habsburg administration.

In Italy Field Marshal Radetzky was left very much to his own resources, and like Windischgrätz formed his own judgment of the situation. The situation in Italy was different from that in Austria north of the Alps, because the whole country had not only risen in revolt, but the individual revolutions had also united under the leadership of Piedmont to expel Austria from the peninsula. This in its turn created the possibility of French intervention and diplomatic complications, but Radetzky acted with confidence. Having evacuated Milan and sought refuge in the Quadrilateral, he compelled the Italians to take the field and soundly defeated them at the battle of Custozza on 25 July 1848. Charles Albert, powerless to defeat the Austrians in the field, was compelled to seek a diplomatic solution of his problems, by which through the mediation of the powers Austria might be induced to relax her hold upon Lombardy-Venetia (see below p. 282). In Croatia a colonel of the frontier regiment, Jellačić, was appointed Ban and began to lead the Croats in the fight against the centralizing policy of the Magyars, with or without the approval of Vienna. The Croat Diet which met in Agram (Zagreb) on 5 June acted as a focal point of Slav resistance in southern Hungary (see below p. 270).

For these reasons, while Habsburg power was at its nadir at the centre, the dynasty's basic strength began to assert itself on the periphery. By July there was a growing appearance of normality in Vienna. The elections to the parliament were held on 6 and 9 July, and on 19 July the Archduke John, who had returned temporarily from Frankfort, formed the liberal Doblhoff-Wessenberg ministry. In fact, the situation following the restoration of authority in Galicia, Bohemia and Italy seemed to be sufficiently under control for the Emperor to return to the capital. The parliament, which was opened by the Archduke John on 22 July, consisted of 383 deputies, of whom the majority were Slavs, but it was not national questions which proved the main subject of discussion. Many of the deputies were peasants or persons representing peasant interests. It was their aim to obtain the abolition of labour services and dues in money and kind in order to free the peasants from their economic dependence upon the landlords, and with it the destruction of patrimonial jurisdiction (*Unterthänigkeit*). Discussion took place upon what principles emancipation should take place, and at length on 31 August it was agreed that the landowners should receive nothing for their loss of lordship, but should be given a moderate indemnity for the loss of services and other dues. When the decree of emancipation was promulgated on 7 September 1848 the peasants showed no further interest in the revolution. It had yielded for them what they wanted, and it remained for the government to ensure that the terms of the decrees were carried out. All that remained of the Austrian revolution was a sullen and rebellious capital.

The most acute of the problems which faced Austria was the revolution which was in progress in Hungary, covering all its acts for the moment with the plea that it was acting in the name of the Emperor in his capacity of King. There were nevertheless tensions, and on 15 September 1848 twelve Hungarian deputies appeared in Vienna to ask the parliament's mediation in the disputes which had arisen between Hungary and the Crown and between the Hungarians and the Croats. On 17 September took place a great debate in Vienna, and the parliament took the decision by 186 votes to 108 not to admit the Hungarian deputies. In short, the deputies of the hereditary dominions of the Habsburgs could offer no aid to the revolution in Hungary. At this point the affairs of Austria and Hungary became inextricably intermixed. It was to prove that, if the middle-class deputies of Austria could not find common ground with the Hungarian parliament in Pest, then both revolutions would fail to produce the liberal freedoms to which everyone aspired.

Hungary in 1848–9

The Hungarian revolution of 1848 had roots which stretched into the past to the battle of Mohacs of 29 August 1526 when Louis II, king both of Hungary and Bohemia, fell in battle with the Turks. By a treaty of doubtful legality concluded in 1514 the Jagiellonian and Habsburg dynasties had agreed that if either should expire the other should succeed to the vacant dominions. Upon this treaty the great Austrian Empire had been founded. In Bohemia opposition was extinguished by the battle of the White Mountain in 1620, but the Hungarians had never been subjected to the same control. The presence of the Turks and the existence of Transylvania kept alive a spirit of independence.

The seventeenth century had been the era of revolt against the Habsburgs. The eighteenth century, on the other hand, had been a period of reconciliation. The dynasty had acquired the prestige of successful wars against the Turks. The country had been freed from the infidel. There was in fact a marked contrast between Hungary and Bohemia. In Bohemia the nobility wished to obtain the restoration of the ancient Czech privileges or at least the constitutions of 1627. During the war of the Austrian succession the Bohemian nobles had shown an inclination to co-operate with the elector of Bavaria. For this reason Maria Theresa was determined to stamp out noble opposition. Hungary, on the other hand, was loyal to her and it was therefore more difficult for her to find an excuse to attack the liberties of the nobility. Maria Theresa's policy was, therefore, one of infiltration, which sought to emasculate the Hungarian opposition, if it should ever arise, by attracting the high nobility to the Court in Vienna. The Hungarian Diet was summoned only very rarely. It in fact was not called between 1763 and 1780.

Under Joseph II the policy of the Crown changed from one of infiltration to one of direct attack. Joseph II refused to hold a coronation at Pest, which was in direct violation of the treaty of Szatmar of 1711. He, moreover, proceeded to follow a policy of centralization and encroach upon the constitutional liberties of Hungary. The result of his policy was to arouse opposition which amounted to a political renaissance. Opposition was expressed in the *comitats*, or counties, which were now reinfused with political life. The constitutional argument employed was that Joseph II, having refused coronation in Pest, had no legal authority for his acts and that, because the succession was broken, Leopold II could not be the legal ruler of Hungary. For this reason the Hungarian diet was called in 1790–1 and the Crown recognized that Hungary should be governed *propriis legibus et consuetudinibus, non vero ad normam aliarum provinciarum* (according to its own laws and customs and not according to the system of the other provinces).

In theory, Hungary's separate existence was recognized, but what in practice emerged was a conflict of systems. On the one hand, stood the absolute Emperor of Austria, on the other, the constitutional king of Hungary. The King had, of course, considerable powers in Hungary, but there were restrictions upon them. The Hungarian Diet gave sanction to the laws, voted a financial contribution and provided recruits for the army. There was no intendant system in Hungary; the unit of administration was the *comitat*, though offices in it were held by the high nobility, who were open to royal influence from their close connection with the Court. At the beginning of the nineteenth century a certain stability had been achieved. The magnates and high ecclesiastics in the upper house of the Diet held the numerous petty nobility in clientage. In the lower house the medium nobility found that they could not exercise any real power, because the *comitats* were dominated by the petty *slachta*, or gentry.

This was the condition in which Hungary found herself when the whole structure of European society began to be transformed under the impact of economic expansion. The old high conservatives were content with the existing system which gave them a position of predominance in the state. The petty nobility feared lest constitutional change should result in the abolition of their tax exemptions. The system of clientage, therefore, tended to uphold the old system. The Hungarian aristocracy found themselves in a position rather different from that of the Polish high nobility. They could continue to enjoy their social status without any of the feelings of guilt which afflicted the Czartoryskis, Radziwiłłs, Potockis and others in Poland who were not entirely proud of the role they played in the events which led to the partitions. From this fact emerges the essential peculiarity of the Hungarian situation. The medium landlords, inarticulate in Poland, in Hungary had political aspirations of their own. Their enemy was the aristocracy, which controlled the *comitats*. It followed that some system of centralization which overrode the *comitats* would permit the medium landlords to emerge as an independent force, which they were not under the old system. There was therefore within Hungarian society a conflict between centralism and anarchical federalism, complicated by a different kind of centralism issuing from Vienna.

It should not be imagined that the Hungarian medium gentry were revolutionaries. They had a stake in Hungarian society which they would not surrender to forces emerging on the extreme left. In essence their policy was that of 'organic work', which in Polish society was a feature of the political views current among the high nobility. Eötvös, for example, was in favour of admitting persons of non-noble persons to the *comitats*. Szechenyi wanted a policy of modernization. As a result of long periods of residence abroad, especially in England, he absorbed foreign ideas; it is significant that the only country in Europe in which the ideas of Jeremy Bentham had any influence was Hungary. Szechenyi saw the sources of Hungarian discontents as lying in the predominance of the nobility and the tax exemptions, but he accepted the existing divisions of society and aimed at removing the causes of dissatisfaction. For him re-education was the prime condition of improvement, though he was prepared to make concessions to the Hungarian peasants. Here was the English constitutional ideal and the evolutionary approach to politics designed to forestall the dangers of revolution which were appearing in the cities.

On the extreme left Hungarian separatism had made its appearance, associated primarily with the name of Louis Kossuth, who appealed to the radical youth of the towns, especially in Pest, and to sections of the lesser nobility. His ideas found expression in the newspaper *Pesti Hirlap*, founded in January 1841. There were two aspects to the policy of Kossuth. On the one hand, he demanded the reform of the constitution, the abolition of the tax exemptions and freedom for the press; these were the traditional demands of European liberalism. On the other hand, there was apparent in his thinking a Magyar chauvinism. Hungary was an indivisible kingdom (*regnum indivisibile*) in which the Magyar people were to be supreme. In short, complete constitutional freedom was to be introduced within the lands which belonged to the Crown of St Stephen as a means of giving expression to the ideal of nationalism.

In the face of criticism and discontent the government in Vienna proved indecisive. The paralysis of government in Austria resulted in the same attitude being adopted towards Hungary as was adopted towards the other provinces before the crisis of 1848. Little was done. Metternich was in favour of some gestures to remove irritations. His second wife was a Hungarian, and he came round to the view that a modicum of reform was necessary in order to canalize Hungarian discontents and make possible the peaceful evolution which the more intelligent Hungarian conservatives wanted. The greatest of all the grievances was the customs barrier between Austria and Hungary. Hungarian economic development was much impaired by this device. The existence of this frontier gave the Austrian industrialists an advantage over the industrialists of other European countries who were required to pay both the Austrian and the Hungarian tariffs.

In consequence, Hungary was regarded in Vienna as an area reserved for agricultural production and therefore as a market for Austrian goods. This was the inferior status which was so much resented by the Hungarian radicals.

The essential features of the Hungarian crisis of 1847-8 were not therefore different from those which may be observed elsewhere, but there was in each of the factors in the revolutionary situation of 1848 a different degree of emphasis. In the political sense Hungary was subject to internal pressures, but in economic affairs the pressures resulted from external control. As the crisis approached the upper classes were split into two groups, the reactionaries who refused all reform of a system which benefited themselves and the conservative reformers, anxious to avoid conflict with the monarchy, but equally fearful of revolution from the lower ranks of society. Among the radicals the psychology of revolt existed, but without some specific act of provocation it is doubtful whether they could ever have made themselves heard. Provocation was indeed offered by the government. Apponyi, head of the Hungarian chancery, wanted to strengthen royal control in Hungary and reduce the power of the *comitats* in order to make government in Hungary effective. What he proposed amounted to increased centralization which would strengthen the monarchy, but which would not benefit Hungary, because the power of decision would as before be exercised in Vienna. As a result the Hungarian moderates and radicals found that they must make common cause. The elections of 1847 witnessed the coalescence of Hungarian grievances, and the revolutions of 1848 put to the test the uneasy dualism which had existed since the eighteenth century.

At the time of the revolution in France the Hungarian Diet was meeting in Pressburg (Bratislava) and in the prevailing excitement Kossuth in a speech of 3 March demanded a responsible ministry in Pest in order to solve the perennial financial difficulties of the state. A motion to this effect was carried in the Lower House, which alarmed the Upper House and caused it to adjourn discussion. The Vienna rising of 13 March 1848, however, caused a strong reaction in Pest. The radical youth appeared on the streets demanding liberal reforms and a revolutionary committee was established. In this situation the Upper House capitulated to the demands for constitutional reform in the Lower House. In its turn the Court in Vienna granted a responsible ministry, the exercise of royal powers by the Palatine and a constitution. In this way was established the constitution of 22 March 1848, by which eight ministries under the presidency of the moderate Batthyány controlled all aspects of the state activity with the exception of foreign affairs. This was more than the dynasty had wished to concede, and an attempt was made by the rescript of 29 March to reserve control of the army and finance to the Crown, but so sharp an opposition was aroused that the Court in Vienna was obliged to defer the question of Austro-Hungarian relations.

From this point the contradictions inherent in the Hungarian situation began to appear. The 'March laws' established a unitary, parliamentary and liberal state. The parliament was transferred to Pest. Electoral districts took the place of the *comitats*. A uniform suffrage based upon property qualifications was established and the privileges of nobility and feudal dues abolished. With these reforms went the incorporation of Transylvania, Croatia and the military districts inhabited by the Serbs. The Hungarian state thus found itself in the position of exerting pressure upon other nationalities.

The essential difficulty of the Hungarian revolution, however, was that it had executed its reforms in the name of the Crown, but its relationship with the Crown was still undefined. Within the Habsburg dominions the forces of the counter-revolution were growing in strength. Windischgrätz and Schwarzenberg, the leaders of the monarchical reaction, were at first fearful of positive action because of the poor morale of the army, but they were encouraged by two factors. The Poles did not appear to wish to contest the right of the Habsburgs to rule in Galicia, nor the Czechs to offer resistance in the lands of the Crown of St Wenceslas. On the other hand, the army was proving loyal. Prague had been brought under control on 17 June and on 25 July Radetzky had won a splendid victory over the Italians at Custozza. A new sense of purpose appeared in the Austrian army and no longer was there a sense of universal collapse which nothing could put right. It appeared now that the army could attack the revolution and win.

Within Hungary the growing strength of the dynasty produced a split in the Hungarian ranks. Batthyány, Eötvös and Deák saw their only hope of survival in acceptance of the principle of legality and therefore of co-operation with Vienna. Kossuth, however, as minister of finance, raised objections. Necessary to the ministry because of the popular support he enjoyed, he complicated its relations with Vienna. He was unwilling to make financial contributions to the central government. Believing in the ideal of a completely independent Hungary, he acted upon the supposition that the Habsburg dynasty would collapse and the German portions of its dominions would be joined in a Greater Germany; every encouragement ought to be given to the Frankfort Parliament, because in a completely united Germany Austria would be reduced to the status of a province. He raised ideological and tactical objections to aiding a dynasty whose policy ran counter to all that was progressive in Europe. How could Hungary supply money and troops for the suppression of the Italian national movement?

Kossuth's faith in the cause of Hungary supposed that all would recognize its justice. He sadly miscalculated the reaction of the Slavs in the military frontier districts and Croatia against the plan of a unitary Hungary. The Croats in particular were a military nation, and there were signs already of an 'Illyricism' which amounted to a desire for some form of Croat autonomy. In the south the Serbs rose in revolt under the leadership of Stratimirović. Jellačić as Ban of Croatia was in a position to rally all the Slavs of the south in opposition to the government in Pest. The dynasty, however, for all its professions of solicitude, would have been prepared to abandon Jellačić if the Hungarians could have consented to remain within the bonds of legality and provide reinforcements for the war against the Italians. Jellačić's policy was revealed to be one of federation. If the Hungarians wished to extend their control over Croatia they would be forced to accept the principle of loyalty to the throne; alternatively, they could concede autonomy to the Croats and defy the Habsburg dynasty. A conference took place in Vienna on 26 July between Batthyány and Jellačić, but it ended in deadlock. Batthyány was uncertain whether he could speak with full authority when he knew that in Pest there was bitter dislike of surrendering the historic claims of the Crown of St Stephen. Failure of the Hungarians to reach an agreement with the Croats sealed the alliance of Jellačić and the Austrian military party. On 4 September 1848 Jellačić was confirmed in his power as Ban of Croatia. Legality would lie with the Croats. The course of illegality lay open to the Hungarians.

The new Hungarian parliament had met on 5 July 1848, and at once showed that it was different in its temper from the diet which had met under the old constitution. Bitter hostility was expressed at the demand for recruits and money to assist the dynasty in its war in Italy. Kossuth openly expressed his opposition and embroidered his arguments with diatribes against the Croats and the Serbs. The command which Kossuth began to exercise over the Hungarian parliament threw the moderates into disarray. Gradually the reactionary group which constituted the Austrian military party began to place their pressure upon Hungary. On 22 August the extraordinary powers which had been granted the Hungarian Palatine, the Archduke Stephen, were withdrawn, which in effect meant that Hungarian measures would be subject to approval from Vienna. The confirmation of Jellačić in his office was equivalent almost to an ultimatum. Batthyány resigned. Szechenyi went mad. Eötvös left for Germany. Deák could offer no advice. Kossuth was left in control and the Hungarian revolution entered its radical stage. Paper money was to be issued. A national army was to be raised. An appeal was launched to the parliament in Vienna, but even before the deputies debated the question whether they might hear the case for a mediation between the Crown and the Hungarians war was opened. On 17 September 1848 Jellačić marched into Hungary. The peasant deputies in Vienna were indifferent to the Hungarian question now that the agrarian question had been solved. The remaining deputies, moderate by instinct, were prepared to do nothing to support a Hungary falling under the control of the radical Kossuth. Counsels of moderation were lost on the Hungarians. An extraordinary commissioner, Count Lamberg, was sent to Pest to negotiate directly with the Hungarians, but he was set upon by a fanatical mob and killed. Up to this moment the dynasty had hesitated to act. Jellačić was not making good progress and had begun to retreat towards Croatia. But for the assassination of Lamberg a compromise solution might at the last hour have been reached, but now on 3 October the Austrian government declared war upon the Hungarian régime.

The Vienna parliament was unwilling to aid Hungary, but radical Vienna was of another mind. When the news was received that

Hungary had been placed in a state of siege the population, which had been in a mood of high excitement throughout September, made its last appeal to force. On 6 October a demonstration took place at the railway station where a Viennese battalion was entraining for the Hungarian front. The incident quickly developed into an armed insurrection, which in two days' fighting placed the city in the hands of the populace under the command of the deputy, Fischof, the left-wing democrat, Tausenau, and the student leader, Hrabowsky. The Czech deputies refused association with the radical movement and left the city. The emperor departed to the security of Olmütz. The insurrection gave the military party the opportunity for which it had waited. Windischgrätz was placed in command of all troops except those serving on the Italian front. By 23 October the city had been surrounded and, in accordance with the rules which had been adopted in Cracow and Prague, Vienna was bombarded into submission. The radical revolution had been crushed and conservatism triumphed. The parliament was removed to the Moravian town of Kremsier, where it would be safe from popular pressures. A new ministry was created under the control of the triumvirate of Schwarzenberg, who had distinguished himself in Italy, Franz Stadion and Alexander Bach, determined upon the preservation of the Habsburg monarchy's territories. Promises of a constitution upon a unitary basis were held out. In order that the new régime might seem to dissociate itself from the old the Emperor Ferdinand was compelled to abdicate on 2 December, and in his place was put the eighteen-year-old Francis Joseph, who was, it might be argued, not a party to the many brutal decisions which had been made on behalf of the dynasty in 1848. This did not mean that he was slow to learn the techniques which had brought him to the throne. First among the major European states Austria was able to restore authoritarian government.

The Reconquest of Hungary

Windischgrätz proceeded in his own leisurely way to attempt the reconquest of Hungary. He was better at bombarding cities than conducting a vigorous campaign in the field. Pest fell without a fight on 5 January 1849, but from this moment the fortunes of the Hungarians began to revive under the dictatorship of Kossuth. In April a Hungarian counter-offensive drove Windischgrätz out of the country, and the capture of Vienna seemed almost within the Hungarians' grasp. At this point they made a capital military error. Instead of pursuing the Austrian army to Vienna, Görgei, the commander-in-chief, diverted his troops to lay siege to the fortress of Buda, which was still in Austrian hands. In the meantime Radetzky had defeated the Italians for a second time at the battle of Novara on 23 March 1849. The Italian situation no longer presenting problems, Radetzky could spare battle-trained officers to take charge of the Austrian armies in Hungary in place of what has been described as the gerontocracy of Windischgrätz. From the point of view of Nicholas I of Russia the time had come for decisive action. He had been careful to offer no provocation to the German revolution in 1848, but this did not mean that he wished to permit Germany to unify herself. On 27 March 1849 the Frankfort Parliament offered the Imperial crown to Frederick William IV, who, though he rejected the offer, nevertheless was himself on 15 May 1849 to announce his intention of finding his own solution of the German Question (see below p. 289). If the Austrian monarchy could be restored it would be able to speak with authority in the Germanic Confederation and act as a counterweight to Prussia. There was also a subsidiary motive in Nicholas I's mind. Large numbers of Poles were serving with the Hungarian army, and in the event of a Hungarian success it seemed likely that they would raise the standard of revolt in Russian Poland. For external and internal reasons Nicholas I was ready to respond to Austrian appeals for help. In May 1849 Russia agreed to send into Hungary an army of 150,000 men under Field Marshal Paskevich without demanding any form of political compensation in return.

The revitalized Austrian army under General Haynau and the Russian army converged upon the Hungarians. In the face of this overwhelming opposition the Hungarian commander-in-chief, Görgei, quarrelled with the dictator, Kossuth, over the actual method of surrender. Kossuth resigned his powers as dictator, and on 13 August 1849 Görgei made his surrender to the Russians at the town of Világos. This gesture was intended to be symbolic of Hungarian resistance, demonstrating that they had been defeated by foreign troops from whom they expected better treatment than from the Austrians. The Hungarian army was handed over to General

Haynau, who to the disgust of the Russians interpreted his powers more widely than they had hoped. As many as 467 persons were executed for their part in the rising, including thirteen generals. Such treatment was not the kind likely to lead to conciliation. The capitulation, the Hungarians insisted, was not to be mistaken for the crushing defeat which the Czechs had received at the battle of the White Mountain in 1620.

The Habsburg monarchy had nevertheless achieved a great victory. It had perhaps not conquered the national instincts of the constituent peoples in its empire, but it had conquered the radical left. The Germans lost faith in the ideal of a Greater Germany. The Slavs, menaced by germanization or magyarization, could hope for a better future only within the framework of the monarchy. Even in Hungary there was a group which sought conciliation. The party of Kossuth remained as strong as ever. Deák and Eötvös for the future were to work for self-government within the empire; they would not fight the dynasty, but rather use it to combat their own radical opposition. Destroyed was the revolutionary spirit. The politicians with whom the Habsburgs would be compelled to deal in the future would not be the men from the barricades of 1848.

The Italian Revolution of 1848

There was in Italy before 1848 a deep consciousness of the need for change, but there was small agreement upon the means by which unification might be achieved and the principles upon which the new political system should be based. Upon one fact alone politically conscious Italians were agreed, and that was that the removal of Austria was the prime condition of any form of unification. The events of 1831 and the equivocal behaviour of Francis IV of Modena had given an impetus to the growth of republican feeling. Guiseppe Mazzini in 1831 put princely sincerity to the test in a public appeal to Charles Albert of Savoy for a war upon Austria, but it not unnaturally made no impression and passed unheeded. Charles Albert never lived down the reputation he had won in 1821, when Piedmont under his leadership had risen against the Austrian intervention against Naples. Mazzini called upon him to side with the revolution or pay the price. Since Charles Albert was required to establish a democratic constitution and admit the sovereignty of the nation, the solution offered by Mazzini was unattractive to a prince who inherited the paternalist inclinations of his dynasty. Failing to obtain a response, Mazzini proceeded to found the association of 'Young Italy', which would appeal to the youth of the nation to achieve independence. When it was discovered that Charles Albert was by no means sympathetic to this society's activities, Mazzini decided to take revenge. This was to assume the form of nothing less than an expedition into the dominions of Charles Albert, which was to be the signal for an uprising throughout the peninsula. On the night of 31 January–1 February 1834 a force of a few hundred revolutionaries, of whom the majority were Poles, crossed Lake Geneva under the command of General Ramorino, disliked by the Poles for his incompetent handling of a Polish army corps in 1831 and disliked by Mazzini, lest he obtain the glory of victory instead of himself, and landed in Savoy to proclaim the liberation of Italy amid the French-speaking peasants of the province. Most of the time spent in the operation seems to have been occupied in rowing on the lake. This farcical episode ended amid mutual recriminations and the return of Mazzini's force to Switzerland. He was expelled from the Swiss Confederation and went into exile in London.

Mazzini is often supposed to have rendered an invaluable contribution to the unification of Italy, but he in fact never had a strong following in Italy itself, though he certainly had some influence upon the revolutionaries of other countries. 'Young Italy' played no part in the Italian struggle because Mazzini was discredited as a political leader after the comic-opera affair of 1834. Nevertheless, there were throughout Italy persons who looked towards a republican solution of the Italian question, describing themselves as 'Mazzinians', 'Democrats' or 'Republicans'. Their activities gave some cause for alarm to the Austrian government in Lombardy-Venetia, but repressive action was taken in a dilatory fashion. What Mazzini and persons who thought like him did achieve was to alarm their own compatriots. The solution which they put forward was the calling of a constituent assembly for the whole of Italy and the erection of a republic based upon universal manhood suffrage. Such views gave rise to deep misgivings. If the republicans adhered to the Mazzinian doctrine of constant conspiracy no progress could be made in a period when the rest of Europe was being transformed by the new technology. There was great interest in material progress throughout Italy. From 1839 on-wards there was a spate of scientific congresses. In 1839 was con-structed a railway in Naples, the first in the peninsula and that in a state which was not the object of universal admiration. Everywhere agricultural societies sprouted. There was nothing uncommon in these developments, and as elsewhere a political conclusion was drawn from them by men of moderate opinions. For them an end must be put to plotting which would lead to repression. Italy should build up her material resources in order that she might the better be able to take advantage of her independence when she obtained it.

One of the most influential writers of this time was the Turin priest, Gioberti, who came under the influence of the romantic catholicism current in Europe which made the Pope as the head of a universal religion the champion of the poor. In his *Primato Morale e Civile degli Italiani* (The Moral and Civic Primacy of the Italians), published in 1843, Gioberti, as the rubbishy title of his book suggests, took over much of the clap-trap current in republican and extreme nationalist circles. Italy was declared to be the home of dynamic men, Dante, Vico and Buonaparte. Christian Rome, it was declared, had created modern civilization and was the moral and spiritual centre of the world. Having thus paid lip-service to the ideas of left, Gioberti went on to point out that Italy had been too long divided and that there-fore only a federal solution of her problems could be entertained, a solution which should be reached by peaceful means rather than by force. At the head of the Italian federation should preside the Pope, a somewhat unattractive solution if it is remembered that the Pope was Gregory XVI, the most reactionary of the pontiffs in the first half of the nineteenth century and universally disliked, but in this new scheme, Gioberti argued, the monarchs of Italy might play their part, especially the King of Piedmont-Sardinia. There was indeed much sound sense in Gioberti's ideas. This orientation, which went by the name of 'Neo-Guelf', offered an alternative to the unitary solution of the republicans and took into account the wide regional variations in Italy between the north and the south. It was, moreover, a solution which could be put forward openly because it threatened no régime. There were, of course, other solutions. Cesare Balbo, in his *Speranze d'Italia* (Hopes of Italy) of 1843, hoped for a federal solution under the leadership of Piedmont-Sardinia, because that state alone possessed an army worthy of the name and for that reason was best equipped to fight Austria. Massimo d'Azeglio, a Piedmontese noble, however, rejected federalism on the grounds that misrule in the Papal States was so scandalous that leadership must be placed in the hands of Charles Albert, who had a good record of administrative reform and sought actively to encourage trade. There was certainly nothing in the thinking of such men as these to encourage revolution, but revolution was in the air. Italy no less than the rest of Europe in the 1840s began to experience the political stresses attendant upon the rise in food prices. In the general discontent Italians blamed the system of government, and their hardships were transformed into the expression of political grievances.

The situation changed suddenly in 1846 with the election of Pope Pius IX on the death of Gregory XVI. Metternich was to remark cynically that 'we expected everything except a liberal Pope'. The subsequent interpretation in Italy and elsewhere was that Pius IX was at the outset a liberal, who afterwards became a reactionary. The interpretation of his actions is not made easy by the supposition that he was in fact a liberal at all. The circumstances of his election point to another interpretation. There were two strong candidates for the papacy, Cardinal Gizzi and Cardinal Lambruschini, but Gizzi was considered too advanced a thinker, while Lambruschini was too closely identified with the pro-Austrian party. The choice therefore fell upon a moderate who fell between these two extremes, Cardinal Mastai, who took the name of Pius IX. Pius IX was a compromise candidate, acceptable to the left and right wings of the Conclave.

The policy of Pius IX was designed to cut the ground from under the feet of the extreme liberals and radicals by a policy of timely concessions which would make revolution unnecessary. The coercive system of Gregory XVI was abandoned and a series of measures undertaken to take the sting out of radicalism, but Pius IX's good intentions were misinterpreted from the outset. In the popular mind he was believed in fact to be a liberal. In July 1846 he granted an amnesty and appointed as his Secretary of State, Cardinal Gizzi, who was well known for his progressive views. He gave orders that gasworks and railways might be constructed in the papal states, against which Gregory XVI had turned his face. The Austrian government grew anxious and occupied the papal town of Ferrara as a precautionary measure, a step which they claimed a treaty right to make. Undoubtedly Metternich committed a political error, because this unilateral action at once aroused the national hostility of the Italian political class and seemed to erect the Pope as a symbol of national regeneration. The eyes of all Italy were turned upon Rome and the Pope held in general admiration. Even those obstinately protestant powers, Great Britain and the United States, decided to enter into direct diplomatic relations with the Pope. Pius IX was from the outset placed in a false position. In popular imagination he was a liberal, but he could not go too far for fear of meeting with the opposition of the Cardinals, while he himself did not intend to go too far lest by granting a constitution for the Papal States he erect an assembly which might try to limit his sacerdotal powers. Pius IX could never forget that he had two functions. He was at once an Italian territorial ruler and the universal monarch of the Roman Catholic Church. The limit of his concessions was the so-called *Consulta* of 14 October 1847. This was an assembly which could give the Pope advice upon the administration of the Papal States, but it possessed no powers. Pius IX intended to keep in his own hands the temporal functions of the Papacy.

In January 1848 the wave of revolutions in Italy began. A separatist revolt in Palermo was the spark which caused an explosion throughout the peninsula. The régimes in all the petty states of Italy were obliged to make concessions to the liberal opposition. In the words of a contemporary 'it rained constitutions'. For all the paralysis of government in Vienna in the years before 1848, the viceroy in Austrian Italy, Field Marshal Radetzky, had managed to preserve the efficiency of the Austrian army under his command. When the news of the rising in Vienna arrived in Milan on 17 March the population gave vent to its discontents in five days of rioting. Radetzky, uncertain of the situation in the capital and rather than be caught in a city where his troops would enjoy little technical superiority over the mob, withdrew to the security of the Quadrilateral, the four fortresses of Pieschiera and Mantua on the Mincio and Verona and Legnano on the Adige. Radetzky wished to encourage the revolution to raise its head and come out into the open country, where his professional troops could easily defeat it. Milan and Venice fell to the

Italian insurgents, and Charles Albert under the pressure of public opinion declared war upon Austria on 24 March 1848. A provisional government was established in Milan, and it appeared that all Italy was to be united.

It should, however, be remembered that the new rulers in the Italian states were men of moderate political opinions. They had two objects in their policy, on the one hand, to expel the Austrians from Italy and, on the other, to prevent their own domestic radicals from obtaining power. The great difficulty of the Italian revolution was its lack of a disciplined military force. The Piedmontese army was well trained, but its troops were too few to engage the Austrians. In consequence, a rabble of volunteers joined the Piedmontese army, bringing with them democratic notions of what a revolutionary army's discipline ought to be. Of the Tuscans it was said that 'discipline appeared to them slavery unworthy of one who combats for freedom'. In fact, the revolutionaries were drawn mainly from the educated classes in Italy. The key position in the situation was occupied by Pius IX. If he were to adhere to the national cause he would strengthen the moderates against the radicals and at the same time place the support of the peasantry behind the national movement. Pius IX went as far as he dared to assist the Italian movement. In January 1848 he admitted lay personnel to the government of the Papal States. On 14 March 1848 he yielded to the extent of granting a constitution. In the all-important Italian Question, however, he stopped short of making a declaration of complete support. He himself had no wish for Austria to dominate Italy and would have been willing to co-operate with the other Italian states upon a federal basis, but he could not make war upon Austria. It would have been fatal to the prestige of the Papacy if the Pope made war at all, especially when the Austrian army contained an overwhelming majority of Roman Catholic soldiers. Pius IX did his best to warn the Italians. In his allocution of 10 February, in which he called upon God to bless Italy, he was careful to point out that Rome's prestige was spiritual and not based upon physical force, but the allocution made an opposite impression upon the public mind. It appeared that Italian unification had papal blessing. Pius IX privately warned Charles Albert that he could not join the war, and finally on 29 April 1848 declared openly in an allocution that the Supreme Pontiff in virtue of the nature of his office could not make war. By the spring Pius IX was meeting with serious political difficulties. The radicals were accusing him of being hostile to the national cause, and their deliberate misinterpretations found an audience in the unemployed of Rome. 1847 had been a year of high prices, but the political troubles had caused a decline in the tourist traffic upon which so many of the poor depended for their livelihood. Here was the raw material for a radical revolution. On the other hand, the landlords of the papal states were financially worse off and at the same time hard pressed by taxation for what they declared to be the Pope's bellicose foreign policy. Caught between the extremes of left and right, Pius IX sought to win over the party of law and order, the moderate liberals. In August 1848 the administration of the papal states was taken over by Count Pelegrino Rossi, a partisan of French constitutionalism of the Orleanist pattern. His nomination only deepened the crisis. Rossi was condemned as an anti-clerical by the reactionaries and as a dictator by the radicals. In the meantime ominous signs had appeared in southern Italy. The revolutionary in Naples had shown itself to be predatory in its attitude towards government. The middle classes regarded the new government as being merely an instrument for the distribution of patronage. Against this concept the masses in Naples reacted with startling violence. Riots occurred on 15 May, and there were demonstrations in favour of the old system. The mob cried, 'Viva il Re assoluto!' (Long live the Absolute King). The army turned against the revolution, and the Neapolitan troops, which had marched north to fight against the Austrians, were recalled. The success of the Italian revolution now depended virtually upon the ability of the Piedmontese army and its undisciplined reinforcements to defeat the Austrians.

There was at the outset little confidence in Vienna that Austria, in view of her many commitments, could maintain her position in Italy. An important role in the Italian question was played by Great Britain. Britain desired Austria to be strong in areas where British interests were affected, but in Italy she was not concerned, except to exclude French interference. From the British point of view, if the Italians could erect a viable state and keep out the French, then the aims of British policy would be equally well served. The Austrian diplomat, Hummelauer, was sent to London to seek some compromise, and was on 23 May 1848 prepared to offer the autonomy of Lombardy-Venetia and on 24 May to concede independence for Lombardy. The British cabinet was unwilling to commit itself entirely to the Austrian plan, and on 3 June 1848 offered mediation if Lombardy and parts of Venetia were given up. The policy of the French Republic was circumspect. The French leaders held the realistic view that the creation of a large state on the southern frontiers of France was not in their best interests because such a state would exclude the eventual cession to France of Savoy and Nice. The situation was altered dramatically when Radetzky took the offensive. On 25 July 1848 the Italian army was defeated at the battle of Custozza and Charles Albert was compelled to evacuate Milan and seek an armistice, which was granted him on 9 August.

At this point the concealed cleavage in Italian thinking was revealed. Charles Albert did not wish for French intervention, because France would demand of him cessions from his own territories, but the Italian movement was not disposed to consider the purely dynastic views of the House of Savoy. The revolutionaries were ready to call in France if the larger aim of Italian unity could be achieved. The second phase in the Italian revolution now began. The argument was advanced that the revolution had failed because the moderates had acted with insufficient vigour. They claimed that if the radicals had been in power they would have achieved success. For this reason the Italian left was able to lever the moderates from power. In October 1848 a left-wing victory occurred in Tuscany and Montanelli became president of the council and the demagogue, Guerrazzi, took the ministry of internal affairs. The moderates under Ricasoli were for the moment set on one side. In November Rossi was assassinated in Rome and there were demands for a constituent assembly. In the face of left-wing democracy Pius IX took refuge in Gaeta. Even in Piedmont there were changes. In December Gioberti came to power in Turin at the head of the 'Democratic Ministry'. The aim everywhere in the North was the summoning of a constituent assembly and the attainment of Italian unity. The responsibility of power, however, confronted the radicals with its realities. Guerrazzi now tried to control the mob at Leghorn, which he had formerly incited. The flight of Pius IX meant that there could no longer be any hope of enlisting the aid of the peasantry. The radicals in Rome deposed the Pope and established their own Roman Republic on 9 February 1849, but Pius IX drew attention to his international position and had already on 7 February called upon the Catholic powers for aid against the revolutionaries.

The Austrian government, heartened by the victory of Custozza, was less prepared to grant concessions in Italy, but it was essential to keep the French out of Italy. On 2 September 1848 Austria declared her readiness to accept an Anglo-French mediation in Italy, an action which for the moment saved French prestige. When at the end of October 1848 the Austrian government had brought under control its domestic revolutionaries in Vienna a new tone was adopted. It was now suggested that neither France nor Austria had any desire to erect a strong state in Italy and that the best course for both parties was the restoration of the *status quo*. The advent to power of Louis Napoleon Bonaparte in December 1848 as the apparent champion of law and order in France introduced a certain conservatism in French policy. The new foreign minister, Drouyn de Lhuys, was a conservative who believed that an alliance of France and Austria would serve as a check to the adventurous instincts of Louis Napoleon. This disposition to compromise was complicated by the popular image of the Bonapartes, who were in public imagination committed to the revision of the treaties of 1815, and the demands of the French clericals. Louis Napoleon therefore wavered between a policy of prestige and the maintenance of parcelization both in Italy and in Germany, which would serve the interests of France better than the intangible possibilities of minor territorial gains.

The result was a diplomatic deadlock which excited Italian passions. As the possibility of a diplomatic solution grew more remote demands grew for a reversion to the old policy of independent action, *Italia fara da se*. Under pressure of public opinion Charles Albert was compelled to renew the war and the Italian army met with disaster at the battle of Novara on 23 March 1849. Having committed himself to a forward foreign policy and met with failure, Charles Albert accepted responsibility and in order to save his dynasty abdicated in favour of his son, Victor Emmanuel, who signed an armistice with Radetzky.

The central regions of Italy were now open to Austrian intervention. The Italian revolution could not long survive the defeat in the north, but Louis Napoleon found himself in a difficult position. The Pope had appealed to the Catholic powers. Louis Napoleon owed much to the support of the French clericals, while the French radicals disliked the Austrian domination of Italy. It therefore appeared possible for France to intervene in Italy to satisfy both elements. The power of the Pope could be restored and the Austrians kept out of the Papal States. In April 1849 a French expeditionary force under General Oudinot was sent to occupy Rome, but at once a complication arose. The forces of the Roman Republic under Mazzini and Garibaldi resisted the French advance, with a consequent outcry in the French radical press. For the moment the French attack upon Rome was called off, but when the French elections of May 1849 revealed a victory for the clerical right it appeared safe for the French army to occupy Rome. In this manner the Roman Republic was suppressed and the temporal power of the Pope restored, but the French involved themselves in more difficulties than they hoped to solve. Louis Napoleon had believed that it would be possible for Pius IX to revert to his policy of moderate reform. It was hoped that the Pope would concede an amnesty, permit some secularization of the administration and introduce the *Code Napoléon*. Pius IX, however, never a convinced liberal, was now of the opinion that the policy of concession had led to disaster and that the only course open to him was reversion to the policy of Gregory XVI. The pro-Austrian Cardinal Antonelli was appointed secretary of state and the liberal phase in the Papal States brought to an end. The French found themselves against their will in the position of defending the old régime and yet unable to withdraw from the false situation in which they had placed themselves.

The year 1849 saw a split in the educated classes of Italy. The church had been closely linked with the people in the eighteenth century and there had been little reaction to the dechristianization which was apparent elsewhere in Europe, but with the failure of the revolution attention was now drawn to the position of the Church. There were 60,000 priests and 220 bishops in a population of 25,000,000. This seemed an obstacle to the achievement of Italian unity. Pius IX was regarded as the enemy of unification, at the head of a vast vested interest with extensive property in the hands of a clergy not distinguished for its intellectual attainments. The Jesuits were openly anti-liberal and anti-Italian. Everywhere clerical control was increased, whether in Naples, Tuscany or Lombardy-Venetia. By fresh concordats with the Papacy the old régimes linked themselves with the Church as a bastion of the existing system. The one exception to the rule was Piedmont. From the troubles of 1848 Savoy inherited a constitution. The prestige of the dynasty was severely shaken and it was compelled to abandon its authoritarian system in favour of a policy of management. Radetzky did not impose a punitive peace upon Piedmont, because he realized that the new king, Victor Emmanuel, would do his best to sustain the conservative order in Piedmont. Piedmontese politics now were determined by an alliance of the monarchists under Cavour and the anti-clerical left led by Ratazzi. The clue to the preservation of monarchical control lay in the satisfaction of anti-clerical feeling. In 1850 were introduced the celebrated Siccardi Laws which limited the powers of the clergy in Piedmont. For this reason a contrast was created between the Papal States, where clericalism was rife, and the apparently enlightened Piedmont. The French general, Lamoricière, declared 'nothing will be done in Rome until four monsignori have been hanged on the four corners of the city'. The illusion was created that progress depended upon Piedmont, but the government of Victor Emmanuel retained its paternalistic instincts. Anti-clericalism was a mere tactical deviation. Piedmontese opinion turned towards a solution of the Italian question, which permitted unification without exciting social discords. Such a solution could be found only in diplomacy. The moderates in the other states of Italy were not slow to form their opinion of the new situation. Ricasoli in Tuscany had come to the conclusion that unity could be achieved only if direction were given from the top. The weakness of government in 1848-9 had given rein to indiscipline. The people at large appeared indifferent to the national cause. Therefore unity might be achieved by any means, provided that the existing order of society were preserved. The federal solution was now set aside and opinion among the moderates veered to a unitary programme under the leadership of the house of Savoy. No one had much admiration for Cavour and the Piedmontese monarchists. It was to be the upper classes of Italy who should determine the future form of the state and Piedmont seemed the safest choice for them.

Prussia and the Problem of German Unity, 1848–50

The Prussian parliament was elected on 1 and 8 May, the same days upon which the Frankfort Parliament was elected, but the Prussian parliament was more democratic in its composition than its counterpart at Frankfort. One explanation of this fact is that the notables normally elected to the former Diets had been selected to go to the National Assembly in Frankfort, which left the way open for men of humbler origin to act as representatives in what were considered regional and therefore inferior legislative bodies. The policy of Frederick William IV was to co-operate with the Camphausen–Hansemann ministry and wait for the opportunity to reassert his power. Continuing unemployment required a policy of public works, on the one hand, to keep the working class quiet, while, on the other, a civic guard was raised from which the workers were excluded. Undoubtedly the workers feared reaction, especially when Prince William, the King's brother, who had been virtually exiled for a period, was allowed to return. The reactionaries were beginning to raise their heads. Ludwig von Gerlach began to take up the idea of founding a newspaper to express conservative views, the 'Journal of the Cross' (Kreuzzeitung), and bringing together the landed proprietors to offer resistance to the liberal policy of the ministry. The new régime found itself under pressure from right and left. On 14 June 1848 the Arsenal was broken into and an attempted rising by the Berlin mob was put down only by the prompt arrival of a battalion of Royal Guards. The propertied classes began to fear for their lives and look more and more to the protection which the state could provide.

The first crack in the liberal régime appeared on 17 June, when Camphausen resigned upon a constitutional issue and left Hansemann as the leading minister to carry on the struggle to induce Frederick William IV to submit to the advice of his constitutional advisers. In fact, within Prussia the forces of right and left were evenly balanced. The reactionaries formed their so-called *Junkerparlament* to protect the interests and fiscal immunities of the nobility. In the Prussian National Assembly attacks were made upon the right wing, even to the extent of a proposal being made on 31 October 1848 for the abolition of titles of nobility. The King, moreover, was to lose the phrase 'By the Grace of God' from his own style and title. The

violence of the left frightened the moderate bourgeoisie. On
1 November 1848 Frederick William IV took the decision to resist
the Assembly and dismissed the liberal ministry, appointing in its
place the ministry of Count Brandenberg, the so-called 'Bastard of
Prussia' for his being a natural son of Frederick William II, with Otto
von Manteuffel as minister of the interior. On 9 November the order
was given for the National Assembly to remove itself from Berlin to
the quiet provincial city of Brandenburg. A state of siege was proclaimed, but there was no effective challenge to reaction. On 5 December the Assembly was dissolved and a new constitution was promulgated. Once more Frederick William granted a responsible ministry
and accorded his subjects their fundamental civic rights, but now the
parliament was to consist of two chambers, an upper chamber elected
in accordance with a high property franchise and a lower chamber
elected by indirect universal suffrage by all males over the age
of twenty-four years. The king, however, reserved to himself the
right of veto on legislation and of legislating by decree. All real
power was now reserved to the Crown, and the ministry was
composed of reactionaries. Almost simultaneously with Austria,
Prussia moved towards a conservative solution of her internal
problems. The larger question of German unity still remained
unsolved.

While the two great German states, Austria and Prussia, were wit-
nessing the re-establishment of royal power, the Frankfort Parliament
was considering its own solution of the German problem. There were
those who favoured the proposal that Austria should lead the new
Germany. The victory of the Austrian state in Italy and the possibility that it would soon see its authority restored throughout in its
dominions seemed to give an assurance that the Germans everywhere
would maintained their liberties and even exploit a vast central European state, in which they would be safe from Slav domination. The
fact remained that Austria continued to exist as a state, and
Schwarzenberg from the first insisted that the entire Habsburg
dominions should be admitted to the new German state. In this sense
Austria would have a dominant voice in the affairs of Germany. This
seemed to offer an authoritarian régime, which was scarcely acceptable to the partisans of a liberal constitution. Heinrich von Gagern,
on the other hand, believed that Germany should be constituted upon

a narrower basis. Austria should remain as a state in association with Germany, but Prussia might assume leadership of the non-Austrian portions of Germany. It would be a simplification to suppose that the conflict of view lay between the supporters of a 'Big Germany' and those who proposed a 'Small Germany'. Neither Austrian nor Prussian leadership was satisfactory to the democratic left wing. Monarchical government by either power would be the negation of the egalitarian ideals which inspired German liberalism. That the final decision of the Frankfort Parliament should have come down on the side of Prussian leadership contains no more significance than that the German liberals of 1848–9 chose the course of what they considered prudent in the light of the constitutional, international and social problems which existed in Germany.

On 27 March 1849 the Frankfort Parliament voted in favour of a hereditary monarchy and on the following day by 290 votes to 248 abstentions declared in favour of offering the Crown to Frederick William IV of Prussia. There was certainly pressure from within Prussia upon Frederick William, but he persisted in the view that the transformation of Germany could take place only by the collaboration of the princes and that Prussia could not act in defiance of Austria. On 3 April he announced that he was willing to discuss Germany's problems with the German governments, which the deputies of the Frankfort Parliament interpreted to be his virtual refusal of the Crown. Rejection of the parliament's offer in this way meant that Frederick William IV looked to a more conservative solution of the German question than the bourgeoisie and radicals, but, even if this had not been the case, he had no choice in the matter. If he had accepted the throne he would have found himself committed to the creation of a unitary German state in defiance of both Austria and Russia. In the event of a war he would have been isolated, and Prussia, so far from creating a united Germany, would have stood herself in danger of dismemberment. There was little point in arguing that Austria was heavily committed in Hungary and that Britain would have adopted a favourable attitude to German unification; British policy was normally pro-Austrian in view of the dangers to British influence in the Near East. The view sometimes advanced that France would have accepted German unification for territorial compensation to herself is to stretch hypothesis to the limits of credibility. The plain truth was that within Germany only the petty states were willing to accept Prussian leadership. The larger states, especially Bavaria, Saxony and Hanover, had no wish to be subjected to the control of the Hohenzollern dynasty and its North German official class. The disappointments of 1849 roused the German left wing once more to activity, and demands were made that the constitution agreed upon at Frankfort should be put into operation. The majority of the deputies were not themselves willing to appeal to force, even though on 4 May 1849 the states were invited to adhere to the constitution and elections were called for the 15 July. Disturbances occurred in Rhenish Prussia, Westphalia, Silesia, Dresden, the Palatinate and Baden, but the German left wing could not summon sufficient strength to make any impression upon the established governments. The Frankfort parliament took refuge in Stuttgart, but the government of Württemberg in July dispersed it.

There was disappointment within Prussia that the king should not accept the imperial crown. It was felt that the least he could do was to recognize the authority of the Frankfort parliament. On a motion of the deputy, Radbertus, on 21 April 1849 the Prussian parliament voted in favour of recognizing the National Assembly, but Frederick William IV was in no mood to tolerate opposition in the spring of 1849. The Prussian parliament was dissolved, and on 30 May a new constitution was promulgated. The *octroyé* constitution of 1849 was to remain in force throughout the nineteenth century and disappear only with the fall of the Hohenzollern dynasty itself in 1918. The electorate was divided into three groups according to the amount they paid in direct taxation. Each group was accorded one-third of the representation. In this manner the representation of the poorer sections of the community was very much reduced and that of the great estate owners and the big bourgeoisie much increased. The constituencies, moreover, were never redrawn, with the result that as the urban centres grew with the expansion of Prussian industry their representation remained static; the representation of the rural areas, where often the population was to decline, remained exactly what it was in 1849. In effect, the Crown entered into a fresh alliance with the propertied classes against the militant democrats of the towns. Upon this basis the junkers of Brandenburg and Pomerania were able to enjoy an electoral influence out of all proportion to their social significance. It is small wonder that the Prussian constitution was sarcastically referred to as 'the fig-leaf of absolutism'.

Simultaneously with these constitutional changes Frederick William IV, under the advice of his minister, Radowitz, himself announced on 15 May 1849 his intention of seeking a solution of the German question. Conferences were held with the representatives of Saxony and Hanover, and on 29 May agreement was announced upon a draft German constitution. Prussia was to be granted leadership in external affairs, and the country was to be controlled by a common administrative council; there was even to be an element of popular representation. The agreement of Saxony and Hanover to this proposal was made conditional upon the assent of the other German governments, which in view of the known dislike of Bavaria for control from the North was a reservation of considerable importance. In August 1849 the Archduke John resigned his post of Vicar of the Empire, and upon a motion of Nassau it was suggested that the states which had grouped themselves around Prussia should proceed to hold elections to a fresh National Assembly. Hanover and Saxony protested that in fact not all the German states had joined the union; what had really occurred was the achievement of a virtual Prussian hegemony north of the river Main. When elections were held on 1 January for the parliament to be called in Erfurt, Hanover and Saxony seceded from the union. At the same time the Austrian minister, Schwarzenberg, began his campaign for the restoration of Austrian influence in Germany. Schwarzenberg's aims were rather less modest than those of Frederick William IV. It was his object to bring the whole of Germany under the domination of Austria.

Schwarzenberg's plan was for a directory to be established in Germany, consisting of seven states, Austria, Prussia, Bavaria, Saxony, Hanover, Württemberg and the two Hesses jointly. Having obtained the accession to this plan of Bavaria, Württemberg, Saxony and Hanover, he was able to turn the tables on Prussia and invite a conference of the German states to meet at Frankfurt on 10 May 1850. Germany in this way appeared to divide herself into two camps, and Austria and Prussia came to the point of war. In this situation one complication at least was resolved. The war against Denmark for the possession of Schleswig-Holstein had been renewed on 3 April 1849 only to be halted by a fresh truce on 10 July 1849. On 2 July 1850, however,

Prussia agreed to a definitive peace with Denmark and deserted the Germans of Schleswig-Holstein. Prussia could not afford to keep alive a struggle, which might lead to diplomatic complications when she was faced with a crisis of a major order in Germany. In this situation Britain adopted an attitude of reserve. Certainly Palmerston had no objection in principle to a solution of the German question upon the lines proposed by Prussia, which seemed better than the Greater Germany at which Schwarzenberg aimed, but when in November 1850 Radowitz tempted Britain with a reduction of the Zollverein tariffs in order to obtain an alliance for Prussia he showed no interest. The attitude of France towards Prussian leadership varied. The foreign ministers, Drouyn de Lhuys and de Tocqueville, were willing to concede Prussia supremacy north of the Main, but they did not wish to permit the complete reduction of Austrian influence. The prince-president, Louis Napoleon Bonaparte, revealed a trait which in the end was to be his undoing. He had his own policy independently of his principal ministers and dreamed of revising the treaties of 1815. The situation in Germany seemed to offer the chance of pushing France's frontiers forward on the Rhine. On 15 June 1850 Persigny was to offer a French alliance in the event of an Austro-Prussian war, in return for which France was to receive the Bavarian Palatinate. It says little for the statesmanship of the Bonapartist clique that they could have made such a proposal to Prussia after so much had happened in Germany since March 1848 and when Prussia herself was standing for the rights of German nationalism. It was, moreover, a grave miscalculation of the state of feeling in France, which was in 1850 pacific after the troubles of 1848. The decisive factor in the situation was the attitude of Russia. It was the policy of Nicholas I to encourage neither the Prussian solution of the German question nor the proposals of Schwarzenberg. Russia desired to establish an equilibrium in Germany between the two major German powers. In May 1850 he warned Frederick William IV that Russia would intervene against whichever state was the aggressor, though it was emphasized that the state which began hostilities would not necessarily be deemed to have committed the aggression, but no tangible aid was offered to Schwarzenberg when he made his approach to Russia. On the whole, the influence of Russia was thrown against Prussia by the concentration of troops on her eastern frontier.

As the result of an incident in Hesse-Cassel in November 1850 a trial of strength was made. Prussia mobilized, but Schwarzenberg submitted an ultimatum to Prussia to disarm. The result was the celebrated Punctation of Olmütz of 29 November 1850, by which Prussia consented to the restoration of the former Germanic Confederation, but Schwarzenberg then discovered that he could not exploit his victory, because the influence of the powers was thrown against any attempt to extend Austrian influence. It had been his hope that Austria with Hungary might be included within the Zollverein in order that a vast economic area might be created in which Austria might be the dominant unit, but such a proposal met with opposition. In fact, Prussia was able to enlarge her influence economically because in September 1851 Hanover agreed to join the Zollverein by 1 January 1854 and was followed by Oldenburg and Brunswick. Though Austria had achieved a political victory, Germany was united economically under the leadership of Prussia. The whole question was complicated by the reforms undertaken by Carl Ludwig Bruck in Austria in 1850. The tariff frontier between Austria and Hungary was abolished in the interest of producing a homogeneous commercial system. Thus the Germans of Austria found themselves wedded by self-interest to a different economic system from that of their fellow countrymen in the Confederation.

There was little to choose between the régime imposed in Prussia under the régime of Manteuffel and that prevailing in Austria. Reaction triumphed with the victory of the Crown, the bureaucracy, army and gentry, but at least Frederick William IV maintained the constitution of May 1849. There was no reason why he should have abandoned so convenient a façade which gave him the appearance of being a constitutional king without many of the limitations which a constitution normally imposes upon a monarch's power. On 13 December 1851 the Austrian constitution was abolished, one of the last acts of Schwarzenberg before his death on 7 April 1852. Nevertheless, the régime which he had inaugurated was continued under the minister of the interior, Alexander Bach who imposed upon the Habsburg dominions a system of rigid centralization. An attack was made upon Hungary. Croatia, the Banat and Voyvodina and Transylvania were administered as separate provinces. German was imposed as the official language in the lands of the Crown of St Stephen. It would have been as if the most doctrinaire of the Josephine bureaucrats had come into their own, if it had not been that the régime concluded the concordat of 18 August 1855 with the Roman Church. Clerical control was now extended to education and all questions concerning marriage placed in the hands of the church. Even ecclesiastical property confiscated by Joseph II was restored. The Church entered into an alliance with the Habsburg dynasty for the maintenance of the existing régime. Whatever might be said of the Prussian system, it at least was free of clerical control. The finances, moreover, of Prussia presented a picture of orderliness, where in Austria chronic difficulty was as ever met in balancing the budget. On balance, in spite of the humiliation of Olmütz, Prussia emerged with greater credit than Austria from the revolution of 1848. At least Frederick William IV had made some effort to achieve the wider unity which most politically conscious Germans desired. The apparent completeness of the Habsburg victory gave an illusion of basic strength which was subsequently to lead Austria to disaster.

Louis Napoleon Bonaparte and the Establishment of the Second Empire

While Austria and Prussia wrestled with their problems, the Prince-President of France, Louis Napoleon Bonaparte, was pursuing his own devious ends. At the beginning of February 1849 Pius IX made his appeal to the Catholic sovereigns to restore his power. Falloux and the Catholic clericals pressed the government to act to save him from revolution, but when in March 1849 Radetzky defeated Charles Albert at Novara it seemed that the salvation of the Pope would be effected by the Austrians. Louis Napoleon was therefore placed in the position of being required by the clericals to save the Pope and by the liberals to prevent the Austrians from intervening in the Papal States, but to send a French force was actually a violation of the French constitution, which forbade French troops to intervene between a ruler and his subjects. Being a gambler by instinct Louis Napoleon sent a French force under General Oudinot to Rome, but on 30 April the French were fired upon by Garibaldi's men and what appeared at first to be a military promenade became a war. Oudinot declared war upon the Roman Republic, and the government in Paris was condemned by 328 votes to 241 for its conduct. For the moment it seemed that there might be a revival of the republican left, but on 18 May 1849 elections to the Legislative Assembly were at last held. New prefects certainly had some effect in managing the elections, but complete control was certainly beyond their grasp. Out of a total of 750 deputies, 500 conservatives were returned, while the republicans of February 1848 virtually ceased to be an important factor. On the other hand, the red republicans under Ledru-Rollin were able to return 180 deputies, mainly from the large towns, where the working class since June 1848 had lost all faith in the liberal bourgeoisie. This unexpected result revealed to the propertied class that the victory which had seemed so secure in 1848 was in fact incomplete. There was therefore a tendency to look for means of combating the red menace.

The elections over, Louis Napoleon could authorize Oudinot to throw the Italian republicans out of Rome. It was upon this question which the red republicans decided to put the reconstructed government to the test. On 11 June 1849 Ledru-Rollin tabled a motion accusing the government of violating the constitution, which was defeated by 361 votes to 203, but he believed that he could force the government into submission by appeal to the people of Paris. Once more on 13 June 1849 an attempt was made at a coup d'état, and once again the forces at the disposal of the government proved sufficient to deal with the situation. The people of Paris may have voted for the extreme left, but they were no longer prepared to sacrifice themselves. Ledru-Rollin was able to muster only 6,000 supporters. Within a few hours order was restored and Ledru-Rollin compelled to take flight. Provincial demonstrations at Toulouse, Perpignan, Strasburg, Lyons and elsewhere proved of little avail. The only result of Ledru-Rollin's ill-starred attempt to seize power was to encourage the moderates and conservatives to hurry through fresh measures to limit the power of the left.

Orders were given for the exclusion from the National Guard of persons suspected of left-wing tendencies. On 19 June freedom of association was suspended for one year and the government empowered to prevent an assembly which seemed likely to threaten public security. Fresh restrictions were placed upon the press and the threat of an immediate state of siege and military control suspended over the heads of prospective demonstrators. Falloux in June 1849 proposed a bill to give the clergy greater control over education.

There were even anti-clericals who now saw in religion a bulwark against socialism. Four archbishops were to be placed upon the governing body of the University of France, while the clergy were to be represented on the provincial educational councils. Relative freedom was granted to religious bodies wishing to found schools; no certificates of qualifications were to be required for teachers in them. Departments and communes could convey their school premises to religious orders and thus escape the obligations of themselves providing for education out of their own funds. Falloux's bill became law on 15 March 1850. It was the first stage in a campaign to win the allegiances of Frenchmen for the Catholic Church. The effort and energy which went into the expansion of clerical education was impressive, but equally astonishing is the fact that anti-clericalism did not disappear beneath the wave of religious fervour which swept France. The truth is that bad clerical education is itself a seedbed of anti-clericalism, and it was upon this foundation that Louis Napoleon was prepared in part to base his régime. Before the Falloux Law came into force Louis Napoleon had in January 1850 secured to the prefects the right to appoint teachers in the primary schools under the control of the state. Henceforth the schoolmaster was to be the servant either of the church or the state.

In October 1849 Louis Napoleon revealed that he intended to speak with greater force in public affairs by the dismissal of the Odilon Barrot ministry and the substitution of a new ministry from persons not sitting in the Legislative Assembly. No president of the council of ministers was appointed which indicated that the president himself intended to direct affairs and to take into his own hands all the powers which the head of the French state could exercise. The Assembly, in part absorbed by its pursuit of a clerical system of education, in part out of fear of challenging his authority, allowed this change to take place without protest. Of far greater concern were the supplementary elections held on 10 March 1850 to replace the deputies who had been deprived of their seats as a result of the attempted coup of June 1849. No less than twenty-one out of thirty-one constituencies returned leftists, to the shock and horror of the conservative majority, which believed that it had extirpated the radical left wing. The conclusion which was drawn by Assembly was that universal suffrage lay at the roots of France's troubles. In May 1850 a bill was introduced to revise the franchise. Henceforth to exercise the vote an elector was to be required to be a permanent resident in his canton for three years. The franchise could not, however, be exercised by persons convicted in the courts, sentenced for offences during their military service, or guilty of any act of violence against the authorities. By these restrictions it was hoped 'to reduce the electorate by 3,000,000. In June 1850 the bill became law, and with it was passed an extension for one year of the restrictions upon the liberty of assembly. In July 1850 further restrictions were placed upon the liberty of press. From the point of view of the conservatives it could only be a question of time before the monarchy was restored. Negotiations were opened with Louis Philippe and with the comte de Chambord, the legitimist candidate. Louis Philippe died in 1850, which removed an obstacle to a reconciliation between the two groups of the monarchists, but the comte de Chambord insisted that he could take the throne only if he were to rule 'By the Grace of God'. Not for the last time did Chambord put an insuperable obstacle in the way of a royalist restoration. Chambord destroyed all possibility of a monarchist reunion by his insistence upon a form of words which even his most devoted supporters recognized would discredit him with the majority of Frenchmen.

While the conservatives of the Assembly were playing their own game of politics, the president, Louis Napoleon, was playing for higher stakes. As the elected representative of the people he sought to separate himself in their imagination from the ministers and the deputies of the Assembly in the first months of office, nor did he allow himself to be tainted with the reactionaries' measures in 1850, which were represented as the legislation of parliamentary committees. All the time he was extending his influence in the administration and in the army. During the course of 1850 he made a number of visits to the provinces, making speeches and claiming that he represented popular sovereignty. By the beginning of 1851 he felt strong enough to make a demonstration against the high command of the army, which remained republican or Orleanist. General Changarnier commanded contrary to the law both the garrison of Paris and the National Guard, as well as being a deputy of the Assembly. On 9 January 1851 Louis Napoleon dismissed Changarnier. Having shown his mettle, he then proceeded to prepare a campaign for the revision of the constitution which would permit him to be nominated for a second term in the elections of 1852. From the provinces of France came a series of petitions for the reform of the constitution. The petitions were discussed in July 1851 by the Assembly, and many of the deputies considered that the re-election of Louis Napoleon was the lesser of many evils, but, though the vote to amend the constitution succeeded, it did not obtain the necessary two-thirds majority laid down by the constitution. The alternative before Louis Napoleon was a coup d'état.

The preparation of a coup d'état did not present many difficulties. There were officers of high rank who had served in the war in Algeria and who were ready to return home to make their fortunes in politics, especially Saint-Arnaud, who would take over the ministry of war. Around the president were a clique of adventurers, Rouher, the president's half-brother Morny, Mocquard, Fleury, Maupas and Persigny. On the one hand, play could be made of the danger which a presidential election might bring from the side of the extreme left wing. On the other hand, the president could pose as the defender of the rights of the people by requiring the assembly to rescind its law limiting universal suffrage of May 1850. When the ministry refused to submit his proposal to the assembly he dismissed it and replaced it with a ministry of his own in which Saint-Arnaud was made minister of war. On 13 November 1851 the assembly refused to modify its electoral law. On the night of 2 December 1851, the anniversary of the battle of Austerlitz, a military coup d'état was carried out. Leading opponents were arrested during the night and a decree posted dissolving the assembly and the council of state, declaring invalid the suffrage law of May 1851 and summoning the people to declare its wish upon the change of the constitution in a plebiscite. Some barricades were raised, but resistance was quickly crushed. The deputies of the assembly attempted without success to declare the president's action illegal. In the provinces there was scarcely any protest at all. There was, moreover, scarcely any enthusiasm for the coup, but enthusiasm could easily be manufactured.

The real founder of the new régime was the president's half-brother Morny When he took over the ministry of the interior he carried out a purge of mayors, schoolteachers and other public employers who would not join in advising a positive vote in the forthcoming plebiscite. A rigid control of the press was maintained. No members of unrecognized political associations were to be allowed to vote. Morny thus put into effect the very same system of elections which the members of the assembly themselves wished to adopt, but with the essential difference that a vote in a plebiscite permitted only approval or disapproval. A negative vote would still leave the next course undecided, and the tendency of the voter was to regard opposition to a proposal as a vote for anarchy. As it was, there were few who could openly advise the electorate. About 27,000 known opponents of the Bonapartist coup were arrested, of whom some 9,000 were transported to Algeria. The result of the plebiscite of 21 December 1851 was a foregone conclusion. The new constitution was approved by 7,500,000 votes to 640,000 against.

The new constitution which came into force on 14 January 1852 placed all effective power in the hands of the president. The president was responsible for all appointments in the state. It was he who nominated the members of the council of state which drew up the drafts of laws. The senate, which was chosen by the president, might revise the laws and even propose fresh ones, but its discussions were private. The Legislative Body, consisting of some 250 members, elected by a new electoral law which excluded republicans, voted the laws and taxation, but was required not to give any account of its proceedings. In the elections of March 1852 an overwhelming majority of official candidates was returned. Against 253 deputies returned on the official list there were 4 legitimists, 1 independent and 3 republicans, who refused to attend. When the Legislative Body was installed on 29 March 1852 Louis Napoleon Bonaparte made the fatuous remark which was subsequently to be held against him: 'The dictatorship entrusted to me by the people terminates today.' The people merely returned the deputies whom the prefects ordered. With the acceptance of authoritarian government it was but another step towards securing the fortunes of the Bonaparte family, when on 2 November 1852 France was proclaimed to be an empire and approval obtained in the plebiscite of 21 November, in which 7,800,000 voted in favour and 250,000 against, with 2,000,000 abstentions. The plebiscite, theoretically the instrument of the popular sovereignty, was made the instrument first for the abolition of such meagre civil liberties as the Legislative Assembly had been willing to permit and then to elevate the adventurer, Louis Napoleon Bonaparte, to the dignity of the Emperor Napoleon III, Emperor of the French. He was truly the heir of Napoleon I in the sense that it was the administrative system of the First Empire which permitted him to create a clientele out of nothing and reduce the powerful royalist groupings to nothing. The opposition did not, however, disappear. The French Second Empire represented merely a change of personnel at the top, just as Louis Philippe had been able to create a group of Orleanists. Often the change meant little more than the advancement of a different member of a local family of prominence. The tragedy was that, though the Bonapartist faction knew how to manage France, it was deficient in statecraft. Napoleon III wished to win a great reputation for himself and was prepared to take risks to achieve it.

1849: The Triumph of Reaction

Everywhere in Europe reaction triumphed, but it took on a different appearance. Austria abandoned its traditional Josephine concepts and leaned heavily upon the Church. The Prussian monarchy retained its constitution, to which it was thereafter to pay lip-service, because it gave a certain specious dignity to what was otherwise the preservation of authoritarian monarchy. France remained under the rule of conservatism, but with a fresh colouring of plebiscitarian democracy, which enabled the shifty dictatorship of Napleon III to plead that all his acts were undertaken in the name of the people. Italy remained cowed but unrepentant under the rule of authoritarian monarchs, except in Piedmont-Sardinia, where the king enjoyed the reputation of being a moderate liberal, though his instincts remained authoritarian and his actual powers only slightly more curtailed than those of Frederick William IV. What had occurred was the collapse of moderate liberalism. No longer were the moderate liberals to challenge the old régime. The year 1848 appeared full of disillusion. The internal forces of the expanding European states had proved insufficient to shake off the control of the traditional ruling classes.

In two important countries the situation was different. In Britain fear among the middle classes gave way to confidence, and with the upsurge of the economy they were prepared once more to consider reform. The threat of the working classes had proved a mere chimera.

In Russia, however, the revolution of 1848 had evoked only the slightest echo. Neither St Petersburg nor Moscow had reached that state of economic and social development which could have given birth to revolutionary uprisings upon the scale apparent in the cities of France and central Europe. Conscious of their own weakness and at the same time aware that they themselves would have to pass through the same phase as the rest of Europe, the Russian intellectuals began the debate upon the future development of their country. Opposition to the régime in the 1840s had been limited to salon society, but with the closer control exercised by Nicholas I in and after 1848 criticism began to make itself felt. There were men who thought that Russia ought to turn her back upon the rest of Europe and seek her own destiny, the so-called Slavophils. There were the Westerners, who believed that Russia should accept the science and technology of the west, but should be determined to succeed where western European liberalism had failed. It would be unwise to draw too fine a distinction between these two orientations, but it nevertheless remains true to say that Russia was deeply involved in the revolutions of 1848, not only diplomatically but also mentally and morally. Nicholas I was aware that times were changing even in Russia, but preferred to fall into line with the prevailing mood of conservatism in the other European states; it was only on his death in 1855 that he was conscious of the fact that he had let the chance of himself assuming the initiative slip from his hands. To his successor, Alexander II, he bequeathed the task of modernizing Russia.

The defeat of European liberalism seemed to call a halt to the orderly development of Europe under the aegis of constitutional government, but the policies of states had changed. Austria abandoned the cautious policy of Metternich and began to speak in international affairs with authority. The France of Napoleon III sought opportunities to give an aura of majesty to the parvenu régime of the Bonaparte clan. Prussia had received a humiliation and was a less certain ally of Austria and Russia. It was out of the clash of international rivalries that the liberalism of 1848, soured and embittered by its experiences, was to find fresh expression. Gone were the expressions of hope for the improvement of humanity's lot. The cosmopolitanism of European Liberalism, even in the darkest moments of 1848, had found its defenders. In its place was put the narrow nationalism which the victory of reaction kept hidden. The new internationalism of the working classes, first to receive concrete expression in the foundation of the International Workingmen's Association in London in 1864, was a tender plant and slow to grow. Between 1848 and 1871 modern industry continued to expand. In 1860 the Cobden–Chevalier treaty between France and Britain ushered in an epoch of free trade, because the other European states lowered their tariffs. The era of the Cotton Millennium, the dream of the Manchester manufacturers, appeared to be dawning, but in reality a battle had been lost. The future of Europe was left in the hands of the conservatives, by whatever name they might pass. While the propertied classes breathed their sigh of relief when the revolutions were safely passed, aggressive conservatism began to prepare for a fresh struggle.

5: The Destruction of the Balance of Power

The Powers in Conflict. I. The Crimean War

The events of 1848 were caused by an upsurge of popular discontent which it had been proved armies could control. The power of the state was bound to increase as the railway network grew throughout Europe. Local food shortages could now easily be averted and the danger of an element outbreak of revolution avoided. Troops, moreover, could be transported from tranquil areas to the scenes of disturbance. Consideration of internal problems soon gave way to the invention of means to re-draw the map of Europe by diplomacy and war. Problems of foreign policy, freed from the social questions with which they had been entangled in 1848, came to the fore. The House of Savoy smarted under the shame of military defeat. The military party in Prussia under Prince William, the heir presumptive to the throne, looked forward to the day when the army would be strong enough to defy the forces which had imposed the Punctuation of Olmütz. The parvenu Bonapartist régime dreamed of giving permanence to its rule by a successful foreign policy. New forces were at work which intended to destroy the *status quo*. To one power alone it seemed that nothing had changed. For Russia the old policy of vigilance remained to be carried out. Central Europe was to be kept under control and European Turkey in a state of quiescence. The weapon which Nicholas I used was diplomacy. The Russian army was impressive merely upon the parade ground, lending weight and authority to Russian diplomacy by its fine appearance. Russia was not short of men. The population in 1853 amounted to about 70,000,000, but there were only 1,049 km of railway in the whole country. Her finances were defective. Out of a total expenditure of 313,086,000 roubles in 1853, 103,479,000 was devoted to the army and 20,751,000 to the navy, but public education absorbed only 2,831,000 roubles. By contrast, 52,589,000 roubles were paid in interest on the state debt. While the outward show of Russian power remained constant, she was in fact falling behind the other European powers because they were making greater material progress as the progress of industrialization was accelerated.

The testing time for Russia came with the re-assertion of French activity in the Near East. Napoleon III decided that he could win popularity for his régime by taking up the interest which his uncle, Napoleon I, had shown in the Levant. The ostensible reason for conflict between France and Russia was the claims which both countries had upon the Holy Places in Palestine, the churches of the Holy Sepulchre and the Virgin in Jerusalem, the church of the Nativity in Bethlehem and the place of Golgotha. Both the Latin and the Orthodox churches had pretensions which in the confusion of Ottoman policy had at one time or another been satisfied. In February 1852, however, the keys of the church at Bethlehem and the grotto of the Holy Manger were under pressure handed over to the Latins, and further concessions were made in the following December. This was not an issue which would in normal circumstances prove the cause of a great war, but it was symbolic of a threat to Russian influence in the Ottoman Empire. Nicholas I knew that Great Britain looked upon the extension of French influence in the Levant with no greater pleasure than Russia, and in January 1853 raised the question of the future of Turkey with the British ambassador, Hamilton Seymour, in the hope that the two countries might reach a mutual understanding. This move was entirely in accordance with the spirit of the conversations held in Windsor in 1844 and seems to have given the then British foreign secretary, Lord John Russell, no cause for alarm. On 9 February 1853 Russell replied that he did not believe in the imminence of a Turkish collapse, though Nicholas had described Turkey as being 'very sick', but he assured Russia that Great Britain would consult her in the event of need. Yet from this despatch began the tragic series of mistakes which brought Russia to war with Britain and France. Upon the copy of Russell's despatch delivered to Nesselrode Nicholas I wrote:

C'est une assurance précieuse, car elle prouve quelle parfaite identité d'intentions existe entre l'Angleterre et la Russie.

In fact, there was no identity of views.

The next step in Russian diplomacy was to put to the test the various rights which Russia had obtained under the treaty of Kutchuk

Kajnardji (1774) and all the subsequent agreements with T rkey up to the treaty of Adrianople (1829), by which Russia appeared to have the privilege of intervening on behalf of the Christian subjects of the Porte. An observation corps was formed in Bessarabia and the Black Sea fleet at Sevastopol held in readiness as if to intimidate the Turks. On 5 May 1853 the Russian envoy, Prince Menshikov, presented to the Sultan a demand that Russia's rights should be confirmed. The British ambassador, Stratford de Redcliffe, though regarded in St Petersburg as being anti-Russian, in fact advised the Turks to give the requisite assurances, but from the outset the Turks grasped a fundamental fact of the situation. If in the last resort Russia made war upon Turkey, then the western powers would be compelled to intervene to uphold the Ottoman Empire at the Straits. In consequence, the Porte refused to give Menshikov satisfaction, and he accordingly withdrew on 21 May.

The diplomats and statesmen now moved automatically towards an unnecessary war. The British government never entirely trusted Russia, who it believed intended to convert Turkey into a vassal state. On 13 June 1853 the British fleet arrived at Besika Bay to give the Turks moral support. On the following day it was joined by the French fleet. Napoleon III was less blind to the consequences than the government of Lord Aberdeen. Fundamental to French thinking was the belief that a conflict in south-eastern Europe would give Austria cause for concern and that, if Austria were to join forces with Britain and France, the solidarity of the three central and eastern European powers, Austria, Prussia and Russia, would be broken and French policy would be able to free itself from the shackles imposed by the Vienna treaties of 1815. The inner designs of French policy were evidently not perceived by Nicholas I. Determined to establish Russia's rights, on 27 June 1853 he ordered the Russian army to occupy the principalities of Moldavia and Wallachia. This move was not technically an act of war, but it might easily have caused the outbreak of hostilities. In order to prevent war the British, French, Austrian and Prussian representatives agreed on 1 August to a compromise solution in the so-called 'Vienna Note', which recommended to the Sultan that he should remain faithful to the letter and spirit of the treaties of Kutchuk Kajnardji and Adrianople with regard to the Christian religion and seek Russian and French consent for any changes he might make. This formula was acceptable to Russia, but the Porte declared on 19 August that it would make itself responsible for the protection of the Christian religion. In other words, the Porte took advantage of the crisis to assert the Sultan's exclusive sovereignty. In order to avert war Nicholas I and the Austrian emperor, Francis Joseph, agreed upon a fresh formula on 24 September by which Russian rights and Turkish obligations to protect the Christian religion should receive equal recognition, but there was in London a fear that a Russian invasion of Turkey was imminent, especially when the French ambassador warned the British government that there was danger of rioting in Constantinople. On 23 September 1953 the prime minister, Lord Aberdeen, and the foreign secretary, Lord Clarendon, without cabinet approval, decided to issue an order to the British fleet to pass through the Straits to Constantinople. By now the Turks understood that the probable support of Britain and France gave them freedom of action. On 4 October Turkey declared war upon Russia, in spite of the fact that Stratford at first refused to carry out the order to bring the fleet up. The Russian attitude was that the Turks might declare war, but that Russia was not thereby necessarily at war with Turkey, but on 23 October Omar Pasha attacked the Russians in the Principalities and on 1 November Russia declared war upon Turkey, whereupon the British and French fleets entered the Bosphorus. To the vacillations and obscurities of diplomacy was added the factor of emotion. The Turks not unnaturally decided to create a diversion in the Caucasus, where Russia had perennial troubles with the inhabitants of the highlands. When a Turkish naval expedition was sent in the direction of the Caucasus the technically superior Russian Black Sea fleet intervened and on 30 November destroyed the Turkish squadron off Sinope. The so-called 'Massacre of Sinope' aroused a storm of fury in Britain. Under the pressure of public opinion Lord Aberdeen now consented to send the British fleet with the French fleet into the Black Sea to contain the Russian fleet at Sevastopol. When in January 1854 the ships of the western powers entered the Black Sea they presented to Nicholas I a challenge inconsistent with the honour of a great state, and he in consequence withdrew his ambassadors from London and Paris. The severance of diplomatic relations placed Britain and France in a difficult position, and on 27 February 1854 they presented Russia with an ultimatum that she should evacuate the Principalities and, when after a month no reply was received from Russia, they declared war, a military alliance having been concluded between France, Britain and Turkey on 12 March.

The cause of the war lay in the deficiencies of European diplomacy and the concealed machinations of French policy, but it was in fact a war without a theatre of operations. Having brought about a war by diplomacy, the western powers now sought to bring it to an end by the same means. On 9 April 1854 an agreement was made between Austria, Prussia, Britain and France that the *status quo* should be upheld in Turkey and the Principalities, while on 20 April Austria and Prussia concurred in a policy of armed neutrality, by which Prussia would aid Austria if she were attacked by Russia, an action which Russia, ever mindful of the dangers of war upon two fronts, did not intend to take. In the meantime British and French troops were landed at Varna to protect Constantinople against Russian attack. On 3 June Austria demanded the Russian evacuation of the Principalities, to which Russia complied on 3 August and thus permitted the Austrian army to occupy them. In this way it became impossible for Russia to intervene in European Turkey, but the Russian compliance with the Austrian demand revealed considerable dexterity. Russia complied with the terms of the western powers' ultimatum of 27 February 1854. Theoretically, therefore, there now was no longer cause for war, but the British and French governments had man-oeuvred themselves into a position in which they must fight at least one battle in order to placate public opinion at home with a splendid victory.

The obvious target for an allied attack was the Russian naval base of Sevastopol. On 14 September an Anglo-French force of 57,000 men under Lord Raglan and Saint-Arnaud, later succeeded by Canrobert, landed at Evpatoria in the Crimea, the success of the landing being marred by the fact that the French troops arrived in steam-ships, but their supplies were sent by the slower sailing ships. This was the hallmark of the entire campaign. Inefficiency, shortage of supplies, unimaginative tactics and disease had long been among the occupational hazards of soldiers, but now the telegraph brought the readers of newspapers in daily contact with the defects of con-temporary military organization. Pressure of public opinion made it doubly desirable for a splendid victory to be won. Sevastopol was not taken. The battles of Alma, Balaklava and Inkerman were fought with the minimum of skill on both sides, and the allies, unable to defeat the Russians in the field, were compelled to winter in the Crimea without proper provision having been made for a winter campaign.

The war, which had been undertaken to produce a victory, now compelled the allies to seek the methods of diplomacy to extricate themselves from the consequences of their action. The answer to their dilemma was the participation of Austria in the war. Austrian policy was now controlled by Buol, who was alarmed by the dangers which war presented. When Austria demanded the Russian evacuation of the Principalities, Buol simultaneously required the allies to state their own war aims, which in fact had not been formulated. After some discussion Austria, France and Britain agreed on 8 August 1854 to the 'Four Points', which required a European instead of an exclusive Russian guarantee for the Principalities, the improvement of navigation on the Danube, the revision of the Straits Convention of 1841 'in the interests of the balance of power' and, lastly, European protection for the Christian subjects of the Porte. Buol knew that the inclination of Austria to give her support to Britain and France was causing Russia great annoyance and was not anxious to join in an alliance with the western powers, but upon the receipt of the false news of Sevastopol's fall, which would satisfy British and French opinion and make the conclusion of a peace possible, Buol agreed to sign on 2 December 1854 a defensive alliance with Britain and France, with the addition that Austria would declare war upon Russia if she did not accept the Four Points; Buol had in fact already received news that Russia would accept the Four Points, which meant that Austria would not be placed under the necessity of making war upon her. The Austrian alliance, therefore, did not bring the western powers any real advantage. A fresh diplomatic campaign was accordingly undertaken to induce Austria to enter the war upon their side.

The diplomacy of the situation revolved upon the interpretation of the third of the Four Points, the revision of the Straits Convention 'in the interests of the balance of power', which privately Britain and France agreed meant the destruction of Sevastopol, but which they informed Austria meant the end of Russian predominance in the Black Sea, an altogether milder conception. The western allies were guilty of practising a deception, which gave the Russian ambassador in Vienna, Prince Alexander Gorchakov, an opportunity to use to his own advantage. Gorchakov by-passed Buol and sought the aid of the emperor, Francis Joseph, asking him to agree that acceptance of the Four Points would not require any infringement of the Tsar's sovereign rights. Francis Joseph agreed that this was a reasonable request to make, and by accepting it made it impossible for Britain and France to secure the destruction of Sevastopol by diplomatic means.

From the Russian side peace became possible when on 2 March 1855 the Tsar Nicholas I died. The new emperor, Alexander II, might without loss of prestige bring the war to an end. In Britain, however, the government of Aberdeen fell in January 1855 and was replaced by that of Palmerston, which after the secession of its Peelite members committed itself to a more warlike policy. The conference at Vienna, which began on 15 March 1855, to discuss terms of peace proved abortive. Buol and Lord John Russell sought a compromise solution of naval limitation, but the French foreign minister, Drouyn de Lhuys, agreed with Palmerston upon a scheme of neutralization of the Black Sea, which they hoped would be unacceptable to Russia and force Austria into the war. When Drouyn de Lhuys arrived in Vienna, however, Buol would have nothing to do with this plan and put forward his own plan, which in essence amounted to a demand for a Franco-British guarantee to Austria. Drouyn, himself, was in favour of an alliance with Austria, which he believed would curb the ambitions of the shifty and adventurous Napoleon III, and was therefore prepared to accept Buol's proposals, but Britain was not ready to undertake a policy of maintaining the integrity of the Austrian Empire. The French minister of war, Vaillant, for his part, insisted upon the vigorous prosecution of the war until a brilliant victory had been obtained in order to restore confidence in the French army; a solution by diplomacy was not enough. Drouyn resigned and was replaced by Napoleon I's bastard son, Walewski. Gorchakov in view of the allies' difficulties declared that Russia would not accept limitation and therefore on 21 April the conference in Vienna was adjourned *sine die*.

The western allies had no alternative but to carry on the unpleasant war in the Crimea. It was not until 8 September 1855 after repeated attempts to bombard the fortress into submission that the Russian army under Prince Mikhail Gorchakov at length decided to evacuate Sevastopol, but when once the allies' objective had been won there remained the problem of bringing Russia to submission. It was beyond the capacity of Britain and France to undertake an offensive on the scale of Napoleon I's campaign of 1812. There were further desultory bombardments and raids, but only diplomacy could provide a solution to the dilemma of the allies. The Austrian foreign minister, Buol, came to the conclusion that the one means of bringing to an end the unhappy episode was for Austria herself to intervene. He believed that Austria had already given such offence to Russia that Austrian policy should henceforth be based upon an understanding with Britain and France. It was therefore agreed that Austria should present an ultimatum to Russia. On 28 December 1855 the Austrian ambassador, Esterhazy, delivered his ultimatum to Russia, requiring a cessation of hostilities and agreement to the neutralization of the Black Sea. Alexander II in his heart felt that Russia ought to continue the war, but on 15 January 1856 the Russian council of ministers advised him that acceptance of the Austrian ultimatum, though it might in the first instance be humiliating for Russia, would rescue her from the isolation in which the war had placed her. Continuation of the war would lead only to renewed checks and disasters, while peace would permit Russia to recuperate her forces and undertake a plan of internal reform. Prudence rather than inclination determined the Russian course of action. In this way the Austrian ultimatum was accepted and a peace conference assembled in Paris on 25 February 1856. Thus ended a war which was neither glorious for the belligerents nor in the long run decisive in the settlement of the Eastern Question. It was nevertheless of profound importance for the future history of Europe.

II. THE TREATY OF PARIS, 1856.

The treaty of peace was signed in Paris on 30 March. Russia was obliged to surrender southern Bessarabia, which deprived her of her command over the mouth of the Danube, now placed under the control of the riparian states. The provisions of the Straits Convention of 1841 were confirmed, but Russia and Turkey were henceforth to be allowed to maintain only light vessels of war upon the Black Sea. The Black Sea was neutralized by the absolute prohibition of the stationing of battle fleets in its waters. Neutralization of the Black Sea was in fact highly disadvantageous to Russia. In theory Russia enjoyed an equal status with Turkey, but the facts of the case were entirely different. In the event of future disputes Turkey would obviously have the support of Britain at least, and the British fleet would be able to enter the Black Sea. The whole of southern Russia would be exposed to the attacks of British forces, while in the Caucasus aid could be given to the dissentient highlanders, who never accepted Russian rule with equanimity. Russia could never permanently submit to a situation in which she was open to the danger of sudden attack, and it was thereafter a permanent aim of Russian foreign policy to secure the cancellation of the Black Sea clauses of the Treaty of Paris.

III. Austria after the Crimean War

In 1849 Russia had intervened in Hungary to restore the power of the Habsburg Monarchy, but Austria had shown small gratitude in the crisis of the Crimean War. It was the belief of Buol that after the assistance Austria had rendered to Britain and France in bringing the war to an end she could for the future base her security upon an alliance with them. In fact, Buol had made a mistake of capital importance. The wartime alliance of December 1855 related only to the immediate circumstances. The alliance concluded by Britain, France and Austria on 15 April 1856 guaranteed only the integrity of the Ottoman Empire in order to prevent future Russian penetration of the Balkans. It was not a guarantee of the Austrian Empire as a whole. A new situation had therefore arisen. Though Austria and Russia had not always acted in concert before the Crimean War, Russia had valued Austria as an ally in the maintenance of the *status quo* in central Europe. Now that support was withdrawn. At the peace conference in Paris, in which the Piedmontese had taken part because they had sent a small force to participate in the war in the Crimea, it was revealed that in principle Britain had no objection to modification of territorial settlement in Italy. The French, moreover, exhibited some equivocation, which revealed that they were not prepared to adopt an attitude of permanent hostility to Russia. It was in reality Austria which lost the Crimean War. No longer was it certain that she could count upon support for the maintenance of her position in

Germany and Italy. The policy of strength adopted by Buol had achieved the very object which it ought to have been his object to avoid, the weakening of the international influence of Austria.

IV. RUSSIA AFTER THE CRIMEAN WAR

Alexander II has often been represented as a liberal and as the 'Tsar-Liberator', but sycophantic phrases should be allowed to disguise the fact that he held views upon the role of the Russian monarchy which were identical with those of his father, Nicholas I. Peace was made in 1856 in order to obtain a breathing space. Nesselrode, who had guided Russian foreign policy for so long under Nicholas I, retired, and his place was taken in April 1856 by Gorchakov, reputedly anti-Austrian and pro-French in his views, but in the last resort it was always Alexander II who took the final decision. There was indeed little room in which Russia might manoeuvre in the field of international politics. Since the reign of Peter the Great the rulers of Russia had adopted a forward foreign policy, seeking, as a precautionary measure, influence in the states beyond the frontiers of Russia, but now the military weakness of Russia had been revealed. Russia was still interested in the affairs of western and central Europe, but she could no longer impose her domination upon Germany. The close relations of the Romanovs and the Hohenzollerns had proved of little use during the Crimean War, because Prussia was powerless to offer aid. Diplomatically therefore Russia began to look towards France to rescue her from her isolation. An understanding with France would break the solidarity of the wartime coalition. Internally Russia was required to concentrate upon the development of her material resources in order to provide the basis for a more successful policy in the future. The expansion of the Russian economy meant nothing more nor less than the abolition of serfdom, which in its turn had repercussions upon Russian foreign policy. The abolition of serfdom was fraught with difficulties. It could not be carried through if the gentry were to be alienated, but it was equally dangerous to impose upon the peasantry burdens which would cause them to break out into revolt. The promulgation of the act of emancipation would in all probability lead to widespread disturbances. The Russian regular army, therefore, was compelled to look to the interior of Russia and assume the role of a force designed to preserve public order. In these circumstances it could no longer be used as the instrument of a forward foreign policy. It was, moreover, dangerous to enlist more soldiers from among the peasantry on the eve of agrarian reform, for that would be nothing less than to put arms into the hands of the class whose interests were most likely to be infringed. Dislike of Austria and the practical necessity of preventing social disruption within Russia therefore created in Europe a diplomatic vacuum. In Italy Austria was to find no one to uphold her interests. In Germany Russia could in effect no longer support the system of princely particularism which alone gave Austria influence in the Germanic Confederation.

Even before the conclusion of the peace Alexander II began his campaign for the initiation of reform. A milder system of government was introduced in the areas of mixed nationality in the provinces of Western Russia, and Mikhail Gorchakov was appointed Viceroy in the Kingdom of Poland. On 30 March 1856 Alexander II addressed the Moscow nobility and appealed for their co-operation in reform, declaring that 'it is far better that it should come from above than below'. What Alexander promised the gentry was that the existing structure of society in Russia should be maintained and demanded that they should use their initiative while they still had it, lest procrastination lead to their being deprived of their social predominance by the rise of a revolutionary movement in the future. Russia was to achieve her transition into the modern world with the preservation intact of her conservative forces.

V. The Emancipation of the Russian Serfs, 1861

There had been discussion of the peasant question in Russia under Nicholas I, but the deliberations of the secret committee created in November 1839, in which the leader figure had been Count Kiselev, had given rise to many rumours and caused disquiet among the gentry. Nicholas I gave the committee to understand in February 1841 that he would not support any project which infringed the rights of the landlords, and in April 1842 he informed the council of state that he had no intention of freeing the peasants in view of the serious unrest in Europe. The only measures taken to protect the peasants were in the provinces of western Russia, where the gentry were predominantly Polish. Here from 1844 onwards an effort was made to give written form to the obligations of the peasants in order to prevent excessive exploitation.

It was difficult to get the Russian landlords to consider reform at all. In some areas the landlords agreed that reform was necessary, but that the time was not yet ripe, while elsewhere estate owners wished even to increase labour services. It was only in areas where the landlords could find a ready market for their crops that they were willing to consider reform at all. This was especially true of the landlords in the three Lithuanian *gubernii* of Grodno, Kovno and Vilna, who were predominantly Polish, but the Poles wished to carry out emancipation in a manner detrimental to the interests of the peasants. Since 1807 the *Code Napoléon* had been in force in the area which in 1815 became the Kingdom of Poland; the Code recognized only two conditions of tenure, ownership and tenancy. As a result of the reforms of 1817–18 in the Baltic provinces of Livonia and Estonia the German landlords enjoyed a similar position. It was this system which the Polish gentry of Lithuania wished to introduce, vesting the title to the soil in the landlord and converting the peasantry into tenants. This would have created a system similar to that of England, but as in Ireland, so in Russia, there was a conception that the landlords and the peasants were the joint owners of the soil. The Secret Committee established in St Petersburg in January 1857 realized that the aspirations of the Polish gentry might easily lead to a *jacquerie*, but the decision was taken to exploit the readiness of the Poles to consider reform. On 2 December 1857 instructions were given to the governor-general of Lithuania, Nazimov, that committees to discuss reform were to be established in Grodno, Kovno and Vilna, but three principles were laid down in advance. The title to the land was to be vested in the landlord, but the peasants were to be given the messuage in which their houses and buildings stood and they were to receive sufficient land to discharge their obligations towards the state. The peasants, moreover, were to be organized in a rural commune, under the control of the landlord. There was also to be an efficient system of tax collection. The Polish gentry were indeed disappointed by the proposals to give the peasants security of tenure, but their discussions served the Tsar's purpose at least of setting in motion the laborious process by which the Russian landlords were familiarized with the problems presented by reform. Gradually throughout Russia committees were established in each *gubernia*.

Reform in the provinces of the old Russia was by no means as easy as it was in the areas which had once been under Polish dominion. In the truly Russian provinces there existed a system of repartitional tenure by which the lands of the village were periodically divided among the villagers every twenty or twenty-five years, upon the basis not of individual ownership, but according to the size of the peasant family. There were good historic reasons for this system dating from the epoch when the Tatars raided and ravaged Russia. The system was perhaps not as deeply rooted in Russian sentiment as has sometimes been supposed, but it presented a difficult problem for the agrarian reformers. The solution ultimately adopted was to give the ownership of the village lands in such areas to the peasant commune as a whole. The discussions did not proceed easily, and there were divisions among the officials in St Petersburg, but it was they who protected the peasants from the excessive claims of the landlords. Unlike the monarchy of Louis XVI in the France of 1789, the Russian autocracy was ready to hold its nobility in check. It was the Tsar Alexander II himself who maintained the impetus towards reform. In 1858 he made a tour of the larger cities of Central Russia. He overrode obstructive officials and demanded that the draft scheme of emancipation should be completed by 22 October 1860. On 19 February–3rd March 1861, the sixth anniversary of his accession to the throne, Alexander II signed the statutes of emancipation and a fortnight later with pomp and ceremony the liberation of the serfs was proclaimed in the churches of St Petersburg. The scheme of emancipation followed the lines laid down in the Nazimov Rescript of 2 December 1857. The peasants were to remain serfs for two years, but were to constitute a commune for each estate, with its own assembly and alderman. The communes were to be grouped into a canton. Disputes were to be settled by arbitration committees, composed of local landlords, from whom there could be appeal to the district commission and the commission of the *gubernia*. In the areas where individual peasant holdings were the rule the law presented no insuperable problems, but in the areas where repartitional tenure applied serious difficulties existed. The government undertook to assist the peasants to purchase their arable land if they paid a deposit of 20–25 per cent; the government then issued bonds to the value of 75–80 per cent of the land to the landlord. The peasants were required to redeem this bond at 6 per cent interest over a period of forty-nine years. In the areas where repartitional tenure existed this system meant that the peasants could not leave the village until the communal obligations had been discharged, a factor which limited the mobility of labour and to some extent retarded the growth of the Russian national economy.

The peasants did not receive the news of emancipation with joy. All over Russia there were disturbances, and especially in the more highly developed areas of Lithuania and White Russia. Personal representatives of the Tsar were sent into each *gubernia* to supervise the maintenance of order. With difficulty the crisis of 1861 was overcome and the modernization of Russia could begin. At varying speeds the ministries of the Interior, Finance, War, Education and Justice began to pursue reforming policies. By 1866 legal reform had been completed and a hierarchy of courts established, which removed many of the abuses of the old system of police jurisdiction. By the law of 13 January 1864 some measure of local government was conceded by the creation of the *zemstva*. A *zemstvo* was a council which existed in the district, while for the *zemstvo* of the *gubernia* the district representatives elected members from among themselves. The electors were divided into three classes, the landowners, the townspeople and the peasants, and a complicated system of indirect election followed which gave the landlords a slight social predominance. These were mere crumbs of concessions to the Russian people, but they did permit the growth of initiative from the bottom. Some progress was made in the field of education to combat the problem of illiteracy. Russia was at last on the move, but the progress of reform could not be anything else but slow. Throughout the 1860s Russia was weak. By 1870 the railway network had grown to 10,731 km and the beginnings of breaking down the isolation of much of Russia were evident, but a great deal had yet to be done. By 1870 the population had risen to 84,500,000 by comparison with 73,600,000 in 1861, but this growth was not matched by a parallel growth of the gross national productivity. In consequence, Russian statesmen tried to avoid international complications which would serve only to expose their country's weaknesses.

The Unification of Italy, 1859–61

Austria's equivocal and hostile attitude towards Russia during the Crimean War lost her support which might have availed to preserve her position in Italy. Italy since 1815 had been a power vacuum, which Austria had filled at the price of maintaining that very division which lay at the roots of Italian discontents. In the struggle of 1859–61 Italy was in part to be united under the house of Piedmont-Savoy. By a curious trick of fate Austria's defeat was to weaken her own internal position and create the conditions of a power vacuum in central Europe itself. From 1859 onwards the Austrian government was to maintain itself in an ever-deepening crisis by recourse to one subterfuge after another until the final collapse of the monarchy in 1918.

I. FRANCE AND THE ITALIAN QUESTION, 1859–60

The Piedmontese monarchy had decided that there was no solution to the Italian question except by calling in the foreigner. The Piedmontese army had revealed its worth in 1848 and 1849, but it was too small and weak by itself to drive Austria out of Lombardy and Venetia. Reinforced by volunteers from the other states in Italy, it was still no match for the Austrian army. The alternative therefore for Victor Emanuel and his leading minister, Cavour, was to seek the aid of France, even at the price of making cessions to her. The possibility of making territorial gains at the expense of Italy was already in the mind of Napoleon III before the end of the Crimean War. Piedmont had tried to ingratiate herself with the western allies by sending a division of troops to the Crimea, but she obtained nothing positive from the war. Before Napoleon III could consider an adventure in Italy he had first to secure the diplomatic isolation of Austria. In essence, this meant the establishment of an entente with Russia.

To achieve an understanding with Russia was not possible immediately after the conclusion of the peace of Paris in 1856. There were Frenchmen like Morny who believed that Russia would offer France a vast field for capital investment, but an immediate understanding with Russia would automatically have led to a deterioration of France's relations with Britain. Nevertheless, though no agreement was found, the French and Russian statesmen admitted in principle that an understanding was desirable. In September 1857 Alexander II and Napoleon III met at Stuttgart, and conversations were held between Gorchakov and Walewski. Nothing was signed, but an understanding of a negative nature was achieved. The two sovereigns agreed not to enter into mutually hostile coalitions, while they would concert measures if the Turkish Empire should seem likely to break up, and their representatives in the Near East would accordingly seek to act in harmony. Alexander II declared that he would not aid the Austrians if they were turned out of Italy and there was some discussion of concentrating 150,000 men on the Galician frontier in order to create a possible second front for Austria, but Gorchakov avoided any closer definition of the aid which Russia might give to France in the event of a war in Italy. A sensitive question in Franco-Russian relations was the problem of Poland. Traditionally French public opinion of left and right was sympathetic towards Poland, but Poland clearly affected the vital strategic interests of Russia. Some concessions were made to the Polish upper classes from 1857, but this was a problem which Alexander II considered to be his private concern and not a subject for international understanding. 'They dared to speak of Poland to me!' he declared indignantly after the Stuttgart meeting. Nothing more than a vague agreement resulted from the negotiations of 1857.

In January 1858 the Italian conspirator, Orsini, attempted to assassinate Napoleon III, which might have led to a crisis in the relations of France with Piedmont, but Napoleon III, while deploring attempts at assassination, chose nevertheless to treat the cause for which Orsini stood as a great one. Cavour responded by tempting Napoleon III. The possibility of a marriage between Victor Emanuel's daughter, Clotilda, and Prince Napoleon, son of Jerome Bonaparte, was dangled before him, an offer undoubtedly attractive to the parvenu Bonapartes whose origins were gentile only in the inexacting social conventions of Corsica. In return for the territorial expansion of Piedmont in Italy Cavour was prepared to cede Savoy, long aspired to by France on account of its French-speaking population. Agreement was reached in principle at the secret meeting at Plombières between Napoleon III and Cavour on 20 July 1858. The marriage compact was agreed and a common war against Austria planned upon the basis of creating a federal Italy consisting of four basic units,

Upper Italy, by which was meant an expanded Piedmont, the Papal States, the Two Sicilies and a new Kingdom in Central Italy, in return for which France should obtain territorial compensation. The task of Cavour was to exacerbate the relations of Piedmont–Sardinia with Austria, while Napoleon III was to prepare the way diplomatically. The diplomacy of 1858 reveals the shifty character of Napoleon III. Instead of opening negotiations through the regular channels of the French ministry of foreign affairs he sent his cousin, Prince Napoleon, to Warsaw in September to confer with the Tsar and Gorchakov, with strict instructions to reveal nothing to Walewski, the Empress Eugénie and Fould. His object was to obtain the benevolent neutrality of Russia, but very soon a serious cleavage in the points of view of Russia and France began to appear. The ultimate objective of the French was the revision of the treaties of 1815, whereas the Russians wished only for the modification of the Treaty of 1856 and the cancellation of the hated Black Sea clauses. Napoleon III might have been willing to accommodate the Russians, but, when the foreign minister, Walewski obtained news of the negotiations which were being conducted behind his back, he was compelled to point out that France could not lightly throw away the gains which she had so recently won in the Crimean War, while Russian assent to changes in the territorial settlement of Italy would seem to show that recognition was required and admit the validity of treaties of 1815, which it was the object of French policy to deny. Any understanding with Russia which amounted to an alliance would, moreover, complicate the relations of France with Great Britain. Gorchakov for his part wished merely to localize the dispute in Italy, because on reflection it seemed that Russia lacked the strength to cancel the Black Sea clauses. While he valued an understanding with France, the situation in Prussia was changing. On 7 October 1858 a permanent council of regency was set up in Prussia to act on behalf of the deranged Frederick William IV and effective power had passed into the hands of Prince William, who it was supposed might strengthen Prussia and ultimately proved a better ally than the unreliable Napoleon III. The result of the negotiations was the agreement of 3 March 1859, by which Russia promised her neutrality, but made no stipulations with regard to the Black Sea clauses. This was very much less than France had hoped for.

An alliance was signed between France and Piedmont on 19 January 1859 and a campaign of provocation was opened against Austria. Britain offered her mediation. Russia on 18 March proposed a congress on the Italian question, aiming at getting herself into a neutral position and at the same time providing a forum for discussion of the Eastern Question. The Austrian attitude was that a congress to discuss Italy would inevitably lead to a humiliation, and therefore the decision was taken in Vienna that Piedmont should be put in the wrong before a congress could meet. For this reason Austria asked that Piedmont should disarm before a congress met, a suggestion which received the support of Britain. Napoleon III vacillated and for fear of offending Britain advised Piedmont to disarm, but the Austrian government over-reached itself. The Austrians desired that the Piedmontese submission should take place as a result of pressure from Vienna. An ultimatum was therefore delivered to Piedmont, which solved the dilemma of Napoleon III and Cavour. By rejecting the Austrian ultimatum on 26 April 1859 the Piedmontese enabled France to come to their rescue against what appeared to be an act of aggression by Austria. On 29 April the Austrian offensive against Piedmont was launched and French troops began to pour into Italy. The Italian campaign of Napoleon III had nothing in common with the famous campaigns of Napoleon I. Within a fortnight both France and Austria brought masses of men into Italy on the railways, whereas such a concentration in the Revolutionary and Napoleonic wars would have taken at least two months, and this in spite of the fact that the railways were not entirely complete. The troops arrived on the battlefield in good physical condition and were no longer at the mercy of the haphazard supply systems of earlier wars, though the evacuation of the wounded still left much to be desired. On 4 June 1859 the Austrian army was defeated at Magenta and again at Solferino on 24 June. As a result the French and the Piedmontese found themselves in possession of Lombardy.

The speedy defeat of Austria at once created a situation of extreme complexity. France had not founded her action upon any solid diplomatic system, and Austria hoped that Britain and the German states would come to her aid. The Conservative cabinet of Derby in Britain wished to uphold the treaties of 1815, but for all its dislike of Italian nationalism it could do little because it was a minority government holding office while the Whig–Liberal majority were composing their differences. The limit of Lord Derby's action was the Circular of 2 May 1859 declaring that Britain would do no more than offer her mediation, and a warning was issued to the German states that they could not expect British aid if they went to war with France. This was a policy which Russia could with safety support, and from the Russian side pressure was put upon Prussia not to intervene in the struggle. There was some movement of troops on the northern Austrian frontier in Galicia, but this was not serious enough to influence Austrian policy. The key to the situation was Prussia. Prussia did not wish to estrange German feeling by leaving the German power, Austria, to her fate, but von Schleinitz insisted that Prussia should stay out of the war, while the ambassador in St Petersburg, Bismarck, even went as far as to suggest that Prussia should use the opportunity to hold Austria to ransom. The Prince Regent, William, however, felt obliged to make some show of good will, and on 24 June proposed mediation on the basis of the *status quo ante bellum*, with a conference to discuss the possibility of internal reform in Italy. Of greater importance was the calling up of six Prussian army corps, which would present a serious menace to France with her best troops engaged in Italy. On 10 June 1859 the British conservative cabinet fell and was replaced by the Whig–Liberal coalition under Palmerston. Palmerston was willing to remove Austria altogether from Italy, and the foreign secretary, Russell, was prepared to accept the French plan, by which Lombardy should be surrendered and an independent archduchy created in Venetia, but the British cabinet was suspicious of France, and Queen Victoria, whose influence upon foreign policy was not negligible in these years, was both pro-Austrian and pro-Prussian. In these circumstances Britain could be little more than neutral.

On 8 July 1859 Napoleon III concluded an armistice with Francis Joseph at Villafranca. Many reasons for his sudden retraction from the war have been put forward, including the assertion that he was so sickened by the slaughter of war that he wished for humanitarian reasons alone to put an end to hostilities. This reason was scarcely one to influence a Bonaparte. It has been suggested that he saw a strong reaction in Central Italy in favour of union with Piedmont-Sardinia that continuation of the war might lead to the creation of too strong a state on France's south-eastern frontier. This solution seems well grounded in *raison d'état*, but of even greater importance was the fact that on the Rhine France could mobilize only 120,000 men, whereas 406,000 Prussians were being assembled, who could be reinforced by the smaller states. There was no doubt of the reasons for Francis Joseph's desire to end the war. He feared revolution within the Austrian Empire if the prestige of the dynasty were shaken by further defeats. In a multi-national army some of the regiments might be unreliable if disturbances broke out in the homeland.

Napoleon III and Francis Joseph met personally on 11 July 1859 to agree upon the preliminaries of peace. Lombardy, with the exceptions of Mantua and Peschiera, which were ceded to France, who in her turn was to cede this territory to Piedmont-Sardinia, but elsewhere the *status quo* was to be restored. Upon this basis a definitive peace was to be negotiated at Zurich. The French had therefore not driven the Austrians from Italy. The Austrians were left as before in possession of the Quadrilateral. Furious with rage Cavour resigned his prime-ministership.

II. The Piedmontese Conquest of Italy 1860–1

France withdrew from the war with Austria, and by the treaty of Turin in March 1860 exacted her reward from Piedmont in the form of the cession of Savoy and Nice, but Napoleon III had set in motion a movement which he could not control. Central Italy was in flames. In August and September 1859 Tuscany, part of the Papal States, and the petty duchies declared in favour of union with Piedmont. Discontent was never absent from the Two Sicilies, and Guiseppe Garibaldi, the most famous of the Italian revolutionaries and one of the Triumvirs in Rome in 1849, in May 1860, with an improvised force of a thousand men, the celebrated Red-Shirts, landed in Sicily. In the north a kingdom consisting of Piedmont-Sardinia, Liguria, Lombardy, Tuscany, Bologna and the duchies had come into existence upon the basis of a monarchical solution. In the south the landing of Garibaldi in Sicily seemed to foreshadow a republican solution. Cavour, who on 20 January 1860 had resumed the reins of government in Piedmont, had no love for Garibaldi's republicanism or for the motley gang of radicals whom he had gathered together. In Sicily Garibaldi's adventure was crowned with astonishing success. The resistance of the Neapolitan army melted before him. The morale of the Neapolitan army was low, for no other explanation can be offered of the fact that 20,000 men were unable to prevent Garibaldi's scratch force, even though it had grown to about 3,000, from taking the Sicilian capital of Palermo. Powerless to hold out in the face of the local population's hostility to rule from Naples, the Neapolitan General, Lanza, requested an armistice and agreed to evacuate the island. Palermo fell on 27 May. By the end of July Garibaldi was master of almost the entire island. Having achieved this success, he found that the Piedmontese government, at first cautious lest the expedition should provoke an international crisis, was willing to annex Sicily and to supply him with money. A commissioner was despatched to the island to place the civil government upon a proper footing. Garibaldi knew that the government in Turin lacked his own adventurous spirit. It feared the consequences of allowing Garibaldi to invade the mainland, where it might find itself in open conflict with the French garrison in Rome. Yet Victor Emanuel who had small love for Cavour, gave him his private encouragement. Thus far audacity had yielded dividends, and Garibaldi was prepared to maintain the momentum of the Italian revolution. On 22 August 1860 Garibaldi landed on the mainland with 3,500 men, and once again, in spite of an apparently invincible Neapolitan force barring his way, succeeded in carrying all before him. Once more the morale of the Neapolitan army proved to be low. On 7 September Garibaldi was able to enter Naples with a handful of men. This was not a conquest of Naples, but a promenade. The Bourbon garrison in Naples paid him military honours as he entered the city. All that remained between Garibaldi and the unification of Italy was the Papal States, but that was a formidable obstacle.

The impression had been formed in Italy that Cavour had no real heart for the struggle and that at all points Garibaldi had justified his concept of a popular revolution. Now Cavour resumed the initiative. Victor Emanuel intrigued with Garibaldi behind his back, but Cavour made it plain that there could not be two masters of Piedmontese policy in this dangerous situation. Garibaldi was publicly demanding Cavour's resignation and had now invaded the Papal States, evidently in the belief that he had Victor Emanuel's support. Cavour therefore ordered the Piedmontese forces to enter the Papal dominions officially in an effort to check Garibaldi's march north, an explanation which lulled the suspicions of Napoleon III. It was Cavour's intention to interpose the Piedmontese army between Rome and Garibaldi's men, but Garibaldi was already in difficulties in his attempt to cross the Volturno valley. On 12 October he succeeded in overcoming a counter-attack aimed at the reconquest of Naples, but he could make no further progress north in spite of this success. On 21–22 October Naples and Sicily declared for union with Piedmont, and on 4 November the papal Marches and Umbria followed their example, but already on 25 October 1860 Victor Emanuel had met Garibaldi at Caianello, and the latter agreed to surrender his conquests. On 9 November 1860 Garibaldi withdrew from the scenes of his triumphs and returned to his solitary home in the island of Caprera. Behind the king had come the northern generals and the officials to organize the new created Kingdom of Italy: Victory lay with conservatism.

III. THE KINGDOM OF ITALY

All that remained to the Pope was the area around Rome, the Patrimony of St Peter. The Risorgimento was not yet complete, but a large new state had come into existence. What had not been created was a nation. Sicily had as ever autonomist aspirations. The Neapolitan masses had disliked some of the features of Bourbon government, but this was not to mean that they had any love for the harsh, exacting government introduced by the northerners. What had happened was a Piedmontese conquest of Italy. In the south a reaction occurred, in which a certain nostalgia for the old easy-going days of the Bourbons appeared. Brigandage was to spring up everywhere in the south, which amounted to a resistance movement occupying the attention of almost the entire Piedmontese army.

On 6 June 1861 Cavour died and was succeeded in the prime-ministership by the Tuscan, Ricasoli, a man of iron will, who intended to tolerate no disorder in the country. It was Ricasoli who persuaded the king and the cabinet to set up in Italy a strong system of centralized control. Cavour had paid some deference to the regional differences and permitted Naples and Sicily to have their own government as Lieutenancies, while in Tuscany a separate government had survived. Ricasoli established fifty-nine provinces, each controlled by a prefect responsible to the ministry of the interior.

THE UNIFICATION OF ITALY 1848 ~ 1870

SWITZERLAND

GENEVA

SAVOY
To FRANCE
1860

NOVARA
(1849)

TURIN

K. of
SARDINIA

GENOA

NICE

To FRANCE
1860

TYROL

AUSTRIA

LOMBARDY

MAGENTA 1859
MILAN

1859

PARMA
1860

MODENA

1860

LUCCA

VENETIA

1866

CUSTOZZA
1848
VERONA
SOLFERINO (1859)
LEGNANO
MANTUA

VENICE

TRIESTE

CROATIA

FERRARA

BOLOGNA

RAVENNA

ROMAGNA

BOSNIA

ADRIATIC
SEA

DALMATIA

LEGHORN

FLORENCE

TUSCANY
1860

1860

PAPAL
STATES

ANCONA

CASTELFIDARDO

CORSICA
(FRENCH)

1870

MENTANA

ROME

PONTECORVO

GAETA

1860
BENEVENTO

NAPLES

SARDINIA

TYRRHENIAN
SEA

KINGDOM of the TWO SICILIES

PALERMO

ASPROMONTE

MESSINA

REGGIO

1860

0   50   100
Miles

MEDITERRANEAN SEA

This was nothing less than the Napoleonic system, in which the government could interfere in every aspect of local life and could make certain that its candidates were returned at the parliamentary elections. Government became an exercise in the arts of political management, by which the middle class was to be satisfied with the distribution of patronage. The Risorgimento came to be synonymous with corruption. The memory of the manipulation of the plebiscites of 1860–1, by which the various constituent portions of the country had joined in union with Piedmont, gave the impression that unification was founded in fraud. Upon this was heaped the dislike created by the heavy taxation necessary to sustain an ambitious foreign policy, because the Patrimony of St Peter and Venetia still remained outside the Italian Kingdom. A large army and, later, a navy bore heavily upon the resources of Italy, where in so much of the country the population was poor and wretched.

The unification of Italy has given rise to much pious literature, in which Victor Emanuel, Cavour and Garibaldi emerge as heroes. In fact, they created an Italy in which political power was exercised by the upper classes and the state was milked to keep the middle class satisfied. The burden logically was borne by the inarticulate poor. Nevertheless, the power vacuum in Italy had now been filled by the Italians themselves. In the international scene Italy counted for something as a power in her own right. Italy's strength was, however, more apparent than real.

IV. Austria after Defeat in 1859

The battles of Magenta and Solferino weakened the position of the Habsburg dynasty within Austria. There has since 1815 been in Austria two strands in official thinking. Metternich and Windisch-grätz had believed that stability could be found upon the basis of conciliating the regional nobilities, who were represented in the provincial diets. From these diets might be created a central consultative assembly to advise the Crown. Such a scheme was in effect to give more power into the hands of the regional feudal nobility at a moment when Austria was entering the era of industrialism. The Austrian empire, however, was well drilled in the attitude of mind of the eighteenth century, with its progressive Josephine centralism. Kolowrat, Schwarzenberg, Kübeck and Bach had believed that the object of the empire ought to be the destruction of feudalism, the modernization of the economy, the improvement of the administration and justice and the raising of the standard of life in order that it might be proved to the populations of the Empire that the dynasty had still a function to perform. Nevertheless, there was much common ground between these two points of view after 1850. Both attitudes shared the belief that the dynasty rested ultimately upon the army, the bureaucracy and the support of the Church.

In the crisis of 1859 the dynasty turned first to the conservative school of thought which sought its solution in the conciliation of the historic nobility by granting some local autonomy. This is the explanation of Agenor Gołuchowski's appointment in August 1860 as chief minister in place of Bach and the production of the October Patent of 1860. Under this new constitutional system the local diets, representing the three orders of the nobility, the bourgeoisie and the peasants, were to send delegates to the capital to a central parliament, or 'Reinforced Reichsrat'. This solution met with the opposition of the Josephine bureaucracy and the liberal German bourgeoisie. The richest area in the Empire were the Czech lands of Bohemia, Moravia and Silesia, which would dominate the Habsburg system, while at the same time surrender the less-developed provinces to the territorial magnates. Even stronger opposition was met with from the Magyars of Hungary, who took their stand upon the legality of everything that was done in 1848. For them the Crown of St Stephen must be restored and Transylvania with the province of the Voyvodina joined with Hungary; within the new system Croatia might enjoy local autonomy. The Hungarian leaders, Eötvös, Deák, Andrássy and Koloman Tisza took their stand upon their country's national rights and refused to attend the Parliament in Vienna. Gołuchowski's October Patent proved unsuccessful in face of such formidable opposition, and the Emperor therefore performed a political somersault. The centralist, Anton von Schmerling, produced his own February Patent of 1861, which provided for a central parliament of 343 members, of whom 120 were to be elected from Hungary, 26 from Transylvania and 9 from Croatia, while from Bohemia, Moravia and Silesia were to be elected a total of 92 members. The members were to be elected by the provincial diets, but the constituencies were so drawn that the Germans were assured of a majority. To this system the Magyars refused to agree, while the Czechs withdrew from the Reichsrat in June 1863. The February Patent therefore never really had any political validity. It provided merely for a rump parliament, in which the Germans were the strongest element. The system was only a façade for absolutism. On 27 June 1865 Schmerling fell from office, when the dynasty in the face of an international crisis once more reverted to the concept of conciliating the regional nobility. The new cabinet of Count Richard Belcredi was commissioned to find some means of finding stability in the face of a mounting threat from Prussia.

V. THE CRISIS IN PRUSSIA

The Prussian mobilization of 1859 had revealed many deficiencies in the army, which would have led to disaster if war had broken out. French observers of this period saw no reason to compare their own army unfavourably with that of Prussia, a thought which gave them an inner satisfaction which in turn produced in their minds a dangerous complacency. With the establishment of a permanent council of Regency in Prussia in October 1858 to exercise the powers of the deranged Frederick William IV Prussia was ruled by a professional soldier, Prince William, who understood the techniques of war and was anxious to translate the industrial revolution, which was occurring in Prussia, into military terms. Prussia already possessed a network of railways, the strategic importance of which was realized by the more intelligent Prussian officers. The existence of railways meant that large numbers of men could be deployed upon the battlefield, but it equally meant that the maintenance under arms of vast forces would create a great financial strain. The common factor in the thinking of such generals who realized the opportunities, which the transport revolution presented them, was the desire to maintain the smallest number of men under arms in time of peace and the largest number in time of war. As early as 1858 Albrecht von Roon was proposing the creation in Prussia of regional commands with cadres of specialist officers, which in time of war could be expanded into regular regiments. For Roon the territorial force, or *Landwehr*, was useless as an instrument of war and, as the events of 1848–50 had shown, not entirely trustworthy from the political point of view. At the best the *Landwehr* could be only a reserve for the reinforcement of the regular regiments of the line. The confusion which was evident for all to see in 1859 led to the appointment of von Roon as minister of war.

The difficulty which confronted the Regent in his search for reform was the need for money. The Prussian Parliament (*Landtag*) was required to provide an extra 9,000,000 thalers a year for military reform. The Liberals in the lower house of the Parliament were not opposed to an increase in Prussia's army, but they were concerned with the details of reform. The proposed new system meant the expansion of an officer corps already large in its influence, and at the same time the virtual destruction of the *Landwehr*, which was to some extent responsive to civilian influences. What was at stake was the precarious constitutional freedoms of Prussia under its *octroyé* constitution. The Liberals therefore proposed that the period of military service should be reduced from three to two years, the *Landwehr* scheme revised and the army financed by annual military votes of supply. The Regent, from 1861 the King William I, as an officer, resented civilian interference in a matter which he regarded as the professional responsibility of the military, and, as a monarch, had no intention of submitting to a system of annual military budgets which would bring his dynasty and the military caste under the control of a parliament. The Liberals were not themselves willing to push matters to a crisis, lest they open themselves to the criticism that they had not got the national cause at heart. In the first instance, therefore, they agreed to grant the money required for the new regiments on the understanding that their detailed demands would be met. The Crown accepted the money voted and proceeded with its reorganization upon the lines which it had already determined. Outraged by this cavalier treatment, the Liberals in the parliament on the next occasion refused to vote further supplies for the army. With the rejection of the budget William I was involved in a conflict with his subjects. His first course was to dissolve the parliament, but the elections resulted only in a defeat for the Conservatives, the element which he relied upon to carry his measures through. The crisis was therefore deepened and the King presented with two unpleasant alternatives, abdication or a coup d'état. The advice of Roon was that the King should call upon Bismarck, the ambassador in St Petersburg, a man known for his violently conservative views, who

favoured the adoption of the most ruthless measures for the preservation of the Hohenzollern dynasty's power, but the King hesitated.
He knew that Bismarck was in favour of a unification of Germany
under Prussian leadership. It was no easy choice which lay before the
King. Bismarck undoubtedly had the resolution to meet the constitutional challenge, but the fear that he would add to it a crisis
in international relations caused the King to hold back. Evidence of
his doubts is that on 29 May 1862 Bismarck was transferred to the
Prussian embassy in Paris, as if he were consigned permanently to an
ambassadorial career; the appointment was annoying to Bismarck,
who began to despair of becoming Minister-President, though it was
undoubtedly useful to him in the sense that he was for a short time
able to observe at first hand the devious processes by which French
policy was formulated at the court of Napoleon III. At length
William I decided to summon up his courage and call upon Bismarck.

On 8 October 1862 Otto von Bismarck-Schönhausen, having
been appointed temporarily on 23 September, became Minister-
President of Prussia. The great reputation which Bismarck was
subsequently to enjoy should not be allowed to disguise the fact that
he was regarded generally as a man who would seek desperate
measures to rescue the Hohenzollern dynasty from the difficulties
with which army reform had confronted it. From the first Bismarck
made it clear to the Prussian parliament that he was the agent of the
Crown, who would interpret the *octroyé* constitution as he wished.
The brutal theory which he expounded was that, if a constitutional
deadlock arose, the Crown was permitted to exercise its powers to
carry on the government of the country. In other words, the dynasty,
if the citizens of the country opposed its political aims, could exercise
virtually autocratic powers. In a debate of 29 September 1862
Bismarck exposed his political philosophy in all its crudity:

> Prussia must reserve its strength for the favourable moment, which
> has already more than once been missed. The great questions of the
> day will not be decided by speeches and resolutions of majorities—
> that was the blunder of 1848 and 1849—but by blood and iron.

The speech was a clear declaration that Prussia intended to seek the
unification of Germany, not by consent and agreement, but by conquest. In the new Germany Prussia was to be the dominant power,

and within Prussia the monarch was to govern with only a façade of constitutionalism.

The lower house of the Prussian Parliament responded to Bismarck's appointment by rejecting the budget of 1862, but the more conservative upper house decided to accept it. Bismarck therefore declared that in the existing impasse the Crown would continue to govern. On 27 January 1863 the lower house voted an address to the throne which accused the ministers of violating the constitution. Bismarck stoutly defended the powers of the Crown and denied to the elected assembly the right to control its actions. As in Italy, so in Germany, conservatism began to prepare itself for the solution of political problems by violence.

The North American Crisis

I. THE CIVIL WAR IN THE UNITED STATES

While William I and Bismarck were labouring to bring into existence a great modern army by design, vast forces by a curious chapter of accidents and with faltering steps began to assemble themselves in the New World. The election of a Republican president in 1860, Abraham Lincoln, threw the United States of America into confusion. Slowly a crisis was reaching a climax. The issue which divided the states of the union was slavery. In theory each state was sovereign and subject to its own laws, but it was a contradiction in terms that a citizen of an indissoluble union could be free in one state and unfree in another. The slaves were the Negroes employed upon the great cotton plantations and latefundia of the southern states. The cruelty of slavery was often more theoretical than real; indeed, there were European peasants in the nineteenth century who fared worse than many a Negro in the slave states. Slavery was nevertheless arbitrary and an affront to human dignity. It was unfortunately the institution upon which the prosperity of the largely agrarian southern states was built. It is estimated that the population of the union in 1850 was 23,000,000, of whom 3,200,000 were slaves without civic rights, at the mercy of about 350,000 owners, good and bad.

The agitation for the abolition of slavery began in the Northern States, where it did not exist. The question became more acute as the United States advanced westwards. Could slavery be instituted in newly acquired territories? Thus Texas, which already possessed slavery when it entered the union in 1845, could be a slave state, but California, New Mexico and Utah, acquired from Mexico in 1848, did not have this institution. In consequence, some compromise was reached in 1850 under the guidance of Henry Clay, which confined slavery to the states where it already existed: Texas, Louisiana, Arkansas, Missouri, Mississippi, Alabama, Georgia, Tennessee, North Carolina, South Carolina, Florida, Kentucky, Virginia and Maryland. For the sake of respectability, however, the slave trade was abolished in the district of Columbia, in which the federal capital, Washington, stood, wedged between the two slave states of Virginia and Maryland. There was no hope of lasting peace in a situation such as this. The novel of Harriet Beecher Stowe, *Uncle Tom's Cabin*, published in 1852, achieved a world-wide popularity and stirred American conscience deeply by its criticism of slavery. Negroes with initiative could always seek the refuge of the non-slave states, but as articles of property they could be returned to their masters. The compromise of 1850 in fact only struck deeper into the consciences of the Northerners.

It was, however, practical issues which brought about the struggle. The compromise of 1850 prevented the entrepreneurs in the slave states from exploiting the upper Missouri valley, though this was an area open to settlement by free men. In 1854 the speculator, Stephen A. Douglas, proposed in Congress that Utah and New Mexico should be permitted to decide for themselves whether or not slavery might exist, while the two new territories, Kansas and Nebraska, might be developed by slave-owners. Douglas was concerned merely to develop fertile areas, but his action aroused a storm of protest in the Northern states and, when the bill was passed by the Senate in March 1854, the anti-slavery agitators felt that they must go over to the attack. The Republican Party appeared on the scene to uphold the principles upon which the constitution of the United States was alleged to be based. Abraham Lincoln emerged as a leader of national importance, though he cloaked his opposition to slavery with hints of compromise which might permit a gradual abolition. The United States were gradually drifting into war. In 1859 John Brown and a small group of exalted followers organized a raid into Virginia with the aim of freeing and arming the slaves, only to be arrested by the

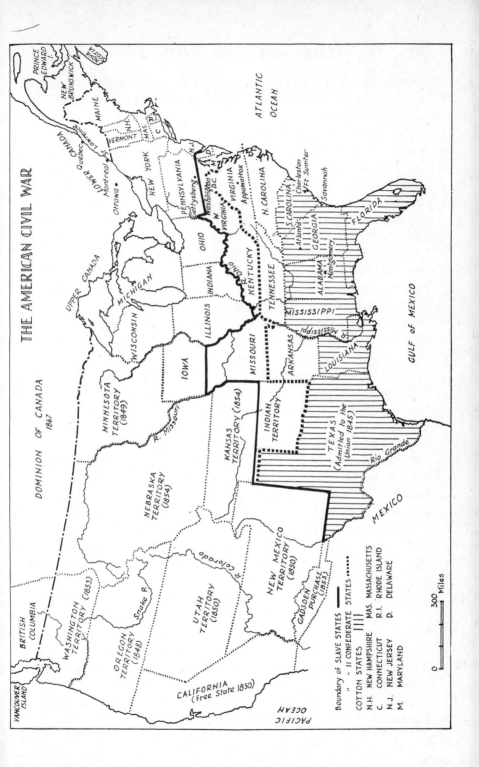

THE AMERICAN CIVIL WAR

PRINCE EDWARD I.

NOVA SCOTIA

NEW BRUNSWICK

MAINE

CANADA

LOWER CANADA

Quebec

Montreal

Ottawa

UPPER CANADA

VERMONT

N.H.

MAS.

R.I.

C.

NEW YORK

ATLANTIC OCEAN

PENNSYLVANIA

N.J.

D.

M.

Washington D.C.

Gettysburg

W. VIRGINIA

VIRGINIA

Appomattox

N. CAROLINA

Charleston

Ft. Sumter

S. CAROLINA

Savannah

OHIO

Ohio R.

KENTUCKY

TENNESSEE

Atlanta

GEORGIA

FLORIDA

INDIANA

ILLINOIS

Montgomery

ALABAMA

MISSISSIPPI

Mississippi R.

LOUISIANA

GULF of MEXICO

MICHIGAN

WISCONSIN

IOWA

MISSOURI

ARKANSAS

DOMINION OF CANADA 1867

Missouri R.

MINNESOTA TERRITORY (1849)

KANSAS TERRITORY (1854)

INDIAN TERRITORY

TEXAS (Admitted to the Union 1845)

Rio Grande

NEBRASKA TERRITORY (1854)

Colorado R.

Snake R.

WASHINGTON TERRITORY (1853)

OREGON TERRITORY (1848)

UTAH TERRITORY (1850)

NEW MEXICO TERRITORY (1850)

GADSDEN PURCHASE (1853)

MEXICO

BRITISH COLUMBIA

VANCOUVER ISLAND

CALIFORNIA (Free State 1850)

PACIFIC OCEAN

Boundary of SLAVE STATES .... " " CONFEDERATE STATES ━━━━━

COTTON STATES ||||

N.H. NEW HAMPSHIRE   MAS. MASSACHUSETTS
C.   CONNECTICUT   R.I. RHODE ISLAND
N.J. NEW JERSEY   D.   DELAWARE
M.   MARYLAND

0   300   Miles

authorities. Brown and six of his supporters were hanged, whereupon they became the heroes of the North and celebrated for ever in the song *John Brown's Body*.

The theoretical struggle which was being waged in fact bore no relation to the balance of social forces of the United States. The south was predominantly rural. The north was developing an industrial power, which was within decades to challenge the productivity of European industry. In strangely modern circumstances the struggle represented the irreconcilable contrasts of the great industrial age and a system as old as that of ancient Greece and Rome. In 1860 Lincoln was elected president, in his misty way committed to the abolition of slavery. In the spring of 1861 there would come into power at the head of the union a man who would in the last resort be obliged to make a stand against slavery. The south was compelled to offer resistance to the principle that all men are equal. In fact, not all of the southern states were prepared to deny the equality of man, nor were all of the citizens within those states, which nominally opposed the abolition of slavery, so devoid of humane feeling that they relished the prospect of a conflict upon a question of elementary human rights. It was the lower regions of the south which exhibited extremism and called for secession from the Union. South Carolina declared against the Union on 20 December 1860 and set the pattern for the remainder of the south. On 12 April 1861 an attack on Fort Sumter in Charleston harbour against the Federal forces was launched by the troops of the Confederate States of America, organized in February 1861 under the presidency of Jefferson Davis.

President Lincoln headed the poll on popular votes, but the votes of his opponents, Douglas, Breckinridge and John Bell, outnumbered the votes which he had obtained. The issue of personalities was immaterial. The majority of the United States citizens voted for the maintenance of the Union; only Breckinridge demanded secession, and he obtained only one-fifth of the total vote. If war had not broken out, Lincoln would have been unable to secure the abolition of slavery, because the majority in Congress would have been hostile to such a step. Lincoln was in fact cautious and had declared against interfering with slavery where it existed. Missouri, Kentucky, west Virginia and Maryland did not join the Confederacy; Arkansas, Tennessee, Virginia and North Carolina joined with extreme reluctance. On 16 July 1861 the Federal forces were defeated by the Confederates at Bull Run in the northern part of Virginia. From that moment onwards there could be no solution of the problem until one side or the other had won a total victory. More was at stake than the existence of the Union which had constituted the United States of America. The whole of the North American continent was in a state of dissolution.

II. MEXICO AND THE FRENCH INTERVENTION

The history of mainland Spanish America after its severance of the link with the mother country revealed all the contradictions present in the founding of the individual republics. Mexico in particular suffered from chronic anarchy, which arose from the reluctance of the large landowners, of whom the largest was the Church, to part with their privileges. The communal villages of Indian Mexico had been distributed among the conquerors in the form of *encomiendas*, or, virtually, fiefs, over which the Spanish Crown had exerted some supervision, intended to preserve the arable lands to the native population, but the lands of the demesnes, or *haciendas*, were in fact enlarged at the expense of the peasants until by the end of Spanish rule one-fifth of the population owned all the land. Independence was therefore to give power into the hands of the colonial upper class, which saw independence of Spain as the means of establishing its own dominance. There was nevertheless an intellectual class which detested the system which had arisen and looked across the frontier to the inspiration of the United States. The politics of Mexico in practice were decided by the political views of the army, which carried out one coup d'état after another. Texas had revolted against this system of government and seceded in 1836, joining itself with the United States in 1845. As a result of the war with the United States of 1846–8 a vast tract of territory was lost by Mexico, which included California, admitted as a free state of the union in 1850, and the New Mexico and Utah territories, and enlarged by the so-called Gadsden purchase of 1853, a rayon of territory added to New Mexico.

The social inequalities of Mexico and the incompetence of the régime gave rise to a liberal movement, which in view of the Church's privileged position was necessarily anti-clerical. In 1857 the Liberals succeeded in imposing upon Mexico a new constitution which afforded the citizens the traditional freedoms of a European liberal system, but in addition forbade civil and ecclesiastical corporations to own landed estates. In consequence, all the forces of the old order, the estate owners, the Church and the army, allied to overthrow the new system. In March 1858 Zuloaga, the leader of the Clerical-Conservative Party, forced the Liberal president, Comonfort, to resign and himself took his place as head of the government in Mexico City, but the vice-president of the Liberal government, Benito Juárez, in accordance with the rules of the 1857 Constitution, proclaimed that he had automatically succeeded to the powers of president upon the resignation of Comonfort, and forthwith proceeded to establish a government at Vera Cruz. A civil war ensued in which Juárez based his policy upon the nationalization of all Church property and the dissolution of the monasteries in order to satisfy the demands of the native Indian population. In January 1861 Juárez had succeeded to the extent of being able to occupy Mexico City.

The periodic disorders of Mexico excited the interest of four powers, the United States, Great Britain, France and Spain. In the United States there were circles which were frankly annexationist in their attitude towards Mexico, but the outbreak of the American Civil War in 1861 for the moment reduced the United States' international influence greatly. Great Britain was principally concerned to secure the commercial interests of British subjects. Spain for her part still retained the memory that she had once ruled Mexico, and there were hopes that she might from her base in Cuba attempt a reconquest. The France of Napoleon III saw in Mexico an area for the extension of French influence at a moment when the civil war in the United States had temporarily suspended the Monroe doctrine. There were enemies of Juárez who saw a means of securing his overthrowal by foreign intervention in appealing to the self-interest of the powers and to the clericalism of the European reactionaries, who looked with horror upon Juárez's stripping the Church of its property.

In October 1861 an agreement was reached by France, Britain and Spain for a joint intervention in Mexico as a result of the Mexican government's defaulting upon the public debt, but, whereas from the

British point of view no actual territorial acquisitions were desired and were expressly disclaimed in Article II of the convention, the Emperor Napoleon III and his advisers were weaving a cunning plot in collaboration with opponents of Juárez for the establishment of the Emperor Francis Joseph's brother, the Archduke Maximilian, upon the throne of an Empire in Mexico. In this manner French influence would be increased and at the same time France brought into friendly relations with Austria, whom she had so recently fought in Italy. It quickly became clear that there was more in French policy than a desire to enforce the resumption of interest payments to the foreign holders of Mexican bonds. In 1862 Spain and Great Britain withdrew from the expedition and the French were left to pursue their own ambitions. In the summer of 1863 French troops occupied Mexico City, and in 1864 the Archduke Maximilian arrived to take up his Empire of Mexico.

A strange situation followed. Maximilian was installed in Mexico City, to adopt a policy which was far more enlightened than his conservative supporters within Mexico desired. Maximilian realized that he could not rescind the agrarian legislation of Juárez without at the same time forfeiting his claim to being a monarch above party politics. On 27 December 1864 he confirmed the confiscation of ecclesiastical property and inaugurated complete religious freedom. The last thing which the papal nuncio, Meglia, expected was that a Habsburg prince should be so ungrateful to the Church. There was enough of a Josephine Habsburg in Maximilian for him to order that no papal bulls and briefs should be published in Mexico without his approval. By recognizing the basic justice of Juárez's policy Maximilian lost the support of the clergy. In theory, the troops of Juárez melted before the French army under Bazaine, but in fact they remained under arms as guerrilla bands. On 2 October 1865 Maximilian issued the order that Mexicans captured with arms in their hands should be tried by court-martial and on condemnation shot. In 1865, however, the United States once more became a great power when the Confederate States submitted to the government of President Lincoln. No longer was it possible for France to support Maximilian, and the decision was taken in August 1866 to withdraw the French forces. Maximilian clung to his Empire, deserted when the last French troops marched out of Mexico City on 5

February 1867. The troops of Juárez could now reassemble to destroy Maximilian's régime. Captured, he was condemned to death and on the morning of 19 June 1867 executed by a firing squad. In the eyes of Juárez and his supporters this could be the only end for the author of the decree of 2 October 1865.

III. BRITISH NORTH AMERICA

The opening of the Civil War in the United States and the establishment of a French-sponsored empire in Mexico were events of grave concern for British statesmen. With regard to the American Civil War Britain on 13 May 1861 proclaimed her neutrality, an equivocal step, because it seemed to place the North and the South upon an equal footing, whereas the government in Washington claimed that it alone could speak for the United States. It accordingly appeared to the North that Britain had granted the South belligerent rights. In consequence, there was a growth of anti-British feeling in the North, which threatened Britain with grave dangers. The North contained twenty-three states with 22,000,000 inhabitants. It was the North rather than the South which had attracted the immigrants and which had established an industrial society with 22,000 miles of railways. The South remained rural and agrarian, with only 9,000 miles of railways, serving the needs of a population of little more than 9,000,000, of whom 3,500,000 were Negro. The North, moreover, controlled the navy, with which the export of cotton to Europe, and especially Lancashire, could be halted. In theory the shortage of cotton, which reached its height in Lancashire in the autumn of 1862, causing distress and unemployment on a large scale, ought to have disposed the British government towards a policy of breaking the Northern blockade of the Southern ports. In fact, Britain acted with extreme caution. Great offence was given when an American warship stopped the British steamship, the *Trent*, in November 1861 and removed from it two envoys of the Confederate States on their way to the United Kingdom. A fierce protest was drafted, but under the influence of the Prince Consort the message was toned down by the addition of a suggestion that perhaps the captain of the American ship was exceeding his orders. From her side Great Britain exhibited some carelessness in permitting the Confederates to order the building of ships in British dockyards. The *Florida* sailed from Liverpool in

March 1862 and did some damage to Federal shipping until she was destroyed in 1864. More famous was the *Alabama*, which at the end of July 1862 put to sea, where she wreaked such damage that the Federal government demanded compensation—the celebrated *Alabama* claims. English law was obscure on the question of building vessels of war in Britain for use against other states, but Lord Russell, the British foreign secretary, took good care not to permit similar incidents in the future.

The caution of Britain is explained by the magnitude of the imperial problem which faced her in North America. Britain still possessed a great colonial empire in the North American continent, which she had been unable and perhaps unwilling to weld into a coherent unit. The attitude of British politicians was that the inhabitants of the colonies could look after their own affairs, but in adopting a policy of *laissez faire* they found that when the American Civil War broke out they could not in fact defend them against attack. There were three groups of provinces. In the east were Nova Scotia, New Brunswick and Prince Edward Island, which were commercial and maritime in their outlook. In the far west stood Vancouver Island and British Columbia, whose interests were naturally turned towards the Pacific. In the centre were Upper and Lower Canada, joined in union since 1841, whose point of view was continental, directed towards the acquisition and development of the Hudson's Bay territories and the prairie provinces. There were vague notions of union, first seriously considered in 1858, but no understanding could be reached. The French Canadians in particular were conscious that a union would make them a minority in a British country. The American civil war, however, and its tensions to some extent resolved British difficulties. The possibility of an Anglo-American conflict revealed the impossibility of defending these provinces against a Northern attack. Britain reinforced her garrison by some 15,000 men, but the North was enlisting the largest and most efficient army which had ever been assembled by a modern industrial state. At first it seemed that the Confederates would be able to hold out, but gradually the superior social and economic organization of the North began to make its weight felt. On 3 July 1863 the Confederate general, Robert E. Lee, suffered a disastrous defeat at the battle of Gettysburg in Pennsylvania, from which the Confederate cause could never recover. In May 1864 the Federal general, Sherman, began his celebrated march through Georgia, laying the country waste as he went, reaching Savannah in December. He then turned north into South Carolina and North Carolina. On 9 April 1865 Lee eventually surrendered at Appomattox. The achievements of the Northern armies found the United States with 500,000 men under arms, who could be employed to restore their international influence and, indeed, invade and seize British North America.

There were two courses before Britain during the American Civil War. She might have supported the South, which would have resulted in the partition of North America. France might have established herself in Mexico, while the Confederate States might have created a slave empire which possibly could have expanded in the Caribbean. In this event the North would have laid its hands upon the whole of British North America. The other alternative was to support the cause of the North, which was taken up in Britain by John Bright, who for reasons of humanity declared that no British government could uphold the institution of slavery. In spite of all the hard words which were exchanged on both sides, it was in fact this course which Britain adopted.

The inhabitants of British North America had never shown much inclination to defend themselves, and they were now presented with the obvious fact that the home government could lend no material aid. The French Canadians, moreover, saw that the danger of their being submerged in a British state was outweighed by their becoming an even smaller minority in an English-speaking state of far greater proportions, if the North should invade the British territories. As a result, an impulse was given to the creation of a Dominion of Canada upon a federal basis. The monarch would be the titular head of this state, but within it the individual provinces would continue to some measure to enjoy their separate identities, while obtaining the strength which resulted from union. The *Alabama* claims were still outstanding, and Charles Sumner went as far as to propose in the Senate that they should be used as a reason for an attack upon the British provinces. Irishmen, who had no reason by cause of British policy in Ireland to love Britain, on demobilization from the Federal forces were prepared to provoke a war by making private attacks upon these territories, as they did in 1866. In 1867 was founded the

Dominion of Canada, which by the fact that it was a virtually sovereign state with its own foreign policy could not be held responsible for the policy pursued in London.

The *Alabama* claims remained a bone of contention, but the slow work of Anglo-American reconciliation began. In reality the Federal victory in the civil war gave the United States a hegemony in the whole of North America. There were new lands to be developed in the west, and the Americans themselves desired British capital to assist in this task. The long years of war, moreover, produced a sense of weariness in the North. Gradually the tension resolved itself into bickering and argument, which was not made easier by the aggressive attitude of sections of Canadian opinion. Britain was prepared to settle her differences honourably with the United States. It is not a mere coincidence that Russia sold Alaska to the United States in 1867, the year in which the Dominion of Canada was created, nor that the Emperor Maximilian's empire in Mexico collapsed at the same time.

The American civil war was not only a struggle to resolve domestic issues. It became in the course of time a great contest to decide upon the future organization of North America. It is for this reason that the policy of Great Britain in Europe was necessarily weak in the 1860s. All the time British statesmen were compelled to look over their shoulder at the New World while dramatic events were taking place in Europe. The Crimean War resulted in the retraction of Russian influence in Central Europe. The American civil war contributed to an identical weakness in British policy with regard to Europe. When therefore the ingenuity of Bismarck in creating a united Germany is praised it should be remembered that general world factors favoured him. The greatest threat to European peace from the British point of view seemed to be presented by France, and British statesmen therefore on the whole favoured a solution of the German question which would create a power strong enough to hold France in check.

The Struggle for Leadership in Germany

The Polish Insurrection of 1863 and the end of the Franco-Russian Entente

The first essay of Bismarck in the struggle for leadership in Germany was not in fact as brilliant as his apologists subsequently claimed.

On 21 January 1863 an insurrection against Russian rule broke out in the Kingdom of Poland, that portion of the former Duchy of Warsaw which had been ceded to the Tsar in 1815 and ruled by him as King. Alexander II intended that agrarian reform should be carried out in the Kingdom as well as in the Empire itself, but in Congress Poland the legal system remained the *Code Napoléon* introduced in the regions in 1807. Under this code there were only two conditions of land tenure, ownership and tenancy. The Polish landlords professed to believe that there was no need for agrarian reform, but members of the radical left-wing groups contested this view. Knowing that the peasants in Poland, just as the peasants in Ireland, considered that they and the landlords had a joint right to the soil, the Polish radicals proposed that an insurrection should be called which should as its first act grant the peasants their freeholds unconditionally and promise the landlords compensation from a state fund. In anticipation of the Russian decree of emancipation of 1861 the left wing had sought to force the landlords themselves to grant the peasants their freeholds in order to forestall the Russian administration, but the Russian government was content to base itself upon the co-operation of the Polish landlords, and as a result of disturbances in February and April 1861 introduced into the administration the Marquis Alexander Wielopolski. Wielopolski was unpopular in all ranks of Polish society, but the landlords were prepared to tolerate him as long as he carried out some scheme of agrarian reform which favoured themselves. In May 1861 Wielopolski succeeded in obtaining a decree for the abolition of labour services and their conversion into rents, fixed at temporary rates, but he fell foul of the Catholic Church in Poland when he promised tolerance for all religions including the Jews. The bishops were to some extent in the hands of the lesser clergy, who shared the same aspirations as the radical left wing. Fresh disturbances in October 1861 led to the temporary removal from office of Wielopolski, but in the summer of 1862 he was appointed 'Head of the Civil Government', and the Tsar sent as Viceroy his brother, Constantine, whose presence would be a guarantee against the work of conciliating the Polish upper classes being frustrated by the local military commanders. By the summer of 1862, however, the radical strength had grown considerably and even the upper classes feared to antagonize the left wing by open collaboration with Russia. Wielopolski therefore convinced Constantine and the Tsar that the only way out of their dilemma was to remove from the scene altogether the left-wing organization. In September 1862 it was announced that, when conscription was introduced again in the Kingdom of Poland, its operation would be limited to the population of the towns and certain elements of the rural population, mainly estate workers, the section of the Polish community which most favoured radical reform. Instead of removing the threat of revolt, the decree actually provoked an insurrection in January 1863. There were in fact too many persons involved in the conspiracy for them all to take refuge abroad as Wielopolski hoped they would. After much heart-searching the National Central Committee in Warsaw called its rising for 21–22 January.

An insurrection against the Tsar as King of Poland was technically his own concern and there were no grounds for the powers to interfere, but into this situation Bismarck stepped with great recklessness. In his search for an understanding with Russia he sent General von Alvensleben to Congress Poland to offer Prussian collaboration in the crushing of revolt, but he met with a frosty response from Constantine and Wielopolski, who in view of the ample forces at their disposal and the comparatively weak opposition offered by the insurgents, did not need Prussian aid. Alvensleben therefore went to St Petersburg, where on 8 February 1863 he was able to conclude with the Tsar, though against the wish of the foreign minister, Gorchakov, a convention for mutual collaboration along the frontiers of Prussia and the Congress Kingdom. In Berlin Bismarck undoubtedly exaggerated the strength of the insurrection and began to throw out hints that, if Russia were obliged to withdraw, Prussia would herself be obliged to occupy part at least of the Congress Kingdom.

Until the conclusion of the Alvensleben convention of 8 February the Court circles in Paris had shown little interest in the Polish revolt, which was an embarrassment to Russia, who still had a vague understanding with France amounting almost to an entente. When the news of prospective Prussian intervention was received in Paris the French government became highly excited. The Congress Kingdom was set up under the terms of the treaty of Vienna of 1815, and therefore all the signatory powers of that Treaty, of whom France was one, could claim a voice if its provisions were in any

way set aside. Poland was a catholic country and excited the sympathies of the French clericals, but the revolt was one of the Polish
left wing and aroused strong emotions in the minds of French
liberals and radicals. There was clearly popular demand that something should be done to alleviate the lot of the Poles, while in the
tortuous minds of the men who controlled the Second Empire there
was a realization that, if anything were to be done on behalf of
Poland, it would take the form of the coercion of Prussia. In other
words, France could attack Prussia in the Rhineland and perhaps in
the course of intervention on behalf of the Poles herself achieve some
of the longstanding ambitions of her own foreign policy. Soon
France began to put out feelers for united action to Britain and
Austria for common action in Berlin, hoping that by setting in
motion a diplomatic *démarche* military measures might follow.
Immediately the international position of Prussia was endangered
and Bismarck offered his resignation, but William I was in no
position to dismiss the minister who was his own last resort. Therefore Bismarck was compelled, as discreetly as he could, to extract
himself from the muddle he had created.

In this he was aided by the British government. Palmerston and
Russell decided that the situation was so dangerous that Britain must
act with France, but direct a joint protest to Russia on the grounds
that Article I of the Final Act of the treaty of Vienna empowered
them to make an appeal on behalf of the Poles, an interpretation
which Russia had always contested. In this way France, for the sake
of joining with Britain, was induced to protest to Russia, with whom
she had her tenuous entente. The Russians at first played for time
and offered the Poles an amnesty, which the insurgents rejected.
Gorchakov asked what proposals France, Britain and Austria might
make for the better government of Poland. On 17 June Britain and
France made their proposals for an amnesty, a restitution of the
constitution of 1815, the admission of Poles to official posts, liberty
of conscience, the use of Polish as the official language and a regular
system of recruiting. Similar, but not identical, suggestions were
made by Austria on 18 June. The notes of the powers were analyzed
by the Russian council of ministers on 8 July 1863, and the decision
was taken to call their bluff. Austria clearly wanted no complications
in her Polish province of Galicia, while the British foreign secretary,

Russell, had made most pacific statements in the House of Lords, which indicated that the British cabinet was not in a warlike mood. Russia replied by declaring that she was willing to enter into an understanding with Austria and Prussia when order had been restored in Poland for the better government of the Kingdom, which was in effect a polite refusal of the three powers' representations.

There is small truth in the view that Bismarck stood by Russia in 1863. The reverse was true. William I wrote despairingly to his nephew, Alexander II, of his inability to help him or give the slightest aid. He could do little more than offer the advice that the Russians should appeal to the peasants against the insurgents. It was in fact this solution which was adopted. In March 1863 the *ukaz* of 1861 respecting the peasants of the Lithuanian provinces was modified. All connection between the manor and the village was destroyed and the peasants considered the owners of the land in return for paying a quit-rent. This system was extended to the south-western *gubernii* and to the *gubernia* of Mogilev and parts of Vitebsk. In an area where the majority of landlords and Christian intelligentsia were Polish by speech the Tsarist government was ready to conciliate the peasants. In March 1864 Nikolai Milyutin's radical scheme was adopted for the Kingdom of Poland, by which the peasants were given their freeholds without the obligation of paying rent or compensation to the landlords. In short, in the Kingdom the Russian government adopted and improved upon the programme of the Polish insurgents. Certain reform from the hands of the Tsar was better than problematical reform from the insurgents. The agrarian programme of the Polish insurgents ceased to have any meaning, and in the course of 1864 the insurrection petered out. Not Prussian support, but appeal to social forces within Polish society had enabled Russia to extinguish the Polish revolt. Yet so great had been the threat that the Tsar Alexander II thought at one time that it might be necessary to grant Russia itself a constitution in order to buy off domestic opposition, and actually instructed Valuyev to make concrete proposals. No less than 700,000 men were put under arms to subdue the Polish revolt. Diplomatically once more the relations of the powers exhibited a fluidity. France's importunate intervention on behalf of the Poles brought to an end once and for all her slender understanding of 1859 with Russia.

The Conflict of Austria and Prussia

I. THE FRANKFORT CONFERENCE 1863

In the light of the constitutional difficulties which beset Austria after her defeat in the war against France in Italy, the foreign minister appointed in 1859, Rechberg, decided that the safest course for the Habsburg monarchy was to work for a reconciliation in Germany. This could mean nothing less than the acceptance of Prussia as the equal of Austria within the Germanic Confederation. In this policy he was opposed by Schmerling, who was a centralist within the Habsburg dominions and determined to preserve Austria's leading position in the Confederation. Austrian policy therefore tended to speak with two voices.

The plan devised by Rechberg was one for re-infusing life into the Germanic Confederation in order to make it an acceptable institution. It was proposed that a standing committee should be set up with a chamber selected from the various parliaments of the individual states. For a discussion of this plan a conference of the German princes was called for Frankfort on 16 August 1863. The majority of the German kings and princes supported the Austrian initiative. The King of Prussia, William I, was sorely tempted to appear in Frankfort, if only out of politeness to Francis Joseph, but Bismarck made the non-attendance of the King a question of principle. The policy which Bismarck had been called upon to implement in 1862 had the ultimate aim of Prussia's aggrandisement. There could therefore be no question of accepting even a position of equality. He persuaded the King of Prussia not to attend the conference, and in this way to demonstrate that he was firmly determined to seek a Prussian solution of the German problem. Without Prussia, the most powerful German state, nothing could come of the Austrian initiative.

II. THE SCHLESWIG-HOLSTEIN QUESTION

Austria and Prussia were soon brought together by the problem of Schleswig-Holstein. The Duchies were governed by the London Treaty of 1852, to which the German Confederation was not a party. By this agreement the great powers recognized that the King of

Denmark held the Duchies of Schleswig, Holstein and Lauenberg and that the Danish Monarchy was indivisible, but required that the King of Denmark should recognize the autonomy and indivisibility of Duchies and not in any way to infringe the rights of the Germanic Confederation; Holstein and Lauenberg were to remain part of the Confederation. The King of Denmark had no direct male heir, and under the Salic Law the duchies ought to have reverted to Christian of Augustenburg, but he was induced to abandon his claims for 2,500,000 thalers. Nevertheless, it could be argued that, though a father might make a renunciation, it was not necessarily binding upon his sons. To this complicated situation was added an internal difficulty. Danish nationalism was as strong as that of any other European people. The 'Great Denmark' party demanded that Schleswig should be incorporated into Denmark, leaving Holstein and Lauenburg with a separate constitution as part of the German Confederation. To this demand Frederick VII submitted on 30 March 1863. In this way a unitary Danish state was created and Holstein left as an autonomous appendage. The new system was an evasion of the London Treaty of 1852 and a challenge to the German Confederation. Within Germany there was a strong reaction, and Frederick of Augustenburg declared that he had never recognized his father's resignation of his rights. On 15 November 1863 Frederick VII of Denmark died. Within the Prussian parliament there were demands that the rights of the Duke of Augustenburg should be recognized. Everywhere in Germany public opinion demanded action.

France, Britain and Russia were parties to the London Treaty, and therefore had a right to be consulted in the crisis which had arisen between Denmark and the German Confederation, but Napoleon III, having failed to make much impression upon French public opinion by his handling of the Polish crisis, used the Schleswig-Holstein crisis to raise the question of a European conference to settle outstanding political problems. His proposal, expressed in the form of a circular of 4 November 1863 to the European powers, met with scant sympathy from the British government, which had no intention of permitting a wholesale revision of European frontiers in the interest of France. Russia was herself suspicious of French aims and declined to be a party to a plan proposed by Napoleon III, who had so recently devoted his energy to embarrassing Russia during the Polish crisis. There was therefore small likelihood of the Concert of Europe acting to procure a solution of the Schleswig-Holstein Question. It was certainly bad tactics on the part of Great Britain to express sympathy for the Danes, because that gave the Danes the impression that Great Britain, linked to Denmark by the marriage of the Prince of Wales to the Danish princess, Alexandra, would give material aid to them. In fact, the international situation was such that the Schleswig-Holstein Question was left to the German powers themselves to settle.

From the point of view of Rechberg, the Austrian foreign minister, the crisis seemed most opportune, because he could use it to promote his policy of reconciliation with Prussia. By a common understanding in the Schleswig-Holstein crisis they might go on to act together in German affairs generally. Prussia refused to permit a Federal execution authorized by the Diet and ignored warnings of Great Britain against taking independent action. On 16 January 1864 Austria took the decision to go to war against Denmark in alliance with Prussia to seize Schleswig-Holstein. The war which followed ended with the inevitable victory of the Austro-Prussian armies, and on 30 October 1864 Denmark, completely isolated, was compelled to surrender the duchies of Schleswig and Holstein to Austria and Prussia, who disregarded the claims of the Duke of Augustenburg. The real question for Prussia and Austria was the division of the spoils.

On 22 August 1864 the two monarchs, Francis Joseph and William I, met at Schönbrunn to discuss this question. Bismarck and Rechberg thought that a friendly settlement was possible. At this stage Bismarck would have been content for the moment with a division of power in Germany, if Prussia were left in control of Schleswig-Holstein, but Austria obviously wanted something to show for the efforts that she had made in the war. It was suggested to Prussia that she might cede to Austria the county of Glatz in Silesia, but to this William I refused to agree on the grounds that this arrangement would be contrary to the will of its inhabitants. Rechberg was more concerned with the cementing of an alliance with Prussia against the French, which would in effect amount to a Prussian guarantee of Austria's possessions in Italy and the Dalmatian coast, but he was hampered in his efforts by the opposition of the counsellor for German Affairs, Biegeleben, who refused to draft a treaty. The essence of Rechberg's policy was a 'Little German' solution, whereas Biegeleben was a partisan of the 'Big German' policy. Commercial questions also served to complicate Austro-Prussian relations. In the Zollverein treaty of 1853 the problem of Austria's entry into the Prussian commercial system was left open. Rechberg wished the clause allowing for Austria's ultimate entry to remain when the treaty was renewed in 1865. Bismarck himself advised that a concession should be made on this point in order that the pro-Prussian Rechberg might obtain at least one success and be retained as foreign minister by Francis Joseph, but William I was a man with a mind of his own and decided that the clause should not be renewed.

It was the commercial question which brought about a cabinet crisis in Austria. The Austrian council of ministers decided to send a sharp note to Berlin protesting against Prussia's attitude towards a future entry of Austria into the German commercial system. This step was taken against the advice of Rechberg, who was compelled to resign. In moments of crisis Francis Joseph tended to turn to men with whom he was upon good personal terms. On 27 October 1864 Alexander Mensdorff-Pouilly became foreign minister, an amiable general, who had been governor of Galicia, but a man with little experience in the field of international affairs. For this reason he fell under the influence of Biegeleben. In a memorandum of 19 October 1864 Biegeleben had argued that the real enemy of Austria was Prussia, and therefore an alliance with France was necessary, but Francis Joseph was the real master of the situation in Austria. On 31 October 1864 he ordered the continuation of the search for a Prussian alliance and the avoidance of European complications. As a result, there was for the moment a stalemate in the efforts of the two powers to solve the Schleswig-Holstein Question. At length on 21 February 1865 Bismarck proposed that the Duke of Augustenburg should be established in the Duchies as a compromise solution, but that Kiel and Rendsberg should be held by Prussian garrisons. This was a suggestion for which Francis Joseph had little sympathy, and for the moment he began to veer towards the policy which had been put forward by Biegeleben. Acceptance of Bismarck's scheme would certainly have presented Austria in a poor light, but at least it would have held in check for the moment the annexationist tendencies of Prussia. To leave the Schleswig-Holstein Question open, however, encouraged Prussia to consider a solution by force. Bismarck now gave Roon, the minister of war, instructions to examine the problems which war with Austria would present. At a meeting of the Prussian council of 29 May 1865 Bismarck and the chief of staff, Moltke, declared in favour of war, though the Crown Prince Frederick urged the need for conciliation. In this situation William I was for the moment undecided.

In July 1865 there were political changes in Austria attendant upon the fall of the centralist Schmerling, who believed that Austria had a role to play in Germany. The new ministry of Belcredi, 'The Ministry of Counts', was conservative in its outlook and therefore favoured co-operation with Prussia. Their desire for conciliation resulted in the treaty of Gastein of 14 August 1865, by which Prussia purchased Lauenberg for 2,250,000 thalers; Prussia was to govern Schleswig and Austria Holstein; while Prussia was to garrison Kiel and Rendsburg and control the military roads to them. This was a compromise solution negotiated without the knowledge of Biegeleben. In effect, Austria obtained a breathing space in which to improve her own internal position and to reconsider the international situation.

This fact did not escape the attention of Bismarck. He now knew that he had to be certain that France would not intervene in Germany in the event of a war between Prussia and Austria. In October 1865 he visited Biarritz in order to meet Napoleon III. Evidently enough was said to excite the appetite of the Emperor, but nothing as definite as the Plombières agreement of 1859 between Napoleon III and Cavour was concluded. The choice before France was whether she should assist Prussia in return for territorial gains or continue a policy of seeking to maintain a divided Germany, the course advocated by Walewski and Drouyn de Lhuys. On 8 April 1866 Prussia negotiated with Italy a treaty of alliance to last for three months; in the event of war Italy was to receive Venetia. For Bismarck the alliance with Italy was of small political significance; its main purpose was to draw off one Austrian army and make a Prussian victory easier in the principal theatre of operations in central Europe. The attitude of France was the decisive factor. It was Austrian policy to keep France neutral. Proposals were made that in the event of an Austrian victory Austria herself would cede Venetia to France for transmission to Italy, while Austria would find compensation in the annexation of Silesia. It was urged that in this way Napoleon III would obtain the glory of having completed Italian unification, while the power of Prussia would be much reduced by the loss of the rich Silesian industrial basin. This was in theory everything that France could require, but the proposal depended upon the power of the Austrian army to achieve it. Napoleon III wavered between two courses, and in the end signed a secret treaty with Austria on 12 June, by which he undertook to remain neutral in the struggle. This was in practice to make no decision at all. Nothing less than armed intervention could have brought France material advantage.

Of Britain Bismarck could be tolerably certain. Britain had enough troubles of her own in North America to wish to intervene in central Europe. There was in Britain, moreover, no objection to the creation of a strong state in Germany which would act as a barrier to subsequent French ambitions. For most Englishmen France was the enemy, and not a hypothetical Germany. Russian statesmen, however, had no illusions about Prussia. Anti-German feeling had a long history in Russia, though it rarely showed on the surface of official exchanges. Rather there was a deep consciousness that Russian interests could not best be served by the creation of a strong state on the western frontier of the Empire. Nevertheless, Russia was occupied with the modernization of her backward economic system and wished above all to make the transition without external complications. The attempt of Karakazov on the life of the Tsar in 1866 was disturbing. The perennial financial difficulties prevented the creation of a modern army to make Russia's foreign policy effective. The best that Russia could do to extend her power was to push her frontiers forward in Central Asia. The main question before Russian statesmen was the revision of the Treaty of Paris of 1856. Suspicion was entertained of French designs in the Balkans. On 23 February 1866 Prince Cuza brought about the unification of the two Rumanian principalities, but he met with difficulties and was deposed. The candidature of Charles of Hohenzollern-Sigmaringen for the Rumanian throne was a threat to Austria, if it meant that Prussia would have an ally in Austria's rear, but the Hohenzollern-Sigmaringens were connected by marriage with the Beauharnais family, and therefore with the Bonapartes. If, on the other hand, Austria were driven out of Germany she would be stronger in the Balkans, where she could concentrate her strength. The situation was filled with unpleasant alternatives for Russia. If France strengthened herself in Belgium and Luxemburg she would be stronger in the Near East. If Prussia won the struggle a powerful neighbour would be established in central Europe, and Austria would be freed from her German obligations, more capable than ever of acting with vigour in the Balkans. In short, Russia could have no policy at all. All that Alexander II and Gorchakov could do was to await results.

Bismarck undertook a campaign of provocation in Germany. On 26 January 1866 a complaint was made that in Holstein Austria was permitting an agitation on behalf of the Duke of Augustenburg, which was a contravention of the convention of Gastein. Austria replied on 9 February, as if to show her strength, by declaring that her alliance with Prussia was at an end, but Bismarck was unimpressed, and on 9 April proposed a plan of reform for the German confederation; a national parliament ought to be elected by universal suffrage to discuss with the German states the new constitution of Germany, which could mean nothing less than Austria would be excluded from membership of the Confederation. On 6 June Prussian troops proceeded to the occupation of Holstein, but to Bismarck's disappointment no resistance was offered. On 10 June, however, Prussia gave a closer definition to her plans for the reform of the Confederation. Austria roused herself for an effort to resist and declared that, because Prussia had violated the treaty of 1815 and disregarded the Federal Constitution, the states of Germany ought to mobilize against her. On 14 June mobilization against Prussia was voted in the Federal Diet. At last Austria was provoked into action, and on 16 June Prussia declared war. On 20 June Italy declared war on Austria in accordance with her treaty with Prussia. There was in Austria's action a certain light-hearted confidence in her capacity to resist Prussia. It is true that with the exception of the battle of Waterloo, when the Prussian army arrived in time to make certain of victory after Wellington's army had borne the brunt of French attack, Prussia had not shown much military prowess since the Seven Years' War, but under Moltke's guidance the Prussian army, in spite of persistent obtuseness among certain commanders, was already adjusting itself to the system of war which the industrial revolution had made possible. Against the Italians the Austrian army could hold its own, and on 24 June the Italian army was defeated at Custozza, but the main Austrian army under Benedek, placed in command much against his will, was defeated at the battle of König-grätz-Sadowa in Bohemia on 3 July. There was certainly muddle and inefficiency on the Prussian side, but the Prussian army was provided with modern weapons, whereas the Austrian army was equipped and trained on the lines of the forces which had fought the Napoleonic wars. The Prussian victory was crushing, but it was not decisive. Austria still had a confident and victorious army in Italy which could be brought up to continue the struggle.

At this point France offered her mediation. On 4 July France informed Prussia that Venetia had been ceded to France for trans-mission to Italy and that she would offer her good offices to find a solution of the Austro-Prussian conflict. Napoleon III's offer con-tained a threat, which he hesitated to implement, but on 7 July after some wavering the French ambassador, Benedetti, was instructed to demand a reply to the proposals of 4 July. Benedetti's appearance at the Prussian headquarters gave some annoyance, but Bismarck could obtain the substance of his aims without provoking a war with France. Superficially Bismarck proposed a compromise solution. Prussia was to be given a hegemony north of the river Main and Austria was to be excluded from Germany. The German states south of the Main were to be independent both of Austrian and Prussian influence. In this way there was to be no unitary solution of the German question, and France might content herself with the belief that she was under no threat from Germany. These terms seemed satisfactory to France, and Austria lost no territory, other than Venetia to Italy, which she was prepared before the outbreak of hostilities to surrender. On 22 July an armistice was concluded, and on 23 August a definitive peace was signed.

In theory the German Question was not solved by the war of 1866. In fact, France had suffered an overwhelming defeat. The surrender of Germany north of the Main to Prussia gave her the power to stand as the champion of German nationalism against French acquisitiveness. On 5 August 1866 Benedetti raised the question of compensation for France, but Bismarck refused to con-sider the cession of German territory. On 16 August 1866 a French request for a secret agreement by which France should acquire Luxemburg and receive Prussian aid if she were compelled to invade Belgium met with strong opposition. The new arrangements in Germany amounted to the dissolution of the Confederation, and in the midst of the problems presented by the reorganization of Germany Bismarck would, perhaps, have been willing to cede Luxemburg, but such a course met with the passionate opposition of the National Liberals in Germany. All that France was to obtain was an international conference, which met in London; its recommendations were that the Prussian garrison should be withdrawn from Luxemburg and the Duchy should be neutralized. France had fallen between two stools. The desire of Napoleon III to make gains as a result of the international crisis was disappointed. France could do no more than watch Prussia re-organize Germany north of the Main. Austria, the defeated power, was compelled likewise to re-organize herself. In the case of Prussia it was merely a question of concentrating power in the hands of the Hohenzollern Dynasty. In Austria the Habsburgs were required to seek a solution of the national questions which had hung fire since 1861. A patched-up solution was necessary to permit Austria to extract herself from the consequences of defeat in order to meet the challenge of Prussia. From what Austria hoped would be a temporary embarrassment emerged a solution which was to last until 1918.

The Reorganization of the German Powers

I. THE CONSTITUTION OF THE NORTH GERMAN CONFEDERATION

As a result of the war with Austria and her allies, Prussia was enlarged by the addition of Schleswig-Holstein with Lauenberg, Hanover, Hesse-Casel, Nassau, the northern part of Hesse-Darmstadt and Frankfurt. Saxony retained her separate identity as she had done in 1815, but she was now virtually controlled by Prussia. The Prussian parliament assembled in August 1866, and a bill was drawn up to provide for the indemnification of the government for its failure to secure a legal budget. The Prussian middle class had no objection to Bismarck's success now that it had been achieved. Bismarck himself intended to use it in a way that would prevent them from ever challenging again the power of the Hohenzollerns. The North

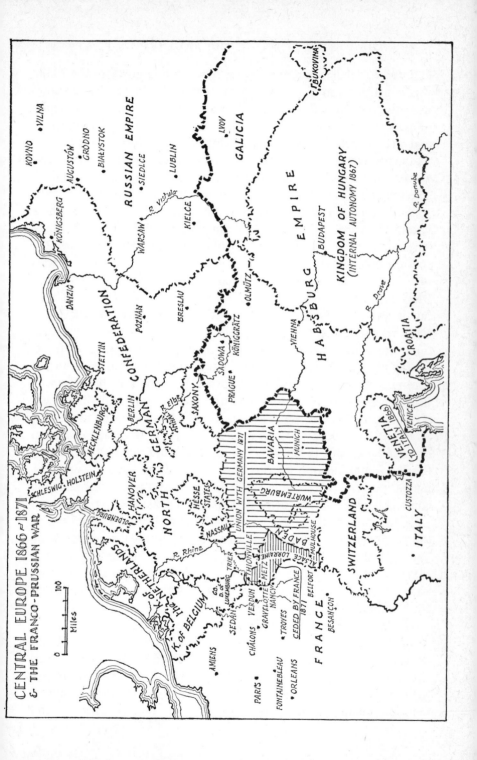

CENTRAL EUROPE 1866-1871
& THE FRANCO-PRUSSIAN WAR

Miles
0   100

•VILNA
•KOVNO
KÖNIGSBERG
AUGUSTÓW
•GRODNO
•BIAŁYSTOK

RUSSIAN EMPIRE

SIEDLCE
WARSAW•
•LUBLIN
R. Vistula
KIELCE•
•LVOV
GALICIA

DANZIG

CONFEDERATION

STETTIN•

POZNAN•

BRESLAU•

OLMÜTZ•

•SADOWA
PRAGUE• •KÖNIGGRÄTZ

VIENNA•

HABSBURG EMPIRE

KINGDOM OF HUNGARY
(INTERNAL AUTONOMY 1867)

BUDAPEST•

R. Drave

R. Danube

CROATIA

R. Drave

MECKLENBURG

BERLIN•

GERMAN

NORTH

HANOVER•

R. Elbe
ANHALT

SAXONY

SCHLESWIG HOLSTEIN

OLDENBURG

HESSE
STATES
NASSAU

UNION WITH GERMANY 1871

BAVARIA
MUNICH•

WÜRTEMBURG

VENETIA
VENICE•
(TO ITALY 1866)

CUSTOZZA•

•ITALY

SWITZERLAND

BADEN

K. OF NETHERLANDS

K. OF BELGIUM

R. Rhine

G.D. OF
LUXEMBURG
SEDAN•
•TRIER
VERDUN•
•THIONVILLE
GRAVELOTTE• •METZ
NANCY•
ALSACE LORRAINE
CEDED BY FRANCE
1871
•BELFORT
•MULHOUSE

CHÂLONS•
•TROYES
FONTAINEBLEAU•
•BESANÇON

FRANCE

PARIS•
•ORLEANS

•AMIENS

German Confederation, which was now formed north of the Main, was constituted in virtue of fifteen treaties of alliance by the component states with Prussia. By February 1867 the general principles of association were agreed upon by a conference of plenipotentiaries, and on 24 February a *Reichstag* assembled to discuss the constitution. At the head of the Confederation was the Praesidium or the executive powers of the new state, which was vested in the King of Prussia. The Federal Council or *Bundesrat* represented the association of the states, in which Prussia enjoyed seventeen out of a total of forty-three votes, but because Prussia was the most powerful unit in the Confederation she was in virtual control of the *Bundesrat*. Beneath the *Bundesrat* was the parliament or *Reichstag*, elected by universal manhood suffrage, a provision which gave the conservative junkers of Brandenburg small pleasure. The *Reichstag* voted the federal budget, but it shared legislative equality with the *Bundesrat*, which could reject its proposals, if it wished. Side by side with these new institutions the constitutions of the individual states remained in force. As far as Prussia went, this meant that the old curial constitution continued to exist, designed to provide a façade for absolutism. If Prussia would not agree to a measure, then it was hardly likely that it would pass through the *Reichstag*. The Federal Minister, moreover, was the Chancellor, who was not responsible to the *Bundesrat* or to the *Reichstag*, but to the Praesidium. He could not be removed by the *Reichstag*, but only by the king, who enjoyed wide powers, promulgating laws, controlling issues of peace and war, and exercising command of the armed forces. In these circumstances no real responsible government could develop. The King of Prussia as the head of the Confederation enjoyed the same relation to the Chancellor as he had with the Minister-President of Prussia, who were one and the same person, Bismarck, raised to the dignity of a count and endowed with an estate at Varzin to give him a status equal with the old Brandenburg nobility.

The conservatives in the Prussia of the pre-1866 epoch might complain that universal suffrage opened the flood gates to militant democracy, but it was not they who had been defeated. The Liberals had been defeated, because executive power now remained beyond their grasp. From this time onwards begins the demoralization of German liberalism. The *Reichstag* had no real significance and gradually degenerated into being a debating shop. The function of the Chancellor was to manage it and secure from it a satisfactory budget. From 1867 until the mid-1870s Bismarck was to rely upon the National Liberal Party, which held a majority. By satisfying their demands in inessentials he could succeed in retaining real power for the dynasty. As time went by it was to become obvious that any man of ambition who hoped to advance in the world could not enter the *Reichstag* to make his career. To obtain political power men sought first economic power in the rapidly expanding industry of Germany, with which to impress a government which understood only the compulsions of superior force. The *Reichstag* was to become a place for the second-rate men who represented the great industrial interests and acted as the marionettes of men more powerful than themselves. Public opinion Bismarck could corrupt. Having overrun Hanover, he obtained possession of the property of the ruling Guelph house, the income from which was used to bribe the press and secure the presentation of news in a form favourable to the government. The so-called 'Reptile Funds' contributed to the glorification of Bismarck and to the growth of the legend of his infallibility. The real architect of victory was von Moltke, who had reformed and fashioned the Prussian army, which could have saved Bismarck from any blunder he might have made in his diplomacy. The army was a state within a state, growing in prestige and excluding the influence of the Chancellor, whom it regarded merely in the light of a person securing the necessary credits for military expenditure. The Chief of Staff enjoyed the right of direct access to the King and was not obliged to consult the Chancellor. Through the military attachés in the foreign capitals it possessed its own channels of diplomatic information. Moltke was the maker of the mass modern army. It was he who gave the new Germany which was being created its military flavour. It is true that William I gave Bismarck his trust and confidence, but Bismarck was still a servant of the state over which William I ruled.

II. THE AUSTRO-HUNGARIAN COMPROMISE OF 1867

War had weakened Austria in 1859 and compelled her to attempt the constitutional experiments of 1860–1. Whereas the peculiar organization of the North German Confederation had been made possible by the victory of conservativism, in Austria the dynasty sought to secure its power in the face of defeat. Francis Joseph did not intend to accept for ever the exclusion of Austria from Germany. There was in 1866 every intention of taking revenge upon Prussia. For this reason a Saxon, Beust, was given the post of Chancellor, with the task of finding a stop-gap solution of internal questions which would permit a forward foreign policy to be resumed. Belcredi had hoped to create an empire based upon an understanding with five elements, the Germans, the Czechs, the Poles, the Hungarians and the South Slavs, but his plans were opposed by the local diets in November 1866. Fresh elections were held and delegates were to be sent to an 'extraordinary Reichsrat', which would in effect become a constituent assembly. Belcredi, however, had failed to obtain the support of the Germans and was therefore succeeded in February 1867 by Beust, who immediately put into effect another solution in collaboration with the Hungarian, Deák.

In July 1866 Deák had declared: 'Hungary asks nothing more after Königgrätz than before it.' There was more in this statement than appeared on the surface. Whereas before 1866 the Hungarians were stating their maximum demands, they were now putting forward their minimum requirements. On 17 February 1867 Count Julius Andrássy became prime minister of Hungary upon the terms demanded by Deák. The constitution and laws of 1848 were restored and a responsible ministry was set up. Upon one question only did Francis Joseph offer resistance. The unity of the army was maintained and with it German as the language of command, the latter not being a very serious demand, because for the majority of the troops this amounted only to some sixty words. Hungary, moreover, enjoyed the protection which a great power might give her, without at the same time being compelled to accept control from Vienna. The Austro-Hungarian Empire created in 1867 had three common ministries, foreign affairs, war and finance; these common functions were maintained by a Hungarian contribution of 30 per cent and an Austrian contribution of 70 per cent, a division of the burden unduly favourable to Hungary. It was laid down that there should be periodic agreements every ten years upon economic affairs. The practical significance of this partial separation was very great. From 1867 the Magyars of Hungary could deal with their nationality problems without fear of intervention by the Crown. Under the constitution of 1848 only 6 per cent of the male population enjoyed the vote. The upper and lower chambers of the Hungarian parliament were in fact dominated by the nobility and owners of large estates. In essence the electoral system of 1848 lasted until 1919. It had been hastily prepared and had resulted in the creation of a large number of rotten boroughs. All manner of electoral chicanery could be employed. In the large constituencies the polling booths were often a great distance away and difficult to reach, especially in the hilly districts. It was the non-Magyar districts of the country which provided the government with its majority. It was always certain of having some 200 members subservient to itself, ready to cheer and clap ministerial speeches. The purely Magyar districts in the centre of the country were on the whole in favour of the liberal-democratic policy of Kossuth and resented the control which the large landowners now obtained over the country, but the Magyar middle class was to some extent equivocal in its attitude towards the government, which everywhere began to carry out a policy of magyarization, cautiously at first, but, as the century progressed towards its end, with strident self-confidence. The hand of friendship was extended to the Croats, who were in 1868 given autonomy in matters relating to their internal affairs, which in essence meant only justice, education and religion. The Croat economy was integrated with that of Hungary and the budget was voted upon in the Hungarian parliament. The Ban of Croatia was nominated by the Emperor upon the recommendation of the Hungarian prime minister. Under the limited suffrage system and in the absence of voting by ballot the Croats could always be brought to heel. The other nationalities, the Slovaks, the Ruthenians, the Serbs and the Rumans, enjoyed no privileges in a state in which Magyar was the official language. In order that the dynasty might turn to what it considered the pressing problem of Prussian aggrandisement, the subject peoples of Hungary were surrendered to the process of magyarization.

On 17 February 1867 the seventeen diets of Austria met and were presented with the accomplished fact of the Compromise, or *Ausgleich*. On 27 February Francis Joseph formally restored the Hungarian constitution. One gain had been made by the inhabitants of the non-Hungarian parts of the Empire. Common affairs were to be dealt with by delegations from the two parliaments. This supposed that Austria proper should have a constitution. The new Austrian constitution of December 1867 in part owed its provisions to the demands of Austrian foreign policy. It is true that the Compromise was concluded without reference to the German parties, but Francis Joseph, intent upon reasserting the power of Austria in Germany, could hardly infringe the privileges of the Austrian Germans. Though the constitution was slightly more liberal than the system introduced by Schmerling in 1861, it was nevertheless intended by Beust and Andrássy that the Germans should have a predominant voice in the parliament, or *Reichsrat*. By skilful 'electoral geometry' a situation was reached by which the Germans, secure in the purely German districts, dominated the Czech lands of Bohemia, Moravia and Silesia; in Carniola, though the Germans were only 6 per cent of the population, they possessed a majority in the local diet. In Istria and Dalmatia the Italians were the dominant nationality, even though they were a minority among the Slavonic population. In Galicia the Poles ruled the roost, while the Ruthenians, about 40 per cent of the population, were virtually without representation in the local diet and therefore in the *Reichsrat*. Up to 1873 the deputies to the *Reichsrat* were elected from the Diets, but even after that date, when direct election was introduced, the curial system, by which classes of the population were represented, rather than heads of the population, was maintained. Under Article XIX of the Constitution of 1867 equality was granted to all races, but the language of the administration remained for practical purposes German. The Czechs, for example, were ready to seek a compromise with the government in order that some coherence might be maintained in the administration. Their view was that officials should be able to converse with the inhabitants of the Czech lands in either German or Czech, but from 1868 the Germans adopted the attitude that their own language was the language of the administration. The practical difficulty remained. Only an official who could converse with the citizens in both German and Czech could be effective. German chauvinism had exactly the opposite result from that which it sought to obtain. Czechs learned German, but the Germans steadfastly refused to learn Czech. For this reason, as time went on, the Czechs began to gain control of the administration in Bohemia, Moravia and Silesia, because they alone could deal with both nationalities. In Galicia the Poles gained the upper hand, because Ruthenian was a language akin to Polish and therefore presented the Poles with no serious difficulties. The language question assumed an importance out of all proportion to political reality. The Austrian Empire might have served the purpose of uniting different peoples of different speech in an economic unity, but stolid refusal to recognize that the citizen wished to have government made intelligible to him could only raise the language question to a point where the very existence of the Austro-Hungarian Empire seemed burdensome to the common man. Desire to meet the government upon the basis of equal validity among mother tongues took precedence over the higher Austrian patriotism which the dynasty sought to promote. The Austro-Hungarian Compromise of 1867 in the long run could only deepen the rift among the constituent portions of the Habsburg Empire and bring nearer its ultimate collapse.

Conclusion

The years between the end of the Crimean War and the year 1867 threw Europe into confusion. The unifications of Germany and Italy were not complete. Russia was seeking to find a way into the modern world. By the Reform Act of 1867 Britain entered into a new phase of her development, which was ultimately to end in complete manhood suffrage. As far as France was concerned, the Second Empire had failed to produce the domination which all Europe had feared since the days of Napoleon I. Napoleon III was deeply conscious of the declining power of France. It remained for the final catastrophe of the Franco-Prussian war to alter the European balance of power. The years 1870–1 were to prove a watershed in European alliances and alignments. In the new conditions the certainties of the past were replaced by the uncertainties of the future. A state of flux caused statesmen to seek solutions to problems, the complexity of which they had barely grasped.

6: Europe and the Wider World

The progress of industrial civilization in Europe required an enlargement of the markets for European goods in the extra-European world. Likewise the United States looked to the world beyond the seas for the sale of American goods. In Asia especially the industrial states began to behave with an arrogance which in the long run created a bitterness and distrust, but it would be dangerous to suppose that crudely conceived economic interpretations can always explain the actions of the powers. It is true that Great Britain raised the question of non-intervention in Spain to the level of a lofty principle in the knowledge that she had conquered the markets of Spain in her American colonies and sought to retain them, but British actions were not always determined by matters of self-interest. Britain was mistress of the seas, but by the beginning of the nineteenth century this implanted in the minds of the political class not only a consciousness of power but also a sense of obligation, which governments in a changed political climate were compelled to respect.

I. AFRICA

By no part of the world was the British conscience stirred more than by Africa. In the eighteenth century the European states had regarded their West Indian possessions, which yielded sugar, as having an importance second to none in their economies. A problem arose, however, because the native populations of the islands would or could not undertake the heavy manual labour required on the plantations. As early as the sixteenth century European adventurers had recourse to the purchase of slaves in West Africa. The African negro was strong and hardy enough to perform the work required of him. Similarly, the development of Brazil was made possible by the source of slaves which Portugal had in Angola. Farther north slavery was extensive in the southern regions of the United States, where it was the basis of a rural economy, producing tobacco and cotton for the European market. In the eighteenth century voices were raised against the institution of slavery, but they met with the opposition of vested interests, because the planters regarded their slaves as capital assets which they had purchased for good money. The tactics adopted by the anti-slavery agitation in Britain under William Wilberforce were first to attack the slave trade itself. The conditions under which the slaves were transported across the Atlantic were foul. The slaves were placed in chains and stuffed into slave ships, where it was certain not all would survive the voyage. In other words, the slave traders were compelled to allow for certain depreciation of their stock during transit, an appalling consideration when a cargo consisted of human beings. The calculation of the reformers was that, when once the slave trade had been put down, the task of securing its abolition first in the British dominions could then be undertaken. One of the last acts of the British 'Ministry of All the Talents' in 1807 was to secure an act of parliament abolishing the slave trade. Thomas Fowell Buxton, Wilberforce's successor in the leadership of the agitation, obtained in 1833 an act of parliament, sponsored by the government itself, which abolished slavery in the British dominions; somewhat later the system of apprenticeship was likewise abolished. It was fitting that slavery should be attacked and abandoned by the country which had done most to promote it in the past and which had seen Liverpool and Manchester thrive on the proceeds, but not all slave traders were British. After the end of the Napoleonic Wars the British government entered upon a campaign to put down the trade by international agreement.

In the treaty of peace signed between the United States and Great Britain at Ghent on 24 December 1814 the two governments undertook to seek the abolition of the trade, though the enthusiasm of the United States was equivocal. Napoleon I may have done little for France by returning in 1815, but his defeat meant that the undertaking which France gave to Britain at the Congress of Vienna to abolish the slave trade was embodied in an additional article to the second treaty of Paris of 20 November 1815. Gradually Britain secured treaties with all the states whose subjects were likely to be involved in the traffic. A comprehensive treaty with Austria, Prussia and Russia was drawn up in 1841. In 1842 Portugal agreed to enter into the system, and France likewise in 1845. In that year a British act of parliament made the slave trade an act of piracy to be tried in the British admiralty courts. Under these agreements the British navy could hunt down and punish the slave traders captured on the high seas. It was one thing to pronounce the end of the traffic and another to bring about its end. Slave trading continued while slavery still existed in the Americas, and the increased risks incurred as a result of the British surveillance were offset by the increased price of slaves.

It should not be imagined that the slave traders were the only guilty parties in this iniquitous commerce. The native rulers of West Africa were tempted by its rewards, and war to obtain slaves became a local industry; there were even African kings who were prepared to sell their own subjects. The stations established in Guinea on the Gold and Slave coasts in the seventeenth and eighteenth centuries to serve as depots for the collection of slaves now saw their functions reversed. They became bases to ensure that slave trading was put down. The vigilance of the European powers began slowly to have an effect upon the economies of the West African states, which could no longer draw large revenues from the traffic in Negroes. In 1843 the British government took formal possession of the Africa Company's stations in Sierra Leone and the Gold Coast. Lagos by the 1850s had become the main slaving centre of West Africa. In 1851 a British naval force restored the king against a usurper on condition that he abolished the traffic in slaves, but it grew up again under his successor, with the result that Britain annexed the kingdom in 1861. In 1871 the Gold Coast formally became British. It could be only a question of time before the British authorities began to extend their authority into the disorderly interior. Such a problem occurred almost immediately after the war. By a convention of August 1814 Britain agreed to restore to the Dutch the colonies, which she had seized while the United Provinces had been under French domination, in order that the new Kingdom of the Netherlands might be strengthened as a barrier to French aggression in Europe, but there were exceptions. Britain retained Cape Colony for strategic reasons; it was before the building of the Suez Canal the key to trade with the east. At once the problem arose of the native populations on the frontier, Kaffirs, who were themselves under pressure from the Zulus. In 1833 a new governor, Sir Benjamin d'Urban, was sent to the province with the task of securing the emancipation of the slaves owned by the Dutch population, but the Dutch viewed the British government with suspicion, and in 1835-7 there occurred the 'great trek' by which 5,000 Dutch settlers left the Cape Colony and crossed the Orange river, where they might establish states of their own and they could create great farms and own slaves. From this movement there ultimately emerged the Orange Free State (1854) and the Transvaal (1852). The Dutch were a hardy race and prepared to defend themselves against the African tribes, while the British home government was extremely reluctant to extend its authority in South Africa; in Natal, however, the territory was in 1843 proclaimed a British colony, lest the Dutch, who had taken refuge there from the Zulus, establish a fresh republic and bring disorder with them. Whether it liked it or not, the British government was compelled gradually to extend its authority in order to maintain order. Behind authority came the European settlers, attracted by a land in which the climate was not ennervating, but more by the discovery that diamonds and gold existed in abundance in the hinterland. Before the 1870s British policy wavered between the need to extend imperial authority over the whole of European settlement and the desire to avoid the expense which this would involve.

The motives of France were somewhat different. The conquest of Algiers by the army of Charles X created exactly the same problem of a troubled hinterland which rendered the French coastal possessions insecure, but there was little disposition among French generals, permanently disgruntled that the prestige of the army won under Napoleon had been so tarnished in 1814-15, to accept a policy of withdrawal which cost alone would seem to have demanded. Instead the French army proceeded to subdue Algeria with a sense of etatistic purpose until Arab resistance was broken in 1847; behind the armies came settlers from France and other Mediterranean countries, and with 1848 and the coup d'état of 1851 the political exiles. What began as a military adventure ended as a colonizing movement. In Guinea, however, etatistic motives combined with political dissent in the republican officer, Faidherbe, who was determined to use a posting, which was a virtual sentence of exile, to build up French influence in West Africa. From taking up his appointment as governor on the Senegal river until his recall in 1865 he extended

French power with the object of dominating the middle reaches of the river Niger. This expansion was carried out largely by the enlistment of native Senegalese troops. In this way began the movement by which Britain extended her control cautiously from the coastal settlements in West Africa, while the French established their domination in the hinterland.

Gradually Africa began to yield up her secrets to the Europeans. This was the great age of missionaries, and the most famous was David Livingstone. In 1853–6 he traced the great river Zambesi to the Indian Ocean. Afterwards he was to explore the lakes of central Africa. His activities excited the imagination of public opinion in both Britain and the United States, and his disappearance was to cause the *New York Herald* and the *Daily Telegraph* to despatch H. M. Stanley to find him in November 1871. The turbulent Richard Burton, upon whose shoulders religion rested more lightly, and Speke in the years 1856–60 began their investigation of the lakes, completed by Samuel Baker by 1864, which proved that the source of the White Nile lay in the great Lake Victoria Nyanza. Exploration, however, did not lead to the extension of British dominions owing to the hostility of the economically-minded home government. It did perhaps induce the Portuguese government to put more order into its government of Angola and Mozambique and therefore define the area of its own claims. The activities of the Europeans in Africa did not seriously affect the African peoples south of the Sahara before 1871. The slave trade no longer played an important part in the economies of the European states, and Africa itself scarcely presented a market for the finished goods of European industry. It was rather to the highly developed societies of the east, where markets did exist, that the great states of the west turned their attention.

II. THE BRITISH IN INDIA

India had once been a great empire under the Moslem Mogul dynasty, which under Akhbar (1556–1605) until the reign of Aurunzeb (1658–1707) had controlled almost all of the sub-continent with the exception of its southern tip, but by the eighteenth century its authority was seriously challenged by the Hindu revival. Mahrattas, Rajputs and the military sects of the Sikhs were making encroachments upon the territories of the emperor. The British East India Company arrived in India at the beginning of the seventeenth century after the Portuguese, French and the Dutch and established itself first at Surat and then in three principal trading points, Madras, Bombay and Calcutta. The rivalry of the French at Pondicherry and the British led to their intriguing in local Indian politics, each side seeking support to oust the other. The result was that both British and French began to raise armies, and during the Seven Years War the French power was broken by the defeat of the Nawab of Bengal at the hands of Clive at the battle of Plassey in 1757 and in the south below Madras at Wandewash in 1760. Traditionally the danger to India had always come from the north, for which reason the Mogul capital was established in Delhi. On the southern periphery of the Mogul empire authority had never been strong and was at the time of the Seven Years War in decline. Gradually the Company began to establish itself as an Indian territorial power.

One Indian state was like another. In 1760 the Company achieved virtual overlordship of Bengal, subject to the payment of a tribute to the Mogul emperor, but Indian methods of government necessarily seemed to British officials arbitrary. Clive was willing to work in collaboration with Indians, but Warren Hastings in 1772 established in Bengal, Bihar and Orissa a purely British administration. Beyond the areas of British control unstable government continued to exist. The Mahrattas gave continual trouble and Tippoo, Sultan of Mysore, proved no better. The consequence was that the British in India were by circumstances led into a policy of nibbling conquest. Under the Marquis Wellesley, who took up office as Governor-General in 1798, a forward policy was adopted and Tippoo overthrown in 1799. Sir Arthur Wellesley, his brother, afterwards the Duke of Wellington, delivered the Mahrattas a crushing blow at Assaye in September 1803. All this was done largely with Indian troops. Gradually during the first half of the nineteenth century British conquest was continued, until by 1856 almost the whole of the Indian sub-continent with lower Burma and Ceylon was brought under control, whether by direct rule or by the appointment of advisers to the native rulers. The ease with which this was done may in part be explained by the fact that only a very small section of the Indian population was affected, the Indian ruling classes, who

were frequently corrupt. The common people of India benefited by
their change of ruler.

It seemed that when a British administrator set foot in India
during the nineteenth century his attitude of mind changed. In the
old days of the eighteenth century the officers of the Company hob-
nobbed with the Indians and many of them took Indian wives,
accepting Indian standards of conduct and behaviour. After 1815 the
climate of opinion began to change. British officials developed the
outlook of the princely despots in eighteenth-century Europe, determined to use their autocratic powers to improve the lot of the
common people and to impose upon the Indians European conceptions of law and order. The governor-general appointed in 1828, Lord
William Bentinck, put down the practice of *suti*, by which Hindu
widows were placed under a moral obligation to throw themselves
upon their husbands' funeral pyres. Equally determinedly he attacked
the sect of robbers who practised *thugee*, the despatch of their
victims to the after-life by strangling in the name of the goddess,
Kali, for which allegedly meritorious service the thugs were rewarded
with such money and property as they carried. No doubt Bentinck's
policy in this respect was humanitarian, but it was symptomatic of a
new outlook, that the native Indians were to receive what was good
for them, whether they liked it or not. Under Dalhousie, governor-
general from 1848 to 1856, grave offence was given to Indian feeling
by his acting up the doctrine that where natural heirs of an Indian
ruler were absent annexation of his dominions on his death became
possible, whereas the Indian feeling was that in such a situation the
ruler might adopt an heir. He, moreover, looked upon misgovern-
ment by native princes with disfavour and deposed the King of Oudh
in February 1856. Dalhousie was an enthusiast for improvements, the
construction of bridges, the completion of the Ganges Canal, the
building of railways and the linking of India by telegraph in order
that physical unification might bring with it actual political unity.
British government was to take on a harsh appearance, rendered less
attractive with the arrival of European women to marry the officials
and officers in service of the Company, which led to a decline in the
free-and-easy contacts which had previously been the rule.

The year of crisis was 1857. The basic problem was the large
number of Brahmins in the service of the Bengal army. As the highest

caste among the Hindus they resented promotion of men from inferior castes, but they were equally conscious of their status in India as the soldiers of a famous army, which they believed now to be in danger of being diluted by the recruitment of Sikhs, Moslems from the Punjab and Gurkhas from Nepal. There was, moreover, fear that, in view of the fact the governor-general was responsible for maintaining British interests in Persia and controlled Burma and Aden, the rocky citadel in southern Arabia, which Britain had seized for strategic reasons in 1839, they would be required to serve overseas, which by Hindu custom would mean loss of caste. A subsidiary and possibly exaggerated factor is the fact that the cartridges for the new Enfield rifle were required to be bitten before being inserted, and they appeared to be greased, it was claimed, either with cow fat, which would defile a Hindu, or pig fat, which would defile a Moslem. As discontent rose among the Indian troops, so the British strength appeared to be in decline. Troops were removed for service in Europe during the Crimean War, and the remaining European troops were always dispersed in small groups. An overwhelming military advantage seemed to lie with the native army.

A series of mutinies occurred in March 1857 and by May Delhi, the Ganges Valley and Bengal were affected; India south of the river Narbada remained largely free from disorder and the Sikhs of the Punjab, who had been brought under control in the years 1846–9, made no movement in sympathy. Not all of the Bengal army was induced to revolt, but it was found wise to disarm some regiments. The mutineers were usually joined mainly by the discontented elements of the old régime, the landowners of Oudh, who resented the treatment they received from British officials, the Rani of Jhansi, Nana Sahib, the adopted son of the deposed peshwa of Poona, and Brahmins who saw the advance of Christianity as a threat to their religious position, of which the abolition of *suti* was an example. The mutiny was marked by the worst features of Indian warfare under the old system. Europeans, men, women and children, were massacred by the insurgents. The British forces dropped all pretence of themselves conducting a war according to recognized European conventions and replied in kind in spite of the protests of the governor-general, Lord Canning. There was an element of panic in the actions of British troops, who often stood their ground against overwhelmingly superior numbers of Indians and were deeply conscious of their isolation. British reprisals were beyond the limits required by a policy of intimidation, and left behind a legacy of ill-will and resentment.

By the beginning of 1858 the authority of the Company was restored in India, but the home government deprived it of its powers and itself assumed direct control, raising the governor-general to the status of a viceroy. More British troops were sent to India. India continued to be subjected to an enlightened autocratic government, and her resources were rapidly developed. No longer was there any pretence of making concessions to Indian susceptibilities. India was now to be unified with English as the official language and English education pronounced superior to anything India could offer. What the British in India set about creating was an official system distinct from and antipathetic to established ways of life among the Hindus. Among the Moslems the cleavage between the governed and the rulers was less acute. The Moslems were on the whole less politically conscious than the Hindus and, moreover, had a religion which had at least some affinity with Christianity. With the Indian mutiny there was among the Hindus a tendency to turn back to traditionalism, whereas earlier there had been a willingness to learn from the European. It was too early to think of an Indian nationalism, but the British administration by linking all the Indian provinces with railways was gradually to give the Hindus a consciousness of brotherhood and strength.

III. SOUTH-EAST ASIA AND THE EAST INDIAN ISLANDS

South-East Asia and the East Indies have never been subject to one universal Empire. It was an area of tropical storms and heavy rainfall, amounting in some places to over 200 inches a year. Most of the region was covered with jungle forests, and the population tended to be concentrated in three centres, Java, Bangkok and Hanoi. On the mainland the culture was Hindu and Chinese, but in the islands Hindu and Arab. From the seventeenth century the Dutch East India Company was the predominant power in the islands, with the administrative centre of its empire at Batavia (Jakarta). The East Indies had been coveted originally because they were a source of spices, but the Dutch had recognized that there was a danger of overproduction which would depress the price on the European markets. They therefore not only preserved their own monopoly of the trade but also confined the production of cloves to the island of Amboina and of nutmeg and mace to the Banda Islands. It was the policy of the Company to destroy surplus spice trees and expeditions were undertaken for this purpose. The result was that the Dutch spread ruin and devastation throughout the area at the same time as they made themselves a power and imposed a measure of unity upon the islands which they had never possessed before. By the eighteenth century the Company was running into difficulties because the dividends it paid to its shareholders were too high, while the costs of administration and the continual wars placed a heavy burden upon its finances. The policy of the Company was to buy spices cheap and sell dear, with the result that the native population could not afford to buy European or even Indian goods. The Dutch therefore never established a considerable market in their dominions, and the company was forced to float loans in order to maintain its dividends.

The policy of the Dutch defeated its ends. The British and French began planting spices in their own tropical dominions, while the more orderly development of British India meant that a powerful competitor was arising. The native population, moreover, in the face of Dutch punitive expeditions frequently took to piracy, which was regarded as an honourable occupation. The crisis of the Company came with the war between Britain and France in 1779. In the following year the United Provinces, controlled by the commercial interests, joined with France against Britain. This action was without much significance in Europe, but it cut off the East Indies from the United Provinces, and for this reason spices accumulated in the east until the end of the war. By the treaty of Paris of 1784 the Dutch conceded to Britain the right of free trade in the Indian seas, and in this manner opened the way to the destruction of their monopoly. The indebtedness of the Dutch East India Company increased from 74,000,000 guilden in 1789 to 96,000,000 in 1791. In 1795 French troops overran the Dutch Netherlands and established the Batavian Republic. The Stadholder, William V, took refuge in England and could do nothing else than place Dutch overseas possessions under the protection of British Government. In 1796 Britain occupied the Cape of Good Hope and Ceylon, but in view of her vast commitments could do nothing for the moment for the East Indies. In 1799 the Dutch East India Company was wound up, but Louis Bonaparte attempted to restore the position. Herman Willem Daendels arrived in Java in January 1808 in order to keep the British out.

Daendels increased the army and enlisted new regiments of native troops to defend the island. Efforts were made to establish a proper judiciary, and a fresh administrative division of the island was made. His Napoleonic zest had one drawback. His policy required money and this was raised by harsh exaction of taxes, which forfeited the loyalty of the local population. Though he was recalled in 1810, the governor-general of India, Lord Minto, decided in 1811 that an expedition must be sent to Java to prevent the French from organizing a base. The British government remained under the obligation to restore the East Indies to the Dutch. It is possible to discern a difference between Lord Minto, who wished only to expel the French, and Thomas Stamford Raffles, who was appointed lieutenant-governor of Java after the Dutch capitulation in September 1811. Minto expected Raffles to administer the island justly, but Raffles thought that he had an opportunity of building up British influence among the local peoples and eventually of bringing the area under British control. He therefore continued the work of administrative reform and attempted to get rid of the worst features in the Dutch system. An effort was made to put down slavery and imprisonment for debt, and the use of torture was forbidden in judicial inquiry. The government was declared to be the owner of the soil and the basis of its finances to be a uniform land tax. In return he was ready to abandon the Dutch eighteenth-century system of forced deliveries of produce and to grant to the native farmer the right to dispose of part of his crops, but such a reform could have been introduced only after a land survey, which would have required time. Raffles soon came under the criticism before the British East India Company, which was bearing the expense of his administration, and he was recalled in 1816. Castlereagh was in any case determined to strengthen the Dutch in Europe and wished to re-establish them in the East as soon as possible.

The British presence in South-East Asia was, however, now established. One of the problems of British rule in the eighteenth century was that the Coromandel Coast, the seas off eastern seaboard of India, were dangerous during the monsoon season of October to November, and it had been British practice to withdraw vessels of war to Bombay, which could not return to Madras before April. This exposed Madras to attack from French warships based upon the island of Mauritius. For this reason there had always been an interest in an alternative base in which ships might refit during the monsoons. At the same time trade with China was growing and a base between India and China was considered desirable. Both Penang and Malacca in the Malay peninsula were considered, but it was Raffles who hit upon the solution of securing in 1819 the lease of Singapore, a virtually uninhabited island at the tip of the peninsula, from the Sultan of Johore. His view was fundamentally a strategic one: 'What Malta is in the West, that may Singapore become in the East.' It was certainly not the intention of the British government to undertake the penetration of Malaya; it was not until 1867 that a forward policy was undertaken there. The fundamental aim was to establish an entente with the Dutch and put an end to the rivalry which might weaken the new Kingdom of the Netherlands. As a result of the Anglo-Dutch treaty of 17 March 1824 spheres of influence were established by the British surrender of footholds in Sumatra and the Dutch undertaking to cede Malacca and not to construct posts in the Malay peninsula. It was British policy to put down piracy and keep the seas clear for the China trade. One curious result of the campaigns against the Dyak pirates in Borneo was that Sir James Brooke established himself as a hereditary absolute sovereign in Sarawak, which did not become a British protectorate until 1888.

The Dutch attempted to repair their damaged fortunes in Java and retained much that Raffles had done during his short administration, including his system of taxation, though with a collective rather than an individual assessment, but they succeeded only in provoking a war which lasted from 1825 to 1830. In January 1830 was established the 'culture system', the basis of which was the concept that the Javanese peasants, ignorant of what crops might yield a profit in the European markets, should receive direction upon what to plant and in lieu of taxation surrender a portion of them to the government. This was in effect the restoration of the forced delivery system of the eighteenth century and, being imposed after the end of the war, was regarded as punitive in its intent. When the Belgian revolution broke out in August 1830 a great strain was placed on Dutch finances to keep the army in the field, and the home government began to rely upon contributions from Java to sustain its cause. A measure of reform designed to improve the condition of Java in this way produced only further discontent. Land laid aside for the cultivation of crops which could be sold in Europe could not be used for food production. Rice famines occurred in 1843 and 1848–50. It was only in 1848, when the home government submitted to domestic pressures, that the affairs of the colonies came under the control of the Dutch parliament. An ordinance of 1854 established from 1856 a governor-general and a council, expressly instructed to ensure that the culture system did not dislocate food production. A number of unprofitable cultures were abolished, but not all. It was only in 1864 that the East Indies budget was submitted to the scrutiny of the Dutch parliament. Dutch policy tended to be mean and narrow and retained much of the spirit of the seventeenth and eighteenth centuries.

IV. THE OPENING OF THE CHINESE EMPIRE

There is a certain similarity between the situations which faced modern India and modern China when the Europeans first reached the Orient in strength. The traditional threat to both of these empires had come from the north. This was a land danger, and therefore in both cases the capitals had been situated in the north. In India the capital was at Delhi, while in China it was at Pekin. The Europeans, however, in both cases came by sea. The administrative structure of these empires was unsuited to meet a danger from an unexpected quarter. Penetration of both the Indian and the Chinese empires presented no insuperable difficulties for the occidental powers.

The vulnerability of the Chinese Empire is to some extent explained by its administrative structure. China was controlled by the Manchu dynasty, which was alien to China and never really accepted by the native Chinese. The Manchus inherited a system of checks and balances, which in effect left all real control in the hands of the Emperor. The supreme organ in the state was the Grand Secretariat, the Neiko, supplemented after 1729 by the Grand Council. They were composed of the Emperor's secretaries and assistant-secretaries. The administration consisted of six Boards: civil appointments,

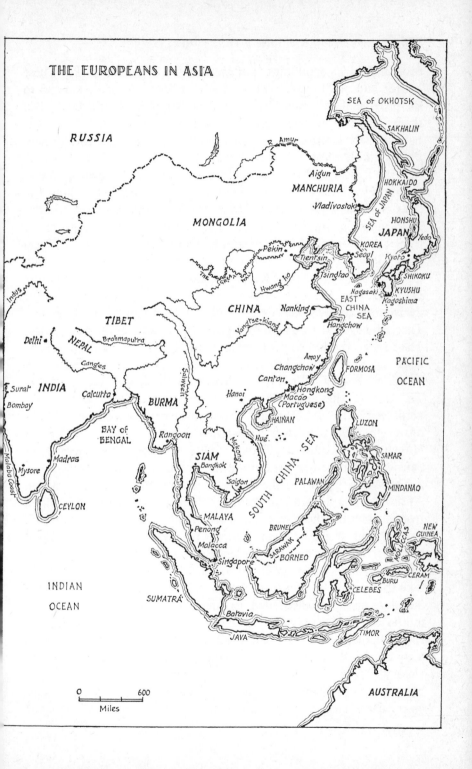

THE EUROPEANS IN ASIA

RUSSIA

SEA of OKHOTSK

SAKHALIN

R. Amur

Aigun

MANCHURIA

Vladivostok

HOKKAIDO

MONGOLIA

SEA of JAPAN

HONSHU

JAPAN

Yedo

Pekin

KOREA

Seoul

Kyoto

Tientsin

Tsingtao

SHIKOKU

THE GREAT WALL

Hwang ho

Nagasaki

KYUSHU

Kagoshima

CHINA

Nanking

EAST CHINA SEA

TIBET

Yangtse-kiang

Hangchow

Delhi

NEPAL

Brahmaputra

PACIFIC OCEAN

Indus

Ganges

Amoy

Changchow

FORMOSA

Salween

Canton

Surat

INDIA

Calcutta

Hanoi

Hongkong

Macao

(Portuguese)

Bombay

BURMA

HAINAN

LUZON

BAY of BENGAL

Rangoon

Hué

SAMAR

Madras

Mekong

SIAM

SOUTH CHINA SEA

Mysore

Bangkok

PALAWAN

MINDANAO

CEYLON

Saigon

MALAYA

BRUNEI

NEW GUINEA

Malaba Coast

Penang

Malacca

SARAWAK

MOLUCCAS

Singapore

BORNEO

CERAM

BURU

CELEBES

INDIAN OCEAN

SUMATRA

Batavia

TIMOR

JAVA

0   600

Miles

AUSTRALIA

revenue, war, ceremonies, punishments and public works. These boards had no authority. They could not send instructions direct to the provincial governors. No single member of the boards controlled them. They simply made recommendations to the Emperor, upon the basis of which orders were issued direct by the Emperor himself. Parallel with these institutions was the Censorate. The Censorate inspected local and central government, checking the memoranda prepared by the Boards and submitting reports direct to the Emperor; the Censorate was empowered to impeach any official in the administration except the Emperor himself. The provinces were governed by governors-general and governors, who were responsible for local administration, public order and the collection of taxes; they reported direct to the throne and were ex-officio members of the Censorate. Under this system political power was so separated that no effective decision could be taken except with the approval of the Emperor. The system worked well enough, provided that there was no urgency. The Emperor could control his dominions easily enough if problems arose north of Pekin, but in the relatively peaceful parts of China decisions were submitted to the process of check and counter-check. The last of the able Manchu Emperors was Chien Lung, who abdicated in 1796. Yet even in his reign there were signs of a breakdown. In 1796 there was a revolt of the White Lotus Society in Hupeh and Szechwan. These revolts revealed that there were deficiencies in the organization of the standing army.

The standing army of the Empire had a pyramidical organization. At the top was the army of the Eight Banners, composed of Manchu troops. Beneath them was the army of the Green Standard, which consisted of native Chinese. Already by the beginning of the nineteenth century there was a tendency to enlist local militia from the provinces. The system employed by the army was to use the militia to take the first shock of attack, then to employ the army of the Green Standard and, if all else failed, to throw in the Eight Banners. In any military contest the allegedly élite Manchu troops of the Empire, the Eight Banners, rarely made contact with the enemy, but it was they who under the pyramidical organization took the credit for any victory. There was by the beginning of the nineteenth century a breakdown of discipline among the regular troops. The government, on the other hand, had reservations with regard to the employment of militia, paid from local treasuries, lest military control should pass from the central authorities into the hands of the provincial governors. For this reason when the Europeans appeared in strength at the beginning of the nineteenth century the Manchu empire was not well equipped militarily to meet the threat they presented.

The European powers met with considerable vexation in dealing with the Chinese Empire. These difficulties arose mainly in the collection of customs dues. The rates were uncertain and officials tended to overcharge Europeans. The Chinese Empire, moreover, imposed limitations upon the ports through which Europeans might trade. The principal port of trade was Canton, but when efforts were made to extend trade to other ports the Chinese system proved equally unsatisfactory. Trade between China and the European states was controlled by the so-called Hong, a monopoly or corporation of individuals entrusted with the purchase of occidental goods. Irregularities arose because when disputes occurred the foreign merchants could not protest direct to the Chinese administration, but must pass their complaints through the Hong, which enjoyed an official status. In other words, the occidental merchants were compelled to make their complaints through interested parties. There were, moreover, restrictions imposed upon the areas of residence of foreigners in China, which proved exceedingly irksome.

The prime difficulty of the occidental states in dealing with China arose from the origin of Chinese diplomatic procedure. For the Chinese the foreigners were originally the barbarian nations of the north. When the Europeans appeared in the south the Chinese central administration attempted to apply the same procedure which they had developed with regard to the nomads of the northern frontier. It was outside all Chinese comprehension that there might be other civilizations in the world as valid as their own and beyond the bounds of possibility that in fact there might be civilizations which exceeded in technical skill the ancient arts of China. In 1793 Britain attempted to establish direct contact with China by the despatch of Lord Macartney's mission to Pekin. Difficulties of procedure immediately arose. Macartney refused to perform the kowtow ceremony before the Emperor, a form of prostration, though in fact the Emperor Chien Lung out of curiosity received him. Extension of trading concessions was nevertheless refused. In July 1816 Lord

Amhert's mission met with equal lack of success. He too refused to perform the kowtow and in view of his inability to fulfil the requirements of Chinese court etiquette he was requested to leave. In July 1834, however, Lord Napier appeared with an order to take a letter direct to the Chinese provincial governor of Kwantung. This in Chinese opinion was an irregularity, because Lord Napier should have acted through the Hong. Chinese officials persisted in the view that the Europeans must observe the correct diplomatic procedure. The basic difficulty remained. The Chinese, confident in the strength of their own position, could not realize that the diplomatic forms developed for relations with frontier peoples could not be applied to the great states which had arisen in Europe. Indeed, the Chinese administration had little impression of the rapid growth of power in Europe. It was supposed by the Chinese that the rest of the world was dependent upon China for supplies of tea and rhubarb.

It should not, however, be thought that ignorance of the true situation in Europe was synonymous with lack of intelligence among Chinese officials. One of the questions which has vexed the relations of China and the West was the Opium Trade. The trade in opium developed in the eighteenth century, and addiction was firmly established in southern China. The problem is to be explained in the light of the British trade system in the Far East. British goods were exported to India, and with the money obtained by their sale Indian goods were purchased, which were then sold on the Chinese market. By this means the British merchants were able to buy Chinese goods for import into Britain. In theory the development of this system of multinational trade ought to have benefited all parties, but in the eighteenth century 50 per cent of the India–China trade was accounted for by opium. When the trade was legal, part of the dues on opium was forwarded to the Chinese treasury, but, when the trade was made illegal, Chinese officials merely imposed the same dues and pocketed the whole of the revenue for themselves. Corruption was not, however, the main problem. It was the drain upon Chinese specie which in fact produced an economic crisis of great magnitude. The result was currency disorder and deflation.

At the beginning of the nineteenth century there were two tendencies in Chinese official thinking. There was the policy associated with Hsü Nai-Chi, who in a memorial of 1836 proposed the legaliza-

tion of the opium trade, but only upon the basis of barter. Opium
might be obtained only by the exchange of Chinese goods and the
drain of specie checked. It was proposed, moreover, that the use of
opium should be prohibited to soldiers, officials and students. Hsü
Nai-Chi saw the problem primarily as an economic question rather
than as a social evil. On the other hand, there was the Chinese official
Huang Chueh-Tzu, who believed in absolute prohibition. He was
in favour of rigorous punishment for the use of opium, which for
him was a source of social demoralization. In the year 1836 the policy
of legalization was adopted, with a consequent expansion of the
opium trade. Abandonment of control led soon to currency difficulties. Therefore in May 1838 Huang Chueh-Tzu obtained the ear
of the Emperor, and a stoppage in the opium traffic was ordered.
The official Lin Tse-Hsü was sent to Kwantung to put down the
trade. He arrived in Canton in March 1839, but already the governor,
Cheng, was enforcing the order for prohibition. This led to a clash
with the British merchants and negotiations with the British agent in
Macao, Charles Elliot. On 7 July 1839, moreover, a Chinese inn-
keeper was murdered by British sailors on Chinese territory. Elliot
himself tried the case. Minor punishments were imposed and the
offenders sent home to England to serve their sentences. The Chinese
for their part demanded that the offenders should be surrendered to
them for trial and punishment. In addition, therefore, to the Chinese
anxiety concerning the effects of the opium trade there arose a conflict of sovereignties, rendered all the more difficult because no
regular diplomatic relations existed between Britain and China.

Lin Tse-Hsü thought that the British authorities would yield to
Chinese demands. The British for their part attempted intimidation
and three Chinese gunboats were sunk. Outraged by this act of war
the Chinese government in January 1840 ordered the stoppage of all
trade with Europeans at Canton. The British government yielded to
the pressure of the mercantile classes in the House of Commons, and
in April 1840 the decision was taken to make war upon China.

The object of the British expedition to the Pearl River was not
merely to blockade Canton. The fleet moved north and on 2 July
attempted to deliver a message at Amoy, but the Chinese, unaware
of the significance of the white flag, fired upon the vessel appointed
to deliver the message. Tinghai was occupied and at length on

10 July the British authorities succeeded in conveying their message, but the Chinese officials who received it dared not report its full contents to the Emperor. For this reason no satisfactory reply was forthcoming and the British fleet sailed to the Pei-Ho River itself, threatening the very capital of the Manchu Empire at Pekin. The approach of the British fleet induced a sense of caution in Pekin, and a promise was made to open negotiations in Canton. When the negotiations opened in December 1840 the Chinese expected that the British would be satisfied with commercial concessions, but in fact a demand was made for the cession of Hong Kong to Britain. This the Chinese plenipotentiary, Chi-Shan, could not grant. In exasperation the British decided to coerce the Chinese and under the threat of force the Chinese consented to the Chuenpi Convention of 20 January 1841, by which Hong Kong was ceded, the port of Canton re-opened, and agreement reached upon direct official contacts; the Chinese, moreover, were to pay a 6,000,000 dollar indemnity to cover the costs of the British expedition.

Once more the comedy of errors was repeated. The convention was repudiated by both sides. From the British home government's point of view the indemnity was too small and the cession of Hong Kong equivocal in the sense that it was made conditional upon the payment of duties. In the Chinese court's view Chi-Shan had exceeded his powers. When the Emperor discovered that Hong Kong had been ceded he decided that the army must be sent to coerce the British. The British for their part occupied strategic points on the Pearl river and compelled the Chinese imperial commander to seek a truce, which was agreed upon 27 May 1841. The Chinese undertook to withdraw their troops sixty miles from Canton, but the Emperor remained misinformed of the real situation. He was given to believe that the British had asked for the truce and therefore gave his assent to it on condition that the British did not resume the opium trade.

The arrival of Sir Henry Pottinger as minister-plenipotentiary in Macao in August 1841 marked a change in British policy. Pottinger's instructions were to avoid negotiations with officials in Canton and to go north to seize ports at the mouth of the Yangtse or the Pei-Ho. His object was to open direct negotiations with the Manchu Court. Amoy and Tinghai were occupied and most of east Chekiang came under British control. The imperial position was now clearly shaken and I'Ching was appointed 'Yang Wei Chiang Chun'—'The General to increase Prestige', but the Chinese Empire was to suffer further humiliations. On 10 August 1842 the great Chinese city of Nanking was stormed. Hitherto the Chinese officials in contact with the British had been unable to convince the Emperor of the serious situation. Now the Emperor at last saw for himself that peace must be made. On 29 August 1842 was concluded the treaty of Nanking. Hong Kong was ceded. The Chinese were required to open the ports of Canton, Foochow, Amoy, Ningpo and Shanghai to Britain. Uniform tariffs were to be paid, and when once the British goods had been taxed at the port of entry they might be transported to any point in the interior without regard to internal Chinese tariffs. In their diplomatic relations the Chinese were to accord British representatives equality, but in fact the indemnity of 20,000,000 dollars agreed by the Chinese pointed to their own inferiority.

The Chinese had paid dearly for their introspective attitude. Opium had been the original cause of the conflict, but the disaster of 1842 would never have befallen the Manchu Empire if it had not been for the Chinese supposition that the whole world was subject to Chinese dominion. Confucius in his desire to promote Chinese unity had stated: 'In the sky there is no more than one sun and above the people there is no more than one Emperor.' By the beginning of the nineteenth century this text was interpreted to mean that the Emperor was the supreme authority in the universe. In the conflict there clashed two differing concepts. For the Chinese law amounted to an administrative decision by the Emperor or his officials, a concept so alien to the British mind with its belief in the rule of law, independent of the executive, that there was no arbitrament except by force of arms. Yet in appeal to superior force Britain made a cardinal error. It was assumed that different legal conceptions, backward techniques and administrative chaos meant that China lacked civilization. British arrogance did not destroy China, because China was too large to conquer. It rather presented a challenge to Chinese civilization, which emerged once more to assert itself against the alien Manchu dynasty. By opening China to western trade Great Britain undermined the authority of the régime, which, though established at the beginning of the seventeenth century, attracted no great loyalty among the native Chinese.

Clearly the financial and economic position of the Manchu dynasty had been considerably weakened, though it is possible to overemphasize this aspect of the question. More important in the first instance was the destruction of the Emperor's prestige. The corruption of the army had been revealed and the technical superiority of the British troops. No longer did the native Chinese hold the Manchus in awe. There arose in China the so-called 'Long Haired Bandits'—long-haired because they refused to grow the pigtail which the Manchus imposed upon all Chinamen as a symbol of loyalty to the régime. Slogans began to arise demanding the expulsion of the Manchus and the restoration of the Ming dynasty. The most serious threat to the Manchus was the rebellion of the Taipings or 'God Worshippers' in the province of Kwangsi. The founder of this sect was Hung Hsiu Chuan, a failed candidate for entry into the Chinese civil service, who in his disappointment turned to a distorted form of Christianity, elevating himself to membership of the Trinity. In this Trinity were God the Father, Jesus Christ, known as the Elder Brother, and the earthly manifestation, the Heavenly King, who was none other than Hung Hsiu Chuan himself, sent to this world to kill all demons and bring about the 'Great Peace'. In 1850 there occurred a clash with government troops, and the Taipings were compelled to raise an army. At first the Taipings were not interested in conquering territory. They marched through the countryside enlisting supporters, who burned down their houses in order that they might have nothing to return to. In March 1853, however, the Taipings established themselves in Nanking and put their ideas into a political form. The Taiping state was based upon a theocratic system, with public ownership of land and the equal allotment of surplus money. The Taipings attracted support because they appealed to the current anti-Manchu sentiment, but their agrarian policy met with the opposition of the peasantry and their western ideology with the dislike of the scholar-administrators trained in the traditional Confucian philosophy. There was, moreover, considerable nepotism within the Taiping régime and before long the appearance of traditional Chinese sensuality. The Heavenly King, Hung Hsiu Chuan, is said to have had no less than sixty-eight concubines and 300 female attendants. There were, moreover, intrigues and disputes among the leaders of the Taiping hierarchy.

The native Chinese resistance to the Taipings is associated with Tseng Kuo-Fan, the Vice-minister of the Board of Ceremonies, who was sent to Hunan to organize the province. Tseng Kuo-Fan realized that he must enlist a militia and train it upon professional lines before he could launch an offensive against the Taipings. He resisted pressure from the Emperor for early action and eventually received from him a letter of understanding. In short, the Emperor admitted the inability of the Manchus to repress the Taipings without Chinese soldiers. Already, therefore, the balance of military power had moved back into the hands of the native Chinese. In May 1854 Tseng Kuo-Fan launched his first offensive against the Taipings, but progress was very slow. Tseng's long campaign against the Taipings had been based upon appeal to the traditional moral values of Confucianism. True to this philosophy Tseng did not use his power to challenge the imperial authority. Nevertheless, the whole pattern of future military organization was now established. In future armies would be raised upon the model of Hunan from the native Chinese population. Internally the Taiping rebellion accelerated the process of the decentralization of power. In the end the real power of the Court was to extend not much farther than the provinces immediately around Pekin.

The treaty of Nanking with Britain and the subsequent treaty of Whampoa between France and China of 1844 were not entirely satisfactory. In February 1855 Great Britain suggested to France that fresh pressure should be put upon China to obtain an enlargement of their trading privileges. An excuse was easy to find. A French missionary was murdered in the interior of China in 1856 and a vessel flying the British flag, the lorca *Arrow*, was seized by Chinese officials. Canton was placed under Franco-British occupation in December 1857 and a small expedition was sent north to the Pei-Ho river to coerce the Emperor. By threatening the imperial capital in 1858 the powers secured their aims with the opening of fresh treaty ports and, above all, the navigation of the great artery of China, the river Yangtse, as far as Hankow as soon as the civil war against the Taipings had ended, but in 1859 the imperial Court refused to ratify the conventions and declined to receive representatives. In September–October 1860 troops of the two powers fought their way into the imperial capital, Pekin, whence the Emperor had

fled. By the treaties of Pekin of 25 October 1860 the Chinese government confirmed the conventions of Tientsin of 1858 and in addition
opened Tientsin itself and Nanking as free ports. China was, moreover, compelled to accept permanent embassies in Pekin. In order
to put China's relations with the occidental powers on a proper
footing a foreign office was established, the Tsungli Yamen, and
relations gradually improved. The western powers for their part in
order to obtain the maximum advantages from the treaties of Pekin
offered their aid to suppress the Taiping rebellion. Levies were
organized under foreign officers, and the Taipings were gradually
driven back. On 19 July 1864 Tseng Kuo-Fan took the Taiping capital
of Nanking.

In theory the authority of the Emperor ought everywhere to have
been restored, but in July 1861 the Emperor Hsien-Feng died in
Jehol, leaving no direct heir. His wife, the so-called Eastern Empress,
was childless, but the concubine, Tzu-hsi, known as the Western
Empress, had a son, Tsai-Ch'un, who was declared emperor, though
he was only five years of age. A regency was therefore necessary,
which was dominated by the Western Empress, who remained the
effective ruler of China until her death in 1908. When the Emperor
died in 1874 another child, Kwang-Hsü, was elevated to the throne.
The administration was demoralized by a central government in the
hands of the Empress's eunuchs. At the top all foreign influences
were resisted. Political power in the provinces was exercised by the
governors, raising their own troops. The Court in effect controlled
only the province of Chili with any certainty. Already the Manchu
system was in a state of decay, but the process by which the Chinese
themselves were to throw off their ancient tradition of accepting
central control by an emperor was to be long and slow.

V. THE OPENING OF JAPAN

There was a superficial resemblance between the system in early
nineteenth-century China and the system in Japan. Both were
virtually closed countries, but here the similarity ended. Within
Japan it was recognized that the Emperor was sovereign, but his
political power had long resided with the Generalissimo or Shogun,
sometimes referred to as the Tycoon, assisted by a council, the
Bakufu. The situation in western eyes was confused. There was even

talk of there being a 'spiritual emperor' and a 'temporal emperor' in Japan, but from the Japanese point of view it was clearly understood that the Emperor was the ultimate sovereign.

The turning point in the history of modern Japan was the establishment of the Shogunate of Tokugawa Ieyasu in 1600. On 21 October 1600 was fought a great battle at Sekigahara in central Japan between two rival groups of chieftains. From this struggle the Tokugawa clan emerged victorious and Tokugawa Ieyasu established himself as Shogun and therefore as virtual master of Japan with the centre of his administration at Yedo (the modern Tokio); it is true that Tokugawa Ieyasu resigned in 1603, but he remained the real repository of power in Japan during his lifetime. In the course of time, however, the Shogun himself found that his powers were circumscribed by the members of the Bakufu. By the beginning of the nineteenth century neither the Emperor nor the Shogun wielded actual direct personal power.

The policy of the Tokugawa Shogunate was indeed a progressive one. Its aim was to put an end to endemic civil war by keeping the feudal lords under control. Nevertheless, the means by which public order was preserved imposed a certain political inertia upon Japan. The feudal lord (daimyo) was controlled by an elaborate system. No arms might be brought into Yedo, for fear of depositing there the instruments of a coup d'état. The feudal lords were themselves required to spend alternate years in Yedo and to leave their families there as hostages for their good behaviour when they visited their fiefs. Nevertheless, opposition was always present in Japan.

The nobles of south-western Japan, who had fought against the Tokugawa in 1600, were permanently excluded from the counsels of state. For them at least there could be no preferment. The peace policy, moreover, of the Shogunate led to impoverishment of the warrior class, the samurai. With frequent civil wars there had always been the possibility of a division of the spoils, but opportunity for such advancement ended at the beginning of the seventeenth century. In consequence, some samurai fell into the clutches of moneylenders and there was the growth of a class of unattached samurai, the so-called *rônin*, who constituted a potential threat to the peace. The Tokugawa Shogunate was extremely sensitive to the possibility of the opposition's getting assistance from abroad. Because Japan was an island, this meant the opportunity of the dissident elements' obtaining artillery and gunpowder from the Europeans. The Japanese were well aware of Europe. There had been a strong Christian influence in Japan in the seventeenth century, which was never entirely to disappear. In 1637, however, the Shogunate adopted a xenophobic policy, refusing permission for Japanese to travel abroad and imposing the death penalty for disobedience. Foreign relations were canalized through a single point of control, the Dutch factory on the island of Deshima at Nagasaki. For all the limitations imposed upon contact with the west, Deshima remained a window on the western world. For this reason Japan was not entirely ignorant of what was happening in Europe, but knowledge was much garbled. In 1716 the Shogunate permitted the importation of foreign books, provided that they contained no mention of Christianity. Weird ideas were current and there was no direction of studies concerning Europe, which were confined to a small literate class. It is difficult to find great differences between the Japanese and the Chinese in their attitude towards Europeans, but, if a difference is to be found, it must lie in the completeness of Chinese confidence in the validity of their own civilization and a certain utilitarian curiosity about the west among a small minority of educated Japanese.

The position of Japan in relation to the European powers and the United States was more favourable than that of China. The United States of America was quick to follow up Great Britain in the exploitation of the Chinese market. It was considered desirable that American ships should, if necessary, be able to put into Japanese ports. The Russians for their part under Muraviev-Amursky were beginning to establish themselves in force upon the Pacific (see below pp. 390-2). They were therefore anxious to draw upon the supplies of Japan for the development of their power in the Far East. In other words, the United States and Russia thought of Japan as a potential friend. It was the Americans who made the first demonstration. In 1853 Commodore Perry sailed into Yedo Bay and announced his intention of returning in the following year to obtain an answer to the requests which he transmitted to the Shogun. These requests amounted to an ultimatum for the opening of Japanese ports to American shipping. Undoubtedly the appearance of the American squadron was a shock of the first magnitude. By Japanese standards the American ships were huge. It appeared that the greatness of American power was out of all proportion to the resources of Japan.

The arrival of the Americans set in motion a political crisis. The Shogunate realized that it could not oppose the Americans, lest a blockade dislocate the seaborne trade of Japan and lead to food shortages in the capital. On the other hand, if the Shogunate failed to offer resistance the Shogun or in his full title the *sei-i hai shogun*—the Barbarian-Subduing-Great-General—would become a laughing stock. The very constitutional system in Japan itself created a difficulty. For all his powerlessness the Emperor was still technically the sovereign of Japan. There was always an alternative régime around which the dissident daimyos might rally. In its dilemma the Shogunate decided to call in the daimyos for consultation, a course of action which had never since its original victory been undertaken by the Tokugawa family. This act amounted to nothing less than a confession of weakness in the face of the foreigner. The arrival of a ship of the Russian navy under Putyatin in August 1853 and again in January 1854 revealed that Commodore Perry's visit was not an isolated incident. Contact with the occidental nations would be the normal pattern of the future. The Shogunate found itself obliged to yield to the inevitable. On 31 March 1854 was concluded between the United States and the Shogunate the treaty of Kanagawa, by which the ports of Hakodate and Shimoda were opened to American ships. In February 1855 a similar treaty was concluded with Russia which opened Nagasaki in addition to Shimoda and Hakodate to Russian subjects, with the privilege of extra-territoriality. It was not long before other nations established themselves in Japan. The opening of the Crimean War in Europe sent British vessels in pursuit of Putyatin. For the Japanese the foreigner had come to stay.

The consequence of the sudden influx of Europeans was loss of prestige by the Shogunate. Its traditional policy had been one of xenophobia, but now it took upon itself the responsibility of admitting western influences into Japan. The imperial court at Kyoto, however, was not involved in the opening of Japan to the occidental powers. Contact with the west was necessary to Japan, but it was equally as contrary to Japanese tradition as it was to the Chinese. Upon the Shogunate fell the odium of admitting the foreigner. It was the Shogunate which began the policy of westernization. It was the imperial court which was to reap the benefit.

A centre of opposition to the Shogunate had always existed in south-western Japan and in the island of Kyushu, which had never reconciled itself to the Tokugawa system. Slogans began to appear of 'Expel the Foreigner' and 'Respect the Emperor'. These xenophobic sentiments were taken seriously by some of the opposition, but they were really designed to complicate the relations of the Shogunate with the foreign powers. Foreign affairs were the key to internal politics. The more the Shogunate was obliged to knuckle under to the foreigner and even to accelerate the growth of western influences in Japan, the more it undermined its own position. The Shogunate tried to meet the opposition half-way by modifying the system of biennial residence in Yedo and the leaving of hostages in the capital. This was a confession of failure which could be remedied only by the equipping of troops on the European pattern to meet the coming struggle. Equally the Choshu clan with its centre at Shimonseki bought western weapons and began to organize troops on western lines, but for reasons of political tactics the Choshu exploited anti-western sentiment.

In 1862 the Emperor Komei took the initiative. An imperial decree was issued ordering the expulsion of all foreigners by June 1863. The outside world might regard the Shogun as the actual ruler of Japan, but for the Japanese the Emperor remained the sovereign. The Shogunate was placed in a position of intolerable difficulty, because the opposition could attack the foreigner with full legal authority. The Shogunate gave verbal assurances that no action would be taken upon the Emperor's decree, but the opposition seized its opportunity. In June 1863 the Choshu batteries opened fire upon western ships passing through the straits at Shimonoseki and similar action was taken by the Satsuma clan on the island of Kyushu. This action roused the occidental powers to retaliation. British and United States warships razed to the ground the capital of the Satsuma, Kagoshima. In September 1864 the Choshu batteries were silenced by British, Dutch, French and United States warships.

Western action consequently forced the hand of the Choshu and the Satsuma. It was evident that the western powers were immeasurably superior in strength to the forces which the opposition could assemble against them. Conflict with the foreigner actually defeated the very aim of the dissident groups. They had hoped to weaken the Shogunate by their action, but it was they themselves who had suffered. It followed that in future military action should be taken against the authorities in Yedo. In 1866 an alliance was concluded between the Satsuma and the Choshu, which was joined by other powerful groups, including the Tosa and Hizen clans and the merchant family of the Mitsui. Behind this alliance stood the imperial court. In 1866 the Emperor Komei died and was succeeded by the Emperor Meiji, who had not compromised by the xenophobic policy of 1862. The way was open for a direct clash with the Shogunate.

The feudal elements in the opposition wished merely that the Shogun should lay down his powers, but there was a progressive element, especially among the Satsuma and Choshu, which had no intention of facilitating a transfer of power from the Shogunate to a coalition of daimyos. Their aim was a complete sweep of the administration and a thorough reorganization of the state on western lines. The ultimate victory was by no means certain. The French representative, Léon Roches, upheld the party of the Shogun; the British representative, Harry Parkes, supported the claims of the opposition. In November 1867 the Shogun Tokugawa Keiki decided to bow before the storm and lay down his powers, handing them over to the Emperor, but this was clearly only a device for the retention of the substance of power by the Tokugawa clan. In January 1868 a great battle was fought near the imperial capital of Kyoto and the Shogun's army was defeated. The result was that imperial authority was restored and Yedo was renamed Tokio—'The Eastern Capital'.

In theory, the 'Meiji Restoration' was the re-establishment of the old régime with its traditional Shinto philosophy. The revolt had been one of the feudal lords against the Shogunate which had deprived them of their influence, but such was the complexity of politics in Japan that the feudal lords within their own fiefs were controlled by oligarchies of young men bent upon a policy of westernization. Men like Saigo Takamori, Okubo Toshimichi, Kido Koin, Ito Hirobumi, Inoye Kaoru, Itagaki Taisuke and Okuma Shinenobu were the real possessors of political power. Determined to establish the power of

Japan upon a firm footing they surprised even some of their closest followers by cultivating the foreigners rather than expelling them. Symbolic of the new development was the visit of Harry Parkes and his retinue to pay respects to the Emperor in his palace at Kyoto. Set upon by fanatical samurai, the delegation was obliged to postpone the presentation of its compliments. The new authorities used the incident to put an end to attacks upon foreigners. Henceforth, it was decreed, samurai who were guilty of such behaviour would be deprived of their rank and executed by the common executioner. If a member of the samurai caste were deprived of his right of ceremonial suicide, Hara-Kiri, his family by tradition would for ever be disgraced. By this means a social convention of old Japan served the purpose of compelling Japanese to adjust their habits to the practices of the west.

The result was surprisingly modern. The old feudal system was destroyed and in its place set up a system of prefectures, vehicles of political pressure which would have done credit to the etatism of Napoleon I himself. The common people were enlisted into the army in contravention of the old system, by which the samurai alone were entitled to bear arms. Some of the samurai were bitterly discontented with the new system which threatened their social position. They refused to recognize that a period of consolidation and development was necessary and yearned for the traditional occupations of war, but the new oligarchy was determined to wait until the moment when it could engage upon a forward policy upon a scale appropriate to the new conditions of European warfare. Japan had first to build up her strength. A straw in the wind was the introduction of compulsory education in 1872, only two years after the first British education act. The Japanese were to become the most educated of the Asiatic peoples and through education the most receptive of new ideas. Where contact with the west brought about the collapse of the Chinese state under the Manchus, in Japan a strong power began to be built, conscious that it would be able to defeat Manchu China when the time came.

VI. FRANCE IN THE FAR EAST

The area in which France showed most interest was Indo-China, the Nguyen Empire of Cochin China, Annam and Tonking, with its capital at Hué, and Cambodia, theoretically a vassal state of Siam. The area was one in which there was considerable Roman Catholic missionary work and the local rulers showed no disposition to accept Christianity in place of their native Buddhism. Minh Mang and his son and successor, Thien Tri, did not realize that western penetration was to be a permanent feature of the future. Britain's success in opening China, moreover, encouraged France to believe that intervention in Indo-China would be relatively easy. During 1843–5 some French missionaries were under sentence of death and their release was secured by French armed intervention, but it was not until 1857 when the Spanish bishop to Tongking was murdered and Spain was willing to offer France a base in the Philippine Islands that a serious intervention could be considered. In 1857 an ultimatum was delivered to Hué demanding religious freedom for Christians, the establishment of a French commercial station and the admission of a French consul. A landing at Tourane, the port of Hué, made no impression, and the French admiral, Rigault, decided instead to lay siege to Saigon. The emperor, Tu Duc, decided that submission was necessary, and by the treaty of 5 June 1862 ceded the three western provinces of Cochin China to France, opened three ports to France and granted liberty to Christian missionaries to enter the country. In August 1863 a protectorate was established by France over Cambodia. By contrast, Siam by the treaty of 18 April 1855 opened her trade to Britain and subsequently admitted other foreign nations. In consequence of her meek attitude and the fact that Britain was happy to see a weak native state on the eastern frontier of her Burmese possessions Siam survived without experiencing foreign rule. France had gained control of the mouth of the Mekong River. Her aims were annexationist, but there was little she could do to exploit her advantage. French energies for the moment were absorbed in Mexico, while in the second half of the 1860s the situation in Europe was already so serious that Napoleon III's régime could not contemplate expansion in Indo-China.

VII. RUSSIA IN ASIA

Of all the imperial powers Russia was the weakest. The rate of industrial growth in Russia was slower than elsewhere, and the resources of the Russian state did not permit grandiose schemes, but there was a deep consciousness even in her weakness after the Crimean War that she could with some reasonable expectation of success use her position in the centre of the Eurasian land mass to enlarge her control over the sparsely inhabited areas on the north and extend her rule into central Asia.

The appearance of Russia in the Far East as a power began with the appointment of Nikolai Muraviev in 1847 to an oversight of affairs on the northern frontier of China. He was a man of some enlightenment, an advocate of the abolition of serfdom and ready to extend the hand of friendship to the United States, whom he looked upon as a counterweight to Britain in the Far East. It was discovered by an expedition of Nevelskoy, who explored the north Pacific area, that the estuary of the Amur river was navigable. Muraviev wished to establish Russian control over the whole length of the Amur river and control the island of Sakhalin. In 1854, with the consent of the Tsar Nicholas I, a Russian expedition proceeded down the Amur river without meeting opposition from the Manchu Empire. By the Aigun treaty of 1858 the Amur river was declared to be the frontier between the two empires, an achievement which caused Alexander II to grant Muraviev the title of 'Amursky'. As a result of Russia's mediation in the troubles of 1858–60 between China and France and Britain the Manchu dynasty conceded to Russia the Ussuri region in 1860, which enabled her to establish a common frontier with Korea, which was then a vassal state dependent upon the Chinese empire. In 1860 was founded the city of Vladivostok or 'Ruler of the East', a name which represented an aspiration rather than an achievement. Between 1858 and 1860 Russia acquired 400,000 square miles of territory inhabited by 15,000 persons. The problem was one of colonization, but conditions in the area were appalling. Criminals and prostitutes were exported to the region and the Amur and Ussuri Cossacks established, but free citizens did not wish to settle in a region which acquired a bad reputation. By 1867 the population had risen only to 65,000.

With regard to the island of Sakhalin and the Kuriles Russia encountered a problem of relations with Japan. On the whole, Russia cultivated friendship with Japan because the land route between central Russia and the Far East was long and arduous and the victualling of Russia's new dominions would depend largely upon the willingness of Japan to provide supplies. In 1867 a condominium was established in Sakhalin, and the nationals of both states were permitted to settle anywhere, for which reason Russia turned it into a penal settlement for convicts. In 1875 the condominium was replaced by Russian control and Japan granted in return full rights over the Kuriles, except for retaining the privilege of fishing the waters around the island of Sakhalin itself. The geographical problems of Russia were too vast for more than a token occupation, while Japan had yet to build up her resources before she could challenge a European power in the Far East. Already, however, the makings of a struggle were present. Both Japan and Russia had their eyes upon Korea and ultimately Manchuria.

In central Asia the possibility of Russian expansion seemed to offer better chances of tangible success. Central Asia had long given Russians trouble, because the nomads raided across the frontiers or plundered Russian caravans. Central Asia was virtually without frontiers. The total population was between four and five millions in 1850, a mixture of Turkic peoples, the Uzbeks, Turkmens, Kazakhs and Kirgiz, and an Indo-European people, the Tadzhiks, who were akin to the Persians. There were three important political centres, the khanates of Khiva, Bukhara and Kokand, exercising a despotic authority where they could. The difference between taxation and robbery was hard to discern. This was exactly the same chaos which from time to time had appeared in India. It was an area with which no proper diplomatic relations could be established, but it was undoubtedly capable of producing colonial goods, especially cotton, for the use of Russian industry. There were, moreover, good reasons relating to Russia's weakness in Europe for penetration of central Asia. The British were nervous of possible Russian penetration in the direction of Afghanistan, lest the security of their Indian dominions might be threatened. The Russian victory over the Persians and the conclusion of the peace of Turkmanchay in 1828 had filled the Indian government with alarm and despondency. When the Sikh ruler, Ranjit Singh, taking advantages of civil troubles in Afghanistan, seized Peshawar in 1834 and the Persians for their part laid siege to Herat, the governor-general, Auckland, decided upon a forward policy to restore Shah Suja, who had been expelled in 1809, and oust Dost Muhammed from Kabul. The campaign of 1839 proved a success, but the occupation of Kabul was to be of short duration. The Afghans compelled the British forces to retreat in 1841–2 and, though a fresh campaign was undertaken in 1842, Dost Muhammed was able to return to Kabul and resume control. It therefore seemed that Afghanistan was a sensitive spot in British foreign policy, and the nearer Russia could approach it the better, because it would provide an opportunity of weakening British pressure in the Near East, if ever an international crisis arose in Europe.

The first effort of Russia to make inroads into central Asia had been the abortive expedition organized by Perovsky from Orenburg in 1839 against the Khanate of Khiva, which led to a reappraisal of the means by which Russia might make her influence felt. There seemed two possible lines of approach. One route lay from Orenburg in the direction the sea of Aral and the river Sir Darya (Jaxartes) in the direction of Tashkent. A second means of penetration was possible from Semipalatinsk towards Lake Balkhash and the river Ili. In 1847 the fort of Aralskoye was established on the sea of Aral, and in 1853 Perovsky captured Ak-Mechet on the Sir Darya from Kokand troops. In this way the Russians were able to organize a line of communications from the sea of Aral half-way to the town of Turkestan. At the same time penetration was achieved from Semi-palatinsk. In 1847 one of the groups of nomads, the Great Horde of the Kazakhs, accepted Russian sovereignty and the fort of Kopal was founded south of Lake Balkhash. Penetration was continued beyond the river Ili, and in 1854 a fort was founded at Vernoye, the modern Alma Ata. At this moment it seemed that the Russian government might be able to unite the posts established by the Orenburg and Western Siberian commands and embrace the whole of the northern part of the area inhabited by the Kazakh nomads, but the Crimean War intervened and there was left a power vacuum in which columns from the Khanate of Kokand levied tribute from the pastoral peoples of the steppes.

The Crimean War caused Russia to turn her back upon Europe politically and turn inwards upon herself. The demands of foreign policy more than ever required the diversion of pressure from the Near East to the Middle and Far East in order that Great Britain should not be able in future to concentrate all her influence at the Straits. The economic crisis of 1857, moreover, affected Russia severely and the area of central Asia became attractive both as a market and as a source of raw materials. Russia was nevertheless cautious. The Viceroy of the Caucasus, Prince Baryatinsky, would have constructed a railway from the eastern shores of the Caspian into central Asia, but Gorchakov considered such a policy likely to provoke British hostility, because it would make possible the rapid movement of Russian troops to the Afghan frontier. The decision was ultimately taken to continue with the policy which had been begun before the Crimean War, because penetration as far as Tashkent would still leave great mountain barriers between Russia and British India. In 1857–8 N. P. Ignatiev was instructed to survey the situation in central Asia. It was discovered that in the khanates there were in fact no armies worthy of the name and that the rulers of these states could not rely upon the loyalty of their subjects. The war in Italy in 1859 delayed a positive decision, but the appointment of Ignatiev to the directorship of the Department of Asiatic Affairs in the foreign ministry in August 1861 was decisive. The question of an approach in the direction of the Amu Darya (Oxus) or along the Sir Darya had largely been a dispute between the military and the foreign office. Ignatiev and the new minister of war, D. A. Milyutin, joined forces to promote the policy of uniting the Orenburg and Western Siberian posts. An added incentive was the outbreak of the Polish insurrection in January 1863 which caused Russia to wish to draw Britain's attention away from Europe, but it was only in December 1863 that the Tsar Alexander II finally made up his mind and determined upon the union of the posts in the spring of 1864. It would be quite wrong to suppose that Russian officers acted on their own initiative without formal instructions, as is sometimes stated. Russian policy was decided only after a long and careful study. What did surprise them was the ease with which their forces accomplished their tasks. Chernyaev advanced along the Sir Darya and Verevkin marched west from the Western Siberian posts. In June 1864 Turkestan was captured and in September Chimkent. In the following year in June Chernyaev took Tashkent by storm. The success of the small Russian forces against apparently overwhelming odds gave some alarm in St Petersburg, lest it give rise to international repercussions, but in July 1867 the fact of conquest was recognized and the Governor-Generalcy of Turkestan was created under General

THE EXPANSION OF RUSSIA
IN CENTRAL ASIA ~ TO 1868

TOBOLSK

PERM

EKATERINBURG

THE MIDDLE
HORDE

SEMIPALATINSK

AKHMOLINSK

ORENBURG

THE
LITTLE
HORDE

LAKE BALKHASH

THE
GREAT
HORDE

ARALSKOYE

VERNOYE
(Fort)

AK-MECHET

SEA
of
ARAL

TURKESTAN

Sir Darya

KASHGAR

TASHKENT

KHANATE
of KHIVA

KOKAND

KHIVA

KHANATE
of KOKAND

CASPIAN SEA

TURKMENS

SAMARKAND

BUKHARA

TADZHIKS

KHANATE of
BUKHARA

MERV

Amu Darya

AFGHANISTAN

KABUL

HERAT

0   100   200   300   400

Miles

Kaufman, formerly Governor-General of Vilna. Samarkand was added to the Russian dominions in 1868, but here Russia called a halt. The Khanates of Khiva, Bukhara and Kokand were allowed for the meantime to remain independent in order that Russian sovereignty might not extend as far as the Afghan border, but they became in effect satellite states of Russia. Russia had now planted her power firmly in central Asia. The advantage was more economic than strategic in the first place, but Russia's victory seemed greater than it actually was, and a corresponding diplomatic advantage was obtained.

VIII. THE EUROPEAN MIGRANTS

In 1823 President Monroe placed a prohibition upon organized settlement by European states in the New World of the Americas, which with France's undertaking in 1866 to withdraw their troops from Mexico received formal recognition. The British navy patrolled the seas and ultimately prevented the shipment of negroes from Africa to southern, central and northern America, though it took much longer to put down the Arab slave trade along the East African coast with its centre at Zanzibar. If the new lands which the explorers had discovered in temperate zones were to be peopled at all, they could be filled only by a natural increase of the population already in them or by immigration. Migration in itself supposed a surplus of population.

The population of Europe in the industrial areas increased remarkably in the years after 1815. In part this may be explained by a decline in mortality attendant upon the introduction of better sewage and provision of good water supplies when steam power was applied to pumping in the towns. There was besides some improvement in medical knowledge. Nevertheless, there could still be epidemics. The cholera of 1831–2 which arrived in Europe from the east reveals that problems of hygiene were not immediately solved, especially when there were renewed epidemics in 1854 and 1866–7. The famine years of the 1840s, moreover, did not encourage a large increase in the population. It seems safer to seek a social explanation for the rise in the population. Before the age of modern industrialism marriage depended largely upon the possession of land. The availability of land, therefore, determined the number of marriages which might take place. Already in France, for example, in the eighteenth century there was a land hunger, and marriage was often delayed, with the consequence that a woman had fewer reproductive years left to her upon her wedding. Small families were the rule in the country districts of France. On the other hand, where labour services were still employed, as they were generally in Eastern Europe and the Habsburg Empire, the distribution of land depended upon the requirements of the landlord for labour. In this way a certain number of large holdings would be allotted for farmers who provided ploughing services and smaller holdings for manual labourers. The mode of agricultural production, therefore, determined the number of marriages and accordingly the number of births. Everywhere in Europe, where this system existed, from the Napoleonic Wars onwards the peasants obtained ownership of their holdings, and with ownership the power to divide them in order to make marriage possible for their children. There tended to be an increase in the rural population of such countries, which gradually produced a system of parcelization, rendering the peasant farm so small that it often could not be subdivided further. On the other hand, some schemes of emancipation of which the best known is the Prussian, resulted in the deprivation of the smaller peasants, who were converted into landless labourers who often drifted to the towns. The Russian decree of 1861 made the village commune responsible for the redemption dues paid to the landlord, which in the areas of repartitional tenure prevented removal from the village, but the system of periodic division placed no artificial or social restriction upon population growth; in fact, it encouraged it, because the amount of land awarded on repartition was based upon the size of the peasant family. In those parts of Russia where repartition was not apparent subdivision proceeded quickly, but Western Russia and the Ukraine did not suffer from serious congestion until the last quarter of the nineteenth century, when the migration to Siberia first began to assume large proportions. On the whole, it is true to say that there was a growth of the population in the countryside following emancipation, but more important still was the abolition of legal serfdom, which permitted the free movement of the peasants within the state.

The first migration was the movement into the towns. The peasants and, indeed, the village labourers of Britain took with them the reproductive habits of the countryside. Possession of a farm in the countryside meant marriage, but in the town it was wages which made marriage possible, and usually at an earlier age, with the consequence that families tended to be larger in industrial centres than in the countryside. There appeared the phenomenon known in Britain as the 'Victorian Family', in which ten or more children might result from one marriage and perhaps even more if stillborn children or children who died at an early age were reckoned in with them. It was not until pressure upon housing became unbearable that the urban family began to limit itself, mainly by the adoption of artificial methods of birth control. The consequence was that there was always a superfluity of labour in the towns as a result of influx from the countryside and a high birth rate, and the frequent depressions of the 1830s and 1840s rendered unemployment all the more severe. The potato famine was especially important, because in Ireland the population, its birth rate high because the Roman Catholic clergy drew its incomes mainly from fees paid at baptism and weddings and therefore tended to encourage early marriage, had for historic reasons come to rely upon the potato as the main source of its diet. The alarming growth of the population did not worry many contemporary observers, who took comfort in the doctrines of Malthus, who in 1798 published his *Essay on the Principle of Population as it affects the future improvement of Society*, which was interpreted to mean that the population would limit itself naturally if it exceeded the means of subsistence. As in economic affairs, so with regard to increase of population, the doctrine of *laissez-faire* might be adopted. In Britain, for example, the appalling mortality attendant upon the Irish famine of 1846 seems to confirm the popularly held opinion of Malthus's theory. The famine years undoubtedly served as a spur to emigration from rural Ireland, but difficulties equally affected the city populations. In 1857 there was a general European crisis which gave the movement a fresh impetus. Between 1821 and 1871 over 6,000,000 persons left the United Kingdom alone, of whom 2,054,578 left in the decade 1851–61, but migration was apparent everywhere in Europe.

The direction of migration varied, while different countries applied different policies. The Italians migrated more or less as they wished to the states which bordered upon Italy or to North Africa. In

Britain, France, Belgium and the Netherlands emigration was un-impeded by the state, but characteristically France, with its lower rate of population growth, did not provide large numbers of emi-grants. In Germany, however, some states viewed with alarm the flow of emigrants from the country and sought to impose restrictions. Nevertheless, the opportunities for the emigrant were great. The slave trade had been abolished and the New World could be developed by free men. The improvement of shipping meant that the voyage was much less arduous. The discovery of gold in California and Australia in the 1850s added an incentive. The main movement of the emigrant population was from western Europe and central Europe. Hamburg, Bremen, Antwerp, Havre and, above all, Liverpool, which took not only British emigrants but also migrants in transit who landed in Hull, became great centres for the collection of men and women ready to settle in the New World. The Irish, English, Scots, Scan-dinavians and Germans went mainly to North America. Between 1850 and 1860 the United States received 2,452,000 immigrants, the Irish remaining in the cities because they were poor, but the Germans and Scandinavians settling in the farmlands in the hope of them-selves obtaining a farm. The English and Scots, being less distinct from the American settlers of long standing, were quickly absorbed into the existing social system and lost their separate identity. With the opening of the American Civil War the movement was tem-porarily halted, but after the victory of the Northern States it was resumed once more. Migration to Canada was avoided by the Irish, who wished for political reasons to escape from British dominion, but it attracted Englishmen and Scots, some of whom nevertheless tended to drift into the United States. There was a movement of European population to Cape Colony, Natal and Australasia. At the beginning of the nineteenth century Australia itself had a bad reputation in the early stages, from its having been a convict settle-ment since 1788, but by the 1850s the various communities of the continent were recognized as colonies with internal self-government and the transportation of convicts finally abandoned in 1866. In 1840 New Zealand became a British colony as a result of the treaty of Waitangi with the native Maori chiefs, which forestalled a French colonization. Australia received in the main English, Scots, Germans and Swiss. By 1850 New South Wales had a population of 350,000 and Victoria 538,000, which is a remarkable growth if it is compared with the development of Maritime Siberia, where the population grew to only 310,000 according to the Russian census figures of 1897. It was not only the Europeans who migrated. From the areas of European penetration non-Europeans were drawn to supplement the labour force. Indians were brought to the West Indies. Chinese were imported into California, British Columbia, Cuba and Peru.

The country which gained most from the population movement was undoubtedly the United States. In 1840 the population of the United States was about 17,000,000, but the continued flow of immigrants opened possibilities of development. In 1842 the boundaries between the United States and the British dominions were established by the Ashburton Treaty, which fixed the boundary on the forty-fifth parallel as the line of demarcation from Maine as far as the St Lawrence along the line of the great lakes and thence along the forty-ninth parallel from the Lake of the Woods to the Pacific Ocean. South of this line to the Mexican border a vast territory lay ready for the creation of a state of continental dimensions, of a power which in its resources would outstrip the European powers when once the area had been linked by railways. The majority of the settlers who came from Europe were at first mainly from the United Kingdom, but they were gradually to be diluted by immigrants from the continent of Europe itself. The result was a long process of fusion from which a distinct United States consciousness was to emerge, even though politics were to be bedevilled by animosities aroused by the civil war and modified by concepts which owed less to inspiration from the institutions of eighteenth-century Britain.

Conclusion

By the 1860s the world had been penetrated by the Europeans. It is possible to speak of a Europeanization of countries which had for centuries remained relatively static. The burst of energy which came from Europe was not necessarily accompanied by love of the European. In Asia, in particular, societies which had different outlooks of mind from those of Europe accepted the technology of the industrial civilization, but the domination which it gave the European states was resented. The superb self-confidence of the Europeans engendered a reaction when once the processes of modern technology had been mastered. This was not a problem which had for the European powers assumed serious dimensions by 1870, but it was to give rise to exactly the same national feelings which on a smaller scale troubled Europe in the nineteenth century. Where the Europeans filled empty spaces they were able to transplant European concepts and traditions, but where they remained in a minority the very technology which they imported was to create the conditions of an ultimate retrocession of power to the indigenous population.

7: The Realignment of European Forces

The construction of the North German Confederation made Prussia the dominant power in Germany, but the balance of the European forces need not have been upset. By the year 1870 Germany was making great progress, but she had not established a significant lead over France. As a result of a programme of intense railway construction France by 1870 had completed all her main trunk lines, which to some extent solved her fuel problem. Coal could be transported from the deposits in the Nord, Pas de Calais, the Loire Valley, Le Creusot and Alais, which made possible the introductión of machinery throughout the country, coal being necessary for machine industry. Coal production is one of the means by which the relative power of the European states may be measured. The annual production of Britain in 1871 was 118,000,000 metric tons, Germany 29,400,000 tons of coal and 8,500,000 of lignite, France 13,000,000 and Belgium 13,700,000. The relative figures for the production of pig iron present a slightly different position. In 1860 Britain produced 3,888,000 tons annually, France 898,000, Germany 529,000 and Belgium 320,000. After 1860, however, pig iron became a less reliable index of power, because in 1856 Henry Bessemer invented his method of cheap steel production, by which hot air was blown through molten pig iron to remove the carbon from it and the correct amount of carbon added in the form of ferromanganese. As a result of the London Exhibition of 1862 the influence of the Bessemer process was felt upon the continent of Europe. It was adopted at Le Creusot and Hayange near Thionville. In this manner French steel production rose from 30,000 tons in 1860 to 110,000 tons in 1869, giving France a total output of wrought iron and steel combined of 1,000,000 tons. While France was in possession of Alsace and Lorraine there was no inevitability of her being overtaken by Germany in the field of metallurgy, but it was an ominous fact so much of her iron ore and metallurgical industry lay in Alsace Lorraine. In the 1860s Germany began to draw level with France, but it was primarily in 1871 when

she obtained possession of the Lorraine ores which were linked
with the coalfields of the Ruhr that Germany began rapidly to overtake France in her industrial progress. The inevitability of French
defeat at the hands of Prussia in 1870 ought not to be attributed
to a superior industrial organization in Germany which was to
emerge after the war, though even before it German enterprise was
an important factor. It was rather in the organization and adaptation
of resources that Prussia drew her advantage.

I. THE CONDITION OF FRANCE UNDER THE SECOND EMPIRE

The adventurous policy which Napoleon III had followed abroad
by the mid-1860s was revealed as having little purpose. The occupation of Rome and the success in the Crimean War were followed by
the failure to find help for the Poles in 1863, the inability to establish
a puppet régime in Mexico and the vacillation which allowed Prussia
to defeat Austria in 1866. Rome, so light-heartedly occupied in
1849, was proving a thorn in the side of France. French troops were
withdrawn from Rome in December 1866, but sent back in October
1867, when it appeared that what remained of the Papal States, the
Patrimony of St Peter, was in danger of being overrun by Italian
revolutionaries. Garibaldi was an expert in the politics of private
initiative, of which his conquest of Sicily and Naples had been the
finest example. With the acquisition of Venetia by Italy there remained only Rome to take. At a battle at Mentana on 3 November
1867 the French forces collaborated with the Papal army in defeating
a force led by Garibaldi, an action which, though it saved the Pope,
did not endear France to Italian opinion any more than the attempt to
lay claim to Luxemburg reconciled German opinion to France. With
the construction of the North German Confederation Napoleon III
and his ministers had completed a cycle of diplomatic errors and
blunders which revealed that they had no fixed or certain principles
of foreign policy at all. Not upon these grounds could the Second
Empire establish any grounds for approval.

Upon the argument of economic development under the Empire it
is equally difficult to point to factors which owed their origin to
measures undertaken by the Empire. France experienced a growth
of her economy which has exact parallels in other European states.
The crisis of 1857 was caused by a remarkably good grain harvest,

which depressed cereal prices, causing a financial failure in the United States. With an expanding economy and drawing upon the goods and equipment of Europe, the United States was a debtor community under the obligation to make remittances to Europe. When the price of corn fell, the farmers could not honour their obligations and there was a corresponding financial crisis in Europe in 1857–8, affecting both Britain and France. With the recovery there was a renewed capital investment everywhere, with a development of finance corporations, which borrowed money in excess of the liquidity of their assets. When shareholders requested to withdraw their money from these corporations they could not sell their assets quickly enough or at a sufficiently high figure to meet their obligations. In Britain there occurred the celebrated failure of Overend and Gurney in May 1866. There was a similar failure in the *Crédit Mobilier*, founded by the Pereire brothers in 1852, because the Bank of France refused to assist it in its difficulties until its principal directors resigned. Whereas in Britain the failure of Overend and Gurney was caused by injudicious speculations, in France the failure of the Pereire brothers might have been prevented if the Bank of France had come to their aid, but the leading financiers in France had little confidence in the permanence of the Napoleonic régime and were not ready to assist a company which was so closely identified with the government. The greatest of Napoleon III's achievements in the economic field was the Cobden–Chevalier treaty of 1860. Tension had arisen in Britain as a result of France's part in the war of 1859 in Italy, and there was a belief that Britain herself would be the next target of French imperialism; hurried preparations were made to meet an attack. In 1859–60 the naval superiority which Britain enjoyed over France was not as great as might be imagined. Technical changes brought about by the construction of iron-clad battleships placed the British fleet in danger of being rendered obsolete. It was not until the famous British battleship *Warrior* was launched in August 1861 that the technical superiority of Britain began to make itself felt again. In Britain there was a conflict in 1859–60 between the Chancellor of the Exchequer, Gladstone, who was determined to reduce expenditure upon the armed forces and the prime minister, Palmerston, who thought adequate provision should be made to meet the danger of a French invasion. The question was in part resolved by the conclusion of the celebrated Cobden–Chevalier treaty in January 1860 between Britain and France which, by establishing a commercial accord between the two countries, took the animosity out of their political relations.

The success of France in the war against Austria in Italy caused Napoleon III to seek to give his government added prestige by the encouragement of trade and industry. This was nothing less than to adopt the Free Trade principles current in Britain, but hardly acceptable to French opinion, which remained as ever strongly protectionist. The treaty, negotiated by Cobden and Chevalier in strict secrecy, received the assent of Napoleon III, who did not submit it to the Legislative Body for consideration, lest it meet with undue opposition. Under its terms France abandoned the policy of prohibiting some imports altogether and agreed to reduce her duties to a maximum of 30 per cent in two years and to 25 per cent in five years, while Britain for practical purposes abandoned all customs dues on imports from France, with the exception of those on wines and spirits. Into this treaty was written a 'most favoured nation clause', by which the two powers undertook to grant to one another any advantage which they might offer a third power. This was the beginning of a series of commercial treaties with other European states and marked a movement towards the lowering of tariffs everywhere. From the point of view of France the Cobden–Chevalier treaty was an act of ruthless surgery. The small inefficient French ironmasters and textile manufacturers could not compete with the influx of British iron and steel and fabrics, but there was, on the other hand, a consequent growth of bigger enterprises and the expansion of railways. In the European sense it inaugurated a period of free trade and with it over a decade of relatively high prosperity and industrial expansion. The year 1860 was the high-water mark of British prosperity in the nineteenth century, but it was not to lead to the complete relaxation of tension for which Cobden hoped.

Napoleon III was increasingly conscious that he must place his régime on a firm foundation. By his marriage to the Empress Eugénie, he had obtained a son and heir in 1856, which seemed to promise a continuity of his line, but there was no basic loyalty to his rule. The French elections of 1857, carried out under the control of the minister of the interior, Billault, resulted in a poll of only 65 per cent of the electorate, of which 84.6 per cent of the votes was cast for the government, which found its support growing in the conservative areas of western France and declining in the more industrialized eastern regions. It was obvious that the towns in particular remained loyal to the republican cause, so much so that Haussmann, the prefect in Paris, who was engaged upon the reconstruction of the city, was in favour of de-industrialization in order to remove a menace from the seat of government. As long as the Parisian area remained an industrial centre there would be mass support for the opponents of the régime. The attempt upon the life of Napoleon III by the Italian Orsini in January 1858 was used as an excuse for a policy of intimidation, but by the beginning of the 1860s it was already noticed that a change was appearing in the climate of French opinion. It was becoming less easy for the prefects to manipulate public opinion, and a sign of the government's anxiety was the decision taken by Billault in 1860 to appoint mayors of the communes before and not after the communal elections, with the result that the mayors appeared to be nothing more than government agents. Under the previous system of appointing them from among the elected members of the councils it at least appeared that they were independent. What was noticeable was the growing maturity of public opinion. When public opinion in the provinces was undeveloped, it was easy enough for the mayor to direct the votes to the candidates whom he considered most suitable, usually the men whom the government suggested to him, but the close identification of the mayor with the government now rendered his advice suspect. Whereas in the early 1850s there was some public support for strong government in view of the disturbed state of the country, the social stability which was achieved by the beginning of the 1860s pointed to the need for some relaxation of authoritarianism.

The tendency was for the government to consult members of the Legislative Body more and more in order to sound opinion. On 24 November 1860 an order was given for the publication of debates and the formulation of an address to the throne, while ministers without portfolio were to represent the government in the Legislative Body. Publicity in itself meant public discussion, and in the view of one section of the Emperor's advisers, the need to permit political opinion to be expressed in a manner which seemed to remove the dynasty from the arena of politics. If direction from above were abandoned, policy would be the target of criticism and not the existence of the Napoleonic empire. The way was paved for 'the Liberal Empire', and the first sign of a general slackening of control was the discussion of individual items of the budget in 1861, but even without concessions the public was making it clear that the old methods of management were no longer in tune with the times. The elections of 1863 revealed that the voters had a mind of their own. The emperor's half-brother, the duc de Morny, a man capable of none too scrupulous financial speculation, but with some talent for conciliation in parliamentary circles, tried to give direction to the domestic policy of the Empire, but his influence upon public affairs was abruptly terminated by his death in 1865, which called a halt to liberalization. It had been hoped by Morny to attract the republican minority of five representatives, of whom Émile Ollivier, Jules Favre and Picard were to achieve great distinction in an assembly which consisted of dull official nominees, to support of the Empire, but now progress was held up, especially when the Emperor Napoleon himself began to ail as a result of a kidney and bladder disease, which made his control over the situation weaker than it had been hitherto. He was still on occasions capable of energy and intelligent action, but now he tended to be smothered by events.

His foreign policy by 1867 was revealed to be full of errors, of which the unification of Germany north of the Main and the withdrawal from Mexico, abandoning Maximilian to his fate before a firing squad, could hardly be brushed aside as inconsequential. At home the pretensions of the clergy grew, fed with papal encouragement from Rome, the most famous of which was the Syllabus of Errors of 1864. This pronouncement made it virtually impossible, in the eyes of Pius IX at least, for a Catholic to hold liberal opinions and at the same time to be a good son of the church. Some Frenchmen reverted to the traditional Gallicanism, but the wave of religious enthusiasm which was sweeping France ensured that the Ultramontane party would remain strong. The crisis culminated in the calling of the Vatican Council in 1869–70 to discuss the problem of papal infallibility. Whereas at the outset Napoleon III had tended to rely upon the clericals, he was now obliged to choose between two sections of them. It was inevitable that, if he wished to liberalize his empire, his choice would fall upon the more liberal sections among the clericals and equally certain that the Ultramontanes, displeased by the reduction of the power of the Pope as a result of the war of 1859, should turn against him, the more so when the Emperor sought to reduce clerical control in the University and in education generally. The opposition of the left began to appear with the removal of controls on the press in 1868. With a forum for discussion the old attitudes of the left could now once more be pronounced. Under the command of Rouher, the minister of state, the French government seemed to founder, even though he was able to keep the Legislative Body under control. First French troops were withdrawn from Rome in 1866, only to be sent back again in 1867 to fight Garibaldi's attempt to overrun the papal dominions. The problem of military reorganization was not faced courageously (see below pp. 415–16). The Empire appeared to be in a state of decomposition.

In the election of May 1869 the French government finally gave up its attempt to influence the return of candidates. There was even some violence in Paris to show that tempers still ran high on the left. For once the votes gave a more realistic picture of the true state of French opinion. The great cities of France pronounced against the government, which was nevertheless still able to muster support. The government candidates obtained 4,400,000 votes and the opposition 3,300,000. The revelation of this basic division ruled out once and for all any further attempt at a coup d'état. The only course left to Napoleon III was to seek reconciliation with the opposition. Rouher was compelled to resign and with him the creatures who had supported him. Napoleon III still had no wish to place his powers in commission and sought a compromise solution, in which he might retain his right to intervene in government affairs and at the same time make his ministers responsible to the Legislative Body. At the end of December 1869 Émile Ollivier was summoned to form an administration representing the majority in the Legislative Body, but the ministry formed on 2 January 1870 was not to be as homogeneous as the Emperor required. It was rather a compromise, secured by the retention of a few former ministers and a coalition of the centre–right and the centre–left. In April 1870 the consent of the Emperor was obtained for the reform of the constitution. The special position of the Senate was to be abolished and the parliament to consist of an upper and lower house sharing legislative authority. The last of the Napoleonic plebiscites was held on 23 April 1870 to approve this change. The French electorate gave its approval by 7,300,000 votes to 1,500,000 with 1,900,000 abstentions. In spite of disagreements and passions, it appeared that the Empire had converted itself into a constitutional monarchy. The Senate and the Legislative Body constituted a parliament based upon a franchise more liberal than that of Great Britain. It was perhaps unfortunate for the ailing Napoleon III that his new experiment was put to the test so early by a crisis of French relations with Germany on the question of the Hohenzollern candidature for the throne of Spain.

II. The Position of Prussia in Germany

With the creation of the North German Confederation Bismarck did not abandon plans for a total unification of the German territories not embraced by Austria. Economic unification had already been achieved, and in July 1867 a Zollverein parliament was proposed to discuss matters of industry and commerce. It was Bismarck's intention that this measure should accustom Germany to thinking in terms of total political association, but in March 1868 as many as forty-nine out of the eighty-five deputies to the Zollverein parliament proved to be opposed to an association beyond that already achieved. Bismarck subsidized the South German press to promote the cause of unification, but during the winter of 1869–70 there was hardening of the opposition to unification. The Grand Duke of Baden, who was connected by marriage with the Hohenzollern family, was ready for closer association, but Bavaria was opposed. In February 1870 the Minister-President, Hohenlohe, who favoured a federative union, was compelled to resign. In Württemberg there was hostility to military reform on the Prussian model. In Hesse-Darmstadt opinion was openly pro-Austrian. Bismarck therefore took the decision that there was no object in pressing for an extension of the German union and preferred for the moment to await events. With the transformation of the French political system in January 1870 it was profitable to adopt a passive role. Napoleon III would undoubtedly not accept the adherence of Baden to the North German Confederation, but the new parliamentary system might force him to pay greater respect to public opinion in France. Émile Ollivier had no wish to interfere in

Germany, except if Bismarck were to attempt a solution by force. For him the line of the river Main had no significance, because Prussia's military power could be made effective beyond it. It was his attitude that the essential error had been made by his predecessors in office and that what might happen in Germany was their responsibility. Nevertheless, the situation changed, when on 15 May 1870 the duc de Gramont was appointed foreign minister in France. He had the reputation for being pro-Austrian, and Bismarck was accordingly less convinced of a policy of seeking an understanding with the Ollivier government when it appeared that France was ready to give her backing to an Austrian effort to keep the South German states within her field of influence. For this reason he was ready to allow another aspect of Franco-German relations to emerge as an alternative line of approach to the question of German unification.

III. The Spanish Throne and the Hohenzollern Candidature

Even in a country as backward and self-centred as Spain there was no immunity from the desire for improvement, which seemed beyond the grasp of the corrupt régime of Isabella, whose scandalous private life added disgrace to inefficiency. There were various political groups, the Carlists, especially in the Basque provinces; the Moderates (*moderados*), who wished to circumscribe constitutional liberties; the Progressives (*progresistas*) and the small group of republicans, but real power rested with the generals, and policies were determined by which direction military opinion took. In the mid-1860s, however, the court camarilla's policy of leaning first on one military group and then upon another lost its charms and recourse was had to a policy of terror, directed against the liberal elements in Spain, which finally brought about the total disenchantment of the army with the Bourbon dynasty. To the end Isabella professed to believe that her policy of firmness would succeed, but in September 1868 the fleet at Cadiz declared against the régime, an action which in its turn brought about a revolution in Madrid. Isabella II fled in haste from the country, and a new régime was established under the regency of Serraño, with Marshal Prim as minister of war. The problem of the new government was to find some means of preserving the unity of Spain. In the view of Prim the best course to adopt was the restoration of the monarchical system, but under a monarch of more enlightened tendencies than the Bourbons.

A subsidiary motive in Prim's thinking was the ultimate aim of securing the union of Spain and Portugal. After much searching for solutions and disappointments the Spanish government hit upon the solution of offering the crown to Leopold of Hohenzollern-Sigmaringen. Leopold was connected by birth with the family of the Beauharnais, which promised good relations with the Bonapartes, Napoleon III himself being a descendant of Alexander de Beauharnais, the first husband of the Empress Josephine, and disposed to look favourably upon Leopold's brother, Charles of Rumania. Leopold was, moreover, married to Antonia of Portugal, which seemed to leave open the possibility of an ultimate Iberian union.

It is difficult to determine exactly at what stage Bismarck first became interested in the question of the Hohenzollern succession to the Spanish throne. Already before the revolt of 1868 there was talk of Leopold's being invited to become King of Spain, and by the beginning of 1869 French hostility had begun to appear. Bismarck evidently knew that the matter might be manipulated to Prussian advantage, but the exact manner in which advantage might be obtained at first eluded him. It appears that, for fear of a strong French reaction against the Hohenzollern-Sigmaringens, William I and Bismarck decided that the affair should be represented as exclusively the concern of the Spanish government and the House of Hohenzollern-Sigmaringen. Very great hesitation was shown in Germany, which was nevertheless sufficiently positive in favour of Leopold's accepting the Spanish throne for the military leaders quietly to perfect their plans for war. At length on 19 June 1870 after much vaccillation Leopold of Sigmaringen decided to accept, but the negotiations were to be conducted in secret, and it would appear from the prorogation of the Cortes on 23 June until November 1870 that the Spanish government did not expect an early conclusion of its arrangements. The envoy employed by Spain in the conversations in Germany, Eusebio de Salazar, was indiscreet enough on his return to Madrid to reveal Leopold's acceptance, and the news reached French ears. On 2 July 1870 Prim was obliged to reveal that the Hohenzollern candidature was being promoted.

When the news arrived in Paris the French ministers affected to believe that a serious threat was being made to French security. Certainly the conspiratorial tactics of Spain were contrary to diplomatic usage, but there was, on the other hand, no evidence of Bismarck's complicity. France could therefore either ask Prussia for her good offices or criticize Prussia for her part in the affair. When information was requested from the Prussian government, the reply was given that no knowledge was had of the matter and that in any case the Spanish government could offer the Crown of Spain to whom it wished, an answer which immediately aroused suspicion, because no German prince, and certainly not a Hohenzollern-Sigmaringen, would accept a crown without first asking the advice of Prussia. The policy of the French government was to use the incident to secure a diplomatic victory by asking the King of Prussia to forbid the Hohenzollern candidature. Bismarck was certainly not the man to permit such a humiliation to be suffered by Prussia and decided that in the first instance discussion of the affair should be avoided and, if France persisted, she should be placed in the wrong by appearing to browbeat Prussia. Evasion was attempted and, when discussion of the candidature could no longer be avoided, the admission was made that Prussia knew of the candidature but was unaware of which Hohenzollern-Sigmaringen prince the Spaniards had in mind. In a crisis the statesmen of the Second Empire rarely exhibited complete clarity of judgment. On 6 July the French cabinet decided that in order to satisfy French public opinion, which was exasperated by an apparent attempt to encircle France, a strongly worded message should be sent to Berlin, and the duc de Gramont in the Legislative Body declared that he expected moderation and a satisfactory reply from Prussia '. . . but if it should be otherwise, strong in your support, gentlemen, and in that of the nation, we should know how to do our duty without hesitation and without weakness'.

In this speech there was a threat of war, the first of the series of diplomatic errors to be made by France. If moderation was to be expected in any quarter it was to be expected from William I, but the King was annoyed, and behind him was Bismarck, who did not shrink from the possibility of war. The King was prepared to offer resistance to French diplomatic pressure, and Bismarck was determined that Prussia should receive no diplomatic humiliation. William I was himself willing to recommend the renunciation of the

Hohenzollern candidature, but Leopold himself was to make the announcement. Renunciation in fact came on 12 July 1870, but it was made in curious circumstances. Leopold could not be found, apparently because he was walking in the Austrian Alps, and the announcement was made on his behalf by his father, Karl Anton. If Bismarck hoped for war there was apparently no longer any likelihood, but the French ministers now began to make further inquiries, whether a father's renunciation was binding upon the son, and whether or not the King of Prussia would give Napoleon III a letter to the effect that he had not meant harm to French interests, which from the French point of view was desirable in view of the excited state of public opinion. This was in practice to demand the formal recognition of a diplomatic victory. To this incautious policy was added a telegram to the French ambassador in Prussia, Benedetti, asking the King of Prussia to give an assurance that Leopold of Hohenzollern-Sigmaringen would not renew his candidature. The authors of this telegram, 'the Mad Improvisation of St Cloud', were Napoleon III and the foreign minister, the duc de Gramont. The French ambassador, Benedetti, sought an interview with William I at Ems, where he was spending his holiday, hoping to extract what Napoleon III desired before Bismarck, who had come from his estate in Varzin to Berlin, could exert any influence. Imperfectly informed of the situation, the King professed his willingness to meet Benedetti during his morning walk on 13 July, but not before he had conversed with Eulenberg, whom Bismarck had despatched to Ems. For Benedetti it was essential to get an early reply in order that some announcement might be made in the French Legislative Body that day. Accordingly, he manoeuvred himself into the path of the King, who, unable to ignore him, was compelled to listen to the French demands. The King was polite and received the news of Leopold's renunciation, but irritated and, without giving any direct undertaking, raised his hat and walked on with the words: 'I have nothing more to add.' This unsatisfactory situation forced Benedetti to request another interview, but the King was determined not to permit more of Benedetti's importunities. Officially he took the attitude that the matter was closed with Leopold's renunciation, but to refuse an audience to an ambassador was a serious matter. The King, moreover, sent an account of the episode to Bismarck with permission to release his rejection of Benedetti's demands to the press. It was contrary to international usage to make a revelation of an un-concluded negotiation, and certainly dangerous in the existing situation to allow a man of Bismarck's known unscrupulousness to report so delicate a matter. William I's action, therefore, points to the conclusion that he himself was prepared to face the consequences of war with France and delivered the actual diplomatic rebuff to France. The function of Bismarck was merely to exacerbate the situation until a war might be forced upon Prussia. The King's telegram of 13 July, the celebrated 'Ems Telegram', was so con-densed by Bismarck to give the impression that France had delivered a virtual ultimatum to Prussia and that William I had to all intents and purposes broken off diplomatic relations. This news when it was received by the German public not unnaturally gave cause for annoyance and indignation, but the annoyance was even greater in France. On 14 July the French council of ministers was still for the most part pacific, but the news that Bismarck had released news of the Ems incident, and in brutal terms, forced them to accept the situation that war was likely, and on 15 July military credits were demanded from the Senate and Legislative Body. In the meantime mobilization was ordered in Prussia. On 19 July 1870 Napoleon III committed the last in his tragic series of blunders by declaring war upon Prussia. The French army was not ready. France appeared to be the aggressor. She was, moreover, without allies. By a light-hearted and irresponsible conduct of affairs Napoleon III and his advisers exposed France to the finest army in Europe.

IV. THE FRANCO-PRUSSIAN WAR: THE BALANCE OF FORCES

The French army enjoyed great prestige, and it was generally sup-posed in Europe that it would swiftly defeat the Prussian forces, but the result was to be different. The fundamental reason for the Prussian victory was that military planning under William I had adjusted itself to the industrial revolution. Under the law of 9 November 1867 the army of the North German Confederation was organized, virtually an expansion of the old Prussian army. The soldiers were conscripted at the age of twenty years and served three years with the colours, then passing into the reserve for four years, before being transferred to the territorial force, or *Landwehr*; on being embodied into the *Landwehr* they could for one year be recalled to the regular field formations. In this way the Prussian high command could draw upon seven or in an emergency eight years' annual intakes, at the same time as having the *Landwehr* controlled by regular officers to meet unforeseen dangers. The Confederation was organized into a series of areas, eight for Prussia itself and six for the other constituent portions, including the former independent states annexed by Prussia, each of them providing an army corps; the Grand Duchy of Hesse was required to raise one division. Though they were not part of the Confederation, Baden and Württemberg copied the Prussian system and in January 1868 adopted conscription. The total number of troops available in Germany in 1870 was impressive. The North German Confederation could raise 15,324 officers and 714,950 men for the regular army, supported by 6,510 officers and 201,640 men in the *Landwehr*. A total of 1,183,389 troops was actually put into the field in 1870, of which 983,064 came from the Confederation.

In the opinion of the French the new Prussian mass army was likely to be too unwieldy to manage, but the Prussian general staff was aware of this difficulty and made studies of it. The general staff trained by General von Moltke differed from all other staffs which had existed hitherto. In the era of armies which numbered only 100,000 men the staffs consisted of adjutants and clerks, but Moltke recruited to his Military Academy the best brains among the officer corps, who were periodically returned to regimental service in order to gain further experience and at the same time to familiarize their comrades with the new ideas. The Prussian general staff already had some experience of the difficulties of moving men by railways as a result of the muddle of 1859. Errors were apparent also in the war of 1866. In 1857, on his appointment, Moltke had little confidence in the capacity of the Prussian army to resist France and planned for a defensive war in which Prussia abandoned the left bank of the Rhine, because he would need thirty-three days in which to mobilize and seven weeks to put an army into the field, but after 1861, as a result of Roon's reforms, he believed that it might be possible to undertake an early offensive and seize Alsace-Lorraine. By 1866 he was convinced that he could open the offensive as a result of rapid mobilization and separate the two French bases of Metz and Strasburg, after which he could continue his advance between the Rhine and the Moselle with the object of compelling the French government to make an early peace. In the final war plans of 1868-9 Moltke planned to put 300,000 into the field in three weeks against an estimated French strength of 343,000, of which 250,000 could take the field at once. The increased tempo of Prussian mobilization plans and their repercussions upon strategy are obvious.

The more intelligent of French observers were well aware of the dangers likely to confront them. After the Prussian victory of Sadowa it was apparent that a great new military power had arisen, and it was considered that among the reforms required was the introduction of a good rifle comparable to the Prussian needle gun, which was subsequently manufactured, the celebrated *Chassepot*, but Napoleon III realized that more fundamental changes were required. In 1866 France had a professional army of 288,000 men, but they had been trained in the colonial type of warfare waged in Mexico and Algeria. At a conference at Compiègne in November 1866 Napoleon III declared in favour of conscription with the aim of raising the army to 1,000,000 strong. This proposal met with the opposition of the minister of war, Randon, who disliked reservists. Civilian opposition was equally hostile because the enlistment of so many men would deplete the labour force and because conscription was in any case unpopular. The government could not afford to ignore public opinion at a moment when the liberalization of the Empire was under consideration. A decision was difficult to reach, and in December 1866 an article in the official newspaper, *Moniteur*, tested public opinion. It proposed that there should be a small intake of conscripts to serve for six years and that those exempt from conscription should serve in the *Garde Mobile*, which was to play a role similar to that of the *Landwehr* in the North German Confederation. This would have made available 824,000 on mobilization with 400,000 in the *Garde Mobile*. Randon continued in his opposition and was replaced in 1867 by Marshal Niel, who unfortunately died in August 1869. Under Niel a modified system was produced in which the conscripts were to serve for five years and then pass for four years into a reserve of ex-conscripts and those who had been liable for full-time service, but called up only for five months. Even this proposal met with opposition, and it was not until February

1868 that it became law. The annual intake was reckoned at 172,000 men, yielding in 1875 a mobilization strength of 800,000, with a *Garde Mobile* in reserve, an instrument of doubtful military value in view of its receiving only two weeks training a year. The inadequacy of the French measures to meet the French threat are obvious. Lebœuf, who succeeded Niel as minister of war in 1869, was less convinced of the need to raise a mass army. It was not a politically encouraging sign when the *Garde Mobile* of the Seine showed itself insubordinate. There was a danger of putting arms into the hands of the régime's opponents. Some progress was made in the manu-facture of the *Chassepot* rifle, a weapon infinitely superior to the Prussian needle gun, but the modernization of the artillery was not seriously undertaken, even though the German firm of Krupp offered to supply breach-loading guns in 1867. The defects of the French army were exposed anonymously by the Orleanist General Trochu in a pamphlet entitled *L'Armée Française en 1867* (The French Army in 1867), but this made little impression upon the authorities. The French generals did not understand the value of staff work and planning. Lebœuf himself realized that careful planning was neces-say, but the appointment of the Ollivier Ministry with its opposition to heavy military spending did not encourage reform. In July 1870 there were 492,585 men available, of which 300,000 could be mobi-lized in three weeks. The numbers and military value of the *Garde Mobile* were difficult to estimate.

The French situation was very difficult, and an Austrian alliance would have been invaluable, even if it had only tied down part of the North German Confederation's army. The French original plan was essentially offensive, with the aim of placing an army across the Rhine to link with the Austrians and in this way to permit the South German states to mobilize their forces against Prussia, but the alliance project came to nothing, in part because Austria wished to declare only a state of armed neutrality in the first instance. The diplomatic circumstances in which the war began ruled out any possible Austrian or South German co-operation because France appeared in German eyes to be the aggressor. The incompetence of French foreign policy resulted in the army's being required to meet unaided the full impact of the mighty instrument of war which Moltke had been creating.

V. The Franco-Prussian War: The Campaign

In spite of the modernity of the situation, the war began in 1870 with an old-fashioned flourish. William I took command of the North German Confederation's troops, for all his seventy-three years of age, though it was generally recognized that Moltke was in effective command. The commander of the First Army, General Steinmetz, was as old as the King and frequently refused to obey Moltke's orders. The Second and Third Armies were commanded by Prince Frederick Charles and by the Crown Prince, Frederick, the latter being in part a diplomatic measure, because German public opinion forced the South German states to take Prussia's side against France, and for their armies to be commanded by the Crown Prince was no slight to their dignity. Within eighteen days 462,000 men took the field, followed at a close distance by the German Princes and a host of war correspondents. With the King went the civil and military cabinets of the Confederation, including Bismarck and Roon. On the French side the ailing Napoleon III was compelled by the Empress Eugénie to take personal command of the armies of Alsace under MacMahon, of Metz under Bazaine and of Châlons under Canrobert, formed into a united force of eight corps. The French mobilization, however, showed how unprepared France was for war. The French generals were probably as good as the Prussian generals, but they received no guidance from a general staff. Units were widely dispersed throughout the country, and the armies were assembled as best could be managed. The supply of food broke down and the troops showed indiscipline. Disaster soon followed.

The Prussian offensive began between the Moselle and the Rhine, and in the first week of August the French army was thrust back from the frontier. Marshal Bazaine was placed in command and withdrew to his base at Metz, exposing Alsace and Lorraine to the German forces. Metz was cut off by the battle of Gravelotte on 18 August and the situation began to seem desperate. Marshal MacMahon and Napoleon III assembled a fresh army at Châlons to join forces with Bazaine, but, for his part, Bazaine made no effective effort to meet them. On 1 September 1870 the French army, having been hemmed in on the Belgian frontier at Sedan, was compelled to surrender to the Prussians. Together with the prisoners they had taken during the battle, the Prussians captured a total of 104,000 Frenchmen with their supply train and artillery. Among them was the Emperor Napoleon III, who was escorted into captivity in Germany. The Second Empire was at an end. The Empress Eugénie and the Prince Imperial took refuge in England, so often the enemy of France and so often a haven of refuge for French politicians.

VI. THE FRENCH PROVISIONAL GOVERNMENT OF NATIONAL DEFENCE

The war against the North German Confederation was lost, but the Legislative Body proclaimed the Government of National Defence under General Trochu and opponents of the defunct government, partly to prevent revolutionary groups from seizing power but also to prolong resistance in order that peace might be secured upon the basis of the *status quo*. The object of the new government was to secure intervention from the neutral powers to prevent the German annexation of Alsace-Lorraine. The minister of the interior, Léon Gambetta, appealed to the people and, when the Germans surrounded Paris on 7 October, escaped from the city in a balloon in order to organize the defence of France from Tours. The resistance which he was able to stimulate came as a surprise to the Prussians, but the campaign was continued. The French even achieved some momentary successes. On 7 November d'Aurelle de Paladines succeeded in retaking Orleans, but on 27 October Bazaine had laid down his arms at Metz, and it could be only a question of time before French resistance was broken. By January 1871 the Prussians were gaining the upper hand and the delegation at Tours transferred itself to Bordeaux. Paris nevertheless continued to hold out in the hope that it would be relieved, in spite of hunger and privation. On 5 January 1871 the Prussians put into operation the device which the Austrians had used to such effect in 1848. A bombardment of Paris was opened to continue nightly until a three-weeks armistice was signed on 28 January. The French forces in Paris had tried to make sorties from the city in October and in January. Each of these attempts had failed and given rise to a disturbing phenomenon. The men of 1848, among them the celebrated Blanqui, had emerged to put themselves at the head of the patriotic struggle in the hope of converting it into a revolutionary movement. On 31 October and 22 January there were even attempts to seize power. The spirit of revolution had not disappeared in Paris and the larger cities, and there were many old grievances among the working class which deeply disturbed the bourgeoisie, who feared the establishment of a red republican régime.

The purpose of the armistice was to permit elections to be held and an assembly to meet to negotiate peace. The elections took place on 8 February. Not all Frenchmen voted, but the composition of the Assembly reflected the mood and social composition of the country. The majority of the deputies wanted peace, and the largest single grouping among them was, as usually occurred when there was no electoral pressure, monarchist, but as ever divided in its allegiances between the Bourbon Comte de Chambord and the Orleanist branch of the royal family. Thiers, who had not been a member of the Government of National Defence, but had instead made a tour of Europe seeking aid for France, was appointed Head of the Executive Power; Gambetta, the protagonist of resistance, had gone into exile, recognizing that he was not wanted. The great danger to the new régime was Paris, where out of forty-three deputies thirty-seven were in favour of a resistance. There were in the city more than 200,000 men under arms. The Assembly judged it wise to hold its sittings not in Paris, but at Versailles. At the same time measures were taken which provoked the people of Paris. The moratorium on promissory notes by which commerce in Paris had been carried on was ended. Rents were made payable and the pay of the National Guard of 1 franc 50 centimes a day was stopped except for the extremely poor. On 18 March Thiers gave orders that the guns in the possession of the National Guard should be removed from the city. The working class of Paris foresaw only their own ultimate coercion by the conservative Assembly at Versailles and refused to submit to this order. Thiers did not make the mistake which Louis Philippe made in 1848. Instead he withdrew all the civil and military authorities from Paris and allowed the revolution to raise its head. The Central Committee of the National Guard found itself the sole authority in the city. On 26 March a municipal government was elected which took the name of the General Council of the Paris Commune, in which the extreme left had a clear majority and achieved an absolute domination because the moderates refused to take their seats. The extreme left consisted of Blanquists, republican revolutionaries of a

Jacobin tinge and seventeen members of the First International, who were socialists, for which reason Karl Marx was to be so interested in the Commune's activity, though it was not consciously Marxist in its inspiration. It was rather that Marx studied the Commune and gave his doctrine of the dictatorship of the proletariat its final form as a result.

In the meantime Thiers reconstituted the French army and on 2 April attempted to seize the city, but the soldiers were repulsed by the forces of the Commune. It was now the turn of the French army to bombard Paris. On 21 May the Versailles army was able to penetrate within the city walls. There followed a massacre of the kind which had occurred in the June days of 1848. The troops of the Versailles Assembly now engaged upon a deliberate extermination of the Parisian opposition, who as in 1848 fought house by house and street by street. Hostages were shot by the Commune, including the Archbishop Darboy, but it was the citizens of Paris who suffered most. About 20,000 supporters of the Commune were killed and 7,500 later deported to New Caledonia. Their final stand was on 27 May at the cemetary of Père-Lachaise, where 147 were shot by the government forces. With the end of the Second Empire came the final effort of the Parisian revolutionaries in the nineteenth century to take command of France. What was to emerge was a defeated and deeply divided France, never again to be capable of arousing fears that she might dominate the continent of Europe. Power in Europe had passed to the Germany which Bismarck and Moltke had created by war.

VII. THE FOUNDATION OF THE GERMAN EMPIRE

Bismarck had followed the armies of the German states to Versailles. The war, which had ended victoriously for Prussia, still left open the German question. The government of National Defence in France had hoped that Europe would be as fearful of a Prussian domination as it had been of French expansionism. On 12 September 1870 Jules Favre issued an appeal for help in the hope that Alsace-Lorraine, which was the most highly industrialized area of the country, might be saved to France, but the neutral powers were not willing to intervene now that France ceased for the moment to be a power of the first order. Before 1870 Austria had not given up entirely the hope of taking revenge upon Prussia, but now the hope of a resurrection of her hegemony in Germany was gone and the Habsburg dynasty turned rather to the reconciliation of the conflicting political forces within Austria-Hungary herself. The Magyars in Hungary breathed a sigh of relief, because it was now safe for them to organize the lands of the Crown of St Stephen without serious fear that the dynasty might abolish their autonomy. In no country was the campaign of 1870 a bigger surprise than in Russia. In Russia France's military capacity was seriously overestimated in 1870. In 1868 Russia had been ready to offer Prussia aid against Austria. Alexander II at first professed delight at Prussia's success, but its significance slowly dawned upon him when he perceived that Russian opinion was shocked by the completeness of Prussia's victory and by the arrogant conduct of Prussian officers. In 1870 Russia had diplomatic aims, but she could not issue more than 572,000 rifles to thirty-five out of forty-one field divisions. This was certainly an improvement upon the situation revealed in D. A. Milyutin's memorandum of November 1867 which estimated that Russia could put only 362,613 properly equipped troops into the field. Milyutin had then argued that Russia could not face war even with Austria, but in 1870 the balance of military power had swung in favour of a Germany dominated by Prussia. The ultimate consequence of the Franco-Prussian war was the decree of 13 January 1875 introducing universal military service in Russia. The more immediate result was the note of 31 October 1870 in which Gorchakov declared that Russia could no longer be bound by the limitation clauses in the Treaty of 1856, which forbade her to maintain a fleet upon the Black Sea. Russian policy was to take immediate advantage of the difficulties of France and not to make any move which would antagonize Germany for the future. Neither Austria nor Britain could in the situation of 1870–1 insist upon the maintenance of Russia's unfavourable position in the Near East. On 13 March 1871 a conference in London declared that agreements to which the major European powers had been party could not be abrogated unilaterally and therefore that assent was given by them to the cancellation of the limitation clauses, an affirmation of a principle coupled with a bowing before the inevitable. Britain was prepared to confess her own powerlessness to determine events in another quarter. She had still not resolved her difficulties with the

United States when the Franco-Prussian war burst upon Europe. With the appointment of Lord Clarendon to the Foreign Office a more conciliatory attitude was possible, and on 8 May 1871 Britain resolved her difficulties with the United States by submitting to the treaty of Washington, which referred the thorny question of the *Alabama* claims to neutral arbitration in return for an amicable settlement of the outstanding differences concerning Canadian pretensions. The year 1871 marks the final concession of hegemony to the United States in North America, which was never again to be seriously contested by Britain. Italy was a power of minor importance which could not have altered the situation in Europe, unless the other powers were prepared to unite against Germany, but she, too, had her problems. While Pius IX's territorial power was slipping from his grasp, he was extending his claims to being a universal spiritual monarch by the decree of Papal Infallibility of 19 July 1870, a vote of the Vatican Council declaring the Pope to be infallible when he spoke in matters of faith and morals, a decision pregnant with difficulties for the future course of politics in Roman Catholic countries. The French troops, however, had abandoned Rome on 19 August 1870, and the defeat at Sedan presented the government of Italy with its opportunity. On 20 September 1870 Rome was taken by Italian troops and the remaining Papal territories incorporated in the Kingdom of Italy, Rome itself to become its capital, but with the Pope in the Vatican palace ever more determined not to permit the lay state to control the Church. The pre-occupations of the European powers with their own problems permitted the German question to be considered in isolation by Prussia and her allies.

There were two questions which were to be resolved. German unification and the peace with France. German unification was not achieved without bickering among the German princes, but in the end the result was an expansion of the North German Confederation into an Empire in which the Crown was given to the ruler of Prussia and his successors. The states which formed the Empire retained their individual institutions, but exercise of their common functions was vested in the Emperor William I and his ministers. On 18 January 1871 the German Empire was proclaimed in the Hall of Mirrors at Versailles. For his services to the new Empire Bismarck was raised to the dignity of a Prince, but he had yet to solve the many practical problems which had to be considered in a new unified country. Prussia had hegemony in Germany, but Germany must still be managed to maintain the Hohenzollern supremacy. France in her extremities was compelled to sign a peace which was onerous. In the face of his domestic crisis Thiers agreed to preliminaries of peace on 17 February, which received their confirmation in the Treaty of Frankfort of 10 May 1871. The least important of the terms was the indemnity of £200,000,000, which at the time seemed enormous. Of far greater significance was the cession of Alsace-Lorraine, which took from her 1,500,000 inhabitants, it is true, partly German by speech, and iron mines, metallurgical industries and textile factories, which were to be integrated with the German economy. France's loss contributed in the succeeding decades enormously to Germany's industrial growth. The rate of industrial growth was slower in France. Germany, the power vacuum, which France had once dominated, now became a powerful and menacing neighbour. Beset with constitutional difficulties of her own, France could not immediately adopt a policy designed to recover Alsace-Lorraine and, though there were many vociferous elements which from time to time raised this question, it was recognized that France could never extend herself to the Rhine again, except as the result of a general European war, from which most Frenchmen instinctively shrank for fear of meeting with fresh disasters.

VIII. The End of an Epoch

The events of 1870–1 mark the end of the problems which occupied the European statesmen since the French Revolution of 1789. The Revolutionary and Napoleonic Wars had paved the way for the unification of Germany and Italy, which had hitherto been open to the penetration of the states which were contiguous with them. Britain and Germany were now pre-eminent in Europe. France was to make a recovery within a decade. Russia was to struggle through the crisis of transition from one form of social and economic order to another. Austria-Hungary was consumed with her own internal problems. The unification of Italy made her a factor in international politics, though only in an auxiliary capacity. She was incapable of great initiative in Europe. The geographical position of Germany and her capacity for developing her resources placed great power in the hands of the Hohenzollern dynasty, guided by Bismarck as chancellor, but even Germany needed time to achieve a viable political system. No power could challenge the new Germany, but for the moment she herself was not a menace to the security of Europe. The security of Europe was determined by the problems which arose in the one corner of the continent which had not experienced transformation, the provinces of European Turkey. Greece, Serbia, Montenegro and the future Bulgaria were yet to undergo upheavals. The Ottoman Empire in the 1860s was aware that her dominion over the Christian nationalities of Europe was being loosened. The bombardment of Belgrade by the Turkish garrison in June 1862 led to a slackening of control. Rumania was created by the union of Moldavia and Wallachia in 1861 by Prince Cuza, to be replaced in 1866 by Charles of Hohenzollern-Sigmaringen, who became the ruler of the Principalities by election, though it was not until 1878 that Rumanian independence was recognized. Even in Bulgaria the Turks were prepared to appeal to native Bulgarian feeling and make minor concessions. The growth of nationalism in the Balkans threatened the Austro-Hungarian Empire, but it was not an insuperable problem incapable of international settlement by the Concert of Europe.

The achievement of Europe before 1871 was that it had expanded into the wider world. The world was being unified and with the opening of the Suez canal in 1869 Europe brought closer to the Orient. Already it appeared that states of continental dimensions might arise. The United States of America were free to develop their resources upon a scale impossible for the relatively small European states. Russia, beset with financial difficulties, could not expand as quickly. China was politically in a state of decomposition, but she was too large for any one European power to do more than detach a province upon her periphery. The technological revolution of Europe was potentially capable of creating in the United States, Russia and China powers of a magnitude out of all proportion to that of the European states. Collectively the European states were powerful, but their national divisions caused them in the long run to surrender the advantages which their high productivity gave them. European civilization transplanted itself in the United States, which for historical reasons was able to expand more quickly than either

Russia or China. While the purely European states resolved their political, though not their internal, difficulties, power peacefully and imperceptibly moved towards the United States.

What Europe created was a system of states in which legislative measures were determined not by ideological principles but by considerations of utility. Modernization signified the creation of the lay state in which men were regarded as citizens and conceded by varying degrees civic equality. Yet almost everywhere the governments in Europe were conservative in their outlook. In no state had the people been admitted to full possession of political power. Even in the most highly developed European state, Great Britain, the limited franchise of 1867 survived until 1885. The *Reichstag* of Imperial Germany was a façade for Prussian control. The French Third Republic had in theory a constitutional government as a result of the evolution of the institutions which emerged from defeat in 1870–1, but the French social system was based upon a compromise among the discordant groups which composed it, none of which was to receive complete satisfaction. Universal suffrage did not exist in Austria-Hungary. Russia remained an autocracy. Nevertheless, there was an erosion of the old values, and no institution was more aware of this than the Roman Catholic Church. In the Protestant countries, where ecclesiastical authority was limited, there was a pronounced growth of religious indifference. Darwin in 1859 produced his *Origin of Species*, and in 1871 *The Descent of Man*, which seemed to prove that Man was an animal who had evolved like other animals. There appeared to be no justification for the supposition that God created Man in his own image. Pius IX, however, refused to permit either lay control over the Church or adjustment of Christian doctrine to the findings of science. The Syllabus of Errors in 1864 listed opinions which a true Catholic might not hold. In 1870 the Roman Church made itself master in its own house by the decree of Papal Infallibility. The Roman Church took its stand upon the defence of authority and traditional values and by its determination retained much of its influence in spite of the advance of the lay state. It is easy to understand why the Roman Church found it necessary to adopt an attitude of resistance, but the decree of Infallibility, though it related only to faith and morals, gave offence both to sections of Catholic opinion and to Protestants. To many

Europeans the defence of spiritual values was irrelevant in face of the atomization of society which was occurring with the creation of the great industrial centres. In order to undertake their defence against the employers, the working classes in Europe began to turn to trade unionism. In continental Europe trade unionism, in contrast with Britain, tended to adopt socialist theories as the intellectual basis of its appeal. Karl Marx was active in the creation of the International Workingmen's Association in London in 1864, which became the First International. As a result of the events of the Paris Commune in 1871, the International became a revolutionary body in the Babeuvist sense of the term, but did not make much progress after its final European conference in Geneva in 1873. Socialism was rather to flourish within the framework of the national states. The state had little to fear from the opposition of the left, because it had at its command ever more effective weapons of repression. In order to impress the state the left had to turn its attention to the creation not of élite, but mass parties which by their very size could obtain parliamentary representation or dislocate the economic life of the community by strikes. The creation of mass parties necessarily was to carry with it the need to make a broader appeal to the people with a consequent reduction in the revolutionary content of political programmes. The growth of Social Democracy in Germany, for example, was accompanied by a progressive tendency to reduce political enthusiasm to a lowest common denominator. In 1870–1 there was no serious challenge from the European working class to the conservative domination of Europe. Provided they used their political victory with wisdom, there was no reason why the conservatives should not retain political power. Yet everywhere the new mass age was to present new problems to which statesmen often brought the attitudes of yesteryear. A powerful Germany, controlled by men schooled in the politics of petty princely courts and the opportunism of Bismarck, was perhaps not well equipped to assume her role as a great power. Austria-Hungary's unity in the face of her serious national problem could be maintained ultimately only as long as the dynasty could replace one compromise by another. Tsarist Russia could not industrialize herself and at the same time retain a form of government in which administrative decisions took the place of law, while the growing urban intelligentsia created by the economic expansion was not even consulted and the working men of the factories denied the right to organize in defence against poor conditions of labour. The subject nationalities of the Ottoman Empire in Europe could not be expected to tolerate for ever a régime which only very slowly adjusted itself to methods prevailing elsewhere in Europe.

Conservatism had won and brought Europe to the threshold of the world in which we live today. An epoch had ended, and with it appeared the uncertainty of the new problems which it had called into existence. As time passed a fresh generation of politicians and leaders came to the fore, reared in the confidence generated by conservatism's peaceful possession of power. Memory of the great revolutionary struggles receded and with it awareness of what had been at stake. Internal problems could now be solved by judicious concessions, but, if external problems led to war among the European states, the conflict of millions of men could lead only to mass slaughter and the disorganization of civilized life. Conservatism had it within its power to prevent the recrudescence of the revolutions of 1848. In 1914 the states of Europe took the fatal decision to put their alliance systems to the test. By 1917–18 conservatism had crumbled and Europe returned to the instability of an earlier age.

Select Bibliography

THE most up-to-date short bibliography covering part of the period embraced by this book is A. Bullock and A. J. P. Taylor: *A Select List of Books on European History*, 1815–1914 (Oxford, 1960). D. Shapiro: *A Select Bibliography of works in English on Russian History 1801–1917* (Oxford, 1962) is also useful. *A Bibliography of Modern History* (Edited by John Roach) (Cambridge, 1968) is useful, but omits important works. Many general histories will contain bibliographies. The best general history of Europe is the series *Peuples et Civilisations—histoire générale* (Edited by L. Halpen and P. Sagnac); the relevant volumes for this period are:

Vol. XIII. Georges Lefebvre: *La révolution française* (translated into English) (2 vols., 1962).

Vol. XIV. Georges Lefebvre: *Napoléon* (1953). (Available in translation, 1968.)

Vol. XV. F. Ponteil: *L'éveil des nationalités, 1815–1848* (1960).

Vol. XVI. Ch.-H. Pouthas: *Démocraties et capitalisme, 1848–1860* (1941).

Vol. XVII. H. Hauser, Jean Maurain, Pierre Benaerts: *Du libéralisme à l'impérialisme, 1860–1878* (1939).

Each of these volumes contains bibliographies. An interesting French series is *Clio*, the relevant volumes being : E. Préclin and V. L. Tapié: *Le xviiie siècle* (2 vols.); L. Villat: *La révolution et l'Empire* (2 vols.); and J. Droz, L. Genet and J. Vidalenc: *L'époque contemporaine*, Vol. I (1815–71). The *Clio* series assesses the present state of studies in any particular problem. Reference may also be made to *Histoire des relations internationales* (Edited by P. Renouvin): Vol. IV, André Fugier: *La révolution française et L'Empire napoléonien* (1954); and Vol. V, P. Renouvin: *Le xixe siècle. De 1815 à 1871—L'Europe des nationalités et l'éveil de nouveaux mondes* (1954).

There are histories of Europe in English. *The Cambridge Modern History*, originally edited by Lord Acton, is in process of revision as *The New Cambridge Modern History*, preserving all the advantages and disadvantages of multiple authorship. The volumes applicable to this period are Vol. VIII, *The American and the French Revolutions 1763–1793* (Edited by A. Goodwin) (1965), *War and Peace in an Age of Upheaval* (Edited by C. W. Crawley) (1965); Vol. X, *The Zenith of European Power, 1830–70* (Edited by J. P. T. Bury) (1960). The *Oxford History of Modern Europe* has yielded A. P. J. Taylor: *The Struggle for Mastery in Europe, 1848–1918* (1954). A recent work is E. J. Hobsbawm: *The Age of Revolution—Europe 1789–1848* (1962), which approaches its subject by themes and assumes in the reader of knowledge of the day to day struggle. A useful work for quick reference is W. L. Langer: *An Encyclopedia of World History* (periodically revised).

The books listed below should not be considered as exhausting the subject. I have assumed that the readers of this book will possess English as a mother tongue and have French as a first foreign language, or will have English as a first foreign language. Books in other languages will, however, be mentioned.

Chapter 1

G. Lefebvre: *Quatre Vingt Neuf* (Paris, 1939), translated as *The Coming of the French Revolution* (Princeton, 1947).
La grande peur de 1789 (Paris, 1932). [Translated as *The Great Fear of 1789* (London, 1973).]
A. Cobban: *History of Modern France*, Vol. I. A good synthesis of the problems of the eighteenth century.
A. Goodwin: *The French Revolution* (1953).
J. M. Thompson: *Robespierre* (2 vols., Oxford, 1935).
The French Revolution (1944).
A. Soboul: *The Parisian Sans-Culottes and the French Revolution 1793–1794* (Oxford, 1964).
G. Rudé: *The Crowd in the French Revolution* (1959).
M. J. Sydenham, *The Girondins* (1961).
R. H. Lord: *The Second Partition of Poland* (Harvard, 1915). A classic, but now somewhat dated.
D. Gerhard: *England und der Aufstieg Russlands* (Munich–Berlin, 1933).
J. Droz: *L'Allemagne et la révolution française* (Paris, 1949).
H. Brunschwig: *La crise de l'état prussien à la fin du xviiie siècle* (Paris, 1947).
R. Herr: *The Eighteenth-century Revolution in Spain* (Princeton, 1958).
A. I. Baranovich, B. B. Kafengauz, P. K. Alefirenko, Y. P. Klokman and E. H. Kusheva: *Ocherki Istorii S.S.S.R.—Period Feodalizma— Rossiya vo ytorov polovine xviii v.* (Moscow, 1956).
R. R. Palmer: *The World of the French Revolution* (London, 1971).

Chapter 2

P. Bain: *La diplomatie française de Mirabeau à Bonaparte* (Paris, 1950).
P. Verhaegen: *La Belgique sous la domination française 1792–1814* (5 vols., Brussels, 1922–9).
D. Thomson: *The Babeuf Plot* (1947).
J. M. Thompson: *Napoleon Bonaparte—His rise and fall* (1952).
P. Geyl: *Napoleon—For and Against* (1949). A useful survey of the vast literature dealing with Napoleon.
F. M. H. Markham: *Napoleon and the Awakening of Europe* (1954). A useful short survey.
G. Ferrero: *The Gamble: Napoleon in Italy 1796–7* (1961).
F. Schnabel: *Deutsche Geschichte im neunzehnten Jahrhundert* (4th edition, Freiburg, 4 vols., 1948–51).
G. P. Gooch: *Germany and the French Revolution* (1920).
H. A. L. Fisher: *Studies in Napoleonic Statesmanship—Germany* (Oxford, 1903).
E. Kraehe: *Metternich's German Policy* (1963).
R. D'O Butler: *The roots of National Socialism, 1783–1933* (1941).
G. Craig: *The Politics of the Prussian Army, 1640–1933* (1955).
G. S. Ford: *Stein and the era of Reform in Prussia, 1807–1815* (1922).

H. Rosenberg: *Bureaucracy, Aristocracy and Autocracy—The Prussian experience, 1660-1815* (Harvard, 1958).

W. C. Langsam: *The Napoleonic Wars and German Nationalism in Austria* (New York, 1930).

E. Driault: *Napoléon et l'Europe* (5 vols., Paris, 1910-27).

Napoleon en Italie, 1800-1812 (Paris, 1906).

E. V. Tarlé: *Le blocus continental et le royaume d'Italie—la situation économique d'Italie sous Napoléon I* (Paris, 1928).

J. Rosselli: *Bentinck and the British Occupation of Sicily, 1811-14* (Cambridge, 1956).

P. Mackesy: *The War in the Mediterranean, 1803-1810* (1957).

A. Vandal: *Napoléon et Alexandre Ier* (3 vols., Paris, 1911).

L. I. Strakhovsky: *Alexander I of Russia* (New York, 1947).

M. Kukiel: *Czartoryski and European Unity, 1770-1861* (Princeton, 1955).

M. Raeff: *Michael Speransky, Statesman of Imperial Russia, 1772-1839* (The Hague, 1957).

E. V. Tarlé: *Napoleon's Invasion of Russia, 1812* (1942).

A. Fugier: *Napoléon et l'Espagne, 1799-1808* (2 vols., Paris, 1930).

H. Butterfield: *The Peace Tactics of Napoleon, 1806-8* (Cambridge, 1929).

V. J. Puryear: *Napoleon and the Dardanelles* (Cambridge, Mass., 1951).

G. J. Renier: *Great Britain and the Establishment of the Kingdom of the Netherlands, 1813-1816* (1930).

R. J. Rath: *The Fall of the Napoleonic Kingdom of Italy* (New York, 1941).

J. Leflon: *La crise révolutionnaire, 1789-1846* (Paris, 1946).

(*Histoire de l'Eglise* (Edited by Fliche and Martin), xx.)

E. E. Y. Hales: *Napoleon and the Pope: the story of Napoleon and Pius VII* (1962).

Revolution and Papacy, 1769-1846 (1960).

C. S. Phillips: *The Church in France, 1789-1848* (1929).

E. F. Heckscher: *The Continental System* (1922).

F. Crouzet: *L'économie britannique et le blocus continental (1806-1813)* (2 vols. Paris, 1958).

A. Cobban: *The Social Interpretation of the French Revolution* (Cambridge, 1964).

R. Cobb: *Reactions to the French Revolution* (1972).

Chapter 3

C. K. Webster: *The Congress of Vienna* (New Edition, 1963).

The Foreign Policy of Castlereagh, 1815-22, (2 vols., 1934).

J. H. Pirenne: *La sainte alliance* (2 vols., Neuchâtel, 1949).

H. von Srbik: *Metternich, Der Staatsmann und der Mensch* (3 vols., I-II, Munich, 1925-6; III, Munich, 1954).

P. R. Sweet: *Friedrich von Gentz* (Wisconsin, 1941).

H. W. V. Temperley: *The Foreign Policy of Canning* (1925).

D. Perkins: *The Monroe Doctrine, 1823-26* (Harvard, 1927).

C. W. Crawley: *The Question of Greek Independence* (1925).

R. J. Kerner: 'Russia's New Policy in the Near East after the Peace of Adrianople', *Cambridge Historical Journal*, v (1937).

C. K. Webster: *The Foreign Policy of Palmerston, 1830–41* (2 vols., 1951).

F. S. Rodkey: *The Turko-Egyptian Question in the Relations of England, France and Russia, 1831–1941* (University of Illinois Press, 1924).

V. J. Puryear: *International Economics and Diplomacy in the Near East, 1834–53* (Stanford University Press, 1935.)
France and the Levant from the Bourbon Restoration to the Peace of Kutiah (1941).

P. E. Moseley: *Russian Diplomacy and the Opening of the Eastern Question in 1838 and 1839* (Harvard, 1934).

H. Dodwell: *The Founder of Modern Egypt, Mehemet Ali* (1931).

W. Miller: *The Ottoman Empire and its Successors* (4th edition, 1936).

B. Lewis: *The Emergence of Modern Turkey* (1961).

By Countries:

Italy

K. R. Greenfield: *Economics and Liberalism in the Risorgimento, 1814–48* (Baltimore, 1934).

G. T. Romani: *The Neapolitan Revolution of 1820–1* (North Western University Press, 1950).

Russia

A. G. Mazour: *The first Russian Revolution, 1825* (Stanford University Press, 1937).

M. Raeff: *The Decembrist Movement* (1966).

M. Zetlin: *The Decembrists* (New York, 1958).

N. V. Riasonovsky: *Nicholas I and Official Nationality in Russia, 1825–1855* (University of California Press, 1959).

C. de Grunwald: *Tsar Nicholas I* (1954).

J. S. Curtis: *The Russian Army under Nicholas I* (Duke U.P., 1965).

France under the Bourbon Restoration

F. B. Artz: *France under the Bourbon Restoration* (Cambridge, Mass., 1931).

C. S. Phillips: *The Church in France, 1789–1848* (1929).

N. E. Hudson: *Ultra-Royalism and the French Restoration* (1936).

C.-H. Pouthas: *Histoire politique de la restauration* (1938).

Belgium

R. Demoulin: *La révolution de 1830* (Brussels, 1950).

H. R. C. Wright: *Free Trade and Protection in the Netherlands, 1816–1830* (Cambridge, 1955).

Poland

R. F. Leslie: *Polish Politics and the Revolution of November 1830* (1956).

Chapter 4

J. H. Clapham: *The Economic Development of France and Germany* (Cambridge, 1921).

P. Lyashchenko: *History of the Russian National Economy* (1947).

S. B. Clough and C. W. Cole: *Economic History of Europe* (New York, 3rd Edition, 1953).

E. L. Woodward: *War and Peace in Europe, 1815–1870* (1931).

France under the Orleans Monarchy

G. Weill: *La France sous la monarchie constitutionelle, 1815–48* (Paris, 1912).
Histoire du parti républicain en France, 1814–1870 (Paris, 1928).

P. Bastid: *Les institutions politiques de la monarchie parlementaire française, 1814–1848* (Paris, 1954).

J. Plamenatz: *The Revolutionary Movement in France, 1815–1871* (1952).

D. O. Evans: *Social Romanticism in France, 1815–48* (1951).

E. L. Eisenstein: *The First Professional Revolutionist, Filipo Michele Buonarroti (1761–1837)* (Harvard, 1959).

N. Richardson: *The French prefectural Corps, 1814–1830* (1966).

A. L. Dunham: *The Industrial Revolution in France 1815–1848* (New York, 1955).

A. R. Vidler: *Prophecy and Papacy: A study of Lamennais, the Church and the Revolution* (1954).

E. Labrousse: '1848–1830–1789: Comment naissent les révolutions', *Actes du congrès historique du centenaire de la revolution de 1848* (Paris, 1948), pp. 1–29.

D. S. Landes: 'The Statistical Study of French Crises', *Journal of Economic History*, X (1950). (A criticism of Labrousse.)

France in 1848 and After

P. de la Gorce: *Histoire de la seconde république* (2 vols., Paris, 1914).

D. C. McKay: *The National Workshops—a study in the French revolution of 1848* (Cambridge, Mass., 1933).

F. A. Simpson: *Louis Napoleon and the recovery of France, 1848–56* (3rd edition, 1951).

H. C. Payne: *The police state of Louis Napoleon Bonaparte* (1966)

A. L. Guérard: *Napoleon III—a new interpretation* (Harvard, 1943).
Napoleon III (1953).

Germany, Austria and Central Europe

K. S. Pinson: *Modern Germany* (2nd edition 1966).

A. J. P. Taylor: *The Course of German History* (1945) (Revised edition 1948).
The Habsburg Monarchy, 1815–1918 (1942).

R. A. Kann: *The Multinational Empire—Nationalism and National in the Habsburg Empire, 1848–1918* (2 vols., New York, 1950).

A. Ramm: *Germany, 1789–1919. A Political History* (1967).

H. von Srbik: *Metternich* (3 vols., Munich, 1925–54).

R. J. Rath: *The Viennese Revolution of 1848* (Texas, 1957).
E. Vermeil: *L'Allemagne du Congrès de Vienne à la révolution hitlérienne* (Paris, 1934) (Translated as *Germany's Three Reichs*, 1944).
R. H. Thomas: *Liberalism, Nationalism and the German Intellectuals, 1815–1847* (1951).
H. C. Meyer: *Mitteleuropa in German Thought and Action, 1815–1945* (The Hague, 1955).
W. O. Henderson: *The Zollverein* (1939).
V. Valentin: *1848—Chapters in German History* (1940).
S. Z. Pech: *The Czech Revolution of 1848* (1969).
T. S. Hammerow: *Restoration, Revolution. Reaction Economics and Politics in Germany 1815–1871* (Princeton, 1958).
L. B. Namier: *1848: the Revolution of the Intellectuals* (1944).
J. Blum: *Noble Landowners and agriculture in Austria, 1815–1848* (1945).
J. Droz: *Le libéralisme rhénan*, 1815–1848 (Paris, 1944).
  Les révolutions allemandes de 1848 (Paris, 1957).
W. M. Simon: *The Failure of the Prussian Reform Movement 1807–1819* (1955).

Hungary in 1848

L. Eisenmann: *Le compromis austro-hongrois de 1867* (Paris, 1904).

Bohemia

R. W. Seton-Watson: *A History of the Czechs and Slovaks* (1943).
E. Denis: *La Bohême depuis la Montagne Blanche* (Paris, 1903).

Italy in 1848–9

H. Boulton-King: *A history of Italian Unity, 1814–71* (1898). (Old-fashioned, but still of use.)
G. Salvemini: *Mazzini* (1956).
E. E. Y. Hales: *Mazzini and the Secret Societies* (1956).
  Pio Nono (1954).
  Revolution and the Papacy 1769–1846 (1960).
R. Aubert: *Le pontificat de Pie IX* (Paris, 1952). (*Histoire de l'Eglise* (Edited by Fliche and Martin), XXI.)
W. K. Hancock: *Ricasoli and the Risorgimento in Tuscany* (1926).
A. J. P. Taylor: *The Italian Problem in European Diplomacy, 1847–9* (1934).

Chapter 5

H. W. V. Temperley: *England and the Near East: The Crimea* (1936).
V. J. Puryear: *England, Russia and the Straits Question, 1844–56* (University of California Press, 1931).
G. B. Henderson: *Crimean War Diplomacy and Other Essays* (Glasgow, 1947).
E. V. Tarlé: *Krimskaya Voina* (Moscow, 1941).
G. Pagès: *La politique extérieure de Napoléon III* (Paris, 1933).

W. E. Mosse: *The European Powers and the German Question, 1848–71* (1958).
The Rise and Fall of the Crimean System 1855–1870 (1963).
C. Friese: *Russland und Preussen vom Krimkrieg bis zum polnischen Aufstand* (1931).
H. Oncken: *Napoleon III and the Rhine* (New York, 1928).

Italy and the Mediterranean

D. Mack Smith: *Cavour and Garibaldi in 1860* (1954).
Garibaldi (1957).
D. Mack Smith: *Victor Emanuel, Cavour and the Risorgimento* (1971).
R. Carr: *Spain 1808–1939* (1966).
R. H. Davison: *Reform in the Ottoman Empire, 1856–1876* (Princeton, 1963).

Germany

C. W. Clark: *Francis Joseph and Bismarck, 1862–1866* (Harvard, 1934).
L. D. Steefel: *The Schleswig-Holstein Question* (Harvard, 1932).
L. D. Steefel: *Bismark, the Hohenzollern Candidature and the Origins of the Franco-German War of 1870* (Cambridge, Mass., 1962).
H. Friedjung: *The Struggle for Supremacy in Germany* (Translation, 1935).
E. N. Anderson: *The Social and Political Conflict in Prussia, 1858–64* (Lincoln, Nebraska, 1954).
O. Pflanze: *Bismarck and The Development of Germany 1815–1871* (1963).
E. Eyck: *Bismarck and the German Empire* (1950).
C. Grant Robertson: *Bismarck* (1917).
F. Darmstaedter: *Bismarck and the Creation of the Second Reich* (1948).
J. Redlich: *Francis Joseph* (New York, 1929).
R. W. Seton-Watson: 'The Austro-Hungarian Ausgleich of 1867', *Slavonic and East European Review*, xix (1939–40).
E. A. Pottinger: *Napoleon III and the German Crisis, 1865–1866* (Harvard, 1966).

Russia

G. H. N. Seton-Watson: *The Russian Empire 1801–1917* (1967).
W. E. Mosse: *Alexander II and the Modernization of Russia* (1958).
B. H. Sumner: 'The Secret Franco–Russian Treaty of 3 March 1859', *English Historical Review*, xlviii (1933), pp. 65–85.
G. T. Robinson: *Rural Russia under the Old Régime* (New York, 1949).
J. Blum: *Lord and Peasant in Russia from the Ninth to the Nineteenth Century* (Princeton, 1961).
P. A. Khromov: *Ekonomicheskiye razvitiye Rossii v 19–20 vekakh, 1800–1917* (Moscow, 1950). (Contains valuable statistics.)
I. Berlin: 'Russia and 1848', *Slavonic and East European Review* xxvi (1947–8), pp. 341–60. (A suggestive essay.)
R. F. Leslie: *Reform and Insurrection in Russian Poland, 1856–1865* (1963).
S. F. Starr: *Decentralization and Self-Government in Russia, 1830–1870* (Princeton, 1973).

Chapter 6

The relations of the European with the Wider World would require a very large bibliography. A few books are recommended here in order to give the student some guidance upon how to begin his reading. For questions of modern Latin American history R. A. Humphreys: *The Evolution of Modern Latin America* (Oxford, 1946) provides an excellent introduction. L. H. Jenks: *The Migration of British Capital to 1875* (1937) deals with British capital investment overseas. S. F. Bemis: *The Latin American Policy of the United States—an historical interpretation* (New York, 1944) is useful. See also J. F. Rippy: *The Rivalry of the United States and Great Britain for Latin America, 1808–1830* (Baltimore, 1929); C. Scheger: *La grande pensée de Napoléon III: l'expédition de Mexique* (Paris, 1939); and D. Dawson: *The Mexican Adventure* (1935).

A. Nevins and H. S. Commager: *America—the Story of a Free People* (Oxford, 1943) provides a good introduction to United States history and contains a bibliography. E. D. Adams: *Great Britain and the American Civil War* (2 vols., 1925) is the standard work on its subject.

D. J. Creighton: *The Road to Confederation—The Emergence of Modern Canada* (1965).

For Africa an excellent introduction is provided by J. D. Fage and R. Oliver: *A History of Africa* (1963). R. Coupland: *The British Anti-slavery Movement* (2nd edition, with a new introduction by J. D. Fage, 1964) and W. L. Mathieson: *Great Britain and the Slave Trade, 1839–1865* (1929) may be read with profit.

For problems of Indian history the *Cambridge History of British India* (Vol. V, 1929 and Vol. 1932) provides a good introduction. For the Far East see W. C. Costin: *Great Britain and China, 1833–60* (1937); P. Renouvin: *La question d'Extrême Orient, 1840–1940* (Paris, 1946); W. G. Beasley: *Great Britain and the Opening of Japan, 1834–1858* (1952); J. K. Fairbank: *Trade and Diplomacy on the China Coast: The opening of China, 1842–54* (2 vols., Harvard, 1953); M. Greenberg: *British Trade and the Opening of China, 1800–1842* (Cambridge, 1951); and E. P. Boardman: *Christian Influence upon the Ideology of the Taiping Rebellion, 1951–64* (Wisconsin, 1952). A very interesting work is Li Chien-nung: *The Political History of China, 1840–1928* (New York, 1956), which presents the problem of opening China to the west from a Chinese point of view. For internal questions of Japan see George Sansom: *The western world and Japan* (1950); *Japan—A short cultural history* (2nd edition, 1952); R. Storry: *A History of Modern Japan* (1960); D. Keene: *The Japanese Discovery of Europe* (1952); and W. G. Beasley: *A History of Modern Japan* (1962). D. G. Hall: *A History of South East Asia* (1955) is excellent. For the complex question of Russia see D. J. Dallin: *The Rise of Russia in Asia* (1950); G. A. Lensen: *The Russian Push Towards Japan—Russo-Japanese relations, 1697–1875* (Princeton, 1959); and R. A. Pierce: *Russian Central Asia, 1867–1917—a study in colonial rule* (University of California Press, 1960), which contains some relevant material in its introduction. M. Edwards: *The West in Asia 1850–1914* (1967) should be consulted.

Chapter 7

For the Second Empire in France see:

J. M. Thompson: *Louis Napoleon and the Second Empire* (1954).

T. Zeldin: *The political system of Napoleon III* (1958). (An attempt at electoral analysis.)

P. de la Gorce: *Histoire du Second Empire* (7 vols., Paris, 1894–1905).

P. Guériot: *Napoléon III* (2 vols., Paris, 1933).

C. S. Phillips: *The Church in France, 1848–1907* (1936).

L. M. Case: *French Opinion on War and Diplomacy during the Second Empire* (Philadelphia, 1954).

H. N. Boon: *Rêve et réalité dans l'œuvre économique et sociale de Napoléon III* (1938).

A. L. Dunham: *The Anglo-French Treaty of 1860* (1930).

T. Zeldin: *Émile Ollivier and the Liberal Empire of Napoleon III* (1963).

For the Franco–Prussian War see:

M. Howard: *The Franco–Prussian War—The German invasion of France, 1870–1871* (1962).

R. H. Lord (Editor) *The origins of the War of 1870* (Harvard, 1924).

G. Bonnin (Editor): *Bismarck and the Hohenzollern Candidature for the Spanish Throne* (London, 1957).

W. E. Mosse: *The European Powers and the German Question, 1848–1871* (Cambridge, 1958).

W. G. East: *The Union of Moldavia and Wallachia, 1859* (Cambridge, 1929).

W. Ebel: *Bismarck und Russland vom Prager Frieden bis zum Ausbruch des Krieges von 1870* (Frankfort, 1936).

L. D. Steefel: *Bismarck, the Hohenzollern Candidature and the Origins of the Franco-German War of 1870* (Cambridge, Mass., 1962).

C. A. M. Hennessy: *The Federal Republic in Spain—Pi y Margall and the Federal Republican Movement 1868–1874* (Oxford, 1962).

V. G. Kiernan: *The Revolution of 1854 in Spanish History* (Oxford, 1967).

Index